Integrating
the Inner City

To: Lisa

Thanks for hosting me
in New Orleans. And for
your commitment to social change.

Toward equity and inclusion!

N⌐/C

Integrating the Inner City

The Promise and Perils of Mixed-Income Public Housing Transformation

ROBERT J. CHASKIN AND
MARK L. JOSEPH

The University of Chicago Press   Chicago and London

ROBERT J. CHASKIN is associate professor and deputy dean at the University of Chicago School of Social Service Administration and director of the University of Chicago Urban Network.

MARK L. JOSEPH is associate professor in the Jack, Joseph and Morton Mandel School of Applied Social Sciences at Case Western University and director of the National Initiative on Mixed-Income Communities.

The University of Chicago Press, Chicago 60637
The University of Chicago Press, Ltd., London
© 2015 by The University of Chicago
All rights reserved. Published 2015.
Printed in the United States of America

24 23 22 21 20 19 18 17 16 15   1 2 3 4 5

ISBN-13: 978-0-226-16439-7 (cloth)
ISBN-13: 978-0-226-30390-1 (e-book)
DOI: 10.7208/chicago/9780226303901.001.0001

Library of Congress Cataloging-in-Publication Data

Chaskin, Robert J., author.
    Integrating the inner city: the promise and perils of mixed-income public housing transformation / Robert J. Chaskin and Mark L. Joseph.
        pages; cm
    Includes bibliographical references and index.
    ISBN 978-0-226-16439-7 (cloth: alk. paper)—ISBN 978-0-226-30390-1 (e-book)   1. Mixed-income housing—Illinois—Chicago. 2. Inclusionary housing programs—Illinois—Chicago. 3. Community development—Illinois—Chicago. 4. Social integration—Illinois—Chicago. 5. Chicago Housing Authority. Plan for Transformation.   I. Joseph, Mark L., author.   II. Title.
    HT177.C4C43 2015
    307.3'4160977311—dc23   2015014463

♾ This paper meets the requirements of ANSI/NISO Z39.48-1992 (Permanence of Paper).

We dedicate this book to Harold Richman, our beloved and dearly missed mentor who brought the two of us together over twenty years ago and whose commitment to social change continues to inspire our work.

Contents

Prologue

Public housing in the United States has been in significant decline over the past several decades, contributing in many cities—perhaps most dramatically in Chicago—to racially segregated neighborhoods of highly concentrated poverty, crime, and physical deterioration. In an effort to respond to these circumstances and counter the negative impact of concentrated poverty on the populations in these neighborhoods, both federal policy and local policy have rethought public housing. Policy responses have included providing vouchers to help families in public housing move to less disadvantaged neighborhoods as well as launching ambitious redevelopment efforts to renovate or, in the most severe cases, rebuild public housing complexes. The new developments replacing distressed public housing are designed as "mixed-income" communities, providing homes for public housing residents and other low-income renters alongside more affluent renters and homeowners, and in some cases including residents of different racial and ethnic backgrounds. Many of these efforts have led to dramatic changes in the built environment, but they have also generated a great deal of controversy and significant social tension.

The Chicago Plan for Transformation, launched in 2000, is the largest-scale mixed-income public housing redevelopment in the United States. Like other efforts of its kind, the Plan for Transformation seeks to respond to concentrated urban poverty and the dramatic deficiencies of public housing by removing residents from failing public housing complexes and remaking these complexes into new mixed-income communities. At the center of the Transformation is an emphasis on integration. As the Chicago Housing Authority clearly states, the intent is "to build and strengthen communities by integrating public housing and its leaseholders into the larger social, economic and physical fabric of Chicago." The mixed-income developments replacing public housing complexes represent the Plan's most concerted effort to realize these integrationist goals and to remake the inner city.

Before exploring in depth the ideas, actors, and actions that lie behind this effort and how it is playing out, in these opening pages we offer a window into the social dynamics that characterize these new communities and that to a large extent condition how fully the integrationist goals of the Transformation are likely to be met. Drawn from focus groups with residents living in one of the new mixed-income developments replacing public housing complexes in Chicago, these conversations provide an introduction to residents' experiences in these communities and their outlook on this bold social experiment to end the segregation of the poor in public housing.

Note that the focus on integration is primarily driven by ideas about the benefits of economic and social integration. Racial integration is not an explicit goal, though race plays into the dynamics to be explored in important, if sometimes complicated, ways. Virtually all public housing residents in Chicago are African American, as are virtually all renters—subsidized and market-rate—in the new mixed-income communities that are the focus of our study. Homeowners are a more diverse group in these contexts, but the extent of racial and ethnic diversity differs from site to site.

What follow are excerpts from two conversations at the same development, one among a group of relocated public housing residents and the other among a group of homeowners.[1] The discussions illustrate some of the central challenges that have emerged and that we will explore further in the chapters to follow.

Minimal Social Interaction: "It's Just Like You're Invisible"

For many relocated public housing residents, the benefits of living in brand-new apartments in safer, revitalizing neighborhoods are offset by the downside of feeling stigmatized and marginalized by their new, more affluent neighbors. Any hopes that residential proximity would bridge differences and build personal networks that might promote access to opportunity are being dashed by the reality of enduring social distance and exclusion.

Sarah: [Y]ou're trying to interact. But it's just like you're invisible. Nobody don't want to recognize you.

[. . .]

Sarah: Say, like you are getting on the elevator. People are coming off the elevator. You speak . . . you just say good morning, good afternoon. People walk right past you . . . like you're not even there. So when it happens two or three times . . . you wasted all this good breath just being nice.

Evelyn: There's mighty few of them that will say hello or "Could I help you do something?" Or I'm coming in with bags or groceries and they would ask me, "Could I help you?" These are students [who might engage], but the grown people look at you just like you're trash. And I have bills, and pay rent and everything else just like they do, even though I'm up under CHA, but I'm still the same person. I think of myself just as good as you or maybe better.

A Clash of Cultures: "Why the Heck You Banging on That Door This Late?"

For many, if not all, homeowners, the benefits of living in handsomely designed condos and townhomes conveniently located just a few minutes' drive from downtown and within walking distance of amenities like lakefront access are offset by disappointment in the prevailing social atmosphere. What they describe as "ghetto" behavior and mentality plays out in a range of perceived incivilities and transgressions, from "hanging out" to littering to inconsiderate, noisy disturbances. These perspectives are broadly representative of the homeowners we spoke with, regardless of race or ethnicity. The homeowners participating in this focus group are all African American.

Edward: There's not that pride in where you are because you're not vested in it. . . . People aren't taking, they don't take as much care in their unit or their surroundings or the common areas or have respect for others. . . .

Deborah: Renters who come from places where they have no sense of pride or have no sense of value for what homeownership means—

Moderator: Okay, so you all have said this, "pride." Tell me, can we get more specific?

Deborah: They hang out.

Edward: Can we say "ghetto"? Can we just use the word ghetto?

Deborah: But we have to define ghetto, you know what I mean. Because, you know, as a homeowner when I come home from a hard day's work or an easy day of work, I really don't want to see people hanging out on the front porch.

[. . .]

Edward: Cultural, that's the way to say "pride."

Frances: And I've actually written the management office about that. Not too long after I moved in, I'm in my unit, somebody's banging on the door. Across the hall from me, somebody's banging on the door. [Banging on table.] I'm watching TV. It's around eleven o'clock at night, so I'm thinking, okay, the person's obviously not at home. [Banging more loudly on table.] Then I hear the banging on down the hall. You know, an hour later, they're still banging on the door and I'm just, like, the person is not home.

Deborah: That's a cultural thing.

Frances: First of all, I'm thinking if they're not home, how'd you get in the building?

Deborah: Well, they buzzed somebody's door, somebody buzzed them in. And that person is at home and don't want to bothered, and they know they're in there. They want to make a point. You should have called the police. I hate to bother the police, but they need to know.

Frances: It bothered me. It really, really bothered me, because I'm thinking a normal person, you know, wouldn't do that. A normal person wouldn't do that. If I go to somebody's house and I ring their doorbell and they don't answer, they're not at home, I leave.

Edward: Somebody with a sense of upbringing and morals and whatever.

Frances: That's not ghetto, as you say.

"Us versus Them" as Systematic Exclusion: "It's Not about Us. Just Take Us out of the Equation."

For many of the relocated public housing residents, the sense of exclusion and separation in the new developments is exacerbated by the lack of inclusion in decision-making entities. While homeowners are able to form condominium and homeowners' associations as exclusive forums where they deliberate and make decisions about life in the new communities, renters have no such associations, and there are no effective mechanisms for cross-income governance.

Sarah: It's set up to look like it looks good on paper or when you discuss it or show it on the screen. But when you put the actuality into it, real people . . . it's not going to work.

Moderator: Why is it not going to work?

Sarah: Because they do this right now. They say, "I'm on the condo association," "I'm on the homeowner association." You're making a difference then. . . . When it shouldn't even be like that, and you're still using the word community. Where's the community part?

Kevin: And if you've got all of these boards that the homeowners sit on, why can't the CHA residents have a board where they can sit on as [residents' council] representatives? That's what I can't understand.

Moderator: So you don't feel like there's any kind of group that is even representing you?

Group: No.

Sarah: You have it, but they won't incorporate it because it's not about us. It's not about us. Just take us out of the equation. . . . It's not designed with us in mind.

David: They even show it when they have the meetings, when we be in the meetings with the homeowners' association or whoever they are. . . . They show the difference in your face. They make the difference. Okay, say for instance if [a CHA resident] raises her hand and she want to talk to a person from the CHA, representative or something. You know, it's like, you hurry up get your question out. And then if the homeowner makes a—they like, "Okay, okay, [to the CHA resident], shush, be quiet. Let her speak because that's a good point, that's a good suggestion that she's doing. Let her talk. Let her talk." And they'll shush you up.

Group: Right. Yeah.

David: And then let you be recognized that you're a CHA person in the meeting. I mean we all can sit together and I don't know who you are or where you live or what you do, you know. And it just shows a difference. It shouldn't be like that.

"Us versus Them" as Self-Exclusion: "You, Yourself, See Yourself as a CHA Person and See Me as an Owner."

From the vantage point of many of the homeowners, the separation that endures in these developments based on race and class is in large part self-imposed. Claiming a lack of prejudice and an openness to engaging low-income residents in the development as "just my neighbor," these homeowners are perplexed by the relocated public housing residents' perceived insistence on labeling themselves as "CHA." They suspect that these people would be happy to be rid of the higher-income residents but realize this would lead to the regression of the developments back to their previous condition.

Deborah: I'll speak for myself; let me speak individually. I'm cordial. I treat and see everyone as a resident. I don't see color until you show me color. I don't see ghetto until you show me ghetto.

[. . .]

Edward: You just my neighbor.

Frances: Right, I speak to everyone.

Deborah: Yeah, if you say something. . . . Yeah, you just my neighbor. . . . So when I see that you, yourself, see yourself as a CHA person and see me as an owner, you have that resistance. I'm just treating you like a person here in my community. Like a neighbor.

Frances: And that's a problem. The labels.

Edward: It is. That's them. And they all, in the meetings, they all sit together.

Frances: And it's us against them.

Edward: And it shouldn't be us against them.

[. . .]

Deborah: But you know they have a sense of pride about who they are.

Edward: That's the thing.

Deborah: They're very territorial. And it's a mentality. If all of us move, they wouldn't care. They'd be like, "We won." They'd be happy to see us gone.

Edward: You're right, because they won. They got new accommodations.

Moderator: What did they win?

Deborah: The community. They win running people out.

Edward: They won a new building with all the bells and whistles.

Moderator: So they don't even want you here?

Edward: They probably don't. . . . That's the human factor. They're concerned for their reasons. We're concerned for our reasons. They're concerned because if I walk away tomorrow, you walk away tomorrow, with no concern for financial repercussions. Because when it gets to a point, like I say, when I can't take it for whatever reasons, I'm out of there, foreclosure or not. But if you turn around and all this turns to no homeowners—because you already don't have a lot of homeowners who own—

Deborah: You're back where you started.

Edward: You're back to a CHA real nice development. And they're concerned about that because—

Deborah: They'll tear it up.

Edward: That's going to bug them more so. See I can up and leave and go get another mortgage somewhere. They can't do that. So they're concerned that if we all leave, their standard of living is going to get worse because it's just going to be another urban jungle.

These conversations provide an initial illustration of the challenging social dynamics emerging in mixed-income developments in Chicago. Although the $3 billion public-private venture has transformed the physical landscape of the inner city, spurring and accelerating revitalization in previously unsafe, deteriorating neighborhoods, the social environments in these emerging communities are characterized by limited social interaction, friction across race and class, and dynamics of exclusion. In the chapters that follow we describe the historical, policy, and theoretical contexts that frame the Plan for Transformation, examine the implementation strategies across three mixed-income communities replacing public housing complexes, and assess the benefits and costs of mixed-income public housing transformation.

PART ONE

ONE

Concentrated Poverty, Public Housing Reform, and the Promise of Integration

Public housing in Chicago has long been recognized as a massive failure of public policy. What began, in this city as elsewhere in the United States, as an effort to provide temporary, decent, and affordable housing to people suffering economic hardship in the wake of the Great Depression became, within a few decades, emblematic of the country's worst concentrated urban poverty and racial segregation. Indeed, the slum clearance and public housing expansion begun under urban renewal in the mid-twentieth century actively *exacerbated* the concentration of poverty and racial isolation.[1]

As the third largest public housing authority in the United States[2] and its most widely recognized calamity—so much so that the federal department of Housing and Urban Development (HUD) placed the Chicago Housing Authority (CHA) under receivership from 1995 through 1999—the problems with public housing in Chicago and the challenges faced (and resilience demonstrated) by its residents have been the subject of numerous scholarly treatments[3] and journalistic exposés.[4] Piecemeal efforts to respond to the most obvious problems—crime, violence, poor sanitation and maintenance, unemployment, concentrated poverty, racial isolation—were insufficient or ineffective at best, intensifying or additive at worst.[5]

In response, after regaining control of the housing authority from the federal government, in February 2000 Mayor Richard M. Daley announced the launch of the city of Chicago's Plan for Transformation, a dramatic and ambitious program to profoundly transform the city's public housing. The largest and most extensive effort of its kind, the Plan for Transformation is part of a broader policy trend, nationally and internationally, focused on deconcentrating urban poverty and addressing the problems that have become endemic to many public housing communities over the past half-century. In Chicago the effort is comprehensive, entailing massive demolition and redevelopment, the relocation of 25,000 households with over 56,000 individuals, and fundamental changes to the institutional roles and division of labor among those responsible for developing, maintaining, and managing public housing. The effort has been significantly aided by the CHA's participation in HUD's Moving to Work program, which provides the housing authority with considerable fiscal flexibility in making strategic decisions about resource allocation. Through these efforts, Chicago's Plan for Transformation seeks, as President Bill Clinton once said of the welfare reform legislation of 1996, to remake public housing as we know it.

At the center of the Plan is a stated emphasis on *integration*—on breaking down the barriers that have left public housing residents isolated in racially segregated, severely economically disadvantaged neighborhoods and, through relocation and community development, incorporating them into the broader contexts, institutions, and opportunities provided by the city as a whole. Beyond its investment in physical development, the CHA makes clear, the Plan for Transformation "aims to build and strengthen communities by integrating public housing and its leaseholders into the larger social, economic and physical fabric of Chicago."[6]

The focus on integration is meant to operate at several levels. It includes integrating public housing residents spatially, both into existing housing in the subsidized private market by providing vouchers and into new developments being built as mixed-income communities on the footprint of large public housing complexes that have been demolished. It includes integrating these new neighborhoods into the street grid and spatial fabric of the city. It includes integrating public housing residents socially into communities with different income groups and housing tenures (renters and owners, subsidized and market-rate) and, to some extent, into more racially and ethnically diverse neighborhoods—although it is important to note that the principal focus is on *economic*, rather than racial, integration.[7] It includes the integration of formerly separate service systems for public housing complexes—policing, sanitation, and social services—into the systems intended for all residents of the city. And it includes, in principle at least, the integration of public housing residents into the normative mechanisms and rhythms of urban life, through engagement in the market and in civil society, in their neighborhoods and in the city at large.

These integrationist claims, however, are fraught with controversy, challenges, complications, and doubt. Critiques have been leveled at the basic theoretical assumptions behind the effort and at how far empirical evidence supports these assumptions. They have included claims and counterclaims about intent and impact, about the promise and limitations of the market-driven logic and neoliberal policy framework under which the Transformation operates, and about the processes, competing interests, and ultimate goals of the policy. Is such sweeping reform an example of urban regeneration or revanchism? Will it generate integration or displacement? What kinds of communities will emerge, for whom, and to whose benefit?

This book interrogates these broad issues, exploring in particular one component of the broader Transformation—the re-creation of urban space and the dynamics of integration through the development of mixed-income communities on the footprint of former public housing complexes. Much research to date on public housing reform, in Chicago and elsewhere, has focused on the history and etiology of public housing's failure, or its relative success, or on the effects of demolishing public housing and relocating residents.[8] In contrast, here we focus on public housing reform as a mechanism of community revitalization and integration—an intentional effort, driven by public policy but relying to a large extent on market processes and operating through public-private partnerships, to reclaim and rebuild neighborhoods while fundamentally reshaping public housing's role in responding to urban poverty.

Seen through this lens, the intent, implementation, and emerging outcomes of what has become a defining policy response to concentrated urban poverty and public housing failure raise a set of specific, fundamental questions. What are the motivating assumptions, arguments, and interests that drive these mixed-income efforts? What is the nature of the new communities being built? What are the strategies, mechanisms, and social processes that shape their community dynamics? What are the apparent benefits and costs to public housing residents? To the city? To addressing urban poverty more broadly?

The chapters that follow will explore these questions in some detail. First we need to set the stage by outlining the key circumstances and arguments—regarding concentrated poverty, public housing reform, and the promise of integration—that shape the Plan for Transformation and similar policy efforts.

Stepping Back: Demographic Change, Deindustrialization, and the "New Urban Poverty"

The problems of concentrated poverty are by now well known and have become orthodox in framing arguments about both the nature of urban poverty and appropriate ways to address it. Catalyzed in large part by William Julius Wilson's seminal 1987 book *The Truly Disadvantaged*, scholarship on urban poverty burgeoned in the 1990s after nearly two decades of relative quiescence. This work reignited debates on the causes and consequences of the urban crisis that raged in the aftermath of urban renewal and that led, first, to a substantial public policy response under the Johnson administration's War on Poverty and, soon thereafter, to significant government withdrawal from policies focused on the problems of urban America.[9]

The emergence of this "new urban poverty" was driven by a set of economic and demographic changes that led to alterations in the nature and pattern of urbanization in most older industrial cities in the United States. Many of these changes began earlier but accelerated with particular force and impact after World War II and came to a head in the 1960s and 1970s. These included changes in the patterns of in-migration to central cities, increased population mobility out of central cities to suburban communities in the greater metropolitan area, changes in the structure of the urban economy and the geographic distribution of economic opportunity, and, particularly beginning in the 1970s, the emergence of other cities, especially in the South and West, as economic and population growth centers.[10] The most dramatic changes can be traced to the 1940s, when investments in the war effort helped move the country out of the throes of economic depression, reinvigorated industrial production, and reshaped the workforce, bringing a significant influx of African American migrants from the rural South to northern cities. Although this internal migration had begun earlier,[11] the prospect of well-paid industrial work in the factories of the North, along with economic dislocation in the rural South, accelerated the process; some three million

African Americans migrated north between 1940 and 1960—double the number that had migrated over the previous three decades.[12]

But as the population of African Americans in northern industrial cities grew, the urban landscape was changing in a number of ways. Housing shortages and policies supporting racial segregation led to severe overcrowding in black neighborhoods and the expansion of black "ghetto" areas.[13] In addition to racial strife, this also led to the increasing exodus of white city dwellers—accelerated by "redlining" and "block busting" practices of banks and real estate professionals—many to resettle in the suburbs that were rapidly growing up around them.[14] Suburban growth was in part fostered by federal policy supporting highway construction, homeowner subsidies, and suburban housing development.[15] In addition, by the late 1960s fair housing laws began to make leaving the central city easier for middle-class blacks, increasing the relative poverty of the neighborhoods they left behind.[16]

In addition to the population exodus, many industrial firms and manufacturing plants left the inner city. Lured in part by tax incentives and the prospect of hiring lower-wage, non-unionized labor, they moved their operations to suburbs, to other regions of the country, and later overseas—aided by international free-trade agreements crafted, in particular, in the 1980s and 1990s.[17] As deindustrialization accelerated, workforce opportunities were limited more and more to an expanded service sector, and employment increasingly bifurcated into high-skill, high-income jobs and low-skill, low-income jobs.[18] The loss of stable, relatively well-paid jobs for low-skilled workers in these deindustrializing cities had particularly deleterious effects on African Americans, who were disproportionately concentrated in the inner city, with few resources for going where jobs were moving, and were facing significant barriers of ongoing discrimination in the workforce.[19]

These circumstances shaped the emergence and consolidation of what controversially came to be called an urban "underclass," isolated in pockets of concentrated disadvantage in neighborhoods characterized by racial segregation, high rates of poverty and unemployment, high proportions of female-headed households, out-of-wedlock births, and teenage pregnancy and high levels of social disorganization, violence, and crime.[20] In many cities—Chicago among them—public housing communities exhibited these circumstances to an extreme. Residents of these neighborhoods thus had to contend not only with the challenges of their own poverty, but with what Wilson called "concentration effects"—the compounding negative impact of being poor and living among the poor, in unhealthy and often dangerous environments with weak physical and institutional infrastructures and disconnected from effective services, supports, and opportunity.[21] Although debates continue about the relative effects of different determinants of concentrated, persistent poverty (e.g., deindustrialization versus racial segregation, structural versus cultural and behavioral factors) and about the most effective means to address it (e.g., "place-based" versus "people-based" strategies), there is general agreement about the influence of these factors, about the persistence of concentrated urban poverty, and about the need for social policies to address it.

Deconcentrating Poverty through Housing and Development Policy

Poverty policy in the United States is multifaceted and includes a range of programs and resource flows—cash assistance, subsidies to offset the cost of food and basic necessities (food stamps, WIC [Women, Infants, and Children]), housing subsidies, health insurance (Medicaid), child care assistance, job training and placement assistance, tax credits (Earned Income Tax Credit and Child Tax Credit), social services—within the context of a residual, and shrinking, welfare state. However, policy oriented specifically toward *urban* poverty has largely targeted housing, urban restructuring, providing services, and economic development. Such responses to urban poverty have been varied, are historically situated, and have entailed a complex and changing interplay among actors in the public, private, and voluntary sectors.

Much of the current policy focus on urban poverty relies on housing and community development strategies to reduce the concentration of poverty in inner-city neighborhoods and improve the environments and access to opportunity of people currently living there. The lion's share of these efforts center on addressing the problems of public housing. Broadly, these policies take two forms. The first focuses on *dispersal*, in which public housing residents are relocated across the urban landscape into neighborhoods meant to have lower poverty rates and higher levels of racial, ethnic, and (especially) economic diversity than those they came from. Dispersal efforts have included the creation of "scattered-site" housing beginning in the 1970s, but most often they subsidize housing in the private rental market by issuing vouchers to cover "fair market rent" above about 30 percent of qualified tenants' income.[22] Rather than concentrating subsidized housing in larger complexes or building smaller, scattered-site developments, each managed centrally by the housing authority, issuing vouchers was meant to help public housing residents access the private real estate market. Unlike project-based subsidies, however, moving to less poor, less racially segregated neighborhoods has been constrained by a lack of landlords willing to accept vouchers, by residents' choice, and by the difference between what these subsidies can cover and "fair market rent" in more affluent neighborhoods with stronger housing markets.

The second approach to poverty deconcentration focuses on place-based *redevelopment*. The national policy framework behind this strategy is HUD's HOPE VI (Housing Opportunities for People Everywhere) program, initiated in 1992 under the George H. W. Bush administration but drawing on earlier experiments (for example, in Boston and Chicago) in reshaping public housing with an emphasis on promoting mixed-income developments.[23] Initially focused primarily on renovating the most severely distressed public housing, HOPE VI quickly began to shift priorities over the first few years, turning more to large-scale demolition and redevelopment as well as encouraging public housing authorities to extend vouchers to move families out of problematic public housing complexes without replacing each demolished unit with a newly constructed unit owned and managed by the housing authority. In addition, HOPE VI efforts were turning more toward privatization and public-private partnerships for developing and managing renovated or rebuilt public housing, as well as for a range of support services.[24] With the 1996 appropriations bill, program goals became explicitly dedicated to deconcentrating poverty, stating that HOPE VI funds should be used to build or provide replacement housing "which will avoid or lessen concentration of very low-income families," a goal that became central to HOPE VI funding allocations going forward.[25] In addition, undergirding the HOPE VI redevelopment philosophy were design principles espoused by the New Urbanist movement, which sought to promote more vibrant, well-integrated social environments through physical planning.

Chicago's Plan for Transformation

Reflecting the objectives, tools, and strategic orientations embodied in the most expansive versions of HOPE VI legislation, Chicago's Plan for Transformation seeks to deconcentrate poverty, promote the integration of public housing residents into less poor, economically diverse neighborhoods in the city, and catalyze urban redevelopment through both dispersal and development strategies. These strategies are harnessed in the service of twin stated goals. One, relying on demolition and re-development, is to fundamentally remake urban neighborhoods that had been dominated by public housing complexes and characterized by extreme poverty, disinvestment, social isolation, and racial segrega-tion, transforming them into well-functioning mixed-income neighbor-hoods. Developed through public-private partnerships, with the state encouraging private action through public funding, tax incentives, and land write-downs, redevelopment is meant to promote in-migration of higher-income residents and attract investment by market actors in real estate development, commercial activity, and community ameni-ties. The second goal, pursued through relocation and dispersal, is to integrate public housing residents into these new communities and into the city as a whole, ending the social, economic, and spatial isola-tion that had characterized their lives in public housing "projects" and giving them access to the opportunities, amenities, relationships, and other resources the city makes available to its citizens. As a response to urban poverty and an effort to address the challenges public housing residents face, both goals rely fundamentally on convictions regarding the benefits of integration as a means to counteract the effects of con-centrated poverty. By removing public housing residents from contexts of disadvantage and settling them in safer, healthier, and more support-ive environments, the intent is to better connect them to resources and opportunity—such as better schools, more responsive services, better access to the workforce, and the opportunity to forge new and positive social relations.[26]

The Plan is wide-ranging. With a price tag of some $3 billion thus far, it includes renovating about 40 percent of the public housing stock, mainly focused on low-rise, peripherally located family developments, scattered-site housing, and developments for the elderly. It also includes tearing down the remaining 60 percent of public housing and relocat-ing many of these tenants into the private market, subsidized by more housing vouchers. Most dramatically, it includes the wholesale demoli-tion and mixed-income redevelopment of the most "distressed" public housing complexes, including all the major high-rise developments that have helped give Chicago's public housing a reputation as a massive policy "disaster."[27]

The development of new mixed-income communities to replace pub-lic housing complexes is only one component of the broader strategy, but it is in many respects the Plan for Transformation's central mani-festation. Although only a minority of CHA residents relocated by the

Transformation will return to the redeveloped sites (ten years into the Transformation, only about 13 percent of those who remained in CHA-subsidized housing had returned to these developments),[28] demolition and mixed-income redevelopment plans have affected the vast majority of Chicago's public housing population since the Plan was announced, driving the process of relocation and consuming by far the largest share of the CHA budget related to the Transformation.[29] In addition to providing "the most visible expression of the Plan for Transformation,"[30] the mixed-income developments also represent the clearest instantiation of the Plan's integrationist goals, providing the greatest control in developing new communities, shaping the built environment and social settings that residents will move into, ensuring some diversity of income and background among community members, and providing mechanisms—through design, unit allocation, property management, and "community building"—meant to promote integration and support inclusion and connection. The nature of the "mix" differs across developments. Most have been guided by a general framework of one-third market-rate (including homeowner and rental units), one-third "affordable"[31] units (including subsidized rentals for low-income non-CHA residents and subsidized homeowner units for qualified middle-income buyers), and one-third public housing replacement units. The relative distribution of units within these broad categories, the spatial distribution of units by income and tenure within developments, and the demographic characteristics of residents living in each differ (sometimes significantly), though in each case these arrangements represent an effort to bring an intentionally mixed-income community into being by targeting specific units to specific populations according to income and public housing status.

Regeneration or Gentrification?

Chicago's Plan for Transformation has been highly controversial, to say the least. Advocates argue that it will improve the quality of housing and increase housing choices for public housing residents, improve the neighborhoods they live in and the quality of life they can support, promote the development of skills and opportunities that lead to self-sufficiency, and end their "economic and social isolation."[32] The mixed-income component of the Plan, as with similar efforts across the country, is particularly lauded as a way to reshape blighted urban neighborhoods, build the human and social capital of public housing residents, and provide safe, healthy environments that help connect poor people to supports, relationships, and opportunity.[33] Thus, in the most positive light the mixed-income component of the Plan can be seen as an effort to promote "positive gentrification"—public policy that harnesses private capital and market forces to attract higher-income residents and regenerate neighborhoods while attempting to protect the right of at least some low-income residents to remain in place and benefit from neighborhood improvements.[34]

Critics, on the other hand, point to a broad range of issues that call into question both basic premises and practical outcomes. Specific critiques focus on both proximal impacts and long-term challenges. These include, for example, the difficulties imposed on public housing residents by dislocation and forced relocation, the disruption of their social networks, and the overall reduction in much-needed affordable housing units. Indeed, the overall stock of public housing in Chicago will ultimately be reduced by about 14,000 units.[35] In addition, there have been a host of problems with implementation—inadequate relocation counseling, poor coordination among implementing agencies, failure to track residents over time, confusion about eligibility requirements and the process for returning residents to new units, lack of available voucher housing, construction delays—that exacerbated these difficulties and placed additional burdens on public housing residents affected by the Transformation.[36] Some of these criticisms of unfair treatment and inadequate support of residents have been the basis of two major lawsuits brought against the CHA on behalf of public housing residents, which generated substantial delays and worsened an already strained relationship between the CHA and resident representatives and their legal advocates.[37]

There have also been more fundamental critiques regarding basic assumptions about the likely benefits of deconcentration, privatization, and mixed-income development,[38] as well as about the intended *beneficiaries*, including claims that they are essentially revanchist schemes focused more on appropriating poor neighborhoods to benefit capital interests and the middle class than on addressing the needs of public housing residents or responding substantively to urban poverty.[39] These claims echo more general critiques of neoliberal urban policy.[40] If proponents see such schemes as good-faith efforts at "positive gentrification," critics believe they lead instead to displacement, invasion, and regulation, "mobilizing city space as an arena for both market-oriented economic growth and for elite consumption practices, while at the same time securing order and control amongst marginalized populations."[41]

Indeed, several scholars have characterized these efforts, in Chicago and nationally, as a contemporary version of the urban renewal of the mid-twentieth century. Although they differ in some respects from the policies of slum clearance and urban restructuring that led, among other things, to the proliferation of high-rise public housing complexes that today's policies are now demolishing, they have similar deleterious effects on those forcibly relocated to make room for investment and redevelopment.[42]

Integrationist Aims and Ends

At this time, Chicago's Plan for Transformation is in its sixteenth year and has recently launched a second strategic phase, referred to as Plan Forward, which is being led by a new CHA chief executive officer, the seventh to oversee the Plan. Major demolition is complete, 85 percent of the CHA's goals for new and renovated housing units (just over 21,000 units) have been reached, and over 56,000 public housing residents have been relocated to either temporary or "permanent" replacement housing.[43] However, the bulk of completed units are senior housing and renovated traditional public housing units, and the production of units in mixed-income developments has fallen far short of the goal. Fewer than half of replacement public housing units (3,415 out of the projected 7,700) had been completed in mixed-income developments as of early 2014. And the pace of production has slowed to a trickle: only 88 units were produced in 2013, and 40 were expected to be produced in 2014.[44]

While some of the aims of the Transformation are being met, at least to an extent, others have failed to materialize. Public housing leaseholders have been relocated to neighborhoods that are safer and less poor than those dominated by the public housing complexes they moved from[45]—although as Lawrence Vale and Erin Graves point out, given the extreme concentration of poverty in their neighborhoods of origin this could hardly have been otherwise.[46] Indeed, in Chicago and other cities engaged in public housing reform, although the neighborhoods that voucher holders moved to are clearly "better"—less poor, more safe, better maintained[47]—most relocated public housing residents still live in neighborhoods that are characterized by high poverty and are almost invariably racially segregated.[48] Those moving to mixed-income communities, given the wholesale redevelopment and repopulating of these sites, have experienced clear and significant improvements in housing quality, the built environment, and community safety; a more robust income mix (at least on the footprint of the development); and the beginnings of broader revitalization of surrounding neighborhoods.[49]

Understanding the question of effective integration—and how likely it is to lead to the benefits for the poor that the policy rhetoric suggests—requires moving beyond what basic indicators of economic well-being, spatial incorporation, and demographic mixing can suggest. It requires understanding the lived experience of public housing residents in their new communities, the dynamics of community life into which they are incorporated, how well their integration provides increased access to resources, organizations, and opportunities they were isolated from in public housing, and the nature of their engagement with their new neighbors and the social networks they represent.

In contrast to strategies relying on dispersal, the effort to remake public housing complexes into mixed-income communities represents the Plan for Transformation's most explicit and intentional effort to realize its integrationist goals (and, more broadly, those of HOPE VI and its successor under the Obama administration, Choice Neighborhoods). Unlike the neighborhoods that voucher holders move into or where scattered-site developments are located, the mixed-income communities replacing public housing developments are highly contrived. Demolition of the public housing that had occupied these sites has generally been total,[50] and in many cases redevelopment entailed the wholesale relocation of residents during the lengthy process of clearance and construction. Although located within broader neighborhoods and intended to be integrated into them, because the development sites are centrally designed and to some extent centrally managed by development teams and property management companies, mixed-income communities provide an opportunity to both shape the physical environment and put in place frameworks and processes—decision-making bodies, rules, contracts, activities—that would have direct and significant influence both in "creating" these new communities and in shaping key inputs that fundamentally condition neighborhood life within them.[51]

Although the effort to remake public housing through redevelopment with an emphasis on economic and social diversity is being carried out on the largest scale in Chicago, the orientation not only has been embraced in other US cities[52] (largely supported by HOPE VI funding) but also represents a broader international agenda that characterizes public housing reform in Western Europe (especially in the United Kingdom, the Netherlands, Ireland, France, Belgium, and Germany), Australia, and Canada.[53] There is a historical logic to this. Public housing in these countries, especially in Western Europe, developed along similar trajectories and in response to the similarly massive social upheavals of the Great Depression in the United States and the two world wars in Europe. In addition, the rapid expansion of public housing in the second half of the twentieth century was part of a broader, transatlantic embrace of what Christopher Klemek calls the "urban renewal regime"[54]—the confluence of a (re)emerging faith in rational, technocratic responses and the need for comprehensive planning to solve complex urban problems, the mounting influence of modernist design principles, and practical alliances among policy entrepreneurs, planning professionals, and social scientists. This regime led to widespread slum clearance and the creation of massive new public housing complexes, functionally segregated from the city and ultimately leading to concentrated pockets of poverty and deprivation in deteriorating, poorly managed developments. The current policies toward integration and mixed-income development across these contexts have thus been shaped by common perceptions of failure and common orientations toward reform, whether seen as a repudiation or as a new version of the urban renewal that created them in the first place.

Interrogating Assumptions and Exploring Reality

Although it is cross-national in scope, understanding in detail how this integrationist agenda and its implementation through public housing reform and mixed-income development are playing out in particular places is critical to gaining insight into its possibilities and limitations and to informing policy efforts and expectations going forward. In this context, Chicago provides a particularly useful case. Chicago is in many ways emblematic of the dynamics of city growth and the problems generated by urbanization, deindustrialization, demographic change, and racial tension that have characterized many cities. "Fordist before Ford,"[55] Chicago pioneered and institutionalized many of the techniques of mass production and labor control that came to typify large-scale industrial production.[56] It exemplified the processes of rapid social change brought about by urbanization and immigration in its early history and has emerged, post-industrialization, as a successful player on the global stage, ranking seventh on the 2014 Global Cities Index—though with a concomitant growth in income inequality.[57] Chicago has also been an important proving ground for much urban poverty policy, including its significant involvement in the urban renewal programs in the mid-twentieth century that led to the CHA's growth as one of the largest public housing authorities in the United States. It has also been central in the development, testing, and reformulation of public housing policy, including being among the first to experiment with mixed-income strategies and serving as a laboratory for public housing development and reform nationally.[58] The scope and variety of the mixed-income effort in Chicago, with nine private development partnerships producing over a dozen major new mixed-income developments, provides an excellent subject for comparative analysis. Specific elements of the Chicago approach to the mixed-income public housing transformation make it particularly interesting: the commitment to including market-rate, for-sale housing in the developments and high levels of physical integration of market-rate and subsidized buildings (and sometimes units within buildings on site); a relocation rights contract to formalize commitments to residents and an independent monitor to oversee its implementation; and the mix of traditional public housing, Housing Choice vouchers, mixed-income housing, and scattered-site housing as possible options for relocating residents.

Grounded in the experience of Chicago's Plan for Transformation, this book examines the assumptions behind the city's effort to re-create urban space that had been dominated by public housing complexes as integrated, well-functioning, mixed-income neighborhoods, and it explores the emerging outcomes. It investigates key dimensions of the design and implementation of the policy on the ground, including the roles and influence of key actors and the shifting division of labor among state, market, and nonprofit organizations; the ideas that inform the design of the built environment as planned, and key aspects of it; the processes of deliberation, decision making, and engagement among professionals and residents in these contexts; the nature and dynamics of interaction, integration, inclusion, and exclusion in these emerging communities and between them and the broader neighborhoods where they sit; and the broader promise and limitations of the strategy for addressing urban poverty and fostering urban regeneration. In doing so, the book both situates the specific case of Chicago's effort in the broader historical and contemporary context of housing policy and community development in the United States and seeks to leverage the analysis of Chicago's experiences to highlight key conceptual, practical, and policy implications for addressing urban poverty more broadly.

Within the broader context of national policy and the local framework of the Plan for Transformation, we look at three mixed-income developments being built to replace large public housing complexes in the city:

Westhaven Park, which replaces the Henry Horner Homes on the city's West Side; Oakwood Shores, which replaces the Madden Park and Ida B. Wells developments on the city's South Side; and Park Boulevard, also on the South Side, replacing the Stateway Gardens development along the State Street Corridor, which was the largest concentration of public housing in the nation before the Transformation. Together these sites offer a useful illustration of mixed-income development in the context of Chicago's Plan for Transformation, providing insight into how these efforts are playing out within different types of developments and neighborhoods, managed through a range of organizational arrangements. (See table 1.1 for a summary comparison.)

We take a mixed-method, comparative case study approach, drawing on document analysis, administrative data, and, most centrally, extensive fieldwork conducted over the course of six years in and around the three mixed-income public housing redevelopments and with actors involved in the Transformation at the city level. Field data include

Table 1.1 Mixed-Income Developments

	Oakwood Shores	Park Boulevard	Westhaven Park
Former public housing site	Ida B. Wells, Madden Park	Stateway Gardens	Henry Horner Homes
Developers	National nonprofit (rental); local for-profit (for sale)	Four local for-profits	Two regional and national for-profits
Social service providers	Nonprofit, delivered by developer and later contracted out to local	Nonprofit, created by developer	Nonprofit, contracted out to local
Total projected units	3,000	1,316	1,317
Relocated public housing units (%)	1,000 (33)	439 (33)	824[c] (63)
Affordable rental units (%)	680 (23)	421 (32)	132 (10)
Market-rate rental units (%)	1,320 (44)	456 (35)	361 (27)
Homeowner units (%)	810 (27)	553 (42)	303 (23)
Units built to date[a]	854	367	1,098
Relocated public housing units (%)	277 (32)	127[b] (34)	788[c] (72)
Affordable rental units (%)	332[d] (39)	106[e] (29)	90 (8)
Market-rate rental units (%)	179 (21)	29 (8)	81 (7)
Homeowner units (%)	66 (8)	105 (29)	139 (13)
Initial occupancy dates	Renters: 2005 Homeowners: 2006	Renters: 2007 Homeowners: 2007	Renters: 2003 Homeowners: 2006

Table 1.1 (*continued*)

	Oakwood Shores	Park Boulevard	Westhaven Park
Select site-specific criteria	Thirty hours per week work requirement; five-year criminal background check; credit screening; residential history check; annual drug test	Thirty hours per week work requirement; five-year criminal background check; credit screening; residential history check	Twenty hours per week engagement requirement; criminal background check; credit screening; residential history check
Guiding legal authority for returning residents	Relocation rights contract	Relocation rights contract	Consent decree
Neighborhood	Bronzeville/North Kenwood–Oakland, South Side Chicago	Bronzeville, South Side Chicago	Near West Side, West Side Chicago
Neighborhood amenities and institutions	Near Lake Michigan, public parks, Hyde Park, and University of Chicago	Near public transit corridor, Illinois Institute of Technology, White Sox stadium, major highway	Near downtown central business district, public transit stop, United Center stadium

[a] Unit counts as of 2014 (Oakwood Shores and Westhaven Park) and 2013 (Park Boulevard) provided by representatives of each development.
[b] Includes public housing replacement units in an off-site rental building, the Pershing.
[c] Includes the Villages, a 200-unit "superblock" of 100 percent public housing units located in the middle of the mixed-income development; the Annex, a 90-unit rehabilitated public housing building nearby; and 261 scattered-site public housing units in the surrounding neighborhood.
[d] Includes 75 units of affordable senior rental housing.
[e] Includes 53 units of affordable rental housing in the Pershing.

in-depth interviews with a panel of residents in the new developments across income levels and housing tenures (public housing and other low-income renters, owners of "affordable" units subsidized with tax credits, and renters and owners of market-rate units). Data also include in-depth interviews with stakeholders in the broader neighborhoods where the developments are being built and with developers, property management staff, service providers, and other professionals (CHA personnel, public housing advocates, city government officials) who have played a particular role in the design, management, and monitoring of the Transformation. In addition to interviews, fieldwork also included observing a broad range of community meetings, programs, events, and interactions both at the three sites and at citywide forums and, in the last year of field research, a set of focus groups with an additional, diverse set of residents. We also draw on administrative data on 16,000 households living in public housing at the outset of the Transformation, including CHA leaseholder data linked with administrative records from a variety of state and local agencies in Illinois, including the Illinois Department of Children and Family Services, the Illinois Department of Human Services, the Illinois Department of Employment Security, and the Cook County Juvenile Court. (For a more detailed description of methods and data, see the appendix.)

The book is organized as follows: Part 1 deals with the theory, history, and context that led to and framed the implementation of the Plan for Transformation. Following this introductory chapter, chapter 2 interrogates theory. This includes the central theoretical lines of argument that provide an intellectual basis for integrationist approaches to addressing urban poverty and public housing reform. Primary among them are sociological theories regarding neighborhoods and social capital, including the role of networks and socially embedded resources that affect social control, social behavior, and access to political and market resources. Also central are New Urbanist planning principles directed toward the potential of well-designed environments (characterized by low-density, mixed-use, "defensible" space and spatial integration) to promote social interaction and social control. In addition to these theoretical moorings (which explicitly inform the Transformation and similar efforts), we draw on two other conceptual frameworks to shape our analysis of outcomes. The first is social exclusion, which calls attention to the social processes and mechanisms beyond informal social relations that lie at the core of social capital arguments—especially the role of institutions and organizational actors—in creating and reproducing marginality.[59] Issues of race, class, and other dimensions of difference and stigma are key to our exploration of exclusion and marginalization in this context. The second framework focuses on the dynamics of "poverty governance" in the context of neoliberalism, which is concerned with how market logics and increasingly robust mechanisms of surveillance and discipline reframe the way social welfare policies contribute to regulating and penalizing the poor.[60]

Chapter 3 places public housing reform policies like the Plan for Transformation in Chicago and HOPE VI (and its successor Choice Neighborhoods) at the national level in the historical context of community development and "community building" efforts in the United States. It then builds on this broader history to situate housing policy as a response to urban poverty, charting the development of public housing in the United States, providing a description and analysis of current policy that seeks to reform it, and laying out the parameters and components of the Transformation that frame action and impact at the local level in each mixed-income development replacing public housing complexes.

Part 2 is the empirical heart of the book. Chapter 4 describes the three sites where our study of mixed-income development took place, including the neighborhood contexts, pre-Transformation dynamics, and organizational arrangements under which redevelopment would "roll out" as implementing the Plan got under way. Chapter 5 details the specific "inputs" that shape the new developments and their efforts to create well-functioning mixed-income communities on the footprint of public housing projects. This includes a focus on the goals and expectations of those responsible for bringing these new communities into being and managing their build-out and the kinds of services, supports, governance arrangements, and "community-building" strategies they adopt.

Chapter 6 then provides an in-depth analysis of the nature of the emerging communities and how well they reflect the ideals of integration that lie behind the Transformation and similar policies guiding public housing reform. It provides a nuanced exploration of the nature of social interaction and relationships among neighbors of different backgrounds, the nature of participation and engagement in community life, and the factors that condition (promote or constrain) interaction among residents of different income groups, housing tenures (owners versus renters), and racial and ethnic backgrounds. It demonstrates that policy assumptions regarding spatial integration leading to social interaction and social capital outcomes for public housing residents are overblown, since social relations for the most part remain distant and are often contentious. These circumstances are shaped by spatial dynamics, differential participation, organizational compartmentalizing, and the enduring influence of institutionalized assumptions about difference grounded in notions of the urban "underclass."

Chapter 7 extends the analysis of social interaction by focusing on critical emerging dynamics around the nature and use of public space, public behavior, and social control in these emerging communities. It shows that the efforts to address urban poverty and public housing reform through mixed-income development generate a set of fundamental tensions—between integration and exclusion, use value and exchange value, appropriation and control, poverty and development—that play out in specific, concrete ways. In particular, community concerns about order and safety and contention around definitions of "public" space, rights of access, and norms of behavior lead to increasingly stringent surveillance, control, and rule enforcement. These dynamics militate against effective integration and contribute to alienating and marginalizing public housing families and other low-income residents in these contexts. Indeed, rather than effective integration, we argue, the experience of many public housing and low-income residents amounts to what might be called *incorporated exclusion*, in which physical integration reproduces marginality and leads to withdrawal and alienation rather than engagement and inclusion.

Chapter 8 takes the analyses in chapters 6 and 7 one step further, examining the relation of the mixed-income developments to the broader neighborhoods where they sit and gauging how well, beyond social and physical integration among residents on the footprint of the development, the Transformation is integrating these new communities into the fabric of the broader neighborhoods and the city. It looks at how far, and in what ways, public housing transformation has been accompanied by broader neighborhood change and the spatial, social, and organizational mechanisms that encourage (or fail to promote) relationships between residents of the development and those in the neighborhood, particularly with regard to cross-class relationships and the integration of public housing residents.

Finally, chapter 9 draws some broad conclusions about the promise and perils of public housing transformation and mixed-income development as a response to concentrated urban poverty and presents some suggestions for both policy and practice. While some of the concrete goals of the Transformation are being met, its broader integrationist goals—and their expected impact on public housing residents—have failed to take hold. Most residents provided with housing during relocation have been moved to generally safer and less poor neighborhoods. In the context of the mixed-income components of the Plan, there have been significant improvements to the housing units and built environment where public housing residents and their new neighbors live, as well as the beginnings of broader revitalization of the neighborhoods surrounding the former public housing complexes. But most residents relocated using housing vouchers are again concentrating in racially segregated, still largely poor neighborhoods. And many public housing residents and other low-income renters moving to mixed-income developments, rather than being effectively *integrated* into these contexts, find that the community dynamics and mechanisms of control are leading to *incorporated exclusion*. With this term, we call attention to the ways the stated aims of integration that lie behind mixed-income strategies of public housing reform are undermined by specific social dynamics, institutionalized narratives, and organizational actions. Thus the broader dynamics of social exclusion that public housing redevelopment is intended to address are instead reshaped and reproduced within the new developments. Informed by debates in the immigration literature about appropriate terminology for understanding integration, we use *integration* here as suggesting some reciprocal interaction and mutual accommodation (a dialectic with each changing and to some extent accommodating to the other) and including formal integration into the social structures and political and economic systems available to citizens at large. We use *incorporation* to describe being (actively, intentionally) merged or folded into society (in this case, specifically, the mixed-income communities and the bridge they are meant to provide to the broader systems and opportunities the city offers) but without necessarily implying changing or being changed, and without necessarily having the broader implications of effective integration. In this way, *incorporated exclusion* both highlights the disjunction between aims and ends and focuses on the actors, mechanisms, and processes that lie behind it.[61]

Adding to these social challenges and shortcomings in the new mixed-income sites and across Chicago's neighborhoods are fundamental concerns about the viability of the remaining planned phases of development and the sustainability of the overall effort. The housing market crisis that began in 2008 has demonstrated the extreme vulnerability of market-driven mixed-income redevelopment and some of the risks and downsides to the neoliberal approach to public housing transformation.

TWO

Theoretical Assumptions and Policy Orientations

Orientations toward poverty deconcentration and the integrationist claims that lie behind them are driving the lion's share of public housing reform policy in the United States. Cities across the country are increasing their use of vouchers to help low-income people move out of high-poverty areas and get housing in the private market. And mixed-income developments—including several major projects in cities such as Atlanta, Boston, Chicago, Kansas City, Louisville, New Orleans, Portland, San Francisco, Seattle, and St. Louis—are at the center of the most ambitious efforts at public housing reform.[1]

As a central part of these efforts, mixed-income development strategies have as much to do with urban revitalization as with addressing poverty. Public housing redevelopment attracts investment and (middle-class) populations back into the central city and offers an opportunity to reenvision, reclaim, and remake parts of the city that have become "discredited," as Lawrence Vale puts it, by poverty, crime, and physical decay, building in their place new, wholesome, reimagined communities.[2] These efforts are also tightly connected to market orientations toward urban renewal policy. To proponents, they are politically viable and economically lucrative strategies to address both urban poverty and urban revitalization. To critics, they are essentially a return to urban renewal, promoting anew the "displacement and containment of poor people of color" and the appropriation of property for market-driven development that benefits the middle class and affluent at the expense of the most disadvantaged.[3]

Debates over intent and likely beneficiaries notwithstanding, the *stated* rationale for these efforts, supported as they are by public policy coupled with the agenda of "transforming" public housing and responding to the needs of its residents, is grounded in a set of ideas that posit the social and economic benefits of integrating the poor into economically diverse, well-functioning, redeveloped neighborhoods. This chapter examines the theories and assumptions that lie behind policies of poverty deconcentration and contemporary public housing reforms in general, and behind mixed-income development orientations in particular. In addition to the explicit theoretical foundations of these policies, we also draw on the concepts of social exclusion and "poverty governance"[4] under neoliberalism. Each of these, in different ways, sheds light on the role of institutional frameworks and organizational actors in responding to, reproducing, and managing marginality. Each of these theories will inform our empirical analysis in later chapters of mixed-income development under Chicago's Plan for Transformation.

Policy Assumptions and Intellectual Moorings: Sociological Theory and Planning Principles

The policy assumptions explicitly informing poverty deconcentration and public housing reform policies are grounded largely in urban sociological theories of concentrated poverty, neighborhood effects, social capital, and social disorganization.[5] Within the context of replacing public housing complexes with mixed-income communities, these policies also draw explicitly on the planning principles of New Urbanism, which argue that aspects of the built environment can be designed to build community, promote diversity, support productive social interaction, and foster effective informal social control.

Concentrated Poverty, Neighborhood Effects, and the Urban "Underclass"

A recognition of the deleterious effects of concentrated poverty and theories about the importance of neighborhoods and their influence on well-being lie at the core of the Plan for Transformation and similar efforts both nationally and internationally. Although it has roots in the earliest sociological inquiry into urban poverty and its focus on slum communities,[6] the current emphasis on urban poverty as a topic of scholarly inquiry and policy response can be clearly traced to the late 1980s, driven in large part by the influence of William Julius Wilson's *The Truly Disadvantaged.*[7] At the heart of Wilson's argument was the impact of major economic restructuring, briefly outlined in chapter 1, that transformed the urban economies of older industrial cities from providing a strong base of manufacturing jobs that offered low- and moderately skilled workers a stable living wage and benefits to providing jobs mostly in the service sector. For low-skilled workers, this shift led to high rates of joblessness or low-wage jobs, often with limited benefits or none, and employment increasingly became less stable and often part-time.[8] These changes disproportionately affected low-income African Americans in these cities, who were concentrated in poor inner-city neighborhoods that had few city services, were disconnected from commercial resources and job opportunities, and experienced significant disinvestment in both physical and social infrastructure, from streets and parks to schools and services. These circumstances were exacerbated by additional disadvantages, including racial discrimination in employment and housing and disproportionate involvement in the criminal justice system (including more vigorous targeting and prosecution).[9] Ironically, some of the victories of the civil rights movement, such as fair housing laws, made conditions worse for the black urban poor, since they helped middle-class blacks leave inner-city neighborhoods. Their exodus removed critical economic resources from what had been vibrant local economies along with the social resources (such as institutional connections, political and market influence, and normative pressure to maintain social control) provided by a stable middle class.[10] The outcome, in Wilson's thesis, was the emergence of an urban "underclass" that faced both extreme deprivation and dramatically constrained access to opportunity. Residents were left socially isolated from "sustained interaction with individuals and institutions that represent mainstream society."[11]

Wilson's argument was largely structural, focusing on a complex set of factors—historical and contemporary discrimination, urban migration, the increasing proportion of youths in inner-city communities, and economic restructuring—in shaping and reproducing concentrated poverty.[12] He provided a vigorous counterargument to conservative scholars and policymakers whose assessment of inner-city poverty focused largely on the behavioral implications of a "culture of poverty"— the internalization by the underclass of a set of values in opposition to mainstream culture. Along with this, they argued that social welfare programs had perverse effects, creating incentives to unemployment and antisocial behavior, from out-of-wedlock births to welfare dependency.[13] Wilson took pains to distinguish between his concept of social isolation and the culture of poverty thesis, stressing that culture in these contexts is a response to structural disadvantage and not an indicator that the urban poor hold fundamentally different values than the middle-class "mainstream." Accordingly, he argued that policy responses to urban poverty need to address structures of opportunity rather than focusing primarily on individual behavior. But his treatment of underclass characteristics—crime, teenage pregnancy, welfare dependency, female-headed households—and his adoption of the "tangle of pathology" language first used in Daniel Moynihan's controversial 1965 report on the Negro family kept culture in the mix.[14]

As our analysis in later chapters will make clear, the institutionalized narrative of a set of enduring cultural differences that are reflected in urban underclass behavior continues to be salient in the mixed-income communities replacing public housing complexes. And significantly, the notion that income mixing will lead the very poor to make positive behavioral changes as they live among middle-class "role models" is the component of Wilson's argument perhaps most directly embraced in the policy rationale for poverty deconcentration schemes, especially for mixed-income development.[15] The essential notion here is that higher-income neighbors will give residents who had lived in concentrated poverty the opportunity to observe alternative ("middle-class") lifestyles and norms, thus promoting positive changes in their aspirations and individual behavior, embracing work, self-discipline, and self-sufficiency.

The mechanisms such role modeling is likely to work through are less than clear. Social learning theory suggests that modeling can be influential where regular association enables repeated observation, where the observer is attentive and perceptive, and where the characteristics of the role model suggest success and accomplishment in ways that have "functional value for observers."[16] This may happen through a kind of "distal role modeling," such as observing others' actions over time (a neighbor going to work every day, a neighbor's kids regularly attending school) or through more proximal interaction, such as direct advice, feedback, and accountability.[17] But while many have found the idea that mainstream role models can change underclass behavior compelling, the underlying assumptions about differences in values, culture, and aspirations driving such behavior have been vigorously contested.[18] Higher-income people, after all, do not demonstrate exclusively productive behavior; people from all income levels may struggle with alcohol and substance abuse or engage in domestic violence and other illegal or illicit behavior. And most people living in poverty have "mainstream" aspirations for themselves and their families yet remain poor despite abiding by the law and adhering to social norms.[19] In this light, expecting that observing "mainstream" values in action will change behavior can be seen as both paternalistic and misguided.[20]

In spite of the controversy around these ideas, mixed-income development responses to urban poverty rely much more heavily on hopes for role-modeling effects than on the more fundamental changes to the opportunity structure, at least at the macro level, suggested by Wilson's structural analysis. But they also rely on a set of broader assumptions about the importance of neighborhoods' influences on those living in concentrated poverty, and on the promise that changing circumstances may offer. These assumptions are informed by a quarter-century of research on "neighborhood effects," largely focusing on the negative impact of living in concentrated poverty, especially on the development and well-being of children and youths.[21]

Although there is still significant debate about the causal link between context and outcome and about the strength of these effects relative, for example, to family influences,[22] a significant body of research demonstrates associations between high-poverty neighborhoods and a range of social problems. Much of this research, particularly early on, looked at the relation between compositional aspects of the neighborhood—especially concentrated disadvantage but also racial segregation, the concentration of single-parent families, homeownership, residential instability, and the absence of relatively affluent families and professional and managerial workers—and a range of negative outcomes, from child abuse to school achievement to crime.[23] Addressing these effects—either by changing neighborhood circumstances or by moving people to more stable, less poor neighborhoods—is seen as a way to support better individual outcomes. But beyond addressing these negative aspects, poverty deconcentration policies, and mixed-income development orientations in particular, stress the positive aspects of "community" that well-functioning neighborhoods can supply by virtue of the activities, mechanisms, and processes that let them operate as social settings.[24]

Community, of course, is a protean idea, frequently invoked but variously defined, and its meaning and relevance in the context of complex urban society and within urban neighborhoods are often contested.[25] Still, beyond their clear relevance as space (delimited geographic portions of a city) and place (areas with recognized identities and at ̈ ̈ that differentiate them to some extent), urban neighborhoods often considered *social* units. They have thus been seen as symbolic and affective units of identity and belonging;[26] as functional sites for producing and consuming social goods and processes such as religion, education, socialization, social control, institutional participation, and mutual support;[27] as contexts for developing and utilizing social norms, social networks, and social capital;[28] and as sites of investment, disinvestment, and political contention shaped by actors in the broader political economy as well as sites of potential mobilization and political action from within.[29] Thus, beyond neighborhood composition and structure, neighborhood effects operate through social processes and community dynamics. "Neighborhood effects," writes Robert Sampson in his groundbreaking *Great American City*, "are not merely the reflection of individual characteristics [but] stem from social-interactional and institutional processes that involve collective aspects of community."[30] Reviewing the evidence on neighborhood effects and the social processes they work through, he and his colleagues note four kinds of neighborhood-level mechanisms that account for differences on a range of social problems. These include social networks and the nature of interaction among neighbors, how fully neighbors share norms and a willingness to intervene ("collective efficacy") in response to neighborhood problems, the presence and use of institutional resources, and the routine activities (and activity space where they occur) that neighbors engage in.[31] In the context of public housing reform and mixed-income development, efforts to build "community" entail shaping environments, opportunities, and social arrangements so as to promote healthy neighborhood life that public housing residents can be integrated into.[32] These efforts, in turn, rest on a belief that social capital, social control, and the built environment can promote community and the benefits that may flow from it.

Social Capital: Networks, Relationally Embedded Resources, and Connections

The idea that people living in concentrated poverty lack "social capital"— the social connections that can provide access to information, opportunity, and the potential for social mobility—is central to arguments about poverty deconcentration and to the rationale for mixed-income public housing reform. The term *social capital* was used as early as 1916 by L. J. Hanifan and in midcentury by Jane Jacobs and Ulf Hannerz, but the construct has become particularly influential since the 1980s, with seminal contributions by Pierre Bourdieu, James Coleman, and—perhaps most instrumental in popularizing it and promoting its use in common discourse—Robert Putnam.[33] Along with its rise in popularity has come a proliferation of uses and meanings as well as a set of important critiques regarding its use and assumptions about its benefits.[34] Most broadly conceived as a "metaphor about advantage," social capital refers to the resources available to individuals based on their position within a social structure—the ways group membership and relational networks provide access to resources and productive capacities that, as Coleman puts it, "would not be attainable in its absence."[35] In the context of arguments for poverty deconcentration, invocations of social capital focus principally on the ways relational networks, and the social resources embedded in them, can provide low-income individuals with the means for social advancement. Much of the perceived importance of social capital in these contexts relies on a distinction between "bonding" and "bridging" social capital[36] and on the evidence for the importance of what Mark Granovetter calls "weak ties." These casual rather than intimate relations that connect individuals to others outside their usual set of relationships have been shown empirically to be critical for social mobility, particularly for learning about and getting jobs.[37]

The argument goes something like this: Poor people, particularly those living in concentrated poverty, tend to have more localized social networks, and their relationships tend to be characterized by network closure and multiplex ties; they are embedded in networks composed of people in similar socioeconomic circumstances, and many people in the network know one another. Since, as Nan Lin points out, people with low levels of any given social-structural resource (social status, economic wealth, political influence) tend to have little access to other such resources as well,[38] these networks provide limited means to foster social mobility. They provide "bonding" social capital and can thus be useful for social support, but given the lack of connections to individuals with wholly other sets of relationships that can provide new flows of information, resources, and connection to opportunity ("bridging" social capital), they are less likely to be able to use their networks, as Xavier de Souza Briggs puts it, to "get ahead" instead of just "get by."[39] Integrating poor people into neighborhoods with higher-income people may thus give them access to the information and connections that higher-income people have—for example, about jobs, child care, financial management, working with schools, negotiating bureaucratic hurdles, getting a response from city agencies. The assumption here is that integration will lead to interaction, and interaction to concrete social and economic benefits.[40]

There is strong evidence that social networks are valuable for both social support and social mobility, particularly by increasing access to employment. For example, Granovetter found that 56 percent of participants in his study of professional, technical, and managerial white male workers in Newton, Massachusetts, used personal contacts to find out about jobs, and respondents believed that information secured this way was of higher quality than that obtained through formal or anonymous sources.[41] Similarly, based on a study of men in upstate New York, Lin and his colleagues found that a similar proportion of respondents got jobs through personal contacts and that resources available through one's social network were significant in explaining occupational status. They found that friends provided better access than relatives to occupational options of greater range and prestige and that the use of weak ties seemed most advantageous for those with lower socioeconomic status, since those ties gave them access to higher-status contacts and occupations.[42] And in their study of women in the Los Angeles labor market, Jennifer Stoloff and her colleagues found evidence that "network bridges"—relationships with individuals of another gender or race or from another neighborhood—improved employment status.[43]

The social capital expectations for poverty deconcentration efforts thus rely not just on spatial proximity, but—even more than assumptions about role-modeling effects—on how propinquity will promote sufficient social interaction to further relationship building that provides at least "weak," casual ties with neighbors whose social networks are different, and potentially more productive for social mobility, than those in which poor people are embedded.

Certainly, proximity can influence network formation, and community of residence provides both opportunities for and constraints on forming and sustaining relationships.[44] Opportunity for contact, proximity to others, and appropriate space to interact in, for example, are important factors that can promote and shape social interaction.[45] However, interaction and relationship building are much more likely to occur among people who share social characteristics, and the greater the social distance between individuals the less likely they are to associate with one another.[46] Promoting social interaction among people from significantly different backgrounds can thus be challenging and requires intentional action.[47] Efforts to meet these challenges often draw on the tenets of contact theory (to which we will return in chapter 6 to frame our analysis of social interactional dynamics in mixed-income public housing redevelopments), which concerns how, through interaction over time and under specific conditions, it is possible to overcome prejudice and conflict between "in" and "out" groups.

But social capital benefits might also accrue more circuitously, not just by direct connections or through specific dyadic relationships, but by tapping into the "positional resources" and the wealth, political connections, and civic influence of higher-income residents that can compel greater attention from external actors.[48] A number of studies have noted the unequal spatial distribution of commercial and municipal services across poor and more affluent neighborhoods,[49] and Sampson and his colleagues, for example, describe the "the differential ability of communities to extract resources and respond to cuts in public service" based on social composition.[50] By attracting higher-income residents into the community, mixed-income developments are thus expected to increase the proportion of local residents who are willing and able to advocate for high-quality goods and services, and their greater spending power is expected to make the community more attractive to retail and commercial development. Higher-income families are also expected to demand better performance from neighborhood schools and property management, since they have significantly more housing options than the poor (and can "vote with their feet" if school and housing quality fail to satisfy). And homeowners' financial stake will attract public and private investment in the community.[51] These factors, along with the likelihood of greater engagement and activism among relatively higher-income residents,[52] may redound to the well-being of the broader community as they garner collective goods such as safer streets, better schools, more commercial activity, better public amenities, and more efficient and responsive city services. In this way the social, economic, and political capital of higher-income residents can indirectly benefit their low-income neighbors even without more direct social interaction that leads to new network connections. Of course, the particular needs and priorities of low-income and higher-income residents may differ substantially, and the unequal distribution of power and resources among residents (and among local organizations acting on their behalf) may magnify such differences so that benefits favor those with more influence. Specifically, as John Logan and Harvey Molotch theorized in their framing of the "political economy of place," tensions and trade-offs between the use value and exchange value of community resources and investments may pit higher-income residents' (particularly owners') interests and influence against those of their less affluent neighbors.[53] Thus the benefits that may accrue to mixed-income communities from the presence or activism of higher-income residents cannot be presumed to equally further the well-being of all.[54]

Social Disorganization and Social Control

Another aspect of neighborhood life that poverty deconcentration policies seek to address—safety and social control—draws largely on social disorganization theory. Social disorganization—"the inability of a community to realize the common values of its residents and maintain effective social controls"[55]—is theorized to be the product of enduring structural attributes of particular neighborhoods that are mutually reinforcing. In their seminal study on juvenile delinquency, Clifford Shaw and Henry McKay demonstrated that variations in rates of delinquency across neighborhoods were highly correlated with factors such as neighborhood poverty, population mobility, physical deterioration, ethnic heterogeneity, and minority (black and foreign-born) status. Patterns of concentrated delinquency remained relatively stable across neighborhoods through the successive in- and out-migration of different groups. Rather than understanding delinquency as the product of culturally determined behavior fostered by particular ethnic groups or as purely individual and amenable to individual-level intervention alone, Shaw and McKay thus argued that both the problem and the solution need to be framed in terms of structurally determined community characteristics and the dynamics of community organization and functioning.[56]

A key element of social organization relevant for social control is the density of local acquaintance networks, which influences how well community members recognize one another and can hold one another accountable.[57] Coleman, for example, noted how network closure could contribute to informal social control by providing the means to level "collective sanctions" and therefore influence and regulate behavior.[58] In the current context this is particularly important with regard to "intergenerational closure" in which, in Coleman's example, parents of schoolchildren who know one another and know one another's children can reinforce each other in both monitoring and responding to children's behavior. Similarly, young people living in neighborhoods where they are known and where antisocial behavior will likely be reported and sanctioned through informal networks are less likely to engage in such behavior. Thus, closed networks (or "bonding" social capital) can be effective not only for social support, but also for social control. Similarly, Sampson and his colleagues note that collective efficacy—the combination of "social cohesion among neighbors combined with their willingness to intervene on behalf of the common good"—mediates between neighborhood characteristics such as concentrated poverty and residential instability, on the one hand, and crime on the other. Higher levels of collective efficacy are associated with lower levels of violent crime.[59]

The social ties necessary to establish network closure or promote collective efficacy need not be intimate or affective relationships; casual or instrumental ties among community members or even attentive, regular observers—"eyes upon the street" in Jane Jacobs's terms—within a broader context of trust and reciprocal obligation can provide accountability.[60] These dynamics can break down, however, in the face of extreme deprivation, or where such networks are overwhelmed by violence, disorder, and lack of trust among neighbors.[61] Concentrated disadvantage and residential instability, for example, are associated with both higher levels of violence and lower levels of collective efficacy, whereas neighborhoods with higher concentrations of affluence and greater residential stability contribute to intergenerational closure and reciprocal exchange among neighbors.[62]

Reducing concentrated poverty entails leveraging the presence of higher-income residents to promote order and neighborhood safety. Their presence is expected to enhance social control and reduce crime for a number of reasons. First, communities with higher proportions of homeowners are likely to be more stable and thus have denser acquaintanceship networks, stronger attachment to organizations that contribute to social control, and greater collective efficacy.[63] Second, higher-income residents are expected to be more likely to exert normative pressure to maintain order and safety in their neighborhood and to enforce rules and protect their investment.[64] Finally, law enforcement and other formal institutions that may contribute to neighborhood social control are likely to be more responsive and active in communities with higher-income people, who have greater political and market influence than the poor.[65]

Although there is ample empirical evidence that higher socioeconomic status, homeownership, and residential stability are positively related to neighborhood social control and lower levels of crime, it is also true that heterogeneity has long been identified with social disorganization and crime and can inhibit the primary ties and flows of communication that undergird many informal mechanisms of social control.[66] In such cases, social control tends to operate less through primary networks and more through local institutions and agencies beyond the neighborhood.[67] While social control mechanisms at these higher levels can be effective, they may also create conflict. As we will explore in detail in chapter 7, such conflict has indeed been generated, driven in part by a "broken windows" orientation to social control, in which outward signs of disorder and a broad range of "incivilities"—from littering to loitering to loud music—are treated as criminogenic and subject to punishment.[68]

New Urbanist Planning Principles

Finally, mixed-income development orientations to poverty deconcentration and public housing reform draw explicitly on a set of concepts championed by planners and architects promoting the principles of "New Urbanism," who argue for the role urban planning and design can play in shaping a built environment that (among other things) supports diversity, promotes social interaction, and ensures safety and civic engagement.[69] New Urbanist principles draw on the searing critiques leveled by Jane Jacobs in response to the massive modernist urban renewal efforts of the mid-twentieth century and reach back to ideas promoted by the Garden City Movement of the late nineteenth century and of "traditional" neighborhood development, championing pedestrian-friendly, mixed-use, sustainable communities that honor local history and vernacular design. By the 1990s, with the establishment of the Congress for the New Urbanism (CNU) and its charter, New Urbanism grew into an influential movement, arguing for an alternative to anomic suburban sprawl and a design response to revitalize the declining inner city.[70]

While much early New Urbanist development focused on greenfield projects that reimagined suburban neighborhoods in the mode of higher-density, pedestrian-friendly, traditional neighborhood design, it has increasingly been used in urban areas. Concentrating on both infill development and, as in the case of HOPE VI redevelopments, larger-scale regeneration, in cities like Chicago it seeks to transform modernist superblocks into more diverse, articulated neighborhoods on the footprint of the former public housing projects, integrating them into the street grid and larger context of the broader community.[71]

As might be expected, New Urbanism has both proponents and critics. Proponents laud it as a "a resilient, practical and well-founded alternative to conventional land development practices," noting its potential to promote economically diverse communities by integrating affordable housing; to shape developments that are environmentally friendly and sustainable; to increase pedestrian travel; to encourage participation, leading to design that is more responsive to community needs and priorities; and to promote positive neighboring, social capital, and collective efficacy.[72] Critics note the limitations of relying on physical development and spatial responses to social and economic problems; the problematic embrace of normative notions of "community" that elide attention to difference and may foster oppression and militate against diversity; the contribution of (particularly greenfield) developments to the de facto creation of exclusive enclaves; the difficulty of realizing New Urbanist goals in low-income communities; the tightly controlled approach to participatory planning; and the way its design preferences reflect "middle class notions of domesticity" and lead to the "suburbanization of the city."[73]

The promise of New Urbanist principles and its realization of the goals it claims to address have yet to be fully evaluated. There is significant diversity among New Urbanist developments, and evidence that they can promote social aims—diversity, equity, community—is limited and mixed.[74] With regard to income diversity, to take just one example, a recent study found that only 15 percent of 152 New Urbanist projects examined included properties "affordable to someone making the Area Median Income" (let alone low-income populations), in large part because few developers are willing or able to finance and support substantial income diversity.[75] Mixed-income public housing redevelopment projects, however, are explicit about affordability while adhering to New Urbanist tenets. They use a complex array of mixed-finance strategies to ensure some level of income mix, and the HOPE VI program has sought to ensure that key New Urbanist principles are applied in such redevelopments by codifying them as criteria to be met by successful proposals.[76]

Probably the most explicit statement of this commitment is codified in a joint publication by HUD and the Congress for New Urbanism's Inner City Task Force that outlines fourteen principles—from a commitment to community involvement in planning, to considering development projects within the broader context of economic opportunity and municipal and regional connections, to a range of specific spatial planning and architectural design guidelines—argued to be central to building community and creating well-functioning neighborhoods.[77]

Particularly relevant here are the claims New Urbanism makes about the importance of neighborhood and the ways design can contribute to "place making" and community building by shaping environments that contribute to social interaction, safety, and social and economic diversity. Indeed, neighborhood is the central construct, seen as a "building block of healthy cities and towns."[78] The vision of neighborhood promoted here is one of diversity, multiplexity, and interaction, where neighbors know one another and take pride in and responsibility for the collective good. Neighborhoods are seen as sites of sociability and exchange, providing easy access to the functions essential to day-to-day life and integrating public, private, and transitional spaces to promote a vibrant community and contribute to a "positive community spirit," where diversity supports the "strengthening [of] personal and civic bonds essential to an authentic community."[79]

Design is seen as contributing to these goals in several ways. Social interaction is to be promoted by attention to both housing and public spaces. Homes are to be oriented outward toward the street, blocks are to be at a small scale (neighborhoods rather than superblocks), and individual dwellings are to be designed with attention to "transitional" spaces (porches are the prime example) that allow for social interaction and observation. Public space is to be integrated into these blocks and the blocks integrated into the broader community, with "streets and public spaces as places of shared use," a variety of parks and open spaces for public gathering and recreation, and civic buildings accessible and appropriately sited.[80] Safety is similarly to be supported by design. The streetward orientation of dwellings, the promotion of mixed-use functionality and activity on the street and in public spaces, the clear spatial delineation of private and public spheres, and the encouragement of neighborly interaction through design all are meant to make space more defensible by increasing informal surveillance (once again, eyes on the street) and individual and collective responsibility. Finally, diversity is to be supported by the design and build-out of a range of housing types— larger and smaller, single-family and multi-unit, at different price points and responding to the needs of people at different stages of life and family—as well as explicit expectations for a range of incomes (from 25 to 125 percent of Area Median Income in the HUD/CNU guidelines, broader yet in some of Chicago's mixed-income developments). In addition, housing design should be sufficiently of a piece—high quality, building on the local architectural vernacular and historical character of the neighborhood, well integrated and cohesive—that significant differences in the status or background of neighbors are not highlighted by what their homes look like.

As we will see in subsequent chapters, while acknowledged as influential in designing the mixed-income developments replacing public housing complexes in Chicago, New Urbanist principles were both selectively engaged and differentially responded to by members of these new communities. Their influence was conditioned by a set of overarching social, organizational, and interactional dynamics that fundamentally challenged the expectations of sociability and community spirit anticipated by champions of New Urbanism.

Supplementary Lenses: Social Exclusion and Poverty Governance

The theoretical frameworks outlined above explicitly inform the rationale and expectations that lie behind poverty deconcentration policies, especially those focused on mixed-income development approaches to public housing reform. To understand how these assumptions are playing out and why, we draw on two additional conceptual frameworks: social exclusion and poverty governance.

Social Exclusion

Like social capital, social exclusion is a multifaceted, fundamentally relational construct.[81] Both social capital and social exclusion, for example, focus on the role of social structure and the nature of agency in engaging in and benefiting from social interaction. Both focus on relational linkages that connect individuals or collectivities to the sources of information and opportunity that are so critical to mobility. And both put forth social solidarity and social cohesion as crucial for alleviating the problems of marginality. Social exclusion arguments, however, call particular attention to the broader social processes and mechanisms—especially institutions and organizational actors beyond the informal social relations that lie at the core of social capital arguments—that create and reproduce marginality. In part because of this, personal agency, state responsibility, and third-sector roles are treated somewhat differently in discussions of social exclusion and social capital, with implications for how they are differentially applied to public policy making in different states.[82] For example, policies informed by social capital often emphasize activating local, interpersonal networks, the types of benefits derived from being embedded in substantively different networks, and the significance of face-to-face interactions. In contrast, policies with a social exclusion orientation often pay considerably more attention to how social relations are shaped by political, economic, and cultural institutions to enable inclusion within the broader society. They also often prefer different means to achieve this. For example, nation-states that predominantly invoke social capital rhetoric in policy making tend to promote non-state solutions to marginality—relying on market actors or civil society organizations, for example—to encourage expanded networks and exchanges, whereas those that adopt a social exclusion lens tend to promote more state-initiated responses that reflect a presumed societal responsibility to build an "inclusive" society.[83]

Social exclusion arguments are more influential outside the United States, but the rhetoric of exclusion finds its place here as well, particularly with reference to concentrated poverty and debates about the "underclass" that, as we have shown, are very much at the center of poverty deconcentration policies in general, and mixed-income development orientations in particular. Moving beyond the instrumentalizing of social relations that lies at the center of social capital arguments,[84] social exclusion suggests a broader focus on integration and inclusion, and on the actors and institutional processes that lie behind the creation and reproduction of marginality.

Although grounded in sociological theory, social exclusion has gained ascendance largely as a *policy* framework and has come to particularly address members of society embedded in extreme and persistent poverty and its associated ills, including withdrawal from civic life and the advantages of citizenship—institutional participation, political enfranchisement, social protection, and equitable treatment before the law.[85] Social exclusion arguments thus focus on the multiple social consequences of economic deprivation, but they also attend to the multiple causes—processes, actors, institutional frameworks, policy, and organizational choices—that help create and reproduce marginality.[86]

Beyond this broad conceptual foundation, however, the discourse on social exclusion has been complex; like social capital, it has many meanings and is invoked in different ways by actors grounded in different theoretical perspectives or adhering to different political ideologies.[87] Although common in policy discourse in Europe and other parts of the world, social exclusion remains a contested idea, given the multiple definitions proposed and, more fundamentally, the question whether it provides much useful conceptual leverage.[88] There are also debates about whether its focus unhelpfully detracts from more fundamental issues of material deprivation and income inequality, potentially undermining support for welfare state provisions.[89] Yet the concept has helped to drive a more refined understanding of poverty, deprivation, and marginality. Further, by emphasizing the centrality of social relations and the crucial role of the state and other institutional actors in producing (and potentially remediating) deprivation, the discourse on social exclusion provides a goad to shape policies that engage a range of stakeholders and recognize the multidimensionality of the problem. This emphasis on process, relations, and actors provides what Amartya Sen calls the "investigative advantage" that lies behind the major contribution of social exclusion as a concept.[90] Although causal agency remains unclear in much of the literature on social exclusion to date,[91] the construct directs us to focus on agents and potential responses beyond the individual and interpersonal, to include institutional and organizational dynamics at both the micro and macro level.

The social capital arguments outlined above clearly lie behind the policy rationales that undergird US housing policy geared toward poverty deconcentration and mixed-income development.[92] Social exclusion is not generally invoked explicitly in the United States in these contexts, but it arguably is equally relevant, given both the population that is the focus of deconcentration policies and the centrality of the rhetoric about integration that characterizes them—particularly with regard to mixed-income development schemes. Public housing communities are typical of the places and populations central to policies targeting social exclusion—they are the "communities left behind" by post-Fordist economic transformation, population mobility, and neoliberal policies.[93] They are the spatial instantiation of "advanced marginality," in Loïc Wacquant's term, characterized by "expulsion to the margins and crevices of social and physical space" by the history and institutionalizing of racial segregation, the generation and reproduction of economic inequality, and both government action and inaction.[94]

Our analysis of the emerging mixed-income communities replacing public housing complexes draws on the insights of social exclusion to examine the institutional mechanisms and organizational behaviors that are important in shaping the opportunities, constraints, and community dynamics that can either promote the kind of integration these policies invoke as a goal or reproduce exclusion and militate against its realization. We will demonstrate that, although mixed-income developments have been effective at changing the built environment and promoting economic (and sometimes, to some extent, racial) diversity in the neighborhoods relocated public housing residents move to (at least on the footprint of the former housing complexes), the interplay between institutional mechanisms, organizational actions, and individual responses within these contexts fosters community dynamics that subject poor people to different kinds of disadvantage and generate new forms of exclusion.

Poverty Governance

The final conceptual lens we turn to for understanding how the assumptions behind poverty deconcentration through mixed-income public housing reform are playing out, and why, is what Joe Soss, Richard Fording, and Sanford Schram call "poverty governance" in its contemporary form.[95] In shaping their argument, Soss and his colleagues build in part on Frances Fox Piven and Richard Cloward's seminal work on the ways state welfare policy serves as much to regulate and control the poor as to ameliorate the effects of material deprivation (let alone attend to the root causes of poverty and inequality) and on Wacquant's analysis of the punitive turn in policy geared to addressing populations of advanced marginality by coordinating social welfare and penal responses.[96] From this foundation, Soss and his colleagues argue that over the past several decades contemporary poverty governance has changed in important ways, centrally informed by race and racialized dynamics and discourses and driven by the confluence of two streams of reform.

The first of these streams is neoliberalism, a theory and set of political-economic processes and practices that privilege market orientations and logics, promote deregulation and privatization, and substantially shift the role of the state from redistributive and provisional social welfare intervention toward market-oriented strategies. Moving away from Keynesian expectations of state responsibility, the neoliberal state supports providing support services through contracting with private firms and nonprofit agencies and through public-private partnerships and a range of collaborative and coproduction arrangements with civil society actors.[97] Rather than representing simple welfare-state retrenchment, these arrangements have reformulated the state as a facilitator of market actors and goals, expanded its reach through collaborations with nongovernmental organizations, and reoriented intervention with the poor in ways that seek to make the objects of social welfare "think of themselves as market actors."[98] Indeed, "living in the market," we will hear a development professional at one site tell us, is very different from living in "the projects," and effecting that transition is one of the goals embraced by those charged with making mixed-income public housing reform work.

The second stream of reform that has changed the nature of poverty governance in recent years is increasingly paternalistic—and increasingly punitive—approaches to managing the poor. Paternalism here refers to the emphasis in state welfare policy on shaping the choices, behaviors, and actions of poor people through social welfare provision that makes receiving benefits conditional on adhering to certain norms and expectations. Programs thus emphasize obeying specific rules and abiding by specific requirements—regarding, for example, work, education, training, abstinence—and institute incentives, penalties, and regimes of monitoring and surveillance to ensure compliance. Beyond regulation, paternalism thus embraces a significantly more directive approach to poverty governance. As Lawrence Mead puts it, under the terms of paternalism, "society claims the right to tell its dependents how to live, at least in some respects. Whereas traditional policy defers to the capacity of clients to live their own lives, paternalism assumes that they need direction by others in order to achieve even their own self-interest, let alone society's. Paternalism thus goes beyond the mere regulation of behavior."[99]

Paternalism explicitly links individual responsibility and adherence to societal expectations for particular kinds of (positive) behavior with eligibility for benefits as well as with a range of punitive responses for noncompliance, including criminal justice intervention and incarceration and the incorporation of "criminal logics of violation and penalty" into social welfare.[100] But it is also, as Soss and his colleagues put it, "a project of civic incorporation that aims to draw its targets toward full citizenship."[101] While zero-tolerance policies, aggressive policing, stringent sentencing, and rising rates of incarceration remove increasing numbers of the poor from effective citizenship and participation in society, social policies providing social and economic benefits within the context of neoliberal paternalism seek to use incentives, rules, supervision, intervention, surveillance, and penalties to direct the choices and behaviors of the poor to make them "more respectable to their fellow citizens and instill them with the self-discipline needed to function as full participants in the community."[102]

This project of integrating the poor into "full citizenship" reflects what Barbara Cruikshank calls the "will to empower," with notions of empowerment embraced, albeit in different ways, by actors on both the right and left politically.[103] Reflective of Michel Foucault's notion of governmentality—governance less by the direct exercise of state power than by a diverse set of tactics and techniques operating through a range of actors and institutions across a variety of social settings—poverty governance in this mode seeks to govern the poor "at the level of the social."[104] It does so through a range of "mundane, little governmental techniques and tools," from case management to training programs to interviews to surveillance, that rely on the work of nongovernmental actors and seek to promote "voluntary" compliance with programs and enlist the poor in developing strategies of self-help and self-regulation.[105]

Regarding contemporary poverty governance, how these efforts play out reflects the convergence of neoliberalism's market orientation (relying on both private firms and nonprofit organizations to contribute through such mechanisms as performance-based contracting) and the disciplinary turn in welfare policy (surveillance, rules, and penalties).

As subsequent chapters will make clear, mixed-income public housing reform exemplifies this dual orientation. Public housing reform under HOPE VI, as Jason Hackworth has pointed out, is in many ways an exemplar of neoliberal urban policy: it couples decreased public funding and substitution of market solutions for direct provision and management with rules, structures, and incentives to "promote 'self-sufficiency,' entrepreneurialism, and private governance."[106] Along with these tendencies, mixed-income public housing reform, in particular, favors the paternalist side of contemporary poverty governance, operating through both state and non-state actors and organizations (the housing authority, the police, developers, property managers, social service providers) as well as more informally (through the normative pressure of higher-income neighbors, the compliance of low-income neighbors, and institutionalized narratives about the underclass). It attempts to shape behaviors, promote self-discipline, and move public housing residents toward a particular kind of citizenship personified by the self-regulated market actor. As with the welfare programs Soss and his colleagues studied, the mixed-income public housing redevelopments we examine in subsequent chapters are tending to similarly "de-democratize" the poor as citizens and conduct them "into positions of civic inferiority and isolation," but in this case through explicitly integrative efforts that shape such exclusion within the context of spatial incorporation.[107]

Conclusion

As we have shown, a clear set of theoretical propositions undergirds poverty deconcentration and mixed-income redevelopment policy, and they will inform our empirical analysis in the chapters that follow. Central among these are the presumed social and economic benefits of integrating the poor into economically diverse, well-functioning neighborhoods. This integrationist approach is grounded largely in urban sociological theories, including Wilson's analysis of the causes and consequences of concentrated urban poverty and its role in producing a socially isolated "underclass." It also comprises ideas about the importance of neighborhoods and the role of neighborhood effects in generating individual outcomes, theories about social capital and the importance of relational networks that can provide access to information and resources, and notions about how social disorganization and its effects (crime, isolation) can result from concentrated disadvantage and residential instability.

Although Wilson's arguments about concentrated urban poverty were largely structural, his ideas regarding the loss of positive role models in the inner city and the characteristics and behavior of a marginalized underclass have been particularly influential in shaping public housing reform. Thus the central components of mixed-income public housing redevelopment policy, including proximity to higher-income neighbors and strict regulatory frameworks of screening and monitoring, are aimed in large part at influencing the behavior of the poor rather than addressing more macro-level structural barriers to social and economic mobility. Bolstering this focus on modifying behavior and shaping community dynamics to support effective neighborhood integration are the planning principles of New Urbanism, which seek to leverage the design of the built environment to influence social interaction and social control.

To understand and interpret how the application of these theoretical orientations is playing out, we draw on two additional conceptual frameworks. The concept of social exclusion helps show how social relations are shaped not only by informal, interpersonal networks but also by political, economic, and cultural institutions. Attention to the punitive orientation and regulatory emphasis of contemporary social welfare policy as poverty governance prods us to focus on the specific mechanisms of control and accountability being employed to reorient welfare recipients (public housing residents, in the current case) toward thinking and behaving like self-regulated market actors. These theoretical approaches inform our exploration and assessment of the strategies and dynamics that have played out in pursuit of the integrationist goals that lie behind mixed-income public housing reform in Chicago. To further contextualize this effort, in the next chapter we situate Chicago's Plan for Transformation in the historical context of community development approaches to urban poverty and the long trajectory of public housing reform in the United States.

THREE

Mixed-Income Development in Context: Urban Poverty, Community Development, and the Transformation of Public Housing

In chapter 2 we situated contemporary poverty deconcentration policies in general, and mixed-income responses to public housing reform in particular, in the theoretical assumptions that guide their implementation and provide leverage for understanding their effects. In this chapter we place these policies in the broader historical context of community development efforts in the United States. We argue that the mixed-income development component of these efforts draws on and reframes a set of assumptions and past practices regarding the importance of neighborhoods and the potential of community-based intervention to address the interrelated needs and circumstances of those living in poverty in disadvantaged urban areas. We then build on this brief review of community development history to situate public housing policy as a response to urban poverty, charting the development of public housing in the United States and describing and analyzing current policy that seeks to reform it. Finally, we situate Chicago's Plan for Transformation within these current policy trends, lay out the parameters and components of the Plan, and describe how they frame action and impact at the local level in mixed-income developments replacing public housing complexes.

Urban Poverty and Community Development in the United States: A Brief History

Although in some sense community development has always been a part of American life,[1] as a focus of planned social policy, community intervention is most often traced to a stream of efforts beginning with the Progressive Era and the early settlement houses at the turn of the last century. It emerged largely in response to the social problems generated by the rapid growth of the industrial city: poverty, overcrowding, crime, intergroup tensions, and urban blight.[2]

Early Community Intervention in the Context of Industrialization

Beginning in the late nineteenth century, in response to the social problems generated in the slum communities rapidly growing up in the industrial cities of the American Northeast and Midwest, social reformers began to experiment with new approaches to responding to urban poverty. Principal among them was founding social settlements in poor immigrant neighborhoods.[3]

Settlement houses were sited in neighborhoods characterized by poverty, demographic heterogeneity, and residential instability, and their approach to working with the people who lived there focused in part on individual behavior and needs and in part on strengthening their neighborhoods. This approach was based on a general conviction that the conditions these individuals lived in were generated by the ecological forces of the industrial city and their negative effects on social organization rather than simply by individual failings.[4] Settlement workers took up residence in the neighborhoods where they worked, providing services and activities that had a strong socializing focus and seeking to promote middle-class values and expectations for behavior among the immigrant poor.[5] And although progressive leaders associated with settlements also addressed broader issues of neighborhood development and social reform,[6] over time settlements concentrated more and more on services, increasingly relying on professional staff and concentrating on the needs of individual clients.[7]

As settlements became more established in the early twentieth century, new forms of neighborhood organizations emerged, including community centers (in which local institutions—especially public schools—also served as neighborhood centers) and "social unit" experiments (in which neighborhoods were organized, block by block, to define needs and coordinate solutions through a system of neighborhood councils).[8] The principal force driving both these efforts, though they had somewhat different emphases and played out in different ways, was an interest in promoting mechanisms for local democracy. These local organizations provided a foundation for citizens' participation at the neighborhood level and an organizational hub for neighborly outreach, interaction and self-help, face-to-face deliberation and planning, and the development of social, cultural, and recreational programs. As with the settlements, rapid professionalizing, here in combination with public officials' resistance to their political activities, led these organizations to focus increasingly, and then exclusively, on professional planning, service coordination, and program delivery.[9]

For the most part, these early efforts concentrated on local, resident-engaged or resident-led planning and provision, with the goal of strengthening community organization and integration. But their limitations, along with the experience of some political organizing in neighborhoods and in other spheres—such as labor organizing in the workplace—generated a shift in strategic emphasis in the mode of community intervention. Beginning in the 1940s, for example, Saul Alinsky famously began organizing communities in Chicago and mobilizing them to engage in direct-action advocacy, using conflict-oriented strategies for political organizing.[10] This included catalyzing new, multi-issue neighborhood organizations, led by neighborhood residents with support from a professional organizer, to initiate community action and demand change from powerful actors like city government, schools, and landlords, fundamentally to alleviate poverty and inequality and gain access to power.

Midcentury Movements: Urban Renewal and Its Aftermath

In contrast to the voluntary sector efforts outlined above, government policy to address urban poverty in the middle of the twentieth century initially tended to be more top-down, emphasizing infrastructure, housing, and economic opportunity. Concerted federal interest in urban policy began under the Franklin Delano Roosevelt administration, which responded to the crisis of the Great Depression in part through large-scale employment and real estate development programs rolled out under New

Deal legislation.[11] These programs invested significantly in building collaboration and coalitions between federal and local government, as well as with actors in both the private and nonprofit sectors.[12] Perhaps most consequential for informing subsequent responses and setting the stage for the current phase of development under HOPE VI and its allied efforts was the urban renewal of the 1950s and 1960s. Urban renewal in this era emphasized slum clearance and the redevelopment of "blighted" inner-city neighborhoods, and to a large extent it privileged redevelopment of the central city at the expense of affordable housing and the needs of low-income residents. Reflecting its top-down, elite-driven orientation, residents living in (and later displaced from) neighborhoods targeted for demolition were not involved in the planning, and because many of the neighborhoods targeted were communities of color, urban renewal was seen by many as racist in practice—"Negro removal" rather than urban renewal, as James Baldwin famously put it.[13] As urban renewal played out, under mounting criticism and sometimes violent protest, several alternative approaches challenged its objectives and methods and attempted to shift activities from slum removal and central-city transformation to alleviating poverty and revitalizing neighborhoods.

The Community Action and Model Cities programs, for example, centered on both service coordination and the need for "maximum feasible participation" of the poor who lived in the neighborhoods targeted for intervention.[14] Indeed, the participatory dimension of the Community Action Program became in many ways the central—and most controversial—element of its design. It also led to significant resistance from city governments and some other local actors because it bypassed local jurisdiction by creating Community Action Agencies through direct federal mandate and because it engaged neighborhood social networks to promote political participation.[15]

Although these programs have been heavily criticized in the years that followed, they had an important impact on the politics of urban policy, established at least the principle of citizen participation as a critical component of redevelopment (despite difficulties in practice and tendencies toward ritual compliance), made issues of race and inequality explicit and incorporated them into the political discourse of development, and advanced a generation of (especially) African American leaders who went on to be influential in local government, private foundations, community organizing, and community development in the nonprofit sector through such mechanisms as the emerging community development corporations (CDCs).

Community Development Corporations and Comprehensive Community Initiatives

CDCs developed beginning in the early 1960s as community-based non-profits focused on both community development and community "empowerment." They were intended to be community controlled (largely through majority resident representation on their boards of directors), to engage in comprehensive community change (through housing, economic development, social services, and advocacy), and to harness market principles and entrepreneurial activity—"corrective capitalism"[16]—to provide collective benefit and pursue collective goals identified by community residents.

In the 1970s, most CDCs shifted to specialize in housing and economic development, partly in response to broader changes in the policy and urban landscape. These changes included economic crises, increased capital mobility, an expanding service sector, changes in the location and management of industry, and new immigration (largely of people of color) that increased ethnic diversity. They also included a political turn to the right, ushering in a neoliberal shift in state policy that lasted into the current century and resulted in (among other things) fewer public resources, a reduced federal role, the devolution of planning and resource allocation to lower levels of government, and an increased emphasis on the private sector, market-oriented responses and voluntary-sector responsibility.[17]

In addition to the shifts in practice these circumstances promoted among existing organizations and actors, new endeavors attempted to build on and revisit some of the approaches of earlier and ongoing efforts. Beginning in the late 1980s, for example, what came to be called comprehensive community initiatives (CCIs) emerged in cities across the country, largely spearheaded by private foundations to promote "comprehensive" neighborhood change and to "build community" by increasing neighborhoods' capacity for planning, advocacy, service delivery, and application of a broad range of development strategies.[18] Through their structure and their strategic focus, CCIs thus attempted to reintegrate the "social"—with an emphasis on social networks and social capital, interorganizational relationships, and "community building"—into a community development practice that had begun to deal more exclusively with physical and economic development strategies.[19]

These orientations, and sometimes specific intervention models, were explicitly followed in subsequent public policy, both nationally and locally. For example, the Obama administration's Promise Neighborhoods and Choice Neighborhoods programs—its two major urban demonstration initiatives—draw explicitly on CCI experiences to address urban poverty through a holistic approach to neighborhood circumstances and collaborative implementation.[20] And the language of "community building," while not foregrounded in early HOPE VI legislation, has become increasingly prevalent in later iterations, working its way into the policy discourse over the course of the early 1990s (again drawing on the ideas and experience of early CCIs), as well as in local variants like Chicago's Plan for Transformation.[21]

Unifying Themes and Overarching Trends

What does this historical trajectory suggest for current policy on urban poverty and public housing reform? A couple of key themes are worth outlining, each reflected or refracted in the rolling out of the Plan for Transformation.

The first theme has to do with assumptions about and orientations toward the local "community" that this history suggests. Different interventions and actions were based on different tacit assumptions about neighborhoods, about the nature of poverty and the relative importance of individual versus structural determinants and responses, and about the relative roles in addressing it of the state, the private sector, and the "community"—from individual citizens to voluntary associations to formally constituted nonprofits. They also engaged communities differently, whether primarily as *context*, to be "taken account of" in ways that inform planning and implementation; as *targets of intervention*, in which particular aspects of the community environment are identified for change or wholesale redevelopment; or as *units of action*, in which community actors and resources are mobilized toward particular change agendas.[22] The Plan for Transformation and other efforts at mixed-income public housing reform have been catalyzed by a recognition of communities' importance as context (as discussed in chapter 2), and they address them largely as targets of intervention in which this context is to be fundamentally transformed, motivated by public policy and carried out through a complex set of roles played by public, private, and community actors.

A second theme concerns the ongoing emergence and adaptation of organizational forms and practices. Community development efforts over time left a legacy both of approaches to practice and of concrete, functioning organizations that continued—and continue today—to operate in urban neighborhoods in a range of ways—though not always as originally intended. In many cities this contributes to a sometimes dense organizational infrastructure—an ecology of organizations and actors—that may complement, support, disregard, or work at cross-purposes with one another. Similarly, actors organized in these different ways place different emphases on what Jack Rothman frames as modes or models of community practice. Some privilege a *planning orientation* focused on rational problem solving and guided by professional expertise and the use of data. Others emphasize a *community development orientation* informed by assumptions about democratic processes and local self-determination (with differing emphases on the kinds of activities or action to be generated—housing, economic development, services, organizing, planning). Yet others are grounded in a *community organizing orientation*, focused on mobilization and claims making, with a more explicit focus on power and shifting power relations through collective action.[23] The Plan for Transformation and other efforts at mixed-income public housing reform draw on and confront this ecology of organizations in various ways, both working with community organizations (such as service providers and CDCs) and encountering (and attempting to counter) resistance from them. In doing so, they take primarily a social planning approach, relying on professional expertise and incorporating participatory planning in limited, controlled, and professionally guided ways.

Although these orientations are often combined in practice, different actors privilege some, and relative emphases have also shifted in general over time. These shifts are driven in part by reassessments of past practice and, especially, by changing circumstances, including macro-structural changes, shifts in governing regimes and policy orientations, and alterations in funding streams and requirements. Related to this is the periodic interplay of action between different actors at different levels; between research, policy, and social action and intervention; between local community efforts and broader social movements; and between governmental and nongovernmental actors. For the most part, government has been most effective at aiding top-down redevelopments of infrastructure and housing that enlist and support market actors and other nongovernmental organizations. It has been less effective at promoting and sustaining participatory efforts and individual social mobility. In the Plan for Transformation and other efforts at mixed-income public housing reform, we see the evolution of practice and responses to shifting circumstances reflecting current general trends toward market-oriented strategies and public-private partnerships, and toward mixed-income developments as an effort both to remake inner-city neighborhoods and to balance the tensions of development and gentrification that are shared by a range of efforts in the public and voluntary sectors.

Public Housing as a Response to Urban Poverty

Current efforts to transform public housing in the United States can be seen as the confluence of two major strands of policy history. One draws on the history of community intervention and neighborhood revitalization outlined above. The other addresses the specific challenge of housing the urban poor and the role of public housing in responding to that challenge. Having set the broader context of community development policy, we now turn to the history of approaches to public housing. Throughout the evolution of these various efforts since the 1940s, several underlying dynamics—racial segregation and marginalization, class and economic exclusion, tensions between a social housing mission and private market interests—have remained constant.

The Arc of Public Housing in the Twentieth Century

Given the well-documented history of the "disaster" of large-scale public housing in Chicago and across the United States over the past sixty years, it is hard to recall its early promise and the horrendous slum conditions it was designed to replace.[24] In Chicago, for example, as Arnold Hirsch reminds us, conditions in the slum communities that public housing in part replaced "were so appalling that decent housing, wherever it was located, was desperately desired by the community, leaders and masses alike."[25] In partial response to this, the 1937 Housing Act authorized and funded the construction of deeply subsidized and locally managed public housing in cities across the nation.[26] The initial low-rise developments built in Chicago in the late 1930s and 1940s seemed like oases of quality housing and social stability in the midst of rapidly overpopulating neighborhoods and provided welcome refuge from the overcrowded, unsanitary, and unsafe tenements—although, as Lawrence Vale points out, this new housing rarely housed those relocated to make room for it.[27] According to Hirsch, when the Ida B. Wells Homes opened on the South Side of Chicago in 1941 there were 17,544 applications for 1,661 units. The high-rise public housing towers that followed in the 1950s and 1960s also initially had long waiting lists of people hoping to move into the modern, spacious apartments.[28] As Vale makes clear, this midcentury public housing construction boom was as much about community-level redevelopment as about building quality housing for individual households, motivated by city leaders' "interest in reimaging and remaking those portions of their cities that damage their reputation, discourage investment, and sustain dysfunctional social environments."[29]

Public Housing Decline

The promise of this new housing was short-lived. Within a few decades, public housing in Chicago had come to exemplify concentrated urban poverty, isolating its residents in increasingly dilapidated buildings amid violence, extreme poverty, racial segregation, and social and economic isolation.[30]

Several factors contributed to these circumstances. First, discriminatory site selection located high-rise public housing only in African American neighborhoods. In Chicago between 1938 and 1953, political and community resistance and adherence to the federal Neighborhood Composition Rule prevented the construction of public housing on vacant land in predominantly white areas.[31] As a result, most public housing projects were racially segregated and built in neighborhoods that were already distressed, lacked services, and offered few jobs. In addition, the 1950s and 1960s saw a surge in high-density developments and high-rise towers. This shift was driven both by the need to accommodate large numbers of households and by the embrace of the principles of modernist design that saw modern, functionally specialized superblocks as an elegant solution to population pressures in rapidly urbanizing society.[32]

Another factor in the rapid decline of the public housing developments was short-sighted planning regarding building design, layout, construction, and maintenance. From the outset, quality was limited not only by available resources (including federal cost-per-unit ceilings), but also by the design principle—adopted to appease private housing developers and their advocates—that government-subsidized housing should not compete with private-sector housing and therefore should be of poorer quality and less attractive.[33] Tenant rents proved sorely inadequate to cover operating expenses, and the larger developments in particular proved very costly to maintain. This resulted in a rapid degradation of the buildings. The complexes were also often segregated from the surrounding neighborhood by building design and street access, creating vast expanses of physically isolated and forbidding living environments.[34]

Beyond these factors, increasing poverty and the increasingly long-term tenancy of residents also contributed to the downfall of large-scale public housing. Several forces converged to promote "the wholesale exodus of the working class and the influx of the welfare-dependent poor" into public housing complexes in the late 1960s and 1970s.[35] These included fiscal crises that caused maintenance and building conditions to decline, increasing social disorder and upheaval in and around the housing projects, and growing welfare rolls and demand from low-income applicants for public housing.[36] This shift was furthered by a number of policies and their unintended consequences. For example, "first-come, first-served" occupancy rules were meant to prevent steering residents to particular projects based on race, but instead they created high demand from families in poverty. A return to income-based rents under the Brooke Amendments initiated in 1969 was meant to protect the working poor from rent increases but instead gave the very poor an incentive to seek public housing and discouraged those with higher incomes from remaining. A fixed cap on rents was instituted by the Chicago Housing Authority as an attempt to retain some working families but was lifted in 1982 in a desperate and "misguided" effort to increase revenues.[37] These changes contributed to both a much poorer public housing population and longer tenancy. By the end of the twentieth century, rather than serving as transitional housing, public housing held many residents whose families had lived there for generations.

Life in "the Projects"

In the context of these changes, a host of problems began to emerge in public housing complexes across the country. By the late 1960s, what came to be known as "the projects" were characterized by increasing welfare dependency, high proportions of single-parent households, and high levels of poverty. On a national level, the number of families with incomes less than 10 percent of the area median increased from 2.5 percent in 1981 to more than 20 percent in 1991. Female-headed households were also becoming more prevalent in public housing, constituting 85 percent of households with children by the end of the 1980s.[38] In Chicago, CHA residents' average income fell to $4,665 (well below the national public housing average of $6,000), 95 percent of CHA residents were African American, and almost 50 percent were under age fifteen. Eleven of the fifteen poorest census tracts in the nation contained CHA developments.[39]

The physical environment of the developments also deteriorated. Residents endured broken elevators, erratic heat and utilities, poor sanitation, vandalism, and increasing numbers of vacant units. In addition, although residents continued to nurture social networks that provided mutual support and showed remarkable resilience in finding ways to provide for their families and build toward a better future for their children,[40] rising crime, drug trafficking, gang activity, violence, failing schools, ineffective police protection, and poor city services all led to increasingly unsafe and untenable conditions.

Early Responses

With the emergence of these problems, a range of responses developed both locally and nationally. One set of responses reflected a community development orientation centered on more inclusive governance and greater participation from public housing residents. Challenged by the dynamics of protest and calls for racial inclusion and participation in the context of the civil rights movement, the federal government responded in part by requiring the creation of local mechanisms for tenant representation and participation in the housing authorities' decision making. In Chicago this entailed creating Local Advisory Councils (LACs) in the 1970s and including residents on the CHA's board.[41] The LACs have been the principal formal mechanism for tenant representation in public housing in Chicago since that time, but their efficacy has often been limited. Residents have played only advisory roles, and in some cases resident leaders have been co-opted through financial incentives and political favors, calling into question their representativeness and influence in decision making.[42] At their most effective, LACs have mobilized advocacy efforts and spearheaded litigation leading to policy changes and institutional concessions, but resident leadership in governance was not able to change the course of institutional mismanagement and social decline.[43]

Another response played out the themes of an evolving ecology of organizations and a shift in division of labor between the state and the private sector as the Habitat Company, a private real estate developer, was named the court-ordered receiver for all new public housing construction in the city in 1987.[44] This response specifically addressed the continued discriminatory siting of public housing in predominantly African American communities. The Habitat Company was able to make some progress in constructing scattered-site housing in majority-white neighborhoods, but the impact was limited by the freeze in construction of major new developments.

A third set of responses reflected a more top-down orientation based on social planning and targeted specific problems. This included a series of local family support programs and social services for public housing residents as well as police interventions in the communities. Social services included drug treatment, job training, and early childhood education. Crime interventions attempted both interdiction and suppression (through police sweeps of buildings and individual units, foot patrols, and arrests) and prevention (through tenant patrols and youth programs). But these efforts were hopelessly overmatched by a tidal wave of social deprivation, crime, and violence, exacerbated by the escalation of the crack cocaine trade. The problems of large-scale public housing were ultimately recognized as too great for such piecemeal amelioration, and major policy changes were sought. The reforms initiated by the federal government at the beginning of the 1990s ultimately set the stage for the launch of the Plan for Transformation in Chicago.

Policy Responses to Concentrated Poverty

As we noted in chapter 1, the federal government turned to two main strategies to deconcentrate poverty from public housing developments: dispersal and mixed-income development. Both strategies were firmly rooted in efforts to leverage the private market as a resource for housing. In dispersal approaches, families are moved out of public housing complexes to subsidized units in the private market (largely by giving them housing vouchers) in metropolitan area neighborhoods that are presumably less economically and racially segregated.[45] Mixed-income development attracts higher-income families to the site of former public housing complexes by replacing them with new developments that include units for both middle-income and low-income families and investing in strong property management and local amenities.[46]

The Dispersal Approach

In the dispersal approach, residents are either given vouchers to use in the private market or placed in public housing units scattered throughout the city.[47] Scattered-site housing had been used by local housing authorities for some time, but it was often constrained by local residents' resistance to having public housing in their communities.[48] Beginning with the passage of the 1974 Housing and Community Development Act, federal housing policy shifted dramatically from a focus on public housing built and managed by local housing authorities to subsidies either provided to tenants so they could shop for housing in the private market or attached to specific units owned and managed by private landlords in order to reduce housing authorities' costs of maintaining physical units and to promote public housing residents' mobility.[49] HUD's most broad-scale application of this policy was through the Section 8 program (originally authorized in Section 8 of the US Housing Act of 1937), now referred to as the Housing Choice Voucher program. The program gives households vouchers that they can use to rent housing in the private market. The federal government expanded the flexibility and scope of the dispersal strategy by making the vouchers "portable" and allowing them to be used across municipal jurisdictions.[50]

Three major programs have promoted the dispersal approach to poverty deconcentration. The Gautreaux program in Chicago was created as part of a court-ordered settlement of a 1966 class action suit brought against the Chicago Housing Authority for enforced racial segregation. Residents selected to participate in the Gautreaux program received vouchers that they could use to move into private-market units in city neighborhoods and suburbs with no more than 30 percent nonwhite populations.[51]

Inspired by the Gautreaux program but aiming explicitly at poverty deconcentration rather than racial integration, in 1994 HUD launched a randomized housing mobility experiment, Moving to Opportunity (MTO), to more rigorously test the effects of using housing vouchers to move public housing residents to lower-poverty neighborhoods.[52] While Gautreaux, MTO, and other dispersal programs are primarily about countering racial or economic segregation, they are also motivated by implicit assumptions that integration into more stable and better-functioning communities would provide public housing residents with a better quality of life and a chance for social mobility.

HOPE VI is the third major program promoting deconcentration through dispersal. This had been the federal government's signature public housing transformation program for eighteen years until its replacement, in 2011, by the Obama administration's Choice Neighborhoods Initiative. HOPE VI was funded and designed to advance the redevelopment of public housing sites, but given the wholesale demolition it entailed, the lower density and mixed-income nature of the replacement housing, and the low rates of return of original residents to the sites, the program is as much about dispersal as about development.[53] (We will discuss the origins and roll-out of the HOPE VI program in greater detail when we turn to the evolution of the mixed-income development approach.)

The Development Option

Mixed-income development has grown in popularity over the past twenty years as a means of deconcentrating poverty, revitalizing inner-city neighborhoods, and addressing the problems of public housing in the United States.[54] Several Western European countries have also used mixed-income housing strategies to revitalize their public housing estates and reintegrate marginalized poor and immigrant families into the broader population.[55]

Mixed-income development is not a new strategy. In fact, as originally conceived and practiced in the 1930s and 1940s, public housing developments in the United States were home to a mix of low-income and working-class families.[56] In the 1970s, the Massachusetts Housing Finance Authority sought to promote "mixed-income multifamily housing" that provided units for households at a range of income levels.[57] The government in Montgomery County, Maryland, promoted the development of several mixed-income housing sites in the 1980s and early 1990s through inclusionary zoning laws. And in the 1980s, private developers began to partner with housing authorities to undertake physical transformations of public housing into mixed-income developments, including Westminster Place in St. Louis by McCormack Baron and Harbor Point in Boston by Corcoran Jennison.[58] By the late 1980s, these efforts influenced a concerted effort at the federal and local government levels to address the failures of large-scale public housing.

In 1989 the US Congress established the National Commission on Severely Distressed Public Housing and charged it with developing a National Action Plan to eradicate severely distressed public housing within ten years. The commission determined that nationwide 86,000 units (about 6 percent of the total public housing stock) were "severely distressed" according to measures including physical deterioration of the buildings, number of families in distress, rate of serious crime in the development and surrounding neighborhood, and barriers to management such as high vacancies and low rent collection.[59] The report proposed several strategies to improve the housing stock, including a commitment to income mixing in order to address the challenges related to high concentrations of extremely poor households. In 1990 Congress approved the Mixed-Income New Communities Strategy demonstration program (MINCS) to pilot and promote this approach. Although the federal government authorized including up to four cities in the program, Chicago was the only housing authority to submit a full proposal under MINCS, and it served as the sole demonstration site.[60] Rosenbaum, Stroh, and Flynn assert that a combination of social science research findings (especially Wilson's work on concentrated urban poverty) and the personal vision and will of former real estate developer and CHA executive director Vince Lane were key to the deployment of a mixed-income approach at Lake Parc Place, the Chicago site of the MINCS demonstration: "[Lane] took Wilson's ideas, informed them with his own experience as a developer, and energetically pushed against a multitude of obstacles to have them implemented."[61] Lane used Wilson's arguments about the concentration effects that result when poor families are isolated among other poor families to argue against simply rehabilitating Lake Parc Place for its existing population.

The current large-scale federal commitment to mixed-income development as a poverty deconcentration strategy was initiated soon after the launch of the HOPE VI program. In 1992 Congress passed the Housing and Community Development Act, which created the one-year Urban Revitalization Demonstration program and allocated $300 million to fund initial planning and implementation of what came to be known as HOPE VI. An additional $750 million in planning and implementation grants was awarded the next year. In its original form, the program was intended to rehabilitate developments exclusively as public housing, but by 1995 the philosophy of the program had shifted to promoting mixed-income redevelopment.[62] The explicit goal of deconcentrating poverty first appeared in the 1996 appropriations bill (and then in subsequent notices of funding availability), stating that HOPE VI funds should be used to build or provide replacement housing "which will avoid or lessen concentration of very low-income families."[63]

How was HOPE VI transformed, in the words of Bruce Katz, then HUD chief of staff, from "a program that initially focused on reconstruction and resident empowerment into one reaching for economic integration, deconcentration of poverty and neighborhood revitalization"?[64] Mindy Turbov and Henry Cisneros and Lora Engdahl provide detailed accounts of the evolution of the HOPE VI program.[65] As Turbov explains, there was a growing recognition inside HUD that most public housing authorities did not have the capacity to strategically apply the up to $50 million in HOPE VI grants and that, even where successful, simply renovating public housing would "[leave each local agency], its developments and residents isolated from the broader community."[66] Outside HUD there was also strong pressure from some influential mayors, housing authority leaders, and private developers for an approach that promoted economic integration on former public housing sites. For example, experienced affordable housing developer Richard Baron was particularly persuasive in making the case for mixed-income development, backed up by the impressive physical transformation his company had achieved with mixed-income redevelopments such as Crawford Square in Pittsburgh and Westminster Place in St. Louis.[67] Several changes to federal policy were enacted to foster the use of HOPE VI dollars to leverage private sector funding to produce mixed-income developments. Atlanta, St. Louis, Louisville, and Pittsburgh were among the first cities to take advantage of the policy changes to use HOPE VI to carry out mixed-finance, mixed-income projects.[68]

By the end of 2009, more than 240 revitalization grants totaling approximately $6 billion had been awarded under HOPE VI. These resulted in 72,718 households relocated, 94,367 public housing units demolished, and 80,130 public housing units rehabilitated or newly constructed.[69] Only 17,382 households (or 24 percent of all affected families) had returned to revitalized units in their original developments by the end of 2008.[70] While commended for the successful physical transformation of public housing sites and for evidence of improvements to the broader neighborhoods in terms of lower crime and increased investment, the HOPE VI program has been widely criticized for reducing the number of affordable housing units, problems in relocating families, delays in constructing new units, and low rates of return of original public housing residents to the new developments.[71]

Operationalizing Mixed-Income Development: Market Logics and Privatization

Mixed-income public housing reform relies on leveraging market processes and private actors to implement redevelopment. It is carried out by directly engaging private real estate developers in public-private partnerships through which they are permitted to build new rental and for-sale housing (for a nominal fee or on a long-term lease) on land owned by the housing authority. Several key changes to federal policy made possible this new role of private developers in public housing redevelopment. First, the Diaz legal opinion, issued by HUD's general counsel in 1994, concluded that nothing in the 1937 US Housing Act prohibited private ownership of public housing as long as private agencies were held to the same rules and regulations as public housing authorities. In 1996, HUD's newly created Office of Public Housing Investments published a new "mixed-finance rule" in the federal register that formally outlined the regulations that would guide these public-private arrangements. And among several key provisions in the Quality Housing and Work Responsibility Act of 1998 were the permanent lifting of the requirement of one-for-one replacement of public housing units and the explicit stipulation that allowed the use of public funds and operating subsidies for projects to be owned by private developers.[72] Private developers would take the lead on design, planning, construction, marketing, property management, and providing social services for all residents.

The strategy of using market mechanisms to leverage and sustain community change goes beyond engaging private developers as owners and managers of the development. Tax incentives and subsidies are used to promote commercial investment and attract residents representing a mix of incomes, including a "middle tier" of workers, such as teachers and other public employees, who could be eligible for subsidies supporting ownership of "affordable" for-sale units. The viability of these developments also relies on attracting market-rate buyers and renters and the demand this population represents for attracting other services and amenities, such as stores and improved schools. The extent of privatization raises questions about the longer-term policy commitment to mixed-income developments as a housing resource for the urban poor. HUD released the "Declaration of Restrictive Covenants" to guarantee that designated public housing units within mixed-income communities would remain so for a minimum of just forty years. In Chicago, the Chicago Housing Authority made land available for private development through a ninety-nine-year ground lease, which could be read as an expectation to maintain (and signal its intent to use) control to ensure that housing would remain affordable over the longer term.

The Chicago Context and the Launch of the Plan for Transformation

The Chicago Housing Authority initiated a foray into mixed-income development right at the beginning of the federal government's commitment to this approach and long before the launch of the Plan for Transformation. In 1988 Vince Lane was appointed CHA executive director and chairman of the board. He was appointed to serve as cochairman on the National Commission on Severely Distressed Public Housing mentioned earlier, had a lead role in designing the MINCS demonstration program, and ensured that Chicago received the first (and only) MINCS grant to experiment with mixed-income development. The grant was used to rehabilitate the Olander Homes on Chicago's South Side, transforming them into Lake Parc Place, which housed a mix of low-income and moderate-income residents. Lane instituted screening procedures for occupancy and contracted out management to a private company. Meanwhile, on the Near West Side of the city, a court-ordered consent decree at Henry Horner Homes required redevelopment of a portion of the public housing complex, ultimately funded in part by a HOPE VI grant, to replace high-rises with low-rise housing and introduce a mix of low and moderate rents. And on the North Side of the city a mixed-income complex called Orchard Park was initiated by private developers as an initial phase of the redevelopment of the Cabrini Green Homes, which received a HOPE VI grant in 1993.[73] But while there were pockets of innovation and redevelopment within the CHA portfolio, by this time the overall public housing enterprise in Chicago was reaching its nadir, prompting the federal government to step in and take over.

In early 1995, HUD began to negotiate with the CHA and city leadership for a full federal takeover of what at the time was widely viewed as the nation's most troubled public housing authority. In May of that year the entire CHA board—including chairman and executive director Vince Lane—resigned and Joseph Shuldiner, assistant secretary for public and Indian housing and a former head of both the Los Angeles and New York City housing authorities, was appointed to lead the CHA. In a press conference announcing the takeover, HUD secretary Henry Cisneros declared that the "national system of public housing is on trial in Chicago" and laid out a plan for CHA's future that focused on combating the isolation of public housing residents.[74] Shuldiner hired new staff to clean up CHA's finances, contracted with a private organization to administer the voucher program, and cut operational expenses. Within three years the CHA received a passing score on the Public Housing Management Assessment and was removed from the federal troubled housing list. In planning for the return of the agency to local control, Mayor Richard M. Daley appointed a new board, and control was officially transferred back to the city in June 1999.[75] As a condition of HUD's withdrawal, the CHA agreed to submit an action plan that would identify the "regulatory flexibility, legislative flexibility, and resources necessary" to move the agency forward and respond to the federal directive to remove failing units from its housing stock.[76] This plan would become the Plan for Transformation.

Launching the Plan for Transformation

On regaining control of the authority, Mayor Daley announced his intention to completely remake the landscape of public housing in the city and to end the "economic and social isolation" of the city's public housing residents.[77] Chicago's Plan for Transformation aimed to demolish 22,000 residential units, including the high-rises that had become nationally infamous as symbols of the failure of large-scale public housing. While most residents of the former developments were to be relocated into the private housing market with vouchers or into other rehabilitated, low-rise public housing developments, there would be about 7,700 units reserved for former public housing residents in the new developments to be built across the city. Mixed-income development would be implemented on a scale far greater than anything previously attempted in the country. With well over 16,000 mixed-income units planned at over a dozen developments around the city, Chicago's effort is almost three times as large as the mixed-income transformation in Atlanta, the next largest to date.[78]

The plan includes several components. At its center is physical redevelopment: demolishing about 60 percent of CHA housing stock, renovating the remaining 40 percent, and constructing new mixed-income communities to incorporate a portion of lease-compliant public housing residents relocated by the Transformation. In addition, it entails privatizing property management, moving the CHA to an assistive rather than management role; providing both Housing Choice vouchers (given to tenants to subsidize the costs of housing in the private market) and project-based vouchers (given to property owners to subsidize the rents of eligible tenants); and a range of social services and support programs. These services and programs focus primarily on case management (particularly concerning housing stability and employment), human capital and workforce development (job training and education, transitional jobs), and youth programs (summer employment, youth development). Many of these services are provided in partnership with nonprofit organizations and city agencies, and the CHA works with for-profit organizations as well (including developers of the mixed-income sites) to promote business ventures and housing.[79] Two main programmatic approaches were implemented over the course of the Transformation to support relocated residents interested in moving to mixed-income housing and those who had moved back: a referral-based model known as Service Connectors active from 2000 to 2008 and an employment-focused case management model known as FamilyWorks operating from 2008 on.[80] In addition, through CHA's inclusion in HUD's Moving to Work (MTW) demonstration program, the Plan includes changes to the regulatory framework that had guided public housing eligibility and governance, including new work requirements and the replacement, in mixed-income developments, of LACs with a centrally staffed ombudsman's office.[81] The permission granted through MTW to combine federal operating and modernization funds and Housing Choice voucher funds into a flexible block grant financing pool, along with regulatory waivers that relaxed conventional program requirements, was critical to CHA's ability to design and launch the Plan.

In February 2000, HUD formally approved the Plan for Transformation, committing $1.5 billion in federal funding to the effort over the next ten years.

Shifting Roles and Responsibilities

The privatizing of public housing redevelopment in Chicago fundamentally changed how subsidized housing was provided at the new mixed-income sites. Four main actors in particular—the CHA, private developers, service providers, and property managers—have undertaken new responsibilities as the Transformation has unfolded at each site. This storyline continues the shifting balance of responsibility among state, private-sector, and community actors and provides more detail about the progression from the social planning phase of the Transformation to its implementation as a public-private partnership.

Privatization has had far-reaching implications for the CHA. The scale and purview of the agency have been greatly reduced. As one indicator, agency staff was drastically decreased, from over 2,500 employees at the launch of the Plan for Transformation to fewer than 500 ten years later.[82] While transferring primary responsibility for the core functions of site redevelopment (financing, construction, leasing, management, and services), CHA staff have been in charge of overseeing the relocation and return of residents and monitoring post-occupancy site management. The shift to a market-driven approach to public housing in Chicago has thus meant not withdrawal of the public sector, but a significant narrowing, shifting, and refining of its role.

To fulfill the social mission of the Transformation, private developers have been called on to move well beyond bricks and mortar, adding the major responsibility of overseeing human services and community building.[83] Thus, in addition to the complex task of financing, construction, marketing, and management, mixed-income developers have had to oversee wide-ranging activities to support residents through relocation, prepare them for a possible return to the development, screen and select those eligible to return, and help residents maintain their eligibility and improve their social and economic circumstances. Complicating matters, the public housing population has turned out to be even more disadvantaged and unprepared for relocation than expected, with high levels of physical and mental health challenges, numerous barriers to employment (including extremely low literacy and skills), and fragile connections to the labor market, if any, in spite of the work requirement for eligibility.[84]

Given this, the social service providers (often nonprofit affiliates or contracted organizations) that work with each development team have had to meet high resident needs within multiple constraints of resources, time, and lack of responsiveness from residents. They have had to work with large caseloads and quickly prepare households for relocation while staying engaged with them and seeking lasting improvements in their circumstances and outlook. Before development, the dispersal of relocated residents to multiple locations across the city and metro region complicated service providers' outreach and ongoing engagement. From the early phases of the Transformation (when they were simply expected to assess residents and provide service referrals), their charge evolved to taking more responsibility for individual cases and, working with property management after occupancy, to building community at the new sites.

Property managers at the sites have particularly demanding roles in the mixed-income context. Screening households and selecting which to accept for residency in the new developments entails maintaining high occupancy (to help the private developer avoid the costs and other problems caused by vacancies) while adhering to stringent screening criteria (accepting only those residents deemed most prepared to live successfully in a mixed-income development). This proved challenging early on, when it was far more difficult than expected to find eligible residents who wanted to return to the new developments. Indeed, some new units remained vacant for up to a year.[85] Because property managers have the most regular contact with residents after occupancy, their roles often extend beyond managing occupancy, lease compliance, rent collection, and building maintenance to collaborating closely with social service providers and promoting community building.

The Relocation and Return Process

The organizational partnerships charged with redeveloping each site operated within the guidelines of an overall process of relocation and return. At the outset of the Transformation, given the local history of broken promises by the CHA and the national experience with HOPE VI displacement, public housing leaders and their legal advocates demanded and negotiated a Relocation Rights Contract that established terms and procedures for relocation from and return to the development sites. In 2002, all 16,846 heads of household who had been living in CHA family household units when the Plan for Transformation was initiated were asked to fill out a housing choice survey to designate their preference for moving permanently into the private rental market with a Housing Choice voucher or for retaining the option to return to a unit in a new mixed-income development or rehabilitated public housing. Almost 90 percent elected to retain their "right to return" to a redeveloped site.[86] Households that retained their right to return were randomly assigned lottery numbers designating the order in which they would be offered a newly constructed or rehabilitated unit that met their household size requirements.[87]

Over the next few years, public housing buildings were emptied for demolition, and residents were relocated to their temporary placements across the city. Social service providers were contracted by the CHA and by private developers working on the new developments to conduct outreach to relocated residents, assess their social and economic status and eligibility to return to a new development, provide information about their housing options, refer them to support services, and help them rectify any issues that would make them ineligible to return to the new mixed-income developments. As new units became available, property managers at the developments made offers to households based on their lottery order, match of household size to unit size, and eligibility. The eligibility criteria qualifying public housing residents for units in the new developments include, in most cases, lease compliance, working at least thirty hours a week, having no unpaid rent or utility bills, passing a drug test, and passing a three-year criminal background check.[88] These selection criteria certainly limit the pool of residents eligible for the new housing, although residents can be designated as "working to meet" eligibility requirements and be accepted to the developments if they are engaged with service providers to address the deficits. They are then given one year to meet the criteria.[89]

The relocation process in Chicago came under fierce criticism from resident advocates, ultimately resulting in litigation. The major criticisms in the early years included the rushed pace of demolition and relocation, limited and constantly changing information provided to residents, and counseling so inadequate that many residents were relocated to high-poverty, racially segregated neighborhoods or to public housing units as physically "distressed" as the ones they were leaving.[90] Despite the "working to meet" option, the stringent selection criteria and relatively short (one-year) period to become eligible left the screening open to broad criticism as a barely concealed effort to exclude much of the relocated population from the new developments. The CHA was criticized for predominantly using off-site rather than phased on-site relocation, entailing more disruption for residents.

Although many causes were beyond policymakers' control, the long delays between initial relocation and availability of new units also greatly complicated the relocation. The CHA was also criticized for ineffectively tracking residents, leading it to lose contact with thousands of residents and making outreach and recruitment difficult and labor-intensive. Inaccurate contact information, stringent bureaucratic protocols, and frequently changing procedures made it hard to determine which residents wanted to return. The CHA also failed to anticipate the severe barriers to engagement and mobility, such as physical and mental health challenges, among a substantial proportion of the families being relocated, and the agency struggled through the first few years of the Transformation with a grossly underfunded social service system and unmanageable caseloads.[91]

Service providers complained that residents' noncooperation—failure to respond to outreach attempts, lack of follow-through on preparations for relocation—was driven by many factors including distrust of the CHA and other public agencies, not believing the impending changes were real, emotional or physical inability to engage, and lack of time and information to be fully prepared for relocation. Some surmised that residents were avoiding the screening for fear an undisclosed individual or family condition would cause them to lose their housing entitlement.[92]

In response to acknowledged shortcomings, the CHA made a series of major modifications over the first ten years of the Transformation.[93] As part of the Relocation Rights Contract, the CHA retained an independent monitor to provide objective oversight and document program challenges and improvements. A relocation program manager was placed at each site for easier access and more in-depth relationships with residents. The pace of the relocation was slowed, residents were engaged much earlier in the process, and information was provided in multiple forms. The housing offer procedure was also reformulated to remove unresponsive residents from the priority list and recruit other residents with higher lottery numbers. While this change may have streamlined the implementation, it also hastened the removal from the official housing rolls of a cohort of residents who, depending on the factors causing their unresponsiveness, were likely some of the most vulnerable among the relocated population.

Conclusion

The mixed-income development component of Chicago's Plan for Transformation builds on a rich history of community-based intervention. Like its predecessor initiatives, the Plan emphasizes the influence of neighborhood resources and conditions on individual-level change. It applies a community redevelopment response to the failures of large-scale public housing and the formidable problems of concentrated poverty that plagued and isolated large portions of the inner city. Once again, as in the urban renewal period that first cleared the land and erected the fateful towers, these communities would be subject to a top-down reshaping of the urban environment through an alliance of federal and local government and private developers. Once again, a community-based intervention with the promise of integration and greater access to opportunity would be implemented with an emphasis on dramatic physical redevelopment supplemented by services intended to provide individual support. And once again, dynamics of race and class, concerns about elevating market priorities and forces over social obligations, and notions of the deserving and undeserving poor would spark controversy and raise fundamental questions about the motivations, intentions, and ultimate beneficiaries of this massive public investment and policy shift.

This time, however, a commitment to economic integration was explicit in the framing, financing, and design of the core redevelopment projects as "mixed-income," in the negotiation of a Relocation Rights Contract intended to protect public housing residents' right to return, and in the establishment and evolution of a highly complicated procedure for resident relocation, services, and screening. The scale of the Transformation—complete demolition of all high-rise towers, relocation of 16,000 households, and the simultaneous construction and populating of more than a dozen new developments—demonstrated how seriously the city approached this latest attempt to remake its inner-city neighborhoods, reshape public housing, and deconcentrate the urban poor. Foreshadowed in the design of the Transformation, however, were elements that would prove highly consequential in implementing it: a focus on individual behavior and circumstances over structural barriers as causes of poverty, the central role of real estate developers and reliance on the private market, and seeing communities and their residents as targets of intervention rather than agents of change.

PART TWO

FOUR

Setting the Stage: The Neighborhood and Development Site Contexts

The Plan for Transformation has unfolded in a variety of neighborhood contexts, with some important differences in how the effort has played out in each place.[1] We examine three mixed-income developments (Oakwood Shores, Park Boulevard, and Westhaven Park) situated in two broad neighborhood contexts, one on the South Side of the city (Bronzeville) and one on the west (the Near West Side). In this chapter we first describe each of the neighborhood and development site contexts, exploring the demographic shifts, institutional landscape, public housing decline, and revitalization trends that preceded the public housing transformation in each area, as well as the dynamics of planning and contestation that shaped development in each. We then review key elements of the design and predevelopment phase of the mixed-income sites and describe the emerging populations across the sites as they have been built out.

Neighborhood Trajectories in Chicago: Decline, Redevelopment, and Contestation

The story of the Plan for Transformation is fundamentally the story of a city coming to grips with a legacy of urban exclusion and inequality that had reached an unsustainable level. As Robert Sampson put it, "The tragic mistake

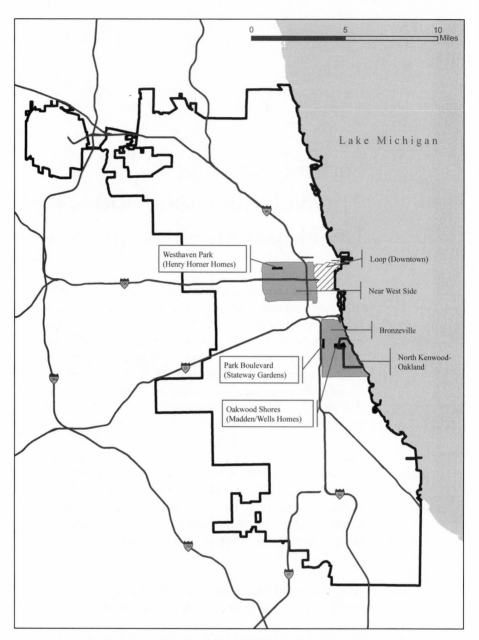

4.1 City of Chicago with locations of focal developments and neighborhoods. In parentheses are the names of the original public housing complexes being replaced.

of designed segregation became too much for even the Chicago City Council to ignore."[2] The overarching question for the Transformation is whether the city's long-standing public housing developments, and the neighborhoods around them, can be remade once more, this time to create a more inclusive array of neighborhoods accessible to all residents of the city. Two mutually reinforcing dynamics have shaped this attempt at inner-city transformation: former mayor Richard M. Daley's quest for "global city" status and the renewed demand for urban living among a growing demographic—first so-called urban pioneers, then young professionals, downsizing empty nesters, and a returning African American middle class with long-standing family ties to the neighborhoods.[3]

In the early 1990s, as the federal government was launching new policies to deal with severely distressed public housing, the local government in Chicago was also experimenting with ways to reverse concentrated poverty more broadly in inner-city neighborhoods, and both corporate and individual investors were beginning to invest in their redevelopment. For example, Mayor Daley's New Homes for Chicago program demonstrated demand for single-family homes even in the midst of high-poverty communities,[4] and African American middle-class residents were drawn to certain historically black areas by the abundance of vacant land, low-priced homes primed for renovation, the historical and cultural significance of the neighborhood, and personal and affective ties among those raised there.[5] Literally overshadowing the nascent glimmers of revitalization, however, were the massive towers of high-poverty public housing that dominated the South Side and West Side landscapes and presented a major impediment to broad-scale redevelopment and renewed market potential. The prospect of removing these public housing complexes, along with the early trends of gentrification, were welcomed in some quarters as hopeful signs of reinvestment and regeneration. But they were also met with organized resistance from some local residents, community activists, and leaders of established neighborhood organizations who anticipated that the low-income population who had lived through the neighborhood's toughest times would be displaced as reinvestment took hold.[6]

The three mixed-income public housing redevelopments we examine in this book must be seen as nested within the broader decline, redevelopment, and contestation playing out across the metropolitan area and in their neighborhoods. Indeed, the redevelopments are complicated by a fundamental, unresolved tension between revitalization dependent on private-sector investment and attracting higher-income residents and the dangers of displacing and further marginalizing an already vulnerable low-income population.

Bronzeville and North Kenwood–Oakland: History, Culture, and Emerging Black Gentrification on the Mid-South Side

Between 1910 and 1930, Chicago's black population grew from approximately 44,000 to more than 233,000, and nearly all of these residents settled in an area that became known as Bronzeville.[7] Confined to this area by restrictive housing covenants until the 1960s—when the black population of Chicago had reached 813,000—African Americans created a self-contained and economically diverse enclave on the Mid-South Side.[8] Both Oakwood Shores and Park Boulevard are in Bronzeville, which, like New York's Harlem, has an important historical legacy as the economic, political, and cultural center of African American life in Chicago.[9]

Local government efforts to redevelop the South Side began in the 1950s with the first wave of urban renewal projects. Large tracts of housing were demolished, and the land was sold at a reduced rate to private developers. This period saw the construction of the Illinois Institute of Technology campus, Michael Reese and Mercy Hospitals, and the McCormick Place Convention Center,[10] as well as construction of Chicago's major expressways and the extension of its commuter rail line through these neighborhoods. All these projects displaced many middle-class and poor black residents. Beginning in the late 1950s, when the CHA moved from constructing relatively small-scale, low-rise public housing to producing larger high-rise and gallery-style towers, the demographics in the neighborhoods where these complexes were built shifted sharply as middle- and higher-income black families moved to other parts of the city and Bronzeville's commercial corridors declined and emptied.

Eventually, with the construction of the Harold Ickes Homes, Dearborn Homes, Stateway Gardens, and Robert Taylor Homes, the State Street corridor at the western edge of Bronzeville held the highest concentration of public housing in the country, and the formerly proud community fell victim to poverty, disinvestment, and crime.[11] Stateway Gardens, now being redeveloped under the Plan for Transformation as Park Boulevard, was completed in 1958. It was in the middle of the public housing corridor and contained 1,664 units in six seventeen-story and two ten-story high-rises covering thirty-three acres.[12] In 1998, all eight high-rise buildings at Stateway Gardens failed a federal viability test, requiring total demolition of the development.[13] By the time the Plan for Transformation was launched in 1999, only 41 percent of the units were occupied.

To the east of the State Street Corridor lies the neighborhood of North Kenwood–Oakland. It is historically seen as part of the larger Bronzeville area, but it is also distinct from the western and central areas of that community. Bordering the Hyde Park and Kenwood neighborhoods to the south (home to the University of Chicago and to President Barack Obama), North Kenwood–Oakland is part of the Fourth Ward, represented through the 1990s and early 2000s by Toni Preckwinkle, who leveraged her strong ties to the university and the politically influential Hyde Park community to wield considerable influence over local development, including how the Plan for Transformation would be implemented in her ward.[14]

The Ida B. Wells Homes, now being redeveloped as Oakwood Shores under the Plan for Transformation, occupies a forty-seven-acre site on the northern boundary of North Kenwood–Oakland. It was among the first public housing developments in Chicago, opening in 1941 and consisting of 1,662 units in 124 buildings, a mix of three-story walk-ups, garden apartments, and row houses. The development, including in later phases Darrow Homes, Madden Park Homes, and Wells Extensions, ultimately amounted to 3,200 units. It sits well to the east of the State Street Corridor and within strolling distance of Lake Michigan and the large lakefront park that stretches most of the length of the city.[15] It is thus in a substantially different neighborhood context than Stateway Gardens, Robert Taylor Homes, and the other public housing developments on the corridor. Conditions at Madden-Wells declined throughout the 1980s and 1990s, as they did at other CHA developments, and by the launch of the Transformation, just over half of the units (53 percent) were occupied.[16]

Efforts to revitalize the South Side began in the 1970s with a small influx of black urban professionals drawn to the area by the many historic and relatively inexpensive homes in need of restoration. With the acceleration during the late 1980s of redevelopment in the South Loop area just north of Bronzeville, a number of community groups joined with area academic and medical institutions to define a redevelopment strategy that would preserve Bronzeville's history and protect its current residents.[17] Specifically within North Kenwood are a set of longstanding and tenacious community-based leaders and organizations, including the Kenwood Oakland Community Organization (KOCO), formed in the 1960s as an association of approximately thirty neighborhood groups.[18] In 1990 KOCO, soon-to-be-alderman Preckwinkle, and other local stakeholders successfully lobbied the city to designate North Kenwood–Oakland a "community conservation area," which gives a Community Conservation Council appointed by the mayor authority over the disposition of city-owned land in the designated area and thus influence over the mixed-income transformation.[19]

These planning efforts established a foundation that would guide the subsequent public housing redevelopment in Bronzeville, including a strong, well-connected base of organizations and institutions with multiple stakeholders, concerned with building on the cultural legacy of the community to draw middle-class African Americans back to the area. Large-scale revitalization required recognizing the early strategic tension between catalyzing homeownership in the neighborhood while preventing renter displacement and articulating the overarching imperative of addressing the public housing developments.[20]

Table 4.1 illustrates the demographic changes in Bronzeville over an eighty-year period. The table documents the extreme population decline from a high of over 250,000 residents in 1950 to just over 65,000 in 2010, the shift to an almost exclusively African American community in the latter half of the twentieth century, and the concomitant decline in a range of socioeconomic indicators. It also records recent signs of revitalization and gentrification after 2000, including a slight increase in racial diversity and a sharp increase in home values.

Within this context are two of the mixed-income public housing redevelopment sites that are the subject of our analysis. The first is Park Boulevard, which is being built to replace Stateway Gardens. The planned 1,300-unit project was developed by a team of four private, for-profit firms—Kimball Hill Homes, Mesa Development Group, Davis Development Group, and Walsh Construction—and was designed to include an equal mix of relocated public housing, affordable, and market-rate units.[21] Unique among the three sites, there were originally no market-rate rental units planned at Park Boulevard, and the core of the design and financing was a substantial market-rate, for-sale component that would constitute 42 percent of all units.

The second is Oakwood Shores, which replaces the Ida B. Wells, Madden Park, and Darrow Homes developments (often referred to collectively as "Madden-Wells"). With a planned 3,000 units, Oakwood Shores was originally projected to be not only the largest mixed-income public housing development in the city, but one of the largest in the

Table 4.1 Bronzeville (1930–2010)

	1930	1940	1950	1960	1970	1980	1990	2000	2010
Bronzeville									
Total population	179,194	200,491	253,471	198,272	166,625	128,163	92,924	78,949	65,276
African American (%)	53.3	53.7	70.8	93.3	90.7	90.7	91.8	88.9	84.3
White (%)	46.4	46.0	26.5	6.1	8.4	7.6	6.3	6.2	9.4
Median annual household income (2010$)			25,398	30,152	34,895	24,624	23,696	27,341	33,072
Families below poverty line (%)					34.0	43.8	51.3	35.6	27.9
Median home value (2010$)		57,473	113,308	128,182	115,491	111,939	143,206	269,354	294,864
Median monthly rent (2010$)		436	389	575	534	386	521	571	736

Sources: Local Community Fact Book for Chicago (1995, 1984, 1963, 1953, 1949, 1938); 2000 Census; 2010 American Community Survey five-year estimates.

entire country. It is being developed through a partnership between a nonprofit developer, The Community Builders (TCB), which has one of the largest portfolios of mixed-income housing in the United States, and a local minority-owned, for-profit developer (Granite Development) that is responsible primarily for the for-sale component. TCB has responsibility for the rental components and (until recently) for providing social services,[22] as well as for spearheading much of the on-site resident engagement and community building. One-third of housing units at Oakwood Shores are to be replacement public housing units, with a slightly higher proportion of market-rate units (44 percent) and a slightly lower proportion of "affordable" units (23 percent).[23] Twenty-seven percent of the units are projected to be for sale.

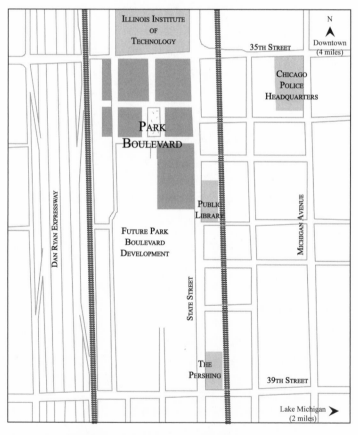

4.2   Park Boulevard development and surrounding neighborhood.

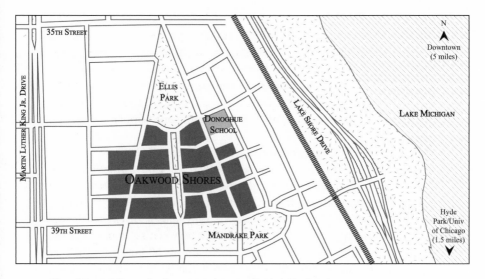

4.3 Oakwood Shores development and surrounding neighborhood.

The Near West Side: Disinvestment and Decline Meet Gentrification and Increasing Racial Diversity

To set the neighborhood context for the third mixed-income development in our study, Westhaven Park, we must look to Chicago's Near West Side, an area that has experienced much the same neighborhood decline, succession, and gentrification as the South Side, but with some key differences, especially regarding racial and ethnic diversity. The Near West Side experienced the same twentieth-century transition from a largely working-class, white ethnic immigrant population living in tenement housing to an increasing number of African American and, later, Latino residents. The population transition lagged and was fueled by the shifts on the South Side as black residents displaced by urban renewal efforts there migrated to the West Side. By the 1990s, the African American population on the broader West Side of Chicago was second only to that in the Bronzeville area in absolute numbers, but without Bronzeville's legacy as a gateway for southern immigration, its early economic vitality, or its rich cultural history as a center of African American life.[24] Although a vibrant commercial corridor ran through the center of the Near West Side neighborhood in the 1950s, the riots that erupted following Dr. Martin Luther King Jr.'s assassination in 1968 destroyed much of it. As in Bronzeville, the West Side African American neighborhoods became a target for urban renewal and large public housing developments in the 1950s, and though there was contention over the large concentration of public housing in the neighborhoods, units in the early developments were in high demand from residents seeking better-quality housing than the crowded tenements being replaced.[25] The city eventually cleared most of the area, leaving vacant lots, sparse businesses, and few jobs.[26] A significant population decline also followed.[27]

Opened in 1957, the Governor Henry Horner Homes, now being redeveloped as Westhaven Park under the Plan for Transformation, were the first development completed during CHA's high-rise era. They were made infamous by the book (later made into a movie) by renowned Chicago journalist Alex Kotlowitz, *There Are No Children Here*. The Horner complex ultimately included 1,765 units, but between 1981 and 1991 the vacancy rate ballooned from 2.3 percent to almost 50 percent.[28] In 1991 a group of residents who called themselves the Henry Horner Mothers Guild sued the CHA and HUD over the conditions at Horner, charging them with engaging in "de facto demolition" by failing to repair and maintain units.[29] In April 1995 the Horner residents' suit was settled through a court-approved consent decree that, by predating and superseding Plan for Transformation policy and stipulations, would set mixed-income redevelopment at Horner apart from other sites around the city in some significant ways. The terms of the agreement included extensive demolition and rehabilitation of Horner Homes into a "mixed-income neighborhood consisting of new and renovated mid-rise and low-rise, low-density homes."[30] It also included the right of existing residents to move into newly constructed units on site or in an existing neighborhood scattered-site complex, or to relocate with a Section 8 voucher.[31] Very important for the mixed-income redevelopment to come, the consent decree established the Horner Residents Committee (HRC), a seven-member resident council of Horner Local Advisory Council members that was legally empowered to negotiate with CHA and development partners on all matters related to implementing the revitalization plan and consent decree, including occupancy standards, resident screening, and appeals of decisions regarding specific residents.

As in the South Side neighborhoods, a turnaround began to take hold on the Near West Side in the 1990s, although, as we noted earlier, the pace of reinvestment was faster owing to the westward path of gentrification emanating from downtown. As in Bronzeville and North Kenwood–Oakland, residents and community-based organizations resisted the external forces looking to influence (and benefit from) the improvement of the neighborhood. Beyond debates over the future of the high-rise public housing, another high-profile area of contention was the city's efforts to build sports stadiums on vacant and (prospectively) cleared land. Neighborhood actors successfully blocked the building of a football stadium and were able to secure more involvement and better neighborhood investments from the building of a new stadium for basketball and ice hockey.[32] Most relevant to the Plan for Transformation was the intensified neighborhood activism and the experience and sophistication local groups gained through resistance and negotiation.[33]

Table 4.2 demonstrates that the Near West Side has experienced a course similar to Bronzeville's—massive population decrease, major racial composition shifts, and socioeconomic decline through the 1990s followed by stabilization, revitalization, and (much more dramatically than in Bronzeville) growth of the white population in the new century. But several factors distinguish the Near West Side from Bronzeville. African American in-migration did not begin to accelerate there until the 1940s, peaked at about 75 percent of the population (versus almost 95 percent in Bronzeville), and has quickly decreased to about a third, with whites in higher proportions than blacks (44 percent) by 2010. While poverty and deprivation reached higher levels than in Bronzeville by some measures (median household income dipped to $17,000 in 1990 versus a low of $24,000 in Bronzeville that same census year), the socioeconomic conditions on the Near West Side have rebounded more quickly. In 2010 the poverty rate was 36 percent lower than in Bronzeville, the unemployment rate 38 percent lower, median home values 15 percent higher, and median rents 27 percent higher. Thus, relative to the South Side, the mixed-income public housing transformation in the Near West Side is taking place in the context of even better-established and faster-paced gentrification. However, much of the development is taking place on the eastern edge of the Near West Side where the neighborhood borders the vibrant West Loop area of the downtown business district. On the western side of the neighborhood, where the Westhaven Park development is located, there is still much more vacant land, less development, and far less commerce.

Westhaven Park is the second phase of the redevelopment of Henry Horner Homes. The development team includes two private, for-profit developers. Brinshore Development, a local firm, and the Michaels Company, a national firm, serve as the master developers, with the rental properties managed by Interstate Realty, a subsidiary of the Michaels Company. Resident supports and services are contracted out to local nonprofit service providers. Units produced in the initial, pre-Transformation

Table 4.2 Near West Side (1930–2010)

	1930	1940	1950	1960	1970	1980	1990	2000	2010
Near West Side									
Total population	152,457	136,518	160,362	126,610	78,703	57,296	46,197	46,419	49,788
African American (%)	16.6	18.9	40.9	53.8	72.2	74.7	67.2	53.2	35.7
White (%)	78.4	80.8	58.5	45.6	25.2	16.3	22.4	29.1	44.2
Median annual household income (2010$)		24,384	29, 349	33,787	19,940	17,131	37,467	51,774	
Families below poverty line (%)					34.7	48.9	52.0	30.1	18.3
Median home value (2010$)		30,980	59,843	91,348	71,936	73,832	187,692	258,845	347,350
Median monthly rent (2010$)		249	290	486	427	283	475	767	1,022

Sources: *Local Community Fact Book for Chicago* (1995, 1984, 1963, 1953, 1949, 1938); 2000 Census; 2010 American Community Survey five-year estimates.

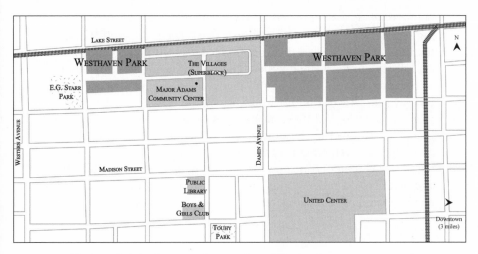

4.4 Westhaven Park development and surrounding neighborhood.

phase were only for public housing residents, so ultimately the site, projected to include 1,300 units, will have a larger proportion of public housing residents (63 percent) than any other site. It will also have the lowest proportion of for-sale units (23 percent).

Launching the Transformation: Design, Predevelopment, and Populating the Sites

Although by the mid-1990s these neighborhoods had each established pockets of revitalization and appeared poised for continued improvement, the persistence of hyper-concentrated poverty in public housing developments in their midst remained a critical barrier to broader revitalization. And though the conditions endured by the vulnerable and marginalized public housing families in these neighborhoods was the rhetorical focus for the citywide Transformation, it remained far from clear if and how they would benefit from the redevelopment of these sites and the regeneration of the neighborhoods.

As we noted in chapter 3, on regaining control of the public housing authority from the federal government in 1999, city leaders and the CHA set about to radically transform public housing in Chicago. As Mayor Daley made clear in public speeches about the planned transformation, his primary stated goal was to end the isolation and marginalization of public housing residents. No longer would the world of public housing represent a separate "city within a city." The most explicit and intentional effort to realize this goal entailed demolishing public housing complexes and redeveloping them into mixed-income developments.

To compare and contrast the predevelopment and preoccupancy processes at each of the three sites, we highlight four activities central to each redevelopment: establishing key actors (including a "working group" to oversee the planning and early rollout of each development and select a development team); financing the developments; designing the developments (including determining the site plan, architecture, and nature of the income and tenure mix); and populating the developments (including marketing, recruitment, and screening).

Establishing Key Actors

The Working Groups

The CHA created working groups as the principal governing mechanism to inform design and oversee implementation at each redevelopment site.[34] Working groups helped to formally engage local community stakeholders in the redevelopment. They helped to select a development team for each site and to establish eligibility criteria for public housing families, and they gave input on development plans (and changes to them). Beyond these initial tasks, they review progress on providing resident services and on community building and engage in general problem solving as the development unfolds. Each working group is convened by a CHA representative who serves as the development manager for that site. Each group also includes other CHA staff (project management, asset management, relocation supports, legal department), representatives of the development team (developer, property manager, service providers), a representative of the Habitat Company (the federally appointed receiver for any new public housing construction in the city), representatives of other city departments (housing, planning, park district, school district), legal advocates (including an "independent monitor" contracted by the CHA to assess adherence to the relocation rights contract), and other community stakeholders such as the alderman representing the ward.[35] Also included on each working group are the president and (often) one other member of the Local Advisory Council (LAC) from the original public housing complex.

Given their central role and the breadth of representation on them, the working groups are a critical locus of control and influence at each site; many of the design decisions and emerging site challenges we discuss in later chapters were debated in working group meetings. Although meetings are chaired by a CHA representative, developers have the most prominent role, providing updates and driving the conversation. LAC representatives and legal advocates are also quite vocal (though not always particularly influential), since this is their most consistent opportunity to voice concerns directly to the CHA and the development team. At Park Boulevard, development problems, delays, and tensions between the development team representatives, the LAC representatives and, on occasion, the social service provider led this working group to have some of the most volatile meetings among the three sites in our study.

Of the three sites, Oakwood Shores was the only one where an alderman exercised leadership and oversight on the working group. Early on, working group meetings were held at Alderman Preckwinkle's office, and she came in and out of them at her discretion, playing an active role when she was in the room. The Oakwood Shores working group had several other strong and influential members including the president of the Community Conservation Council and one of the former LAC presidents for Ida B. Wells, whom the mayor had also appointed to the Chicago Housing Authority Board of Commissioners.

At Westhaven Park, the formation of the working group was conditioned by the overarching framework of the consent decree. Resident representatives from both the Horner Residents Committee and the LAC, as well as the legal counsel appointed to represent residents under the terms of the decree, participate in working group meetings. Westhaven Park has the only working group (of more than ten in the city) at which legal counsel representing CHA residents is a voting member and one of only two (the other being the Cabrini Green redevelopment) where the CHA and the Habitat Company do not have the final say over disputes.[36]

Selection of Development Teams

The choice of development team was arguably the most critical element of redevelopment at each site. All core elements of the process—design, financing, marketing, screening, post-occupancy management, services, and community building—are driven by the development team. The composition of the teams, their internal structure and external partners, the inclusion of any nonprofit partners, and the nature of their experience with mixed-income development all shape their approaches. Although all three teams are joint-venture partnerships formed specifically for the development of these projects, there are important differences among them. Two (Park Boulevard and Westhaven Park) are for-profit development firms, and one (Oakwood Shores) is a not-for-profit organization. One (Oakwood Shores) had in-house capacity to provide services; the others had to contract out that responsibility to other organizations. One had significant national experience in mixed-income development, one brought moderate experience, and one was brand-new to the field.

In January 2001, the working group at Park Boulevard selected the team of Stateway Associates, LLC, a partnership of real estate and construction companies with strong track records in local development but little experience with public housing transformation. Having no existing capacity for resident services and community building, the development partnership decided to establish a start-up nonprofit corporation, Stateway Community Partners (SCP), to carry out those functions.

At Oakwood Shores, the CHA and the working group got off to a false start in selecting a development team. The developer initially selected was a joint venture group led by McCormack Baron Salazar, one of the most experienced mixed-income development companies in the country.[37] As an indication of the CHA's insistence on maintaining a strong hand, it was unable to reach agreement with McCormack Baron Salazar on the terms of the partnership. After several months of planning, the CHA terminated its contract with the group and, in May 2001, requested proposals from a new master developer. The working group turned to a joint venture led by a development firm with significant experience in redeveloping public housing complexes into mixed-income developments, Boston-based The Community Builders, Inc. (TCB). TCB brought a unique corporate structure and organizational philosophy to its task at Oakwood Shores. As the only nonprofit organization to lead a mixed-income redevelopment in the city, it brought a social mission fully and equally intertwined with its business imperative. Furthermore, it was the only lead development company involved in the Plan for Transformation to have its own internal property management and resident services practices, which presented tremendous (though later unfulfilled) promise for successful integration and alignment on site across these core functions.

The Westhaven Park working group selected the developer submission that proposed the highest number of replacement public housing units, a joint venture between a local development company, Brinshore Development, and the national real estate development firm the Michaels Company. This provided the development team with a mix of local contacts and knowledge as well as national experience and access to resources. A subsidiary company would manage the property, and social services would be contracted out to local organizations.

Financing

Although the decision to privatize the redevelopment of public housing, in Chicago and elsewhere, was driven in part by the expectation that private sector efficiency would outperform years of local government incompetence and corruption, another key imperative was leveraging private-sector investment to support the massive costs of the redevelopment. By 2013, more than $3 billion had already been expended.[38] Thus far the three sites we focus on range in total development costs from $145 million at Park Boulevard to $153 million at Westhaven Park and $238 million at Oakwood Shores.

To put these figures in context, the average HOPE VI federal redevelopment grant was $24 million,[39] and the current maximum Choice Neighborhoods Initiative federal grant award for mixed-income redevelopment is $30 million. So these federal program funds must be leveraged several times over to finance these redevelopments. The current estimated total development costs for the Choice Neighborhoods Initiative redevelopments being built in Chicago, San Francisco, and New Orleans are $225 million, $279 million, and $589 million, respectively. As another point of reference, dividing the current total development costs by the number of units produced so far yields a very rough benchmark of about $395,000 per unit at Park Boulevard, $295,000 per unit at Oakwood Shores, and $300,000 per unit at Westhaven Park. In addition to construction of the units themselves, the total development costs generally include the expense of demolition and site preparation, resident relocation and services, and marketing.

Funding to support these costs across sites is complex and includes a mix of public and private financing and loans, tax credits, and development fees. Indeed, mixed-income projects like these are often referred as "mixed-finance" projects because of the variety of funding sources that must be secured to support them.

The scale and pace of the Transformation in Chicago was made possible by financing from the city and its affiliated agencies, which have invested more than $600 million in the Plan for Transformation, including dedicating about half of the city's affordable housing resources, such as the Low-Income Housing Tax Credits described below, to the mixed-income developments in the first ten years of the Plan and about

$74 million in city-funded infrastructure improvements.[40] The CHA also contributed a substantial amount to each site from its development and capital funds. This is a remarkable level of commitment and signifies the priority the city placed on the Transformation. But it also raises questions about the dedication of such a high proportion of affordable housing resources, given the relatively low number of public housing and low-income residents who have been housed in the developments.

Philanthropic sources, like the Chicago-based John D. and Catherine T. MacArthur Foundation and the Partnership for New Communities,[41] have provided critical supplemental funding for investments that could not be covered by development funding. The MacArthur Foundation has contributed over $50 million, including funding for the Partnership for New Communities, which in turn has pooled and distributed $20 million. These philanthropic funds were used for a range of purposes, such as loan guarantees, home purchasing incentives, social services, employment programs, youth programs, and community building, as well as to support data collection, analysis, and research on the Transformation.[42]

Beyond local funding, the development teams at both Oakwood Shores and Westhaven Park sought and received federal HOPE VI grants ($35 million and $18.5 million, respectively), which could be leveraged against private-sector capital.[43] The Park Boulevard developers did not seek a HOPE VI grant to fund the initial phase of redevelopment, thinking that forgoing HOPE VI funding might reduce restrictions and speed up the closing. Informed participants at the development suggest that it ultimately did not, but in lieu of HOPE VI funds, the CHA helped to secure other sources of funding. The Park Boulevard team later was awarded a $20 million HOPE VI grant in 2007 to fund subsequent phases of redevelopment. An ongoing source of federal support will be Annual Cost Contribution payments made to cover rent for relocated public housing residents above the one-third of their income that they pay.

Another key source of financing for mixed-income redevelopment is the Low-Income Housing Tax Credit (LIHTC).[44] Oakwood Shores has leveraged almost $108 million from LIHTC funding, Westhaven Park has leveraged more than $52 million, and Park Boulevard has leveraged about $22 million. While this is a critical part of the financing packages, developers note two major problems they encountered with LIHTC funding. First, the scale of the Transformation in Chicago, with multiple mixed-income redevelopment projects proceeding simultaneously, generated competition among developers for the state pool of tax credits (and also drew tax credits away from projects throughout the rest of the state). The mixed-income developers often found themselves in a queue for tax credit allocation, delaying their projects. Second, as the US and world economies faltered beginning with the housing market crisis that began in late 2007, private-sector interest in LIHTC dropped precipitously across cities, making tax credits less valuable even once they were received.

Finally, another key resource supporting the developments is tax increment financing (TIF), a means of redirecting local tax increases spurred by redevelopment back into further investments in the local area.[45] TIF became a popular tool in Mayor Daley's planning and development department, and all three developments are part of TIF districts. Park Boulevard has obtained $9 million and Oakwood Shores and Westhaven Park have each obtained about $4.8 million in TIF funds.

Besides these more customary sources of funding, each development team used creative strategies to leverage other financing from local government and the private sector. They applied for and obtained affordable housing grant funds from city and state agencies and federal HOME loans allocated by the city. Loans from private banks were particularly important for financing the for-sale portion of the developments. Oakwood Shores has secured more than $58 million in private loans, Park Boulevard has secured almost $35 million, and Westhaven Park has secured about $33 million.

In sum, then, the total development cost of $238 million at Oakwood Shores included $48 million in federal funds, $23 million in local public funding, and $167 million in private investments. At Park Boulevard, the $145 million total included $30 million in federal funds, $22 million in local public funding, and $93 million in private investments. And at Westhaven Park, the $153 million total included $30 million in federal funds, $26 million in local public funding, and $97 million in private investments. Note, however, that the private equity investment across sites is heavily incentivized by federal subsidy in the form of forgone federal taxes through the LIHTC (reducing tax liability on the amount invested in affordable housing dollar-for-dollar).

A final note about financing concerns something of a paradox regarding the relation between the financing for market-rate units and that for affordable units. While it might seem that the market-rate units would generate profit that could subsidize the construction of affordable units, the price structure of the market-rate units and the availability of public subsidy for the affordable units means instead that the public-sector subsidy, mainly the LIHTC, becomes critical for making the entire mixed-income project work. As one developer explained: "It's exactly the opposite [of what you might expect]. The market side needs subsidy,

Table 4.3 Development Funding Sources[a]

	Oakwood Shores	Park Boulevard	Westhaven Park
Federal sources[b]			
HOPE VI federal grants[c] ($)	24,804,572	14,857,000	14,792,288
HOME loans[d]	23,219,497	15,300,000	15,000,000
Local government sources			
CHA funds[e]	14,530,086	13,100,000	19,652,227
Tax increment financing[f]	4,773,000	9,000,000	4,758,833
Affordable housing grants[g]	3,032,563	0	2,033,500
Private sources			
Tax credit equity[h]	107,932,554	22,236,193	52,464,367
Private bank loans[i]	58,084,049	34,850,000	33,402,632
Deferred developer fees	731,165	500,000	2,178,337
Developer and investor equity	0	0	6,103,205
Homeownership sale proceeds[j]	0	29,655,850	1,801,845
Other sources[k]	1,163,491	5,875,537	1,694,988
Total	238,270,977	145,374,580	153,882,222

[a] Reflects expenses for mixed-income rental and for-sale units built through July 2013.
[b] Missing from the accounting of federal sources are the forgone tax payments due to the provision of Low-Income Housing Tax Credits (LIHTC) that are offered as an incentive for raising private equity investments listed below.
[c] Used for rental housing construction only.
[d] Federal block grant funds allocated to the city of Chicago for affordable rental housing construction.
[e] Federal dollars allocated to CHA from the Public Housing Capital Fund and Development Fund; used for rental housing construction only.
[f] Local funds generated from future increases in property tax revenue; used for rental and for-sale housing construction.
[g] State and local grants from sources including the Illinois Housing Development Authority and the Federal Home Loan Bank of Chicago; used for rental housing construction only.
[h] Private equity leveraged from allocation of federal LIHTC and state donation tax credits; used for rental and for-sale housing construction.
[i] Used for rental and for-sale housing construction.
[j] Estimated at time of construction.
[k] Includes accrued interest on public loans, general partner capital contributions, and funds from disposition of retail space.

and there's no vehicle to subsidize the market side. There's a vehicle for the affordable side with the large amount of tax credits, but there's no vehicle [on the market side]. . . . [So] the financing sources that are supposed to subsidize the affordable component are actually going to subsidize the market-rate component."

This does not mean that public financing specifically targeted to fund affordable housing units is being directly reallocated to fund market-rate housing units. But while affordable housing regulation prohibits any direct cross-subsidy of the market-rate units, renting and selling them in revitalizing neighborhoods requires pricing them at a level that would be hard to finance without the public subsidy that makes mixed-income redevelopment feasible. This is easiest to understand in the case of a mixed-income rental building where the tax credit equity can be invested in the construction of the overall building, many components of which (for example, overall structure, HVAC, electricity, plumbing) support both the affordable and the market-rate units.

This brief review of the financing of mixed-income public housing redevelopments makes several things clear: the scale and complexity of resource development in support of the mixed-income endeavor, the level of financial commitment being made by both public and private investors, the considerable opportunity costs given the potential other uses for the funding (particularly affordable housing resources), and the realities of what it takes to produce market-rate housing at scale in high-poverty neighborhoods. In particular, the revelations about the scope of the city's commitment of funds to affordable housing and the need to, in effect, subsidize the production of market-rate units clearly expose the underlying concerns about the pitfalls and trade-offs inherent in market-driven public housing redevelopment.

Site Design

Decisions about design are another core building block in determining the physical and social environment that would establish the character of the emerging neighborhood and shape community dynamics for decades to come. We briefly consider the key concerns that influenced design decisions and the ultimate resolution at each site about architectural style, land use, and unit mix.

The master site plan for the Park Boulevard redevelopment of Stateway Gardens was completed in June 2001 and included 1,316 total units, with one-third set aside for public housing residents, 42 percent being for-sale housing, and the rest being "affordable" rental housing subsidized primarily with tax credits and generally housing a low-income, non-CHA population. Many of the buildings throughout the development were to include a mix of for-sale and subsidized rental units, and the larger buildings were to mix units on the same floor. Development team members expressed concern that there would not be sufficient demand for market-rate rental units at a profitable price point, although after the recession and housing market slowdown hit beginning in late 2007, the team was forced to revise its plans and added a market-rate rental component. The plan called for re-creating the neighborhood street grid, constructing a variety of housing types (town houses, two- and three-flat buildings, and mid-rise condominiums and apartments),

4.5   Park Boulevard features a mix of building designs, including condominium buildings with street-level retail space, three-story walk-ups, and mid-rise elevator buildings. Photo credit: Janet Li.

putting a small playground and pocket park in the middle of the development, and establishing a wide boulevard with a landscaped median along State Street, the major north-south corridor that runs along one border of the development.

A product of seven different architects, the redevelopment plan was awarded a Center for New Urbanism Charter Award in 2002 and the 2007 Community Vision Award from the Urban Land Institute, Metropolitan Planning Commission, Home Builders Association of Greater Chicago, and Metropolitan Mayors Caucus.[46] The master plan also included off-site units two blocks south of the development in a six-story, eighty-unit building completed in 2005 that was a mix of public housing replacement units and affordable rental units subsidized by low-income housing tax credits.

The Oakwood Shores redevelopment of Madden-Wells presented both the design opportunity and the significant challenge of redeveloping one of the largest sites in the city. The master plan covered ninety-four acres and called for the creation of a mixed-income community containing 3,000 total units, including 1,000 public housing replacement units,

810 for-sale units, and 1,190 units of non-CHA rental housing, a mix of tax credit subsidized and market-rate units. Unlike Park Boulevard, for-sale units would be in separate buildings from the rental units, but rental buildings would include a mix of subsidized (both public housing and affordable) and market-rate rentals. The plan proposed to raise funds for a new neighborhood charter high school (in collaboration with the University of Chicago), a field house, and a community cultural center, although in 2013 the financing and build-out of these amenities lagged behind the rest of the development. Incorporating community amenities such as recreational facilities and schools into the master plan for the development is unusual; other sites' master plans focused on housing and, sometimes, retail development, intending to address recreational and community amenities in later phases. Oakwood Shores is bordered on the north and south by two city parks, and a small playground was added in the center of the development. There was some debate within the Oakwood Shores working group between those who preferred a more open, suburban-type layout (made possible by the site's large footprint) and those who wanted a higher-density, more urban design. Ultimately the more urban design (supported by Alderman Preckwinkle) was selected, reestablishing the traditional street grid and aiming to connect the new development to the broader neighborhood. Ironically, the subsequent freeze in the build-out of the for-sale component of the development left large lots open throughout the site and ended up creating a more suburban feel. As we shall see in chapter 8, this makes the site feel less well integrated into the broader neighborhood.

The resulting layout, with a mix of town homes, three-flat and nine-flat apartment buildings, row houses, and single-family homes, does not offer enough land to build the 3,000 proposed units at the density the working group agreed to, which has led to debates about increasing the height of buildings on site, a sensitive subject given the problems encountered with high- and mid-rise public housing in Chicago. Ultimately, two mid-rise buildings have been added to the site: a seventy-five-unit senior building (added in 2011) and (in 2013) a mixed-use apartment building housing a community medical center affiliated with a local hospital.

As we noted earlier, a first phase of the redevelopment of Horner preceded planning for the development of Westhaven Park under the Plan for Transformation. This first phase was initiated in 1996 and completed in 2000 and produced 200 on-site units of public housing known as the Villages of Westhaven, but often referred to by development team members and residents as the "Superblock." The existence of the Superblock has become a major issue owing to its physical location at the center of the redevelopment site, dividing the second phase of redevelopment into two separate sections from east to west.

When plans for the development of the mixed-income component began, the repeal by the US Congress of the one-for-one public housing replacement rule and the announcement of the CHA's Plan for Transformation led to a renegotiation of the number and type of units remaining to be built under the consent decree. To attract private developers, the CHA argued for fewer public housing replacement units and more affordable and market-rate rental and for-sale housing. The Horner Residents Committee opposed this plan as insufficient to accommodate all the public housing residents who wanted to remain on site. The final plan, despite HRC opposition, established that only 36 percent of the additional on-site units to be constructed would be reserved for public housing residents. When complete, the full Horner redevelopment, including units on site and scattered-site units off site in the Near West Side community is projected to consist of 1,317 units: 824 public housing replacement units, 303 for-sale units, and 190 units of non-CHA rental housing, a mix of tax-credit subsidized and market-rate. The

4.6   Oakwood Shores is built at a lower density, with more green space in front of and between buildings, giving the site a suburban feel. Photo credit: Janet Li.

4.7 Westhaven Park incorporates modern designs and materials. Photo credit: Janet Li.

63 percent public housing replacement total is higher than any other mixed-income development in Chicago.[47] Units at Westhaven Park are arranged in a mix of three- and six-flats, two- and three-story walk-ups, and two mid-rise buildings. Except for one of the mid-rise buildings that mixes public housing rentals and for-sale units on each floor, all buildings on the site are either for-sale or rental.

Thus each development team balanced a number of imperatives as it made decisions about site design. They all sought to create an attractive development that broke from the institutional, monotonous look of public housing and would be broadly marketable. They determined ways to reconnect the development with its surrounding neighborhood. And they chose a mix of units by income and tenure meant to achieve both inclusion and marketability while attracting a critical mass of higher-income residents.

Populating the Developments

Having determined the design of the site and secured funds for at least the first phase of redevelopment, development teams and working groups turned to populating the developments. This task had two dimensions. First, development teams had to find, engage, and support those relocated public housing residents who had expressed interest in returning to the development. The three sites presented very different contexts. At Westhaven Park, where a phased relocation process let all Horner residents who wanted to remain on site as new units were developed, the outreach was far easier. By contrast, outreach was most difficult at Park Boulevard, where all relocation and demolition was completed before any new units were built and residents of Stateway Gardens had been scattered across the city, some far from the site. The experience at Oakwood Shores lies somewhere in the middle; while some buildings on site remained occupied during construction, a substantial number of residents of Madden-Wells were relocated to other neighborhoods from the buildings that were demolished first. Second, once teams had engaged potential residents, they had to screen households for the new development and develop marketing strategies to attract families to rent or purchase the units developed for higher-income households.

Recruiting and Screening Relocated Public Housing Residents

As we described in chapter 3, the CHA established a recommended general screening policy—including a work requirement, drug testing, criminal background checks, and credit checks—across the new mixed-income sites to set standards for which resident households could move back into the new developments. But individual working groups were able to modify these general standards when they developed their "site-specific criteria." This is a prime example of a topic where there were strategic tensions along the lines of interest we described earlier. CHA staff, developers, and local community organization representatives tended to push for more stringent screening standards (ultimately exercising more influence and authority), while LAC representatives and resident advocates generally pressed for greater inclusion and access. When the Oakwood Shores working group established screening criteria for the first phase of redevelopment, for example, they included annual drug screenings and a work requirement of twenty hours a week. When the CHA board of commissioners approved a Minimum Tenant Selection Plan in 2004, which established a work requirement in all sites of thirty hours a week, the standard had to be raised at Oakwood Shores. In contrast, the Park Boulevard development team chose not to include drug screening as part of the site-specific criteria. One development team member explained that the team did not feel it was necessary to add that barrier to public housing residents who wanted to return, because the work requirement would identify those who were actively seeking to advance themselves and who would be strong residents. At Westhaven Park, the consent decree guaranteed a right to return for all lease-compliant Horner residents, thus establishing the least stringent screening criteria across the three sites. However, there was still a series of disagreements between the HRC and the CHA about screening, including whether the criteria would be more stringent for residents from other developments (who were not covered by the consent decree), and over the eventual establishment of a tenant selection committee with resident representatives. This is a unique mechanism among the mixed-income redevelopment sites and reflects the greater influence that residents and their advocates hold at Westhaven Park because of the consent decree.

Development team members at all three sites told us that recruiting relocated public housing residents became more time-intensive and costly over time than marketing units to higher-income residents. Many public housing residents did not meet the screening criteria. Indeed, development team members estimated that at some sites as much as 80 percent of the caseload failed to meet at least one of the selection requirements. In addition, many of those who *did* meet the criteria were not inclined to move to the developments. Some had been resettled and were not interested in moving again. Others feared being unwelcome or overly monitored. Yet others preferred not to move into an unfinished, uncertain development or were concerned about the small units in the new developments.[48] Development teams thus had to become more creative and invest more heavily in recruiting relocated public housing residents. They also chose to accept more in the "working to meet" the selection criteria category, which made the process (unintentionally) more inclusive but also entailed helping residents to meet the criteria within the one year allotted and managing a more problem-prone population on site.

Marketing to Higher-Income Residents

Attracting higher-income residents, especially homeowners, was a central requirement for ensuring the market success of these mixed-income communities, and there were some similarities in early marketing efforts of for-sale units across sites. All sites had well-designed marketing websites and listed the properties in a variety of print and online locations. They offered upmarket amenities, such as an extra bathroom, at lower price points than those available in many other parts of the city and

4.8 A billboard advertising the Oakwood Shores mixed-income development emphasizes racial diversity. Photo credit: Mark Joseph.

offered incentives for referrals from existing residents. Most sites targeted early marketing efforts to employees at local universities, hospitals, and other large employers. Developers highlighted the sites' proximity to downtown and other landmarks, such as ballparks and stadiums and, in the case of Oakwood Shores, the lakefront. Racial diversity was emphasized in print materials and billboards at all three mixed-income sites, while the fact that these were former public housing complexes—and would be home to relocated public housing residents—was generally downplayed in marketing materials and interactions with prospective higher-income residents, if they were mentioned at all.

Despite enduring stigma about the former public housing sites and their neighborhoods, the lack of nearby amenities, and concerns about crime, the locations and price points enabled the developments to generate and sustain relatively high rental occupancy—well above 90 percent for both subsidized and market-rate units. As we will discuss further in the next chapter, however, demand for for-sale units was a very different story; although sales started out strong, that market stalled completely with the onset of the nationwide housing crisis in late 2007.

The outreach, marketing, and screening were far more complicated and difficult than anticipated and helped shape the challenging social dynamics to be examined in subsequent chapters. Considerable time and investment had to be dedicated to recruiting public housing residents to return, which pressured the development teams, created tensions between the teams and the CHA, and sapped energy that would be needed in the subsequent phase of property management and community building. The outreach difficulties led recruiters to accept residents in more questionable circumstances, which broadened access to the developments but made it harder to help residents (across income levels) adjust to the new social environment. Furthermore, development teams' general lack of transparency about the nature and exigencies of the mixed-income setting meant that many higher-income residents did not fully understand the nature of the neighborhoods they were moving into and sometimes felt misled.

Emerging Population at the Mixed-Income Developments

These initiatives have led to the build-out and populating of the three sites, providing the foundation for these new mixed-income communities. The population growth has been incremental. In development phases over time, especially at Oakwood Shores and Westhaven Park, the construction of for-sale housing was frozen in response to the economic downturn while rental production continued, and redevelopment at Park Boulevard rolled out at a much slower pace. Indeed, by 2013 only 367 new units had been constructed as part of the Stateway Gardens revitalization. As of 2014, approximately 30 of the for-sale units remained unsold (a casualty of the housing crisis and recession), and these completed units represented only 28 percent of the projected unit total.

At Oakwood Shores, 854 units had been built by 2014. The most recent phase of development includes 48 mixed-income rental units and 28,000 square feet of commercial space, which opened in the summer of 2013. This space is occupied by a local hospital and an outpatient primary care clinic. Plans for the next phase of for-sale housing have been stalled since 2008.

At Westhaven Park, 547 units had been constructed by 2014 in the mixed-income redevelopment phase. When added to the first phase of redevelopment, the Horner revitalization plan is over 80 percent complete. All but 36 public housing replacement units have been delivered—a very important achievement considering the shortfalls at the

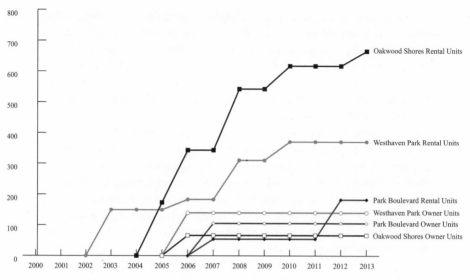

4.9   Mixed-income development units by housing tenure, 2000 to 2013. Source: Developers.

other mixed-income sites in Chicago. A major outstanding issue is the 200-unit Superblock, constructed and populated (with all public housing residents) before the Plan for Transformation, that sits in the middle of the Phase 2 mixed-income development. As we will discuss in subsequent chapters, the Superblock has aroused ongoing contention. In 2014, legal negotiations were proceeding among the CHA, the developer, and the HRC and its lawyers to relocate some of the residents of the Superblock and redevelop it as mixed-income housing, better integrating it into the surrounding new development.

At each of the three sites, the relocated public housing population is drawn primarily from the complex each development replaces.[49] Whereas the high-rise towers of Stateway Gardens were mostly demolished before new construction was initiated for the Park Boulevard mixed-income development, at Oakwood Shores and Westhaven Park some of the buildings from the original housing development remained occupied well after new units began to come online. This enabled some of the residents at those two developments to move directly into the new units without relocating to an interim location off site. At Westhaven Park the consent decree further favored the return of original residents. This, along with the higher portion of planned public housing units completed there, has contributed to Westhaven Park's return rate, far higher than that of the other two developments; 56 percent of Horner residents with a right to return are living at Westhaven Park or in the Superblock, while the corresponding return rates are 10 percent at Oakwood Shores and 9 percent at Park Boulevard.

Official demographics of the population at each site are not available, but we can get a general sense of the emerging population from our random sample of interviewees, descriptions provided by development staff, and CHA leaseholder data. As would be expected given the demographics of the original public housing developments, the relocated public housing population at all three developments is exclusively African American, and household heads are primarily female. Those in our interview sample range in age from twenty-five to seventy and are more likely to have children, and to have older children, than the residents of affordable and market-rate units. They have relatively low levels of employment and education (many are high school graduates, but none are college graduates), and most have an annual income under $20,000. The affordable and market-rate rental population at Oakwood Shores is also exclusively African American, while at Westhaven Park the higher-income rental population is primarily but not completely African American. On the whole, our random sample of interviewees suggests that renters of affordable units are closest in socioeconomic status and life circumstances to relocated public housing residents, though they are somewhat better off. They have modestly higher levels of education (few are college graduates, but most have graduated from high school) and of employment, and they are nearly as likely to have children in the household. Although there were initially no affordable or market-rate rental units planned at Park Boulevard, a rental population (and one that is far more diverse than at the other two sites) is emerging there through three mechanisms. First, some owners are subletting their units.[50] Second, the developer is renting some of the unsold for-sale units to students at neighboring Illinois Institute of Technology. Third, a new 128-unit rental phase has been completed, and there are plans for two more.

As for the emerging homeowner population across sites, Oakwood Shores is the least ethnically diverse; an estimated two-thirds of homeowners are African Americans and about a quarter are white, with the rest composed of Asians and Latinos. Park Boulevard owners are ethnically diverse but are predominantly young, single, and childless, including some IIT students whose parents bought the units they live in and some Asian families who moved from nearby Chinatown. Owners at

Westhaven Park are the most ethnically diverse but again are predominantly single or childless couples, with only a small minority of African American owners, to the surprise of that development team. Owners of affordable units are similar in some respects to market-rate owners and in other respects to renters of market-rate units. Most respondents in all three of these higher-income groups are employed and earn significantly more than $20,000 a year. Owners of affordable units are more likely than market-rate renters but less likely than market-rate owners to earn more than $70,000 annually, and, like market-rate owners, they are in general better educated, with 80 percent having earned a college degree. They are also more likely than market-rate owners, but less likely than renters of market-rate units, to be African American. Census data on the race of residents of the development footprints as well as the broader neighborhoods is presented in table 8.1 in chapter 8, where we will explore in more detail the demographic changes in the development sites and neighborhoods over time.

Conclusion

The mixed-income transformations in Chicago took place in neighborhoods with strong identities forged over decades of in- and out-migration, racial and economic segregation, and several iterations of contentious community planning and renewal. They occurred on public housing sites that, though undergirded by networks of enduring family and communal ties, had descended into disrepair and disorder as severe as any in the country. With the launch of the Plan for Transformation, the CHA and its private developer partners set about the highly complicated task of designing, financing, clearing, constructing, and populating the new mixed-income sites. The development teams had to navigate substantial logistic, legal, and economic barriers within public housing and neighborhood contexts that had an enduring legacy of contestation and marginalization. We turn now to what has turned out to be an even more complex enterprise: designing and implementing the strategies to support relocating public housing residents, managing the properties, and building the communities within and around the new developments so as to promote the integration, inclusion, and advancement that are the stated objective of the Transformation.

FIVE

From Physical Transformation to Re-Creating Community: Development Strategies and Inputs

With much of the original public housing demolished and new apartments and townhomes being built and occupied at the three sites, the development teams and their partners faced a common imperative: to promote the rebuilding of "community" among the new population of residents that was now emerging. This speaks to the assumptions about community, both as a geographic place and as a social setting, that lie behind mixed-income public housing redevelopment approaches. Beyond the physical changes to the built environment and populating the community with a new mix of residents, what were development professionals' goals and expectations for neighborhood life within these new communities, and how did they aim to achieve them?[1] How, and to what extent, would the goal of stimulating market demand through placed-based revitalization be aligned with the social goals of lifting individual households out of poverty and integrating them into an economically diverse community?

Over the first decade of the Transformation, it became increasingly clear to the CHA and its developer partners that simply relocating public housing residents into mixed-income housing would not achieve the desired social goals of integration discussed in the preceding chapters. It would take more resources, more comprehensive service strategies, and more attention to intentionally shaping environments, opportunities, and social arrangements than initially anticipated. And as we shall see in the remaining chapters, even with additional resources and attention, the move from spatial incorporation to social and economic integration would prove elusive.

To realize the vision proponents of mixed-income development have aspired to, development professionals would need to balance generating and sustaining market demand among higher-income residents with promoting the social goals of including and advancing low-income households. This chapter describes the strategies and inputs put in place to help re-create community in each of the three sites and lays the foundation for our analysis of emerging social relations, social organization, and broader integration.[2] We pay particular attention to how some of the underlying theories and concepts discussed in chapter 2—especially the promise of social capital as a resource for individual change and social mobility—are reflected in development teams' decisions on design and implementation. We first examine the vision, expectations, and goals regarding community building among the teams and their key partners. In particular, we focus on the interplay and tensions between market and social goals and explore development professionals' expectations for change at the individual and community levels. We then turn to the strategic inputs they put in place to achieve these goals. We organize our discussion around three main strategic orientations to re-creating community at the sites: providing services to help low-income residents change their economic and social conditions, promoting and managing social relations, and shaping the environment through design, investment, and enforcement of norms and rules.

Vision, Expectations, and Goals

The Plan for Transformation was launched with some bold pronouncements from city and CHA leaders about what it would accomplish, such as Mayor Daley's public statements about ending the reality of a separate "city within a city" and "rebuilding the souls" of public housing residents.[3] As we turn to the strategies used at each of the sites, we begin by considering how housing authority employees, developers, and other local organizations and partners involved in implementing these strategies conceived of the mixed-income redevelopment approach and how it could be expected to "re-create communities that function like communities," as one CHA employee put it.

Balancing Market and Social Goals

Much of the controversy around and resistance to the launch of the Transformation has centered on concerns that privatizing public housing would entail a predominant emphasis on market goals (renting and selling market-rate units, generating a profit from the redevelopment, and making the neighborhoods more attractive for private investment) at the expense of social goals (such as using quality affordable housing as a platform to improve low-income households' social and economic well-being), with the result that public housing residents would fail to benefit from the massive public-private investment in redevelopment.[4] As one service provider put it, expressing skepticism about developers' objectives compared with those of the social service agencies: "I don't think any developer went into this project thinking we're just gonna fix people's lives, people's problems. Folks came in [thinking] we're gonna [make] money. . . . [For] the social service entity, this is about changing lives, building better futures, creating opportunities for people to advance themselves."

For their part, developers asserted that the potential for market success alone was not a sufficient incentive to take on this work. "This is not the easy way to make development money," as one put it. Some already had direct experience with the complexity of mixed-income financing, the contentious politics around public housing redevelopment, and the large risks of such a major commitment to a public-private partnership with an entity with the CHA's checkered history. Others quickly learned. The need to price market-rate units at below-market rates to attract demand squeezes the profit margins on these deals. Given the uncertainty about the ultimate financial rewards of the mixed-income developments, other factors were important in the decision to participate. These factors included the chance to do large-scale real estate projects, being positioned as part of the highest-profile redevelopment work being done in the city, and, according to at least some of the developers, the opportunity to advance the social goals of the redevelopment. Indeed, most development professionals asserted that the social goals were inextricably linked to market success. It would be difficult, they argued, to attract and retain market-rate buyers and renters in a setting where low-income families continued to struggle socially and economically and community life was not stable and well organized.

Given these circumstances, development teams realized they needed to put in place strong services and community supports to help relocated public housing residents improve their circumstances and be successful in these new communities. If not, market demand would decrease, forcing them to lower rents and sale prices and to fall short of the desired range of income mix. Indeed, failing to achieve the social goals of the development, they argued, could lead to higher-income residents' opting out of development and, ultimately, to the unraveling of the "social experiment." In addition, while the Transformation is clearly a market-driven approach to public housing redevelopment, the social mission of responding to concentrated poverty and addressing the failures of public housing was fundamental to receiving government funds and incentives that made the market investments viable and central to the rationale for using public funds and resources to subsidize private developers. The role of the city and the CHA in conveying land (through long-term ground leases) and investing in infrastructure made the mixed-income projects feasible and enabled competitive rents and sales prices.

That said, a market orientation permeates the entire redevelopment strategy, from the developers' private-sector expertise and connections, to the desired market demand for unsubsidized units, to the CHA's intention of getting public housing residents more attuned to "market norms" in terms of occupancy standards and engaging in the world of work. The pervasiveness of a market-oriented sensibility can be seen in how development professionals described the nature of the task at hand. As one property manager noted, "All of our investors are investing this money, and it's a lot of money going into this, and we really want it to succeed. We need it to succeed. We need it to work." Even in discussing the social goals for individual transformation, the objective was often framed in terms of reconnecting low-income families to the "market." As a development team member at Oakwood Shores described their work with relocated public housing residents:

Trying to get them, you know, kind of acclimated to what the market is and then getting them connected to it. . . . When I say "the market," we are looking at family economic profiles and hopefully having them envision a trajectory that really gets them to being stable in the market. . . . You may never have thought to save money and you only make $21,000 a year, but you can. You can save money towards a goal. . . . This is your future. We want people to think this way.

Getting relocated public housing families "acclimated" and able to live successfully in these new contexts was significantly driven by the need to attract and retain higher-income residents. The "mixed-income environment" would need to feel secure and well-managed to remain attractive to market-rate residents. Or, as a developer at another site put it, "People are not moving here because they wanna be part of the social experiment. . . . They're moving here in spite of that." To create a mixed-income community that would sustain market demand, the development teams would need to provide the resources to help lower-income residents be strong tenants and neighbors.

Development professionals thus claim a symbiotic interplay between market exigencies and the stated social goals of the Transformation. First, the social mission validates the public subsidy of private development. Second, market investment and demand promote urban revitalization. Third, success in individual and collective social transformation is critical to sustaining market demand. Achieving the market goals was seen by development professionals to depend on success with the social goals of stable households and an orderly community. Likewise, they believe, if the market venture was not successful, the broader social goals would be compromised. Failure to build and occupy market-rate units would inhibit the production of affordable housing units, and shifts in market conditions or other factors that altered the income and tenure mix of the developments would affect the intended balance across housing categories. This could lead to a downward spiral and the re-creation of low-income neighborhoods that, in the words of one developer, "makes it feel much more like a public, you know, another public housing development."

In sum then, in contrast to critics' and resident advocates' concerns that market and social goals would conflict, development professionals argued that the market and social goals of mixed-income public housing redevelopment were tightly interconnected; neither could be achieved without the success of the other. This underscores how critical their efforts are to promote change at the individual and community level in ways that enhance this synergy—but it also raises questions about how development teams might respond when these goals conflict.

Expectations for Change

Development professionals discussed their expectations for change at both the individual and the community levels. At the individual level, while hoping to stabilize household circumstances, they often had quite modest expectations for advancement among low-income residents—at least among those who had been disconnected from the labor force for much of their adult lives and would have to surmount numerous barriers to achieve a substantially different economic trajectory. Their most common perspective was that, as an initial catalyst for change, living in a new, mixed-income environment could help shift these residents' aspirations about their future, which might then motivate them to address barriers to economic mobility. As a resident association leader in Oakwood Shores put it, "What we wanted to do was not just change where people live. We want to change, to a certain extent, people in the way they view themselves and their community."

While some saw the possibility for adults to change, most were more hopeful about youths in the public housing families. They saw youths as less constrained by counterproductive mind-sets and habits and much more likely to modify their behavior and seize chances for advancement. As a legal advocate involved with the Transformation explained, "I always thought that it'll be the children of the people who are involved that will be the primary beneficiaries of this effort." Such modest expectations for individual change among adults reflect a combination of factors: a growing sense of the severity of social and economic disconnection among relocated public housing residents, the relatively limited resources available to assist them, and the difficulties of initiating and sustaining engagement with these households.

Expectations for what could be achieved at the community level were, in general, similarly measured and pragmatic. Expectations were lower for improving community as a social unit—with benefits provided by social cohesion and interaction—and higher for improving community as place—with benefits in improved quality of life such as safety and amenities.

Those working on the redevelopments were well aware that mixed-income housing was intended to let low-income families live near higher-income families, where they could interact and build "social capital" with neighbors who might have better connections to information and resources and who could model other choices and lifestyles. But not all shared this expectation early on, and among those who did, expectations were soon modified. As a development professional at Westhaven Park noted soon after residents began to move into the development, "In the beginning, I think in our minds success was you have all these people sort of living together and interacting with each other, and that's not always the reality. . . . So now in our minds success is . . . just that people can feel comfortable where they live, they can feel safe, and that they can enjoy where they live regardless what the income mix is."

Indeed, most were skeptical from the beginning about achieving much social interaction between low- and higher-income residents, but even without direct, more intimate social interaction among neighbors, they hoped that casual encounters and distal observation would influence low-income residents' behavior and outlook.

Development professionals were much more confident about the mixed-income strategy's promise to generate a broad range of community-level improvements, including increased safety, better services, and higher-quality amenities. As one developer asserted, "We're trying to build neighborhoods. We're trying to build community. Building the residential unit is one part and, for a lot of it, where the capital money goes, but that's not the point. . . . We want these to be neighborhoods of choice. We want this to be quality housing, schools, parks, transportation, retail, all the pieces that . . . safe, secure. Places that you come to come with your family and stay."

Development professionals thus had no illusions that the grand rhetoric of city leaders regarding transformation at the individual and community level would come easily. They had modest expectations for major changes in social and economic advancement for public housing residents and were cautious about expectations for significant social interaction and cohesion. And they were concerned about the interdependence of the market conditions and social conditions and whether each would be strong enough to support the other, even as they stressed the potential synergy between market and social goals. These cautions aside, they framed their task as fundamentally about building new communities that would be both viable in the market and transformative on the ground, attracting middle-class residents, revitalizing urban space, and promoting the integration of public housing families and other low-income residents into well-functioning neighborhoods and the city they are a part of. These goals informed the strategies they identified and the investments and inputs they developed.

Re-Creating "Community" in Mixed-Income Developments: Strategic Orientations and Inputs

There have been three major strategic orientations to re-creating community within the mixed-income developments across sites. These strategic orientations are differentiated by their primary focus on either the individual, the collective, or the neighborhood level. The first targets specific services and supports to individuals, particularly to relocated public housing residents, in order to equalize opportunity and access, essentially seeking to "level the playing field" in ways that help public housing residents participate actively and effectively as community members. The second strategy tries to directly promote specific activities that foster social interaction among residents, particularly across income and tenure groups. The third attempts to shape the general neighborhood environment to enhance "natural processes" that lead to effective community functioning. Some combination of these three approaches has been used across each of the sites.

Resident Services and Supports as a Primary Input for Re-Creating Community

Although the investment in resident supports and social services was a core component of the Plan for Transformation at the outset, few if any development professionals anticipated the depth of individual and household needs and the difficulties of recruitment and sustained support that service providers would confront in working with relocating public housing families.

Several goals shaped the service strategies the development teams put in place. A primary and fundamental goal was to help relocating public housing residents meet eligibility criteria and maintain lease compliance after moving to the mixed-income community. Given the broad list of screening criteria—employment, credit scores, criminal background, household management, and at Oakwood Shores, drug testing—meeting this goal implied being able to assess and address a wide variety of resident issues.[5] A second core goal across sites was to promote "self-sufficiency" among relocated public housing residents, helping them move beyond relying on social services. Once households were stabilized, had addressed barriers to work, and had secured employment, the goal was to help them become more independent through effective financial management, strategies for saving, and the ability to find a new job when necessary.

Development professionals also sought to change relocated public housing residents' behavior and outlook by promoting "middle-class" norms to prepare them for living in a mixed-income community operating largely in the private sector, under assumptions that govern market and civil-society behavior rather than the more institutionalized, public-sector management of their previous housing. Changing these norms and behavior was also seen as a way to achieve better interaction across groups. Development professionals made the following connection: furnishing strong services and supports to relocated public housing residents would not only promote their individual advancement but would lead to more effective interaction, neighboring, and inclusion. The argument is that if residents from such different socioeconomic backgrounds are to work effectively together at building and sustaining a neighborhood—or even to live separately but harmoniously within it—it is necessary to build the skills, and the individual and family stability, of those who have been socially and economically marginalized. As a development professional put it:

As far as what we're doing, we're all about building a community, because what's happening is this area is changing, and so we want to make sure that our residents are ready for the change and we want to make sure that they're provided with all the things that they're going to need to be able to be successful in this area, because there's going to be a lot of things going on, and being able to adapt is one of the biggest things.

Facilitating such adaptation includes both the household and employment supports described earlier and an effort to change the perceptions and behaviors of relocated public housing residents that are seen to condition the possibility of success. The focus on behavioral changes reflects concerns about community norms discussed above—a work ethic, respect for property, adherence to public decorum—and demonstrates the enduring power of an urban underclass narrative used to characterize public housing residents in general. In addition to individual services and rule enforcement, development team members created programs to provide alternative contexts and opportunities, particularly for young people, that would give them, as one put it, "something positive and constructive to be involved in." But it also includes efforts to change *mind-sets*—in particular, relocated public housing residents' perspectives on their lives, aspirations for their future, and orientations toward longer-term goal setting and achievement.[6] In the words of a development professional at Westhaven Park:

When you really get a chance to go inside of these people's home and you sit down and talk with them and you take five or ten minutes, you realize that the community building, the community itself, the returning residents have issues. . . . So even though they switched housing overnight, their mentality is not switching like their housing has and

111

so, like they say, you can take the person out of the projects but you can't take the projects out of the person . . . and if you don't have enough services to try and transition them mentally, regardless of what community you put them in, it's not going to work.

In pursuit of these goals, a range of services has been made available to residents at each of the sites. These include a combination of programs to build skills and knowledge, remedial and supportive social services, and efforts to reshape both behavior and perceptions seen to prepare them to be "successful" in the private market and to work toward self-sufficiency. Programs and social services include workforce development (including job training and placement), adult education (including GED preparation and financial literacy), health and wellness programs, social support and discussion groups, case management and other specialized treatment services, and youth activities. Many of the adult and youth services are provided through citywide programs designed for CHA residents or available free to them. Services developed and provided on site include case management, financial education seminars, health and wellness programs, social support groups, and many of the youth activities. For most other services, residents are generally referred to other providers off site.

As development professionals at each of the three sites worked to provide the necessary services and supports, they met several key challenges. There was not enough funding to provide the long-term, intensive services many residents needed, even though the CHA substantially increased funding over the course of the Transformation.[7] Limited resources also constrained staff capacity at the service agencies, both in numbers and in training and technical expertise. The magnitude of household needs—physical and mental health care, improved skills and work history, help with credit problems—was exacerbated by the presence in many homes of residents who were not listed on the lease (and technically not eligible for services). Effectively engaging residents in services, particularly in the preoccupancy phase when they were living in temporary locations in various areas of the city, was also difficult for several reasons, including faulty contact information and poor tracking, distrust of the CHA and its programs, and low motivation to participate. These challenges made the resident services dimension of the mixed-income redevelopment process a major, ongoing source of concern and frustration. While each of the development teams struggled with their service strategies at the sites, the CHA was also continually trying to strengthen its Transformation-wide strategy and procedures.

Promoting and Managing Interaction

In addition to providing services to individuals, the development teams have used strategies intended to promote positive and constructive interaction *among* residents both within the development and in the broader neighborhood. Indeed, although expectations for any extensive, meaningful interaction were relatively modest, teams gave substantial weight to encouraging interaction among neighbors across differences in income and tenure. Recognizing that residents likely would not make such connections naturally, particularly given significant social differences, they sought to at least give them an opportunity to get to know their neighbors and work effectively with them, even if they did not develop strong social ties. Although a few development team members across sites advocated adopting a hands-off, "organic" approach and seeing if interactions and connections between residents would develop naturally, most strove to promote community building through a variety of organized activities. These efforts came in three forms: holding community events, launching community projects, and supporting various participatory mechanisms for planning, decision making, and governance.

Promoting Engagement through Social Activities and Events

Development teams have placed the most emphasis on events and activities designed to give residents a chance to interact and build relationships. By appealing to a broad range of interests, the teams hoped to provide comfortable, casual opportunities for residents to mingle and connect. A public housing advocate described the critical role of informal activities that could encourage community cohesiveness: "We have a development that is supposed to be one development, not a development of public housing residents and a development of market residents, so . . . I think it's going to [take] efforts that involve people getting together, doing things that they want to do together or have common interests in."

This notion was echoed by a development professional who worked with all three sites: "So you've got to create the opportunities for participation, and then people will figure out how to participate. The dog walkers will participate with each other. The artists will participate with each other. The parents, you know, with the strollers will participate with each other. The runners will participate with each other."

In the service of these goals, a range of community events has been organized across sites to provide low-key occasions for neighbors from all income levels to meet and interact. All three sites have hosted barbecues, picnics, movie nights, and holiday celebrations and have arranged field trips to museums and cultural events. Each of the sites has sponsored youth sports teams and hosted summer programming for youth sponsored by the CHA. Oakwood Shores and Westhaven Park have organized book clubs. In one of the more innovative programs, the social services partner at Westhaven Park, Project Match, a nationally recognized workforce development agency, developed an incentives program called Pathways to Rewards to encourage residents in goal setting, personal advancement, and community engagement. In monthly small group meetings, participants set personal goals with the guidance of program staff. While adults set goals such as volunteering, paying bills on time, and applying for jobs, their children set educational goals such as improving their school attendance and grades. Community "reward banquets" with dance and music performances were held every three months where participants were celebrated for their engagement and could redeem "points" they had accrued for goals achieved to exchange for prizes such as DVD players, bicycles, and gift cards. The peer support, role modeling, and public recognition at the regular community gatherings were key components of the strategy.

In addition to events sponsored by the development teams, activities in the broader neighborhood also provided occasions for residents of the development to interact with one another and with residents from the surrounding area. A community organization leader at Oakwood Shores described several neighborhood activities meant to promote informal interaction: "We want everybody to come to the farmers' market from all over. . . . The goal for that is that once folks get there and they meet and they start talking about that tomato and that potato, you know it doesn't matter where you live. It doesn't matter what you do for a living. It just doesn't matter. You're there to get a potato. Same thing with our [other] event[s]."

The principal rationale here is to provide space and opportunity for interaction that is geared toward the broadest possible cross section of residents and that is low-cost and easy to take part in. A development professional at Park Boulevard emphasized the need for informal—but intentional—occasions organized around common interests to foster connections across lines of difference that could eventually lead to more effective collective action among neighbors:

So you don't jump into it by just trying to, "Oh, we can get together and do stuff together." I mean, you have to know somebody first. So you create environments that folks can become engaged and begin to break down stereotypic barriers, whether or not it's race, income, culture, any of that stuff, you know. Folks want to live in a nice healthy community, period. That's so like Organizing 101. What's the common interest? What does everybody want? And that's what you can do, but you're going to have to do it in a concentrated way. You've got to know what you're doing, not happenstance.

In practice, many of these activities were occasional or short-lived. Development team members continued to experiment to see which types of activities would more effectively promote participation, but, as we will discuss in detail in the next chapter, it proved extremely difficult to get higher-income residents to take part in most of them.

Engaging Residents through Community Projects

Specific, longer-term community projects provide another mechanism to promote interaction, often organized by development team members around particular interests or tasks. Examples include organizing a "neighborhood challenge" at Westhaven Park to foster planning for community projects among residents, designing and building a playground at Oakwood Shores, and forming a tenant patrol at Westhaven Park to address safety. Unlike community events, projects like these are sometimes looked to as a way of intentionally engaging residents in different roles. For example, they might attempt to interest market-rate residents in community volunteering where they can interact with lower-income residents. Although certain individuals have been strongly involved, it has generally remained hard to engage higher-income residents. Westhaven Park has had the most success at sustaining community projects over time, likely owing to a number of factors: a few dedicated homeowners have stepped up to take leadership on the projects, neighborhood and citywide organizations have been more engaged on the site, and the developer has offered financial and staffing support. For example, a series of community art activities, including the creation of a building mosaic, live performances, and design of an outdoor space aided by an outside group known as Archi-Treasures, has generated relatively strong participation from a broad range of residents. Also at Westhaven Park, a community garden is an important collective project that over time has garnered engagement and leadership from various community actors. The project was initiated by a local residents' association with support from the property manager and some funding from the developer. Eventually, as one resident leader described it, "different people started putting their hands in the garden," and more volunteers took turns caring for the plants.

Managing Participation and Opportunities for Deliberation

A third approach to promoting interaction has been to establish ways for residents to discuss issues about life in the community. Opportunities for such deliberation took many forms across sites, from periodic public meetings to ongoing informal forums and formally constituted associations.[8] These settings have served varied functions. Some have provided informal occasions for engagement, sharing, and developing community activities. Others have performed more particular, sometimes legally required functions. Some have operated specifically on the footprint of the development and others at the broader neighborhood level.

Most common across sites were the condominium boards and townhome associations that were established to assume building governance as for-sale buildings became occupied. As legal entities charged with oversight of building finances and management, these associations have formal roles, procedures, and domains of authority but include only homeowners. They are neither intended nor designed to promote interaction between owners and renters, even when the groups occupy the same building. At Westhaven Park a new organization, the Neighbors' Development Network (NDN), was formed by owners to focus broadly on neighborhood issues such as safety and resident norms and, later, on community activities. The NDN board is made up exclusively of homeowners, but its activities are open to all residents of the site and the broader neighborhood. As we will explore more fully in later chapters, however, although these entities provided a core mechanism for owners to interact and build ties with one another, they generally excluded renters.

At the neighborhood level, there were already in existence a number of additional mechanisms that encouraged residents to engage with one another and with the broader community. For example, prominent in the neighborhoods at all three sites were Chicago Alternative Policing Strategy (CAPS) meetings, public meetings organized by the Chicago Police Department and held regularly in each of the city's police beats. The nature of participation and the tone of discussion at these meetings would concern and frustrate relocated public housing residents, but as mandated outreach strategies by the police department, CAPS meetings were a consistent vehicle for residents to meet and talk.

Beyond forums like these, development teams and their partners launched others, including town hall meetings and block clubs, to promote resident interaction across income groups. These mechanisms have somewhat different functions. Town hall and community meetings largely provide an opportunity for information exchange and planning input; block clubs are meant to promote neighborly interaction and plan resident-led activities. Town hall meetings have occasionally been used at the sites to discuss specific development issues (e.g., parking permits, security cameras) that affect a large group of residents. At Oakwood Shores, the developer supported a short-lived series of "neighbor circles" across income levels among residents living in neighboring buildings and blocks. Residents were encouraged to share their personal backgrounds, discuss their aspirations for life in the community, and identify some common issues they might address together.

Across all three sites, the major point of contention on how to achieve participation and inclusion in the new mixed-income communities has been whether to maintain separate associational structures for the relocated public housing residents. By far the majority of development professionals have argued for trying to "mainstream" them into less segregated modes of representation and deliberation.[9] Reflecting this preference, most reasoned that the Local Advisory Councils (LACs) elected to represent residents in the original public housing developments should not be continued in the new mixed-income developments. CHA leaders shared this perspective and did not support forming LACs in the mixed-income developments. Their main rationale was to promote the integration of public housing residents into the broader community and avoid replicating organized forms of segregation and difference.[10] A community partner at Westhaven Park emphasized the concern about separate entities' being detrimental to community building:

Local Advisory Councils kind of contradict the reality of mixed-income development. If the objective is to get people to begin to function as a community, then you can't have a thing that exists that constantly says, "You're public housing, you're public housing, you're public housing, entitled to different rights." And "You're different, you're different, you're different." And as long as you have that, you can never achieve true community building. So the very nature of Local Advisory Councils will come into sharp contradiction with where these mixed-income communities will ultimately try to get to.

Some also wanted to avoid overly contrived forms of resident organization and work to make sure these new communities function "just like any neighborhood in Chicago." And there were some who felt that avoiding separate structures would reduce conflict between different groups of residents. But most of those who argued for mainstreaming spoke mainly of the need to avoid continued separation. A representative of an advocacy organization explained:

There's tension between the understandable desire on the part of residents to be represented as a public housing group having in many obvious ways different interests from the non-public-housing residents . . . and the desire to produce a social mix in which people aren't identified as public housing residents. How this is going to play out I think remains to be seen. . . . My own instinct about this is that the more the public housing residents think of themselves as residents of the community, that is, the new mixed-income community, and the less they think of themselves as a separate group with the need for separate representation, the better it'll be for them as well as the community in the long run.

The major problem with this stance against a separate structure for low-income residents is that there are, at the same time, separate formal structures set up for the homeowners in these developments. There is an inherent inequity in abolishing housing authority-sanctioned associations for relocated public housing residents but establishing homeowner associations as exclusive entities to represent owners. As a development professional at Westhaven Park acknowledged:

I think [relocated public housing residents] don't feel like they really have an outlet. . . . [T]he only place they would have to go and complain to would be the site manager. That's it. There is no renters' association. Like, there's a condo association but there is no renters' association, so they don't meet. . . . If you had a renters' association that would speak for them and those groups talked, then they could share information back to their groups. But with the [relocated] people, you don't have that. They don't have anybody, they're just out.

One solution could be to create some type of overarching association that includes residents of all income levels and tenures. While the need to form such a governance body at each site was often invoked by development professionals and resident leaders, it was rarely put into practice. Service providers across the sites were often most articulate on this perspective. A development professional at Park Boulevard put it this way:

I'm hopeful that we'll have a more inclusive neighborhood association, one that's not a condo association and not a CHA residents' group. One that includes everybody over here where decisions can be made about a variety of things like, you know, some small to bigger things like setting rules for the park to different sorts of things like that.

Among the three sites in the study, only Oakwood Shores has sustained action toward establishing such an entity. The Bronzeville Oakland Neighborhood Association (BONA) was formed with support from the development team to include representatives across income levels from the mixed-income site as well as from the broader neighborhood, although in practice participation has largely been only from relocated public housing residents. At Westhaven Park, the city Department of Human Relations facilitated an effort to engage residents across income levels throughout the neighborhood, as described by the leaders of a local community organization:

The city Department of Human Relations has stepped in to begin to bring folks together, like the condo owners and towers of Westhaven, the homeowners in Westhaven, public housing residents. So there's been an effort since the fall of last year to begin to create a vehicle where all residents' concerns can be heard. Now, I mean, there may not be complete agreement on ultimate solutions, but it will be an opportunity for everyone to get heard or the stakeholders in various interests to be heard and come up with something that really mirrors what the larger community wants and not just what a particular silo sees as best for itself.

This effort developed over time to include the establishment, in 2010, of an umbrella organization called the Unification Focus Initiative, which hosts open meetings designed to stimulate discussion among a broad range of neighborhood residents—although in practice it has mainly focused on convening various neighborhood organizations.

Shaping the General Environment to Enhance "Natural Processes"

In addition to supplying services to individuals and supporting communal activities and associations, the final major orientation to re-creating community evident in the development teams' approaches has been shaping the general neighborhood environment to provide the groundwork for longer-term, normative community functioning. These have in some sense been foundational efforts, and they have centered on three aspects of community structure and functioning: physical design of residential and communal spaces, shaping community norms and behavior, and developing connections to community institutions.

Efforts to influence community dynamics through design draw on the principles of New Urbanism outlined in chapter 2. Decisions about design were driven by developers, but with opportunities for residents to give input through public forums and charrettes held at each site and through the resident representatives on the working groups. One strategy focuses on the coherence of units, seeking to reduce obvious distinctions between residents by making buildings indistinguishable by tenure type, so that from the outside one would be unable to tell public housing from affordable and market-rate units. A second design strategy addresses the spatial integration of units, meant to enhance positive interaction and reduce potential residential clusters of antisocial activity by dispersing residents of different incomes throughout the development. Together, these factors seek to reduce both the spatial distance between residents of different "types" and obvious markers of social distance, making interaction more likely.[11] These aspects of design are seen as an important foundation for re-creating a "normal" neighborhood. In the words of a developer, "Our mission is to do what we did. To get rid of what was here, to put back units that are indistinguishable from market-rate units. Give people a safe, decent, nice place to raise their families in good conditions with good housing, and deliver market-rate units and affordable-rate units at the same time."

A third aspect of design concerns common space and shared amenities. This approach takes various forms, including common outdoor space, like parks or a town center area, indoor space for meetings and functions, like a "community room" that residents can reserve for various purposes, or local businesses and organizations that cater to all residents. A development professional from Westhaven Park explained how such shared spaces and amenities could lead to a "true mixed-income community":

It's not all about social engineering. It's not all about having a vision for how you want people to relate. It's about, thinking about, naturally what makes communities? Good schools, a good grocery store, you know, businesses that thrive and people will begin to invest in the vision of that community because it's a thriving community. So, be more strategic about that kind of thing, and then you will have natural interactions. You will have natural shared community effort.

As we will demonstrate in the following chapters, however, the development of these shared spaces has been underemphasized and contentious, and expectations for positive "natural interaction" have largely not been realized, especially across lines of difference among residents.

Besides shaping the design of the residential and commercial environment, development professionals also sought to create an atmosphere conducive to community building by establishing expectations for normative behavior and working to enforce them through both informal and formal means. Informally, there is the expectation that public sentiment and collective efficacy will shape public behavior toward "acceptable" norms, particularly about safety and public order. Informal social control in this regard generally aims to influence some relocated public housing residents to behave differently than they did in "the projects." More formally, establishing, monitoring, and enforcing rules play an important role. At one level, this is a basic function of property management, and although development professionals noted the importance of consistency—of establishing rules that apply to everyone—much of the discussion about rules concerned the need to monitor and enforce behaviors among relocated public housing residents. At another level, there is active attention to safety and order, through both community monitoring and working with the police. Establishing and maintaining shared community norms has proved to be a highly challenging and contentious issue, which we will explore in detail in chapter 7.

Finally, development professionals have tried to promote community integration and cohesion by supporting connections to local institutions. In some cases they have primarily helped to strengthen links to existing institutions, such as schools, parks, and police. In others the focus has been on planning for new unifying institutions and amenities such as an arts and recreation center at Oakwood Shores that could attract broad use and promote informal interaction. Such amenities— particularly quality schools—are clearly critical for attracting and retaining middle-income families, and many development professionals see them as a fundamental anchor for relationships. As Oakwood Shores was being developed, for example, the University of Chicago opened a new charter elementary school adjacent to the development. One development professional described the value of the investment in a new neighborhood charter school this way:

This is very simple when you think about kids because . . . the fact that we have home buyers who have kids who are going to that school, those home buyers are going to have to interact and are interacting with renters from that neighborhood. So that's a natural way for them to evolve hopefully into friendships and relationships.

Similarly, at Westhaven Park, a development professional discussed the importance of connecting residents to the local library as a resource:

Well, for example, one of the first things we'll do in the new community room is have an orientation to the community library, where we'll get the staff to come over and create some displays to show exactly what they've got going on over there so that again we get people across the street. The same with Union Park [field house and programs]. Those are just two small examples, but it's a really big deal and the residents are not naturally making those connections themselves.

The strategy of connecting residents to existing local institutions makes sense given the limited resources available to replicate services at the development sites as well as the goal of helping residents engage more fully with the broader neighborhood and city environment. But many of these intended institutional resources and connections have not come to fruition. The arts and recreation center at Oakwood Shores remains on the drawing board, largely owing to other priorities after the onset of the Great Recession. The charter school at Oakwood Shores has been quite successful in terms of enrollment and performance, but the expected synergy and collaboration between the school and the development has not materialized, partly because of misalignment in timing, with the school needing to fill its slots well before units were ready for families to move into the development. And as we will explore further in subsequent chapters, there has been limited engagement by many development residents, particularly relocated public housing residents, in neighborhood institutions such as libraries and community centers.

Conclusion

The development teams and their partners at the CHA and in the community took seriously the need to complement the built environment with a comprehensive plan to re-create community within and around the new developments. While the public housing transformation was to be driven by market actors and market demand, it was also clear to most that the social goals of moving relocated public housing families toward more stable, self-sufficient lives and promoting constructive and supportive interactions among neighbors would be critical to the success of the overall initiative. Each site developed a range of activities intended to provide services and supports (primarily) to relocated public housing residents, encourage social interaction and resident participation, and shape the overall environment so as to sustain a well-functioning and engaged community. Each of these efforts, however, encountered substantial impediments in application and resident response, and most have fallen short of (often modest) expectations. The development teams' efforts to stabilize relocated public housing families' social circumstances at the individual level and prepare them to get and keep jobs were constrained by insufficient resources and capacity, administrative and logistical problems, unresponsive and highly challenged residents, and the unfortunate timing of a major economic recession. The endeavors by development teams and resident leaders to build community, launch community projects, and promote forums for discussion and deliberation, although they served to engage a subgroup of the population, were often short-lived and poorly attended, and as we will explore more fully in chapter 6, they either failed to attract meaningful participation from higher-income residents or excluded renters and low-income residents. And, as chapter 7 will demonstrate in detail, shaping the general community environment to create a sense of connection and shared norms has proved more difficult than expected, and often more divisive.

SIX

Does Social "Mix" Lead to Social Mixing? Emergent Community and the Nature of Social Interaction

Given the neighborhood contexts and strategic inputs described in the previous two chapters, we now turn to the communities emerging on the footprint of former public housing complexes. True to its name, the Transformation has generated dramatic change on the ground, fundamentally reshaping the built environment, contributing to significant demographic change, establishing new organizations, and shaping the circumstances for new social dynamics among neighborhood residents. The gallery-style high-rises, mid-rise towers, and barracks-style housing that characterized "the projects" have been demolished and replaced with new housing that includes a mix of single-family homes, town houses, and multi-unit apartment buildings and contains both rented and owned units. The physical infrastructure surrounding these buildings (streets, lighting, sanitation) has been significantly upgraded and integrated into the street grid, allowing better access to surrounding neighborhoods. Both property crime and (especially) violent crime have been reduced, and streets and public areas are cleaner, quieter, and more orderly. New support services have been established for public housing residents, new activities have been organized to promote community cohesion, and a new organizational infrastructure is developing to address community needs.

In addition to these changes, the public housing residents who have been able to return to these communities are now living among new neighbors, most differing from them in income, occupation, education, family structure, life experience, and (in some cases, at least) race and ethnicity. These differences are critical, since beyond the benefits that the physical, organizational, and infrastructural changes are meant to provide, the effective integration of public housing families and other low-income residents into these new neighborhoods is also meant to leverage *relational* benefits that might accrue to poor people from interacting with higher-income neighbors rather than living isolated in concentrated poverty. But to what extent does spatial integration promote such social interaction? What factors influence the nature of this interaction and its effects? How well does social interaction in these contexts promote the integrationist goals of the Transformation?

This chapter explores the nature of social interaction as it is emerging among neighbors in these new communities and assesses how well the ideals of integration are being met. We focus specifically on the nature and extent of relationships among neighbors of different backgrounds (low- and higher-income, renters and owners, of different racial and ethnic backgrounds) and on the processes, mechanisms, and conditions that shape them. First we briefly review and build on the key theoretical arguments behind the potential benefits of promoting social interaction across incomes, housing tenures, and racial groups and review current empirical evidence on how well poverty deconcentration has promoted such interaction. Next we examine residents' perception of "community" in these new contexts, the extent and nature of their social interactions with one another, and how relational dynamics are changing over time. We then turn to the specific mechanisms, processes, and conditioning factors that promote or constrain relationship building within and across groups and their connection to the kinds of community building efforts outlined in chapter 5.

Theoretical Considerations and Empirical Foundations

Two of the theoretical frameworks we examined in chapter 2, which lie behind arguments for using mixed-income development as a remedy for concentrated urban poverty and the failings of public housing, explicitly concern assumptions about social interaction's effect on social mobility.[1] The first is grounded in social capital arguments. This centers on how integration into more diverse neighborhoods might give poor people access to the networks of relationships their higher-income neighbors are embedded in—and to the information, resources, and opportunities they represent. Rather than their relying on the relatively closed, dense networks typical among residents of public housing, which provided them with social support to help them "get by" but not to "get ahead,"[2] integrating poor people into higher-income populations is meant to help them access the information and connections their higher-income neighbors have.

The second theoretical framework is grounded in the argument that deconcentrating poverty and fostering income diversity will reduce social isolation of the poor by providing "role models" who demonstrate ways of life that can shift poor people's expectations, modify their behavior, and reshape their aspirations and future orientation.[3] Although strong ties or intimate relationships with higher-income neighbors are not considered necessary, it is assumed that there will be sufficient interaction, through repeated observation or regular association, to allow "social learning" to occur.[4] In the context of public housing transformation, the foundational assumptions behind this orientation draw on notions of an urban underclass that embraces a "culture of poverty"—an internalized and self-perpetuating set of values and behaviors shaped in response to poverty and exclusion that are opposed to those held by the middle-class "mainstream" culture.[5] Culture of poverty arguments have been strongly criticized as confusing cultural patterns with the external conditions of poverty itself[6] and as theoretically questionable and empirically unfounded.[7] But we will see that these notions continue to be influential in the emerging communities replacing public housing complexes, particularly among the policymakers and professionals behind their development and the higher-income residents living within them, and they help shape their engagement in and interpretation of social interactions in mixed-income settings.

These expectations for the relational benefits of mixed-income communities rely, at least implicitly, on the notion that tendencies toward homophily—the idea that people are most likely to associate with others similar to themselves—and barriers to interaction among diverse groups can be overcome. Homophilic tendencies have been widely documented by a long line of research, from the early network studies of social anthropologists in the 1920s[8] to large-scale survey research in the second half of the twentieth century[9] to more recent work on organizational contexts, management teams, cultural niches, and neighborhoods.[10] This research provides strong evidence for the power of such tendencies across types of relationships and contexts.[11] Homophilic tendencies can be based on *status*, such as race, gender, education, income, and age, or on *values*, such as attitudes and beliefs.[12] The dimensions of difference likely to create the strongest divides between individuals are race and ethnicity, but these characteristics often reflect and are combined with the structural position of different racial/ethnic groups and their relation to other dimensions like income, education, and occupation.[13] As we shall see, the interaction of these dimensions of difference—race, income, education, social status, perceived values—are particularly apparent as public housing residents relate to their higher-income neighbors in the new communities replacing public housing complexes.

Contact theory offers one response to barriers that reinforce homophilic tendencies. Initially focused on overcoming racial prejudice and promoting intergroup relations but later tested in contact situations that included a broad range of participants,[14] contact theory posits that intergroup contact and interaction over time can reduce prejudice between opposed groups. In its most influential elaboration, Gordon Allport argues that intergroup contact could reduce prejudice when the interaction conformed to four essential conditions: that individuals have equal status, pursue common goals, work cooperatively rather than in intergroup competition, and come together under the auspices of an authority that provides "explicit social sanction" and establishes "norms of acceptance" for intergroup interaction.[15] Thomas Pettigrew elaborates a set of processes through which intergroup contact changes attitudes and reduces prejudice. These include cognitive processes (in which learning about the "outgroup" changes negative perceptions), behavioral dynamics (in which repeating new behaviors changes attitudes about outgroup members), affective tie development (leading to reduced anxiety and, ultimately, friendship), and the reappraisal of "in-group norms and customs" in light of effective intergroup contact.[16] Subsequent research also suggests that prior cross-racial contact encourages acceptance and engagement in more diverse social groups.[17]

A large body of research has substantially supported the contact thesis,[18] although the conditions Allport outlined as essential, while clearly providing an optimal foundation for leveraging the benefits of contact, appear not to be necessary; greater exposure to different groups *in itself* generally leads over time to breaking down barriers and reducing prejudice.[19] On the other hand, *negative* contact can *increase* prejudice, particularly where there is high anxiety, perceived threat, and lack of trust.[20] Indeed, recent research suggests that negative contact may be more influential in shaping intergroup experiences, given individuals' tendency to give negative information more weight than positive information.[21] Negative experiences thus become more salient in shaping impressions about other groups, in part because negative contact "is more consistent with people's expectations about outgroups—at least negatively perceived outgroups."[22]

In our analysis of emerging community relations within mixed-income developments replacing public housing complexes, the influence of factors such as those proposed by Allport and the effect of both direct negative contact and generalized negative stereotypes will become clear. Before turning to this empirical analysis, though, what is the current evidence regarding the impact of poverty deconcentration efforts and mixed-income development schemes on fostering social interaction in these contexts?

Promoting Interaction through Poverty Deconcentration: Current Evidence

Although social relationships and social interaction are central to the arguments that lie behind these policies, mounting evidence provides little reason to expect that groups in mixed-income settings would build relationships—either affective or instrumental—simply because they live together. Most of the research comes from housing mobility studies, which focus on the effects of relocating public housing residents to neighborhoods and suburbs with less poverty and, in some cases, more racial and ethnic diversity.[23] Stefanie DeLuca, for example, in a study of families relocated from Chicago public housing under the Gautreaux program, found that over time—fifteen years after relocation—women *did* report improved social networks that included instrumental exchanges (for example, help with child care and transportation) even though at first it was hard to adjust to the social norms and expectations of the new neighborhood.[24] Other studies, however, are less positive. Ruby Mendenhall, in her qualitative research on Gautreaux movers, found they formed few relationships with higher-income neighbors and made limited use of them to find jobs.[25] Although Rachel Kleit found that residents in scattered-site public housing are as well embedded in their neighborhoods as public housing residents living clustered together and are as likely to know their more diverse neighbors, they are less emotionally connected and less likely to use them to help find a job.[26] Xavier de Souza Briggs, investigating the effects of relocation to scattered-site housing in Yonkers, New York, found little interaction between newcomers and their neighbors,[27] and recent research on social interaction between participants in the Moving to Opportunity program similarly produced little evidence that movers developed anything more than limited relationships with their new neighbors or that they leveraged them for social capital.[28]

So far, less research has focused on social interactions across income groups in mixed-income developments such as those supported by HOPE VI, but the evidence emerging suggests similarly weak relational effects.[29] Across these studies, where social interaction does occur it is more likely between residents of similar social backgrounds. Cross-group interaction tends to be extremely casual. Sometimes there is an exchange of information or favors, but without clear instrumental benefits like information about or access to employment. In a study of a small early (pre-Transformation) mixed-income site in Chicago, James Rosenbaum and his colleagues found some evidence of social interaction among residents of different income levels, but their social distance was less; the range of incomes there was much narrower than in many other mixed-income sites (between 50 and 80 percent of area median income, with no market-rate units).[30] Several studies in both the United States and elsewhere suggest that homeowners and higher-income residents were less likely overall to interact with their neighbors—including other homeowners—than were public housing residents.[31] In her study of the HOPE VI site New Holly in Seattle, although Kleit found greater social interaction and neighboring than in many other mixed-income sites (including among homeowners), neighboring relations were much more likely within the more homogeneous networks of different groups (public housing residents, homeowners, ethnic and linguistic groups) than across them.[32] In addition to social similarity, spatial proximity within the development was associated with more interaction.

Thus, research to date suggests that we need to moderate assumptions about promoting effective relations across groups in these contexts. But there has been little research on the specific mechanisms and processes that promote or constrain interaction and its theorized positive effects, the ways residents interpret the relational context and shape their responses to it, the kinds of communities that emerge, or the relation between efforts to promote social interaction and build "community" and the nature of social interaction on the ground. We now turn to these issues.[33]

Emergent Community: The Nature and Extent of Social Interaction

Redeveloping public housing complexes as mixed-income communities represents the most intentional effort, in the United States and internationally, to integrate public housing residents into economically (and to some extent racially) diverse communities, break down barriers of prejudice and structural disadvantage, and promote the ties between poor and middle-class residents that are theorized to increase the social mobility of the poor. Wide-ranging improvements to the built environment and, in particular, reductions in crime—especially violent crime—should remove barriers to social interaction born of fear and distrust. Making replacement public housing and other subsidized units outwardly indistinguishable from market-rate units should reduce the assumption of social distance between neighbors. And efforts to promote community building and shape these developments into well-functioning neighborhoods reflect several of the conditions Allport suggests are important for optimal intergroup contact. The communities are supported by policy that explicitly promotes integration and positive interaction, encouraging intergroup cooperation through mechanisms and activities such as those outlined in chapter 5. And though these efforts are less specifically goal-oriented than collective endeavors, such as sports teams,[34] that are often cited as optimal contexts for intergroup contact, residents arguably share at least a general common goal of living in relative harmony as neighbors and are (for the most part) aware of the effort at social integration that is at the core of these communities' intent.[35] Equal status among residents is the one condition clearly not met, though as we noted earlier there have been attempts to equalize status among residents, and at least a few factors might help "bridge" status differences. Higher-income African American residents might mediate between low-income black residents and nonblack homeowners and authorities, and youths might connect adults of different backgrounds through the relationships young people develop with other neighborhood children from a range of backgrounds.[36]

In spite of these circumstances, we find that social interaction among residents in these communities—and particularly between residents of different races, incomes, and housing tenures—is restricted, overwhelmingly casual, and of limited instrumental benefit. Most residents describe dyadic exchanges with their neighbors as informal and, while mostly problem-free, notably distant. For the most part they consist of casual greetings and sometimes fleeting conversations—in the elevator or on the way in and out of the house, for example, or while passing on the street, or from balcony to street. For the most part residents describe these exchanges as spontaneous and limited, not likely to develop relationships or contribute to the emergence of community. As an African American homeowner[37] at Oakwood Shores put it, "You know, people are cordial. You know, they're friendly. They'll speak. But there's nothing, no kind of like, you know, sense of community. Nothing that unifies or brings people together."

This anonymity may be relatively comfortable (and, for some, desirable), in that what interaction there is can be described as congenial, or at least not contentious. As a relocated public housing resident at Oakwood Shores described her neighbors, "A lot of them is friendly. Some of them like to stick to their self, which is fine. We speak. And some of them speak and some of them don't. But other than that, it's fine." However, many point out the distinction between "speaking" and "talking," with the former describing most interactions between neighbors: "I don't have any relationships with anybody. We speak and that's it. We don't talk," as a renter of an affordable unit at Oakwood Shores put it.

Although this limited interaction is often described as reflecting the general tenor of life in these neighborhoods, interactions are notably more distant between residents of different backgrounds. Even casual greetings are sometimes constrained—at least between many low-income residents and their higher-income neighbors, especially homeowners and those of a different race or ethnicity.[38] Relocated public housing residents and other low-income renters frequently note that homeowners, in particular, tend to avoid speaking or even acknowledging their presence. As one public housing resident in Park Boulevard described it, "You're trying to interact, but it's just like you're invisible. Nobody wants to recognize you. I know what the problem is. It's them. It ain't me. I can interact with anybody."

Indeed, with the sometime exception of passing greetings, most interactions across sites—and by far most meaningful affective or instrumental exchanges—occur between residents of similar social status. Homeowners tend to interact with other homeowners and relocated public housing residents with one another (and, to some extent, with other subsidized renters). Market-rate renters tend to be less engaged in these communities in general, but they also sometimes describe encounters with neighbors that are among the most explicit efforts to interact with low-income residents, especially with their children.[39] In part this reflects the kind of "middleman" or "middlewoman" status that Mary Pattillo describes among the black urban middle class, when "members of the black bourgeoisie meet the truly disadvantaged."[40] As we will see, this liminality provides the potential for both mediation and conflict.

Although some residents report new friendships, in most cases such within-group interaction remains casual and instrumental. Often the favors exchanged are described as small but important acts of basic good neighboring—"just common courtesy things," as one resident put it— like jump-starting a car in cold weather or helping to carry a heavy package or groceries. In a few cases interviewees described more fundamental assistance, including the "looking out for" one another that is grounded in a more concrete knowledge of neighbors' needs and circumstances. Most often, instrumental exchanges are based directly on their common interests and concerns as owners or renters, public housing residents, other subsidized renters, or market-rate renters. Reflecting on this, a white homeowner at Westhaven Park remarked that the people he lives among are "actually more fellow homeowners than neighbors, if you will."

Indeed (and in contrast to some of the research we cited), homeowner status is often the basis of neighborly interaction and the foundation for instrumental exchange and collective organization. In the words of an African American homeowner at Oakwood Shores:

I like my neighbors. We just formed our homeowners' association, and the neighbors in this courtyard are very close. When we walk in and somebody else is coming in, we usually have a conversation. We usually e-mail each other throughout the day if we find out something new. That's how we kept in touch about things that were going on in our units, because we would e-mail each other and say, "Are you experiencing this? Are you experiencing that? This is what's going on with me."

Similarly, both instrumental and affective ties described by low-income renters overwhelmingly involve relationships and exchanges with other low-income renters. This is particularly true among relocated public housing residents, whose relational networks are largely carried over from public housing. A relocated public housing resident at Westhaven Park, for example, described the help she's received from these carryover relationships:

Neighbors that I've known before, like that were already living in the neighborhood and that I've known from when we stayed in the projects, yeah, they've given me like advice on—like before I started working my job . . . they gave me advice on what programs to look into to help with the light and the gas and, you know, bills and utilities to help me stay up on my feet until I got something really stable, and that keeps me rolling.

Such prior relationships are also largely the source of friendship ties among relocated public housing residents, as one at Oakwood Shores related:

I go to Evelyn's[41] house. Talk to her, drink some coffee, and we sit and watch the people go past. And sometime I go over in the park with them and play cards. . . . And then, I talks to the men and a lady named Donna. Mostly everybody here came from Wells. If they didn't come from my block, they came from another block, another block. And I know everybody but I don't fool with everybody. Certain people I talk to, that's about it.

As the end of this quotation suggests, these carryover relationships are not all positive, and part of the relations among relocated public housing residents, as well as between them and other subsidized renters, is grounded in negative experience that makes them want to distance themselves from specific potentially troublesome tenants and to avoid reciprocal obligations.

Indeed, many of these residents specify that this social distancing is self-protective, a strategy of "keep[ing] myself to myself," particularly in light of past experiences in public housing. As a relocated public housing resident at Oakwood Shores put it:

You don't want too much of that personal interaction because it's like your home is supposed to be like a private area, so if you really get to know these people and you start receiving things from them in any form . . . if that don't work, you're right here in the same building if it don't go right or if you start to—like the lady wanted me to babysit. I don't want that personal—if something goes wrong, that means we got to feud with each other right here in our own building.

Many relocated public housing residents and other low-income renters said this caution is increased given how much they feel their behavior in the new context is scrutinized by both neighbors and development staff—a theme we will return to. The effort to maintain distance from "certain people" and not be associated with the behavior of "problem tenants," often presumed to be public housing residents or their guests, was stressed especially by renters of affordable units. As one such resident at Westhaven Park put it, "I trust my [condo] neighbors, but not the project folks; I know how ghetto people are." Or, in the words of a relocated public housing resident at Westhaven Park, "I keep to myself. That's the best way to be. . . . It keeps you out of a lot of things. . . . A lot of things have not changed [from the projects]."

In contrast to within-group interactions, which can be more or less instrumental, more or less affective, and more or less distant, interactions between low- and higher-income residents are described as almost invariably minimal and distant by the vast majority of people, across sites and regardless of income, race, or housing tenure. Although a few instrumental exchanges across groups were noted—for example, donating unwanted furniture when some homeowners were moving in or out—and many residents described casual exchanges of greetings as noted above, cross-group interactions were rare and largely anonymous. This is the case even among the most sociable, as a relocated public housing resident at Westhaven Park described it: "I pretty much know everybody. . . . I'd say about 90 percent of the people within this small area, *aside from the owners*. I'd say about 90 percent of the people within these two buildings I would know personally and say hi and bye to and have a little conversation with" (emphasis added).

This perceived divide, particularly between lower-income renters and owners, is in some cases a source of middling discomfort, informed by subtle cues and quiet assumptions about race and class. In other cases it generates considerable tension. Indeed, although residents generally described *dyadic* exchanges as relatively trouble-free (though they also shared specific examples of strain, minor altercations, and in some cases outright conflict), many framed relations between low- and higher-income neighbors within a broader context of mistrust, or avoidance, or tension. They described the tenor of such interactions in broad, anomic terms: a general lack of friendliness, some caution toward one another, a sense of judgment being rendered. As a relocated public housing resident in Oakwood Shores put it, "Well there's some people, they think if making this amount and they higher than you, they look—you know, you could walk past and speak and you can tell they don't want to speak or something so you know you ain't on their level or something like that." From the other side of the socioeconomic spectrum, an African American homeowner in Oakwood Shores noted, "I'm still trying to figure out who is who and what is your motive. You know? Are you a worker or are you a person that sits back and reaps the benefits of the workers?"

Given what is known about the relation between residential stability and density of acquaintanceship networks[42] and the anticipated working out of contact theory, one might expect these dynamics to shift in positive ways over time. But while there have been subtle shifts in how some residents, at least, describe the tenor of interactions—"the notion of 'us versus them' is still lingering, but it's not as profound," as one African American homeowner at Westhaven Park put it—for the most part these patterns and the quality of interaction have become more established over time, and in some cases worse. Negative encounters—either experienced directly, witnessed, or discussed among neighbors or at public forums such as CAPS meetings—particularly with regard to perceived infractions of normative expectations for behavior and the use of public space—are influential in shaping these relational dynamics. Rather than a breaking down of barriers and shaping of new relationships across groups, there has been a more general withdrawal, an increasing tendency to keep one's head down. In the words of a renter of an affordable unit in Westhaven Park:

They had a leadership group when I first came here, trying to have people that lived in the condos and [renters] to come together, talk about the community, work out some of the relationship problems that were coming up. . . . Frankly, owners didn't want to have anything to do with renters, and the opposite too—renters didn't want to have too much to do with owners. And it's still a lot of tension here . . . a lot of divide between the people who own and the people who rent. And hardly any interaction between the two.

With rare exceptions, this contrasts with residents' experience (across income levels and housing tenures) in the communities they moved from, nearly all described as more connected and relationally rich, as well as with their expectations before moving. Although most residents had modest expectations for the depth of relational ties they might have with their new neighbors, most would not have anticipated the distance and the undercurrent of tension they are experiencing. As a renter of an affordable unit at Oakwood Shores described the difference, "It feels like it's isolated to me. When we was living in Wells, you see people going to the parks and things, people have cookouts, but you don't see nobody over here."

Or in the words of an African American homeowner at Park Boulevard, "I knew that there would be mixed-income, but I wasn't, I thought that I would have, at least have one or two more owners here. More of a balance, you know? So I kind of feel like the isolated one to a certain degree. Making sure I don't make anyone feel as though I'm different or that I'm more or not—so [I] just tread lightly."

As we will see, distance and tension between groups are broadly felt by residents across different incomes and housing tenures. But the sense of exclusion and the impact of mechanisms that shape and reproduce these tensions are disproportionately felt by public housing residents and other subsidized renters. This is particularly true as they find themselves on the sharp end of an increasing reliance on formal mechanisms of social control and intervention (for example, from property management and the police) in response to the concerns and complaints of their higher-income neighbors.

In addition to the lack of active interaction and the social capital benefits it was hoped to provide, the expectation for role modeling effects—that observation and interaction between very poor and higher-income residents might influence the former's behavior, aspirations, and future orientations—is equally unsupported. This expectation was regularly invoked both by professional stakeholders with some responsibility for developing and managing these new communities and by higher-income residents. As a white owner of a market-rate unit at Westhaven Park put it, "It used to be empty on the sidewalks in the morning, but now there's people going to work . . . and I think that's the whole, kind of somewhat of the point of doing the mixed neighborhood is to show people different ways of life and to be aspiring to have that 9:00 a.m. to 5:00 p.m. job if you didn't before."

In contrast, few relocated public housing residents or other low-income residents embraced the notion that learning from middle-class neighbors (whether passively or actively) motivated them to new behaviors or changed their values or attitudes. Indeed, many were explicit about shared rather than divergent values. As a relocated public housing resident at Oakwood Shores noted, "I eat, sleep, get up, I love my family. I want good things. I want to stay in a beautiful community, neighborhood. I want to have somewhere decent to raise my family. . . . But like I said, my personality, my character, I have very high self-esteem. Nobody could make me feel any less anyway, you know."

In addition, relocated public housing residents and other low-income residents rarely mentioned the instrumental benefits they might obtain by observing the behavior and life choices of their new neighbors. Those who explicitly discussed the benefits of living in a mixed-income community took a more general view of the positive aspects of seeing "how other peoples live," as one put it. But to them the benefits of these new contexts stemmed overwhelmingly from increased safety and better-quality housing. Although some did discuss the ways they were adjusting their behavior and, in a few cases, thinking differently about future possibilities, they were motivated mostly by new responsibilities (e.g., to pay their utilities directly), new opportunities (e.g., for job training), and new regulatory pressures (rules, monitoring, screening, and sanctioning) rather than by having higher-income neighbors as role models.[43] As a relocated public housing resident in Westhaven Park noted, "I have to be productive to keep my apartment and to be living in a really decent neighborhood . . . as opposed to, okay, being kicked out." In addition, these influences often take a punitive turn. As a public housing resident from Park Boulevard noted, the broader change accompanying better housing and a nicer built environment is not always an unambiguous benefit: "The trade-off for my apartment in Stateway Gardens for what they're giving me had belittled me. . . . It's just much cleaner, but I was a clean person in the projects. I want peace of mind and don't want to be belittled by anyone."

Mechanisms, Processes, and Contributing Factors

The findings above largely reinforce and extend those of other recent research on the limitations of cross-group social interaction in mixed-income settings. Whatever interaction occurs between public housing families and other low-income residents and their higher-income neighbors has generally not generated exchanges (of information, support, connections) that yield the social capital benefits theorized in the policy frameworks behind poverty deconcentration schemes or brought changes in values, aspirations, and behavior owing to role modeling.

Why has positive social interaction across groups, and the promised benefits of such integration, been so elusive? As we noted in chapter 5, some specific efforts have been designed to foster interaction and integration. And as we noted above, several of the factors theorized to promote effective intergroup contact are present in these contexts. Yet the cognitive, behavioral, affective, and reappraisal processes that might reduce prejudice and break down intergroup barriers are largely not playing out.[44] In the rest of this chapter we examine the particular mechanisms and processes that direct and constrain social interaction between public housing residents and other low-income renters and their more affluent neighbors and the role these factors play in marginalizing the poor. First we focus on general orientations toward relative anonymity in contemporary urban life and on preferences for partial, provisional connections to neighborhood relationships. Next we explore the way New Urbanist design has been applied in these settings and how spatial allocation of housing units and resident propinquity shape interactional dynamics. Third, we demonstrate how compartmentalizing opportunities for engagement and cooperation largely reinforces division rather than promoting interaction across groups. Finally, we explore how residents and development professionals draw on institutionalized notions of class and race (including the enduring "culture of poverty" narrative) to frame, interpret, and act on assumptions about neighbors and thus shape choices regarding interaction and engagement.

Contemporary Urban Life and Communities of "Limited Liability"

Some of the barriers to fostering interaction across groups—or, indeed, among neighbors in general—are not specific to mixed-income communities. Basic obstacles to relationship building occur in any neighborhood owing to the preferences, pressures, responsibilities, time constraints, and dynamics of contemporary urban living. Sociological theorizing about the shifting nature of community in the face of urbanization and the complexities of mass society has long been concerned with the weakening of primary ties at the local level and the way urbanization influences more distant, secondary ties.[45] Intimate relations are increasingly dispersed across space,[46] and neighborhoods are more likely to be seen as communities of "limited liability" where residents' attachment is contingent, voluntary, and based on instrumental values (connected with investment, function, and use) rather than on affective relations among neighbors.[47] While some people may actively try to connect with their neighbors, most take it as it comes within the broader set of activities and exchanges that make up their day-to-day lives. This is likely to be particularly true for higher-income, more highly educated, working residents. With resources, employment in other parts of the city, and more dispersed social networks, they tend to rely less on local neighborhood assets and relationships than those who are less well integrated into the larger society (e.g., the unemployed, women with young children, the elderly, youths, those with disabilities, ethnic minorities).[48] In the context of these dynamics, a staff member of a community organization characterizes the emergent Westhaven Park in terms of neighborhood rather than community. Expectations for neighborhood interaction are thus situated within basic, circumstantial limitations:

"In neighborhoods, you come, you know, you go to work, you come home, you pretty much stay in your condo, or your apartment or whatever it is. . . . There's interaction, there's human interaction in communities and neighborhoods [but] it's like a giant hotel, people are in and out."

The choice of *whom* to engage with on one's daily rounds is also conditioned by existing relationships, personal proclivities, and specific constraints. Many interviewees across sites, incomes, and housing tenures noted that the demands of work, family, friends, and other time commitments constrain their engagement—or even their inclination to engage—in new relationships. As a community organization staff member in the neighborhood surrounding Oakwood Shores noted, "I think what we have to kind of do is understand that people are not coming into these developments as infants. You know, they already have lives. They already have relationships. This is a place to live. That's what it is for them—a place to live."

Building relationships with neighbors one has little in common with is all the more difficult. A white owner of a market-rate unit in Oakwood Shores—whose professional training might predispose her toward such engagement—illustrated how individual proclivities, personal commitments, desire for privacy, and an orientation toward social life close to home may limit relationship building across social distance even when there arises a rare opportunity for the social learning intended by mixed-income designers. She described an interaction in which a (presumably) relocated public housing resident[49]—a low-income neighbor "on disability" who's "never worked"—approached her while she was watching her kids play and asked questions about her work, her life, and how she reared her children:

It was an interesting interaction. And, but I, this isn't, but that isn't how I want to spend my time—building these types of relationships. I get it. That is the answer. But I don't, I mean, it was great hanging out in the garden. I don't mind doing that at all. I'm not saying I don't want to have that type of interaction with people but it's not the type of friendships I want to, like, put my energy into right now. I just don't have that kind of time.

Beyond basic constraints of time and general inclination, social distance—and its specific implications—also plays a role. She continued:

It's just we're so different. Me and this woman could not be more different. I'm a social worker in a hospital. She is exactly like someone that I interview who comes into the hospital because they're having something, you know, like, tragic happen to them and I need to help them get resources. I mean, it's exactly how it felt.

As we noted above and in chapter 2, intimate ties—or even less intensive affective connections such as those among friends—are not considered necessary to support the exchanges that might provide social capital benefits like access to information about jobs or that might influence aspirations or behavior through social learning.[50] Indeed, as Mario Small points out in a recent exploration of the "core discussion network," individuals rely on a broad range of interlocutors to discuss different kinds of important issues, not just on people they consider "important" to them.[51] Given this, are there factors that can encourage interaction that, if limited, is *sufficient* to promote the relational benefits that poverty deconcentration efforts in general, and mixed-income development in particular, hope to generate?

Several factors emerge in our analysis that might shape such interaction, but in these mixed-income communities they often have a double edge or are implemented amid structural arrangements and enduring divisions that work against their promise. As the analysis below also makes clear, there are differences among the three communities—in size, demographics, the mix and spatial distribution of households, existing or absent neighborhood amenities, and the orientations, capacities, and actions of the development team. These differences produce nuances in dynamics across sites, but they have nevertheless led to quite similar overall outcomes. Race, for example, acts as a more salient proxy for higher-income residents' assumptions about the income and housing tenure of their neighbors in Westhaven Park and Park Boulevard. A larger proportion of homeowners there are not black, but virtually all renters (public housing, otherwise subsidized, and market-rate) are African American. There is a clearer and more strongly felt divide, and more explicit conflict, between higher- and lower-income residents in these same sites. Beyond the dynamics of race, in Park Boulevard this is exacerbated because, at the time of data collection, the income and tenure mix included primarily homeowners and relocated public housing residents—there was no significant component of market-rate renters—and because some development team professionals sought to maintain distance between the two groups.[52] In Westhaven Park, this divide is due in part to the relative size of the low-income rental population (the largest among the three sites), including residents of the Villages (often referred to by residents as "the Superblock"), a set of about two hundred town-house-style public housing units built in the first phase of the redevelopment of the Henry Horner Homes (before the launching of the Transformation), which sits in the middle of the mixed-income development. Also contributing to these dynamics in this site, residents are relatively more organized on both the homeowner side (through activist homeowner associations) and the public housing side (through connections with the Horner Residents Committee, the active advocacy of its lawyer, and the terms of the consent decree under which redevelopment is taking shape). In Oakwood Shores, a similar division and relational distance between higher- and lower-income residents are in general less overtly conflictual, in part owing to the small number of homeowners relative to renters overall, their spatial concentration in the development, and the development team's efforts to engage residents in a range of community building activities and forums—though these efforts largely do not foster relationships between renters and homeowners.

New Urbanist Design and the Promise of Propinquity

As we discussed in chapter 2, design principles of New Urbanism have been influential in shaping mixed-income redevelopments of public housing complexes and are explicitly embraced by the HOPE VI program.[53] Among these are assumptions about how particular design features of the built environment—such as scale, walkability, mixed uses, civic and transitional space—can support social objectives associated with diversity, such as vitality, economic health, equity, and sustainability.[54] Although community building is not explicitly stated as a core principle in the charter of the New Urbanism, community—in particular the ways design can foster social interaction among diverse neighbors—is frequently used "descriptively" in support of other principles.[55] With regard to enhancing the potential for social interaction and promoting community cohesion, propinquity is seen as central:

Related to social and civic bonds is the idea that social diversity within a neighborhood can promote social interconnectedness. When diverse groups are in proximity, there is no requirement for social interaction, but the situation allows the possibility of mixing divergent groups (rich and poor, white and nonwhite). When this diversity happens in a place such as a neighborhood, it is possible that diverse populations can find something they share in common, since they occupy a shared world.[56]

These goals of integration and social interaction are shared across sites, as are a set of basic design choices intended to foster integration among residents of different backgrounds. These include variation in size and type of building (single-family, town house, multi-unit), a mix of homeowner and rental units, and unitary external design (so that replacement public housing, other subsidized units, and market-rate units cannot be differentiated from the outside). However, the spatial distribution of housing types and residents varies across sites. In some cases the distribution maximizes propinquity between low- and higher-income residents; in others there is more within-site separation. The one exception concerns market-rate renters; in both Oakwood Shores and Westhaven Park (the two sites that have market-rate rental units), these residents are more thoroughly integrated throughout the neighborhood in rental buildings that include both subsidized and unsubsidized units. This propinquity, along with shared race—virtually all renters, market-rate, relocated public housing, and otherwise subsidized, are African American—contributes to the more informal cross-class interaction and the more frequently noted efforts to engage with low-income residents that market-rate renters discussed in our interviews.

There is also significant difference between sites in the nature and extent of unit integration within different subneighborhoods. In Oakwood Shores, for example, in its current state of build-out homeowners are largely concentrated in the eastern half of the site, in single-family detached homes or row houses, or in relatively small (six- to eight-unit) condominium buildings. The rental buildings on this side of the site are largely grouped around the perimeter or in rows between the concentrations of homeowner units (see fig. 6.1). This arrangement has clearly given homeowners an opportunity to encounter one another informally in daily comings and goings, but it has done less to promote informal interaction with renters. As an African American homeowner in one of the courtyard buildings noted, "I speak to homeowners because of the way we're set up. We have to interact because we're U-shaped; because of the U-shape you're going to always see people. And then when we exit the building, the minute you walk to the bus stop or you're walking someplace in the neighborhood, if you get in a car you're not interacting with any of the rentals because the rentals are on the corner."

In Westhaven Park, homeowners are concentrated on the eastern and western ends of the site, with mixed-income rentals and the Villages lying between them. However, homeowner and rental buildings are somewhat more integrated at the block level on the west side, and on the east side they are considerably more integrated within a mid-rise, 113-unit building that includes both condominium apartments and units for relocated public housing residents (see fig. 6.2). In Park Boulevard, single-family homes are contiguous along several parallel streets, with

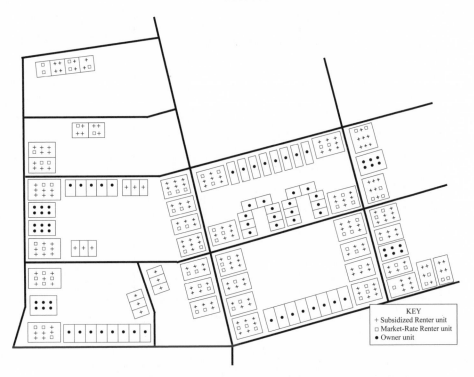

6.1   Oakwood Shores, phase 1, spatial distribution of units by housing tenure. Subsidized
       rentals include units reserved for relocated public housing residents and units rented at
       affordable prices to other low-income residents. Rows of symbols within boxes represent
       units arrayed on multiple floors. To protect anonymity, the diagram reflects the relative
       distribution of units within and across buildings but does not necessarily correspond to
       the actual distribution or location by floor.

multi-unit buildings at the corners. With just a few exceptions, though, multi-unit buildings are integrated, with both rentals (occupied by relocated public housing residents) and condominium units, and most of the current population lives in a highly integrated block of multi-unit dwellings in the northeast corner of the site (see fig. 6.3).

As one might expect, the relative spatial integration in these sites has given groups more chances to interact, at least in the extremely casual ways described above. A relocated public housing resident at Westhaven Park described how propinquity and routine activity shape these opportunities: "Oh, I see them [homeowners] when they be getting—you know, going to work, coming home from work, go shopping, you know. But I just stay on the balcony and stuff like that, and they are walking—when

KEY
+ Subsidized Renter unit
□ Market-Rate Renter unit
• Owner unit

6.2 Westhaven Park, phase 2, spatial distribution of units by housing tenure. Subsidized rentals include units reserved for relocated public housing residents and units rented at affordable prices to other low-income residents. Rows of symbols within boxes represent units arrayed on multiple floors. To protect anonymity, the diagram reflects the relative distribution of units within and across buildings but does not necessarily correspond to the actual distribution or location by floor.

they be walking their pets and stuff. That's when I mostly see them, and like when I go out to dinner and go to the mailbox, I'll see, you know, some coming in."

Although propinquity certainly makes interaction more likely by reducing its "costs,"[57] social distance grounded in differences in race, ethnicity, education, income, or age is critical in determining the likelihood and nature of interaction. Indeed, in seeking to measure the relative effects of physical and social distance between residents in a newly developed New Urbanist neighborhood, John Hipp and Andrew Perrin note how differences in wealth (as measured by home value) reduce the chances that weak ties will be formed among close neighbors in a small neighborhood.[58]

But more than this, propinquity plus significant social distance can throw up barriers to positive interaction. Negative interactions with neighbors were noted more frequently in Westhaven Park and Park Boulevard than in Oakwood Shores, and propinquity clearly generated some of this tension. In Westhaven Park, for example, while living together in the multi-unit mid-rise building gave residents of different backgrounds informal exposure to one another, their shared use of common space occasionally caused problems, as when relocated public housing residents used lobby furniture to socialize or just sit for long periods, to the disapproval of many condo owners. In response, the condominium association removed all the furniture from the lobby, causing consternation among relocated public housing residents and leading to a successful intervention by the developer.[59]

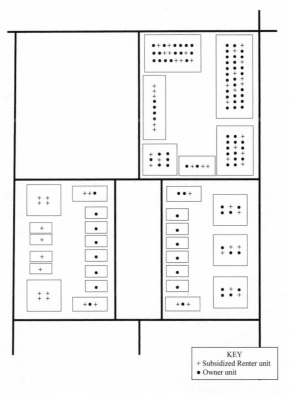

6.3   Park Boulevard, phase 1, spatial distribution of units by housing tenure. Subsidized rentals include units reserved for relocated public housing families and units rented at affordable prices to other low-income residents. Rows of symbols within boxes represent units arrayed on multiple floors. To protect anonymity, the diagram reflects the relative distribution of units within and across buildings but does not necessarily correspond to the actual distribution or location by floor.

In most cases these interactions reflect the underlying distance residents maintain from others, rather than overt conflict. They are also frequently born of higher-income residents' caution and concerns about safety where there is a lack of trust, leading to reciprocal distancing by relocated public housing residents and other low-income neighbors. As a public housing resident at Westhaven Park said, "I don't like for somebody to look at me like there's a problem. . . . You my neighbor [and all I expect is if] I say 'How you doing?' then you say 'How you doing?' I don't like it if [I] speak and say hello and they act like they are so frightened. . . . If my son is holding the door for you—I'm trying to raise a gentleman—you don't just walk in and don't say thank you, or I appreciate that, or anything like that."

Beyond the propinquity (and its double-edged effects) produced by the distribution and mix of units, the nature and quality of public space and amenities were frequently noted as being able to encourage social interaction. But more regularly their absence was seen as discouraging it. A development team member at Oakwood Shores described it this way: "When people are not hanging, those third spaces [are important]—your home, your work and that third space—the school, the park, the coffeehouse. So we're trying to build some of those third spaces where people can just not have to go to a meeting and talk about security, but just go and have a cup of coffee and see each other."

A white homeowner at Westhaven Park similarly noted the lack of such "third spaces": "There isn't—like there isn't a Starbucks, or there isn't a [place] like where everyone goes and it's like, 'Oh, we all live in the same area, and this is where we hang.' There's nowhere to hang. . . . There isn't like a—even our—grocery store. I haven't ever seen anyone at the nearest grocery store."

In contrast, residents and development team members at Park Boulevard noted commercial amenities—a Starbucks, a sandwich shop—as sites of socialization, though the amount of cross-group interaction at these places is unclear. In addition, as we will explore in detail in chapter 7, disputes about what "count" as public spaces, and about what activities are acceptable in them, often lie at the core of more explicit conflict and contribute to a range of both formal (organizational) and informal responses designed to limit (or reappropriate) such spaces and police their use.

Opportunities for Participation and Compartmentalized Engagement

Community activities and forums also can foster cross-group interaction. Organizations involved in developing these communities—developers, property management, service providers, local nonprofits—have supported a range of efforts to build community among residents. They seek to shape an environment conducive to healthy neighborhood functioning, provide services to support successful integration, and create opportunities for residents to engage, interact, and cooperate. Though with different emphases across sites, residents are encouraged to engage with one another either in deliberative forums like community meetings and associational mechanisms or through community activities and projects, from recreational events (such as barbecues, movie nights, and block parties) to community-focused projects (such as cleanups, security details, and gardens).

Although these efforts show promise in principle, in practice they have been less successful in fostering cross-group interaction than in reinforcing connections within groups. With just a couple of exceptions,[60] participation is largely compartmentalized, with relocated public housing residents and other low-income renters taking part in some and higher-income residents (mostly homeowners) in others.

In part this is a question of common interests. As an African American homeowner at Westhaven Park noted, "People in the condo association come together because they are dealing with the same problems in the neighborhood and trying to resolve them. They all want the property to appreciate and have similar frustrations, and this is what has formed their group."

But, particularly with associational mechanisms, this compartmentalization is also a consequence of formal arrangements. Condominium and homeowners' associations, for example, are by definition (and in the former case by law) governing mechanisms of and by owners. Homeowners "come together," at a minimum, because these associations are established to manage and make decisions on their behalf about the upkeep, financing, and rules governing residence in their buildings. As the quotation above suggests, they also have embraced broader issues concerning the development and the larger community where their buildings sit.

Similarly, although not mandated in the same way as for condominium associations, property management at each site has established periodic meetings—mostly attended by relocated public housing tenants and other low-income residents—to engage renters. Rather than serving the same governance or problem-solving functions as condominium association meetings, these sessions are mostly informational, largely devoted (from management's side) to clarifying tenants' rights and responsibilities and the consequences of transgressing rules and (from the residents' side) to expressing concerns and registering complaints. The meetings hosted by the CHA ombudsman, which are attended almost exclusively by relocated public housing residents, play a similar role.[61] Even where broader forums have been organized—such as development-wide or neighborhood-wide "town hall" meetings—participants tend to be largely from one group or the other. As a staff member at a community organization in Park Boulevard noted, "It's like the public housing residents have their own special meetings, and they don't feel welcome at like, I guess, [when] there's a larger meeting. It's like, no, these are your meetings. Those are ours."

The same self-selection is at play in patterns of participation in community activities, events, and projects. With rare exceptions, homeowners and market-rate renters choose not to engage in community activities organized by developers and property management or by community organizations allied with them. This includes a broad range of social events—barbecues, bingo nights, back-to-school events, holiday celebrations, block parties—that attract relocated public housing residents and, to some extent, other low-income renters. This in part reflects differential interest in the activities or associations chosen by those with limited time and existing relationships. As an African American renter of a market-rate unit at Oakwood Shores put it:

I mean, our time right now is just so precious as far as never getting family time or, so I think, I think it would be important to [go to a block party]. But, you know, I'd much rather have my buddies over and hang out in the backyard and drink beer, I mean, than, like, go over and try to make friends with the folks in the neighborhood. But I think it's important. I do, I get that it's important. And I think I would feel very differently if I was living in a community where, like, there's people like me.

But beyond these general preferences, this sorting reflects perceptions that some activities are *meant* for certain residents and not others. A development team stakeholder at Oakwood Shores, for example, noted that activities that attract low-income residents carry a kind of "social service stigma," in spite of their normative nature. An activity organized at Park Boulevard is instructive: When a local development professional was given a large number of tickets to a local zoo and offered them to relocated public housing residents and homeowners alike, homeowners took advantage of the offer while maintaining distance from the "community" nature of the event: "We were given 1,000 tickets. . . . So this is like a ridiculous number, so we offered it to homeowners and said, 'We've got a bus. We're going to go. You can come, or you can just come pick up your tickets and take your whole family if you want.' We've had homeowners that came over and got [the tickets to go by themselves], so you know, okay, sure."

Conversely, some activities—like a farmers' market organized at Westhaven Park—attracted largely homeowners, whether by accident or by design. As the member of a neighborhood homeowners' association put it, "I thought that the farmers' market . . . was an excellent idea. Having said that, it was geared to a specific demographic, and if you did not fit that demographic, you were not made to feel warm and welcome, and their price points further illustrated the audience they were targeting. [Laughing.] How was that for being politically correct?"

Residents and professional stakeholders alike recognize these tendencies and note the paucity of opportunities for residents to come together across incomes and housing tenures. In response, they often invoke the need for an overarching neighborhood association that can engage and work on behalf of all residents. At Oakwood Shores, for example, in response to the developer's efforts to organize owners and renters to work together in an inclusive neighborhood association, the Bronzeville Oakland Neighborhood Association (BONA) was established, but almost all participants are renters. At Westhaven Park, the Neighbors' Development Network (NDN) was launched by a group of homeowners united around safety and public behavior, though it has evolved to encourage youths and families to take part in activities such as a running club and a community garden, which did attract more residents across incomes and housing tenures. Beyond these rare (and limited) exceptions, however, efforts to engage residents across groups, whether in deliberative processes, social gatherings, or community projects, have largely brought only partial and highly compartmentalized participation.

Social Distance and the Dynamics of Difference

A powerful influence undergirding this differential engagement, within-group solidarity, and cross-group distancing is social distance and a set of interpretive processes that shape residents' impressions about their neighbors and their reactions to them. Mild responses to social distance may consist of avoidance, such as not responding to greetings, not engaging in activities, or not using common facilities. In Park Boulevard, for example, an African American homeowner noted the general lack of people in public, but she also limits her use of public facilities when others are present: "Not a lot of people live here, and I don't hang out outside. . . . I come home, and I'm in here so I don't, I don't go over and sit in the park. A couple of times when my son and I did go there, nobody else was there. And then we'll go over there, but typically if people are there, we won't go over there."

Many homeowners are inclined to maintain distance out of caution, a lack of trust in their (poor, black) neighbors, and a general concern about safety. A white homeowner at Westhaven Park explained why she avoids interacting with youths in the neighborhood: "I don't feel like am I going to make a difference if I strike up a conversation, because I don't know that I can trust these kids, because I know what type of upbringing they're getting, and if they're out this late at night, I don't want to build a trust and then get screwed."

In their more virulent forms, these dynamics of difference have created—and continue to reproduce—a more conflictual "us versus them" tension between low- and higher-income residents. This tension manifests itself in different ways. It is perhaps most explicit around rules, monitoring, and sanctions in response to conflicts over normative expectations for behavior and the use of public space, which we will explore in depth in chapter 7. But it is also reflected in resentments about costs and subsidies, use and exchange values, and questions about community "ownership" in the context of relocation and return (among public housing residents) and settlement (by higher-income newcomers).

Tensions surrounding cost burden and entitlement are a quiet undercurrent contributing to this divide. Some owners, at least, harbor a simmering resentment about their investment in their homes in contrast to the deep subsidies provided to their low-income neighbors. This is, in a sense, the other "edge" of the design principle that seeks to reduce stigma by making all units outwardly similar, made more salient by the Great Recession and the loss of home value it engendered. As the staff member of a community organization on the Near West Side put it:

Now, this is the part that I think gets lost in this whole mixed-income fiasco. This woman has to leave and go to work every day, and if she's like the average American, she's probably working a job that she doesn't like. She has to come home every day, after working a job that she doesn't like, to her $300,000 condo that she has a mortgage on, and right next door she knows this woman's got the same thing she has, and doesn't pay squat for it. No one says anything, [but] right below the surface it's grating her, and anyone.

An African American homeowner at Oakwood Shores took a similar position:

I really don't think that it's fair as far as being in the same—I'm not talking like home-owners mixed with renters in a different area, but when they're in the same area, like in the same building, I kind of have a problem with that, because it's like people who are paying huge mortgages that are next to people who aren't. I don't know. I just don't feel like it's fair.

These perspectives are not lost on their lower-income neighbors. Awareness of disparities in wealth or rent and resentment about "entitle-ment" were often noted by relocated public housing residents and other low-income renters. As one in Westhaven Park noted, "Well, us low-income—because they put us as low-income people and people that [are] from the projects because we're paying low, and they own theirs. We rent ours. And like, they put us in a category. So that's what I don't like."

Issues around cost burden are also connected to exchange value prior-ities among homeowners, who are concerned with retaining (and grow-ing) the value of their homes for eventual resale. As with home buyers everywhere, the potential to build wealth through increasing home val-ues was certainly one component of homeowners' calculus in choosing to move into these communities, and to some it was a predominant motivation. A white homeowner at Westhaven Park, for example, noted the centrality of "good investment" claims in her decision to purchase: "We were told that this was a groundbreaking area with this untapped market and blah, blah, blah." But investment orientations also inform how some homeowners frame differences and use specific cues to draw conclusions about "who's who" among their neighbors. In the words of an African American homeowner at Oakwood Shores:

But when it's not your own, you've got this lackadaisical attitude like, whatever. It's like, be invested. And so people that are just, I don't know, riding up and down the street all wild and crazy or throwing, you know, bottles on the floor as they're walking up and down the street, or food, or garbage—it's just like if that was your house you would never do it. So that's how I feel like they're not owners. They don't feel like they have an investment in this area because if they did they would protect [it] like they do their personal belongings.

Also informing these tensions are responses to the hopes for or fears of gentrification—a shared recognition that these new communities are by definition contested turf. Thus relocated public housing residents feel the pressure of a potential "takeover" by incoming homeowners, often of a different race: "They want to take this land, this area from us," is how one resident at Westhaven Park put it. And many homeowners, while hoping the neighborhood will become increasingly middle class, recognize that they may be seen as unwelcome intruders by those who lived in the demolished public housing complexes where their homes now sit. A white homeowner at Oakwood Shores sketched both sides of this tension:

I think you have just people from different backgrounds, and I think people may not interact with somebody that is not, from not the same background as them, and I think it's both ways that they, that maybe renters, they see, like there's many people moving in here that may be, like taking over their community or something like that, or maybe the people who live here look at the renters like, you know, I don't know, maybe undesirable or whatever.

As we've previously noted, a broad range of strategies have been tried to reduce this social distance or obscure its existence. For some (by far the minority), the pieces are in place to shape inclusive communities where such differences are not self-evident and do not define social interaction among residents of different backgrounds. A development team member at Park Boulevard, for example, discussed the benefits of spatial integration as a mechanism for breaking down barriers of perceived difference: "I think, in part, because our buildings are integrated, people generally know their neighbors, and many of our CHA families will not self-identify as CHA and they know their neighbors and their neighbors have no idea if they're CHA or otherwise, because how would you know?"

But this rather sanguine view does not reflect the dominant reality of social dynamics in Park Boulevard or in the other sites. Indeed, residents across incomes and housing tenures use a broad range of cues to make assumptions about the social background of their neighbors, and they act on those cues in specific ways. Higher-income residents, and homeowners in particular, frequently interpret these cues based on the enduring influence of a culture of poverty narrative. Many homeowners and professional stakeholders internalize this narrative and use it as a cognitive frame to organize assumptions about their low-income neighbors, drawing "symbolic boundaries" that distinguish neighbors in terms of specific in- and out-group characteristics.[62] These assumptions are in part informed by observation and in part extrapolated from and integrated into socially constructed notions of the "other": what these people value and how their values inform their life choices and behavior. Some of the cues that shape these responses—particularly in

Westhaven Park and Park Boulevard—are obvious markers of race and income. A white homeowner in Westhaven Park noted:

There's a dichotomy between the renters and the owners. The renters are obviously low-income. They're obviously black. And they're obviously used to living here in public housing. . . . Which means they lived here through some hard times, which means like a lot of them just survived. So they have this history of being like broken and public housing residents and that whole history that comes with that. They're obviously poor or low-income. They're obviously black. And the owners are obviously not black, for the most part. Like we have a few.

Others are geared toward more specific details, such as how their neighbors dress, what kinds of cars they drive, whether they have dogs (which are not allowed in some rental units), and the nature of their daily activity. In some cases these cues are more subtle, as expressed by an African American market-rate renter at Westhaven Park: "I could tell when I first came in, because they were always home. At first you don't pay any attention to that. I'm coming in and out. Maybe they work different hours. I give everybody the benefit of the doubt, but after a while, you're going, 'I always see that lady over there. I wonder if she works.' You just start thinking that."

Still others describe what a number of interviewees referred to explicitly as "ghetto" behavior. Thus, public gathering and socializing (loud interactions in the street, lawn chairs pulled up in front of building entrances, late-night parties) become a sign of fundamental differences in culture and lifestyle and come to characterize the relocated public housing residents as a group. Some residents thus end up (often self-consciously) stereotyping one another and shaping their behavior accordingly. An African American homeowner at Oakwood Shores put it this way:

I guess in theory you're not supposed to be able to tell who's low-income, who's middle-income, who's high-income. But even in this mixed-income neighborhood, you can tell. Do you know what I mean? Renters for example—I mean, I'm sorry I'm assuming a lot of them, or you can assume a lot because you see a bunch of kids on bikes and so forth. . . . I mean that the park's dirty there and clean here; it's not so much safety but it's like they still treat the area like it's the old area—"We ain't got to keep the streets clean. We don't have to pick up the trash"—like it's still the projects.

Responding to outward cues about difference runs the other way as well. In this way the day-to-day behavior of owners—retreating to their homes after work, walking their (often large) dogs, not greeting people on the street, calling the police about the public behavior of neighbors—comes to symbolize standoffishness and unsociability or, more forcefully, opposition to the presence of low-income people.

These cues are not unfailingly accurate, of course, though the set of assumptions that lies behind them is remarkably consistent. As an African American homeowner at Oakwood Shores explained:

> I mean, you can make assumptions based on stereotypes. I mean, that's easy enough to do. But it's not always 100 percent. You know what I mean? There are days when I'm hanging out with my girlfriends, and I'm coming home at 2:00 in the morning from some joint and my music is blaring and we're screaming and acting crazy. People never think those are the homeowners or that's the attorney coming home and making all that ruckus. You see what I'm saying?

Similarly, an African American homeowner at Westhaven Park recounted experiences in which race, in particular, framed the responses of some of his unknown neighbors or their guests to his coming home:

> If someone comes to the door, and if I'm coming to the door with someone at the same time and they don't know me, they're not a resident here, they don't know me, they definitely look at you different. They're afraid. Some of them, they're just plain old outright afraid. You can just tell. Their body language, they're clutching their purses, and they'll let you go through the door first and act like they forgot something so they don't have to go in the elevator with you at the same time. Oh yeah, this stuff is apparent.

Although far less frequently, interviewees also provided examples going the other way, as did this relocated public housing resident in Oakwood Shores: "I've actually had a market-rent person talk to me about a CHA person and didn't know I was from CHA. . . . She was like, 'They move'—the market-rent person—'they move these people in here from CHA, and they don't know how to act.' Now you talking to a CHA—now she's confiding all this in me and I come from CHA."

In expressing these assumptions and responses, different residents stress the relative salience of race, class, and culture or lifestyle, but they are nearly always conflated. Relocated public housing residents and other low-income renters are more likely to focus on race and racism as central, though many also use the word "culture" to distinguish between themselves and others; as a public housing resident at Oakwood Shores put it, "I'm comfortable with my black brothers and sisters [but] . . . now my awareness [is] that there's another culture here, now I need to be paying attention." Higher-income residents are more likely to focus on socioeconomic status and the ways it shapes particular cultural or lifestyle adaptations—very much in line with the culture of poverty narrative. Although race is often acknowledged as a component factor, it is more likely to be downplayed. As a white homeowner in Westhaven Park put it:

Well, I personally wouldn't want to say it's race is the problem. I think it's a socioeconomic thing. But I am seeing that there's more of a cultural difference too that I guess would have to do with race. But I think your culture is based on your economic [status], you know, where you came from. Because we're, we're really a diverse building. You know, there's homeowners of various races. So I don't see race as the problem in the building, but what I do see is, you know, obviously, you know, a different class of people that come in that make me a little uncomfortable—not because of their color but because of their, the way they're dressed and that stereotype I have about them. So that's a problem.

In some cases higher-income African American residents may play a bridging role. Shared race and their own experience of social mobility may help them collapse social distance and interact effectively with their low-income neighbors. As an African American homeowner at Westhaven Park put it, "If you're an outgoing and pretty cool person, you can get a little aura about yourself, and you can talk, because I can walk on both sides of the lane, of the street, because I come from one, and I've migrated to the other side, so that really doesn't bother me."

On the other hand, the dynamics of race and the liminal position that higher-income African Americans hold in these communities sometimes generate complex undercurrents, including what Cathy Cohen describes as "secondary marginalization," in which these African Americans actively push for "middle-class" norms, condemning or policing the behavior of low-income neighbors who transgress them.[63] They also might try to maintain racial and class identity while distancing themselves from "ghetto" behavior despite pressures from lower-income neighbors. The renter of a market-rate unit at Oakwood Shores described this situation:

I'm an African American black female. I have a master's degree. I mean, I don't stunt my growth because of the environment that I'm in, and I talk a little bit to the kids. I give them things to try to draw some attention to myself so that I can communicate with them, but I also have—on the other side of that, I can see that there's some jealousy and envy from lack of understanding because I'm not going to revert to some of their negative ways, which is, you know, the talk, the walk, the clothes. I'm not gonna do that. I'm gonna be me. And my car's been scratched up. My mirror's been broken off. I can't put

my name on the mailbox. They keep taking it off. I mean, going through stuff like that
and it's very frustrating and very discouraging because it's my own people, you know.

There were similar hopes, particularly among professional stakeholders at the developments and early in the life of these communities, that
young people could operate as a relational bridge between residents of
different incomes and housing tenures. This bridging potential, however, has for the most part not moved past the aspirational, and hopes
have dimmed over time. Indeed, in addition to some basic demographic
factors (relocated public housing residents are likely to have more and
older children than their higher-income neighbors) and structural constraints (young people from different backgrounds tend not to attend
the same schools or share programs or facilities) that constrain their
"bridging" potential, youths are often at the contentious core of the
problems of social control that play out in these neighborhoods.

Conclusion

Policy assumptions that spatial integration will lead to social interaction and increased social capital for public housing residents are not
coming to fruition. Social relations in general are cordial but very distant, and there is little interaction across incomes and housing tenures. These circumstances are shaped by spatial dynamics, differential
participation, associational compartmentalization, and the enduring
influence of institutionalized assumptions about difference grounded in
notions of the urban "underclass." Although dyadic relations are usually described as trouble-free, significant tension has arisen across sites,
ranging from a low-key but pervasive "us versus them" attitude between
low- and higher-income residents to more significant conflicts. Some of
these tensions have become muted over time, but with rare exceptions
proximity has not created the foundation for more generative social interactions across groups. Instead, many residents have withdrawn into
relative isolation or homophilous relationships, particularly organized
around homeownership, on the one hand, and public housing status on
the other. For community problem solving and social control, they also
increasingly rely on formal mechanisms that further isolate and exclude
families relocated from public housing and other low-income residents.

SEVEN

Space, Place, and Social Control: Surveillance, Regulation, and Contested Community

Beyond expecting that promoting social interaction will contribute to the social mobility of the poor, proponents of mixed-income public housing reform expect it to improve stability, safety, and order in neighborhoods that once were characterized by crime, deterioration, and disorganization. This transformation is to be accomplished by redeveloping the built environment, screening out problem residents, integrating higher-income renters and homeowners, and establishing organizations and procedures to set rules, monitor compliance, and respond to problems as they emerge.

As we noted earlier, dramatic changes have indeed taken place on the ground, particularly in the built environment and in the safety, security, and physical conditions of the emergent communities. In these respects at least, the new developments are a nearly unqualified good, and public housing residents are virtually unanimous in approving the relative quality of their new housing and the relative safety of these new communities. "You don't have to hide behind anything and won't get shot at," as a relocated public housing resident at Park Boulevard put it. "You can walk to the el station instead of running."

These changes, however, and the social and organizational dynamics generated by redevelopment and demographic change, have also produced fundamental tensions that play out as concrete problems. These tensions—between integration and exclusion, use value and exchange value, appropriation and control, poverty and development—contribute to serious contestation about the nature of community and the rights, privileges, and responsibilities that are shared or differentially enjoyed by community members. In particular, community concerns about safety and order and contention over "public" space, rights of access, and norms of behavior have led to increasingly stringent surveillance, control, and rule enforcement. This atmosphere has militated against the effective integration of public housing residents and other low-income renters and given rise to new forms of exclusion and alienation. And, as might be expected given how race is entangled with the generation and reproduction of urban poverty in the United States,[1] racial dynamics and enduring assumptions about the urban underclass play an underlying, if complicated, role in shaping both perceptions of and responses to these situations.

This chapter extends the analysis of social interaction in chapter 6 by focusing on critical dynamics around the nature and use of public space, expectations regarding behavior, and social control in these emerging communities.[2] First we briefly rehearse some of the theoretical arguments for how mixed-income development and integrating the poor into economically diverse, well-functioning neighborhoods can contribute to neighborhood safety and security and outline some of the foundational tensions affecting how these ideas might play out in the context of mixed-income public housing reform. Next we examine the principal considerations that motivate residents' and development professionals' approaches to establishing social order and regulatory regimes. Third, we investigate the nature of these regulatory regimes and the orientations, processes, mechanisms, and actors that drive and sustain them. In particular, we explore ideas about "market norms" and the influence of a "broken windows"[3] approach to preserving order, the rules and sanctions established to protect that order, and the role different actors and mechanisms (from property management and police intervention to security cameras to enlisting residents in informal surveillance and control) play in maintaining it. Finally, we explore responses to this regime and to specific contentious issues—from differential targeting and enforcement to differential impact on residents based on income and housing tenure—and how these circumstances have helped redirect the integrationist aims of the development policy toward a kind of *incorporated exclusion* of relocated public housing families and other low-income residents. While contributing to the regeneration of the built environment and the *spatial* incorporation of residents of diverse backgrounds, these factors—regardless of intent—shape circumstances that instead reproduce division and contribute to new dynamics of exclusion and marginalization.

Social Organization, Social Control, and Foundational Tensions

As we elaborated in chapter 2, assumptions about how mixed-income development might aid in social control draw, at least implicitly, on social disorganization theory. Reshaping neighborhood context through redevelopment responds to assumptions about how neighborhood effects operate in high-poverty neighborhoods, epitomized by the public housing complexes being replaced by mixed-income communities. A large body of research, for example, finds associations between living in high-poverty neighborhoods in the United States and a range of social problems, including child abuse, teenage and out-of-wedlock births, school drop-out rates, crime and delinquency, and adult unemployment—which may all be associated with weakened mechanisms of social control.[4] Mixed-income developments seek to promote social order by changing the composition, structural circumstances, and social processes in these new communities. Much of this change is expected to flow from the presence of higher-income residents (along with screening out the most disruptive public housing families) and from the accommodations development professionals make to attract and retain them.

Complicating these assumptions are the dynamics of demographic heterogeneity and tendencies toward homophily and withdrawal. Increasing the proportion of higher-income residents, homeownership, and residential stability may improve social control and reduce crime, but it may also generate conflict between groups who assign responsibility for particular conditions or infractions to specific groups "unlike" themselves.[5] Indeed, although there may be broad agreement across class and race about the desire for neighborhood safety and about a broad range of behaviors that would be considered disorderly and unacceptable in *any* neighborhood,[6] the line between acceptable and censurable behavior often shifts where there is dramatic demographic and community change. Thus, Mary Pattillo describes a tendency in gentrifying neighborhoods toward the "progressive criminalization of 'quality of life issues'" and an increasing tendency to censure legal behaviors (barbecuing in public, fixing cars on the street, playing loud music) that some (generally higher-income newcomers) find distasteful.[7] Mixed-income public housing redevelopment—itself a kind of planned gentrification[8]—highlights these dynamics, informed by the enduring power of the urban underclass narrative and driven by processes that are both formal and informal, organizational and individual.

Indeed, although in many ways they reflect other gentrifying contexts, these mixed-income public housing redevelopments differ in several important respects, each relevant to the way such normative debates and social control dynamics might be expected to play out within them. First, each development explicitly aims to promote income mix and integration. Second, because of the way they are designed, built, and managed, there is more formal, centralized control over rules, monitoring, and enforcement than in gentrifying neighborhoods where many actors—renters, homeowners, developers, elected officials, community organizations, public agencies—play multiple roles that are only sometimes coordinated. Third, rather than the infill development and renovation that characterize most gentrifying areas, these developments entail the wholesale demolition and reconstruction of the physical infrastructure. This requires relocation and return, with most public housing residents being moved away, then brought back to the "new" community concurrently with the gentrifiers.[9] Unlike more typical gentrifying neighborhoods where the middle class are the sole newcomers, all residents are in some ways "new" to the redeveloped housing complex, complicating questions of "turf" and rights. Finally, as part of a formal, structured, citywide initiative, these sites are being developed under defined procedures and constraints (a relocation rights contract for public housing residents, an independent monitor), in a highly politicized and litigious environment, under much public scrutiny. These factors contribute to competing visions of the kinds of communities these new neighborhoods should be and of how residents and development professionals should approach the regulation and social control needed to ensure neighborhood stability and order.

Rationales and Motivating Considerations

In thinking about their desire for neighborhood order and the need for standards, rules, and mechanisms to ensure it, both residents and development professionals express a number of reasons for supporting regulation and enforcement. These fall principally into three broad categories. The first, and by far the most salient and widely shared, is concern about crime, safety, and disorder. The second, shared principally by development professionals and homeowners, is concern for the market viability of the communities and the need to protect investment and exchange values. The third is the need for clear community norms and standards of behavior. As with concerns about safety, the need for neighborly norms is widely embraced among development professionals and across residents of different backgrounds, but there is also some disagreement about what those norms should be, what procedures should be used to establish them, how they should be enforced.

Crime, Safety, and Disorder

Safety and security are clearly important for residents in the mixed-income communities replacing public housing complexes (as they are in all neighborhoods), and concerns about crime and disorder lie behind much of their support for rules, surveillance, sanctions, and design features that control and defend space. Worries about violent crime, and about drug trafficking and gangs bringing violence, were shared by development professionals and residents across sites regardless of income, race, or housing tenure, though they were raised more frequently at Oakwood Shores and Westhaven Park than at Park Boulevard and by homeowners and higher-income renters across sites. Westhaven Park residents, in particular, were more likely to be apprehensive about gangs and drugs than their counterparts in other sites, in part because of the "superblock" and its concentration of public housing residents in the middle of the new development. However, perceptions that safety and security have gotten worse in recent years (especially since 2010) were most prevalent among residents and development professionals at Oakwood Shores, where there have been some well-publicized shootings.[10] As we will see, these perceptions have driven a range of responses across sites, from more vigilant rule enforcement by property management, to stepping up policing of public space, to extensive use of surveillance cameras.

Although similarly concerned with these issues, relocated public housing residents we spoke with had a somewhat different orientation than other residents, especially higher-income residents and homeowners. On one hand, they sometimes feared that ongoing gang activity (however reduced) and, more generally, the behavior of unsupervised youths (often assumed to be either former residents of the public housing that was replaced or friends of current residents who live in the surrounding neighborhood) might lead to a return to the negative community

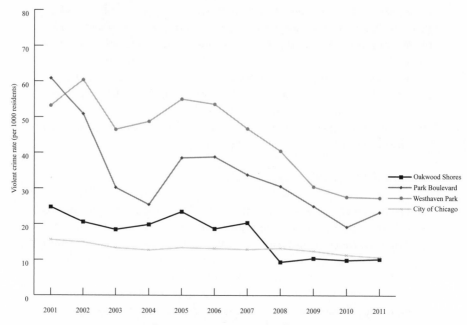

7.1   Violent crime rate, 2001 to 2011. Violent crime includes homicide, criminal sexual assault, robbery, aggravated assault, and aggravated battery. Annual rates are presented for police beats containing the mixed-income developments and the city as a whole. Source: City of Chicago (https://data.cityofchicago.org).

dynamics of the projects—"coming back to the same damn stuff again," as one put it. On the other hand, while other residents frequently discussed the need for more (and more effective) policing, public housing residents were more likely to take a defensive stance, seeking to avoid entanglements ("No one don't bother me, I don't bother them") or getting erroneously caught up. As a relocated public housing resident at Westhaven Park put it, "I caught myself walking up to the park and kept a U-turn right back here. I said, 'I'm not going to no jail.' [The police] go up to talk to some girls I know, and [the girls] got drugs on them. They think I'm there with them. I'm go to jail for them? No thank you. I left."

Although fears about drugs, gangs, and violent crime were salient, however, they were far from overriding. More prevalent were complaints about property crimes and, especially, about a broad range of "incivilities" that stop short of criminality but lower residents' assessment of neighborhood quality of life. Indeed, total reported crime, and especially violent crime, has declined significantly across sites over the course of the Transformation (see fig. 7.1).

In spite of these changes, residents expressed considerable concern about a range of behaviors they tended to frame as security issues. A number of these, discussed in our interviews and focus groups and raised at community meetings, concerned both "quality of life" crimes (such as vandalism and gambling) and more serious criminal acts (such as robbery, burglary, and assault), often seen to be carried out by local youths. Some residents have directly observed such behavior or its impact. Others worry about future infractions. But by far the most common concerns centered not on crime as such, but on particular public behaviors and the improper use of public space. Again, youths are often at the contentious core of these issues, but they are not the only factor. More broadly, homeowners and higher-income renters focus on what they often describe as "ghetto" behavior: hanging out in parks and on street corners during the day and late at night, playing loud music on the street and in cars, yelling and arguing in public, littering.

In some cases these behaviors are seen as threatening or as cover for actual illegal behavior. Public gatherings of (invariably African American) men, for example—on the streets, in vacant lots, playing chess in parks[11]—are frequently seen as indicators of drug trafficking or gang activity, and groups of youths in public, "swarming" home after school, are often interpreted as trouble waiting to happen. A board member of a community organization at Oakwood Shores recounted an exchange at a recent meeting: "He said, '[A group of kids was] hanging out there, and the kids weren't bothering anybody, so I don't see any problem with it.' And I said, 'Yeah, there's a problem with it. The problem is that's how they get into trouble because they're bored. They might not be doing anything today, but that's just not the way children should live.' "

Other residents are more ambivalent, not sure how concerned to be, how threatened to feel, or how best to respond. "It's not illegal," as an Asian American homeowner at Oakwood Shores put it; "there's nothing you could do about stuff like that, but it's just not—it doesn't make for a very friendly environment." But in most cases, concern about such behavior is more a matter of propriety and a desire for order and control in the neighborhood than a response to feelings of threat or danger. As an African American homeowner at Park Boulevard put it, "I feel safe around here, but if someone came to me and wanted to buy my unit [I would sell], because it's not what I bought into. . . . It's the people who hang out on the corner and barbecue, the youths, watching them running from this house to that house. . . . They all know each other." Or in the words of an African American renter of a market-rate unit in Westhaven Park, "I should not have to not want to go outside

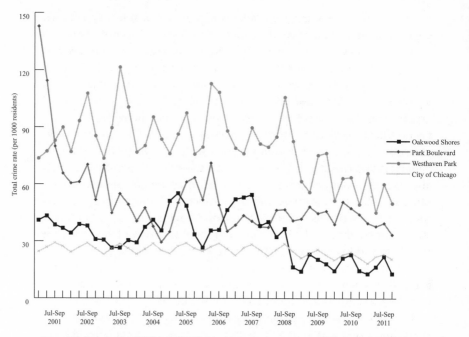

7.2 Total crime rate, 2001 to 2011. Total crime represents reported index crimes (violent and property) and non-index "quality of life" crimes (criminal damage, drug offenses, prostitution, and gambling). Quarterly rates are presented for police beats containing the mixed-income developments and the city as a whole. Annual spikes in crime rates during the summer reflect increases in violent, property, and quality of life crimes. On the whole, property crimes and quality of life crimes are more prevalent than violent crimes in these neighborhoods and the city at large. Source: City of Chicago (https://data.cityofchicago.org)

because . . . there's a bunch of other people out there loitering, hanging out, and doing whatever. Next thing you know, there's garbage all around, and that's not being taken care of."

Regardless of these different responses, the range of behaviors—from clearly criminal to those that cause minor annoyance—are often conflated as issues to be confronted in the name of safety and security. When community awareness of crime is heightened, such as when break-ins or shootings spike or in warm weather when more people are on the streets—as well as when more crime is being reported (see fig. 7.2)—attention to both crime and incivilities is heightened.[12] Thus, at meetings both on the footprint of the development and in the broader community—including more general forums (working group meetings, tenant meetings, meetings of neighborhood associations, park council meetings) and those specifically geared toward crime and safety (CAPS meetings, safety and security committee meetings)—residents' complaints often move seamlessly between worries about crimes (break-ins, drug trafficking, shootings) and concern about incivilities (public gathering, unsupervised youths, noise). At CAPS meetings, which are specifically designed to foster collaboration between the community and the police to reduce crime, police representatives frequently feel compelled to deflect complaints about noncriminal activity and keep the focus on crime. This tendency toward linking incivilities with crime both reflects and supports a "broken windows" approach to addressing safety concerns and maintaining order in these communities. The idea of policing disorder as a prophylactic against more serious crime informs the strategies embraced to address them. This is a theme we will return to.

Market Context, Investment, and Exchange Value

A second consideration motivating support for maintaining order and social control is homeowners' and development professionals' concern about the investment value of their property and about continuing to attract and retain both higher-income renters and buyers and commercial investment. They want a community that is well ordered, well maintained, and stable, where the resources a homeowner invests are likely to increase in value over time and where market-rate renters will feel they are getting comfort and value for their money. Clearly, crime and safety are critical, and a sense of the neighborhood as safe influences whether prospective buyers—as well as current homeowners—feel comfortable and are likely to invest. The opposite is equally true: seeing neighborhood disorder and feeling unsafe make residents uneasy about stability and the soundness of investments. As an African American homeowner and the leader of a local community organization in the neighborhood surrounding Oakwood Shores put it:

I'm investing in this community. I come through here in the evening, still daylight, and you've got these roving bands of kids, and they're just being destructive. They're throwing—if you drive up the new street, Forty-Second Place here, you will see where they have taken the time to break out every one of these new lights that we begged the alderman to give us, acorn lights. Do you know how long it would take for a kid and how many rocks you'd have to throw straight up to break out a light? That's destructive.

These concerns tie directly to calls for rules, surveillance, and enforcement that can help maintain order and protect investments. As a professional stakeholder working for a citywide organization supporting the Transformation noted:

Well, you really have to enforce the rules for the entire premises, both [renters and owners]. If you're not managing the property properly and not enforcing the rules, and across all income spectrums . . . , so I will be clear about that, although there are probably fewer rules if you've bought a house than if you're renting—but if there isn't some consistent enforcement, then the property values will go down, the appearance of the property will be degraded, the desirability of living there, the comfort of people living there will diminish.

But beyond indications of vandalism or other specifically criminal acts, a range of other behaviors are seen as evidence of disorder that provides negative cues for potential investors and higher-income renters, and as ultimately damaging the property values of those who have already invested. These concerns are often raised in both development and homeowners' association meetings, as well as at a range of public forums in the broader neighborhood. Often people object to "loitering" and the very presence of people on the street, especially black men and unsupervised youths. As an African American homeowner in the neighborhood surrounding Westhaven Park put it, "Last night there were seventeen guys down at this place just hanging, seventeen people in front of two of the CHA homes, just hanging around talking and so forth. If anyone drives through this neighborhood and they see that, they're not going to buy a home next door to that. It's not gonna happen." Or, in the words of a local public official, "So, yeah, you may like the kids on the block and think that they're cool and think they should be hanging out but, at the same time, you don't want people driving around seeing them hang out because it may give the wrong impression of the . . . of your property value, you know."

Development professionals share these concerns, for obvious reasons given that, as a market-driven strategy, the Transformation privatizes former public housing developments (transferring property and responsibility for development and management to private developers) in order to create mixed-income communities whose (market) success relies to a large extent on attracting higher-income homeowners. As we will see, the regulatory regimes established to maintain order largely aim to enforce middle-class norms, in part to keep the developments viable in the market, and in practice they target low-income residents. Strategies for accomplishing this aim are ongoing and will be explored in detail below, but they begin with establishing the screening procedures and preoccupancy supports for relocating public housing residents that we described in chapter 5. As one development professional put it, "We try to work through the folks that we have, preparing people for moving into the community. That's a huge part of what we do, because how you start is how you finish. People have to be prepared for living in this community . . . [and] *living in the market* is very different" (emphasis added).

But while considerations of exchange value clearly contribute to homeowners' and development professionals' attitudes toward social control expectations and responses, even more salient—particularly among residents, and particularly emphasized by homeowners and market-rate renters—are expectations regarding *use value* and the norms of accepted behavior that lie behind them.

Norms and Community Standards

Beyond rules and enforcement clearly focused on safety and security (which attend to crime reduction and intervention) and on investment maintenance (which also attend to property upkeep and sanitation), rules and enforcement are also applied to maintaining "appropriate" behavior and controlling the use of public space.

The need for community norms and basic standards of behavior is broadly embraced both by development professionals and by residents, regardless of race, ethnicity, income, or housing tenure. When discussing expectations for behavior and neighborhood norms, most respondents in some way invoked respect and common sense as essential guiding principles. And despite some perceptions to the contrary, most share a set of values. Virtually everyone, homeowners and renters, across income levels, is in favor of a safe and clean environment, and no one wants to be disturbed or awakened by the thoughtless behavior of neighbors or their guests or children. And virtually everyone agrees that rules, and regimes to enforce them, are important and should be reasonable, appropriately specified, and fairly applied. As a public housing advocate put it, "Good strong norms thoroughly enforced, responsibly enforced, understandably enforced are very important, and good management will do that automatically." There is some disagreement, however, over where the line should be drawn between prohibiting behavior and tolerating difference, about who decides, and about apparent double standards.

Indeed, while much of the focus on norms of behavior concerns generally agreed-upon nuisances that impair other residents' quality of life, much of the discourse on maintaining community norms centers on the need to reform what many homeowners, higher-income renters, and development professionals see as the deviant norms, values, and behaviors of low-income renters, particularly relocated public housing residents. As one professional working for a community organization involved in the Transformation put it:

I think by not assisting and altering behavior and putting them in situations where they thought that their old behavior would work and they find themselves on the street. . . . That's work, 'cause you're talking about generational poverty, bad habits. I mean, public housing created a different kind of person, not the average person, and people look at me like I'm crazy when I say that, but when you subject people to things that people in public housing were subjected to—and that it's not normal, it's not natural and then you have to teach, you know that stuff is taught to successive generations, you know, and you've created a different kind of human being, not better or not worse, but different.

The spectrum of noncriminal behaviors to be changed ranges from generally agreed-upon incivilities—noise late at night, littering, loud and obscene language, unruly youths (propping open doors, running through hallways, damaging property, leaving trash in their wake)—to activities that are far more innocuous, such as storing personal items on balconies or hanging laundry in plain view, washing or repairing cars in the street, and barbecuing in public.[13] Indeed, as we noted above, much of the concern focuses on the very presence of people congregating openly for leisure or with no apparent purpose. Again, these orientations are shaped in part by the enduring power of an urban underclass narrative and informed by embedded assumptions about race, class, and culture. As an African American renter of a market-rate unit at Westhaven Park put it, "I think when you start hanging out like that, it makes it look more like a quote/unquote ghetto. So I don't like that." Or in the words of another, "I feel like I work really hard to live here, [and] it angers me when I walk out my door every morning at eight o'clock to go to work and I see the same people just hanging out and staring at me every day when I go to work and every day when I come home. You live in the same kind of standard that I do, yet I go to work and work fifty to sixty hours a week."

These frustrations lead to arguments about rules and enforcement. As an African American homeowner at Oakwood Shores suggested, "You don't have this going on in communities on the North Side. You don't have this going on in white communities, and I don't think we have to deal with it in our community. The loitering, the children just hanging out on our block. . . . They don't live here, so why are twenty-five of them hanging out here? Why are kids just walking in the middle of the street?"

While these frustrations are clear, where to draw the line between the freedom to enjoy neighborhood space and the point where such enjoyment infringes on the rights and enjoyment of others is a matter of contention, as is how appropriate and equitably enforced are the rules established to maintain such norms.

Regulatory Regimes: Orientations, Processes, and Mechanisms

Acting on these considerations, development professionals at each site have established specific rules and processes. They have also connected with existing and emerging mechanisms in the development and in the broader community to establish and maintain regulatory regimes directed toward safety, security, normative behavior, and the use of public space.[14] We now turn to these responses. First we examine the dominance of "market norms" and the "broken windows" approaches that frame them. Next we consider the rules and sanctions that have been put in place and the actors, mechanisms, and processes engaged to establish norms, monitor behavior, and compel compliance.

Market Norms and Broken Windows

Two principal orientations guide the establishment of rules and regulatory regimes to ensure safety, security, and order in these new communities. The first, responsive to the exchange value considerations described above and the market-oriented goals explored in chapter 5, is a concern for what development professionals in particular often describe as "market norms," driven both by the need to attract and retain higher-income residents and by the effort to acclimate relocated public housing residents to the behavior expected in the market and civil society, outside the institutional framework and isolated circumstances of the "projects" they came from. In response to the first concern, norms must be set "for the highest common denominator," as one development professional at Westhaven Park put it. "This is business and a fact of life." In response to the latter, rules and mechanisms for supporting low-income residents in general, and relocated public housing residents in particular, need to be accompanied by efforts to both instruct and enforce. As a development professional at Oakwood Shores explained:

We can set certain rules that are basic management rules, but they have to be market norm management rules. This is not supposed to be prison lockdown management. This is supposed to be market, for market-rate [residents], but also for public housing renters. The point of this is you're making—for public housing families you're transitioning into the market. This is with safety, transitioning with [a] safety net. So part of it that's important is, What is it like to operate with a private landlord? What are the rules that you typically expect? How does that work?

The second orientation is an embrace of the "broken windows" theory of crime and disorder. Definitions of what constitutes criminality are context-specific and change over time, but both normative and relative approaches to crime are generally grounded in the notion of *threat*.[15] Outward signs of disorder (litter, broken windows, graffiti) and expressions of incivility (loitering, panhandling, cursing, unruly behavior, public drinking) are often seen to indicate more fundamental problems with safety and crime, leading residents to assume they may be victimized and providing youths and others inclined to crime and antisocial behavior with "cues" that such action will be tolerated. In racialized contexts such as Chicago, historically among the most segregated cities in the United States, the presence of young black men, in particular, contributes to these dynamics. Along these lines, the influential "broken windows" thesis argues that such disorder *leads* to crime, and that policing disorderly behavior, including "taking informal or extralegal steps to help protect what the neighborhood had decided was the appropriate level of public order," is an effective way of preventing or reducing crime.[16]

Visual cues certainly matter, and research has shown a relation between disorder and perceptions of crime.[17] However, the empirical basis for a causal link between disorder and crime proposed by the broken windows thesis has been challenged. As Robert Sampson and Stephen Raudenbush argue, rather than seeing disorder as a direct cause of more serious and predatory types of crime, both disorder and crime might more appropriately be viewed as consequences of underlying circumstances— such as concentrated disadvantage, residential instability, and a deficit of collective efficacy and social control. Indeed, with the exception of robbery, their analysis suggests that assumptions of a causal relation between measures of neighborhood disorder and predatory crime are in general spurious. Equally important for our analysis, however, is their drawing on Morris Janowitz's definition of social control as "the capacity of a social unit to regulate itself according to desired principles—to realize collective, as opposed to forced, goals."[18] In the new mixed-income communities replacing public housing complexes, however, there is clear disagreement about what "counts" as disorder and what should be viewed as normative enjoyment of community space. As a public housing resident leader argued, "They're acting like we're the problem when our community has been like this. They have a problem with us standing on the corner. We're colored. That's what we do. We gather in groups. We don't have to be [doing] no drug activity or nothing like that for us to gather around."

Acting on broken windows assumptions, at least in some instances, calls into question whether particular expectations for behavior are collectively acknowledged or whether they cross the disputed line between the right to enjoy neighborhood space and infringing on the rights of others.[19]

Development professionals and higher-income residents tend to embrace broken windows orientations particularly when there is heightened conflict or perceived threat (although many recognize the complexity of the issue and find themselves on different sides of the argument at different times).[20] In some cases demands to deal with unsupervised youths and pervasive "loitering" have been extreme. Explicitly invoking the broken windows approach to youth problems at Oakwood Shores, for example, a homeowner and leader of a local community organization suggested emulating the state response to the London youth riots of 2011 by evicting the families whose children are causing trouble in the neighborhood. Indeed, as we will explore below, ramping up evictions and threats of eviction has recently been done across sites, especially at Oakwood Shores and Westhaven Park. But beyond reactions to particular spikes in concern over crime and antisocial behavior, the general response has been routinely curtailing access to public spaces and proscribing daily activities that are deemed unsafe in some way or seen as generating more serious problems down the road. So, as a relocated public housing resident at Oakwood Shores noted, there should be "no loitering [in] the hallways, no playing around on the steps, 'cause kids can get hurt playing in the hallways." And, as we suggested above, the association of a broad range of incivilities with more serious crimes creates a gray area where the one is linked seamlessly to the other. A white homeowner at Westhaven Park made this point unselfconsciously:

I think the message that [property management is] sending is, We care. We want you to live in decent housing, but we also want you to care, but—and we don't want people living in the housing who are going to, you know, mess it up. And that's drug dealing. That's prostitution. That's, you know, selling cigarettes out of the back of your place. That's loitering at, you know, at 2:00 a.m. That's people swinging by in the car with the loud music. You know, that whole kind of attitude.

Similarly, an African American renter of a market-rate unit at Oakwood Shores connected management concerns about safety with broader behavioral expectations: "The security is very, very important to them. They take that very seriously. Just—you can't do this. You can't hang clothes outside. You can't barbecue in those common areas and then things like that."

These approaches toward maintaining order are reflected in specific rules and sanctions and codified in instruments, perhaps most centrally the lease, that ground responses to residents' infractions.

Rules, Regulations, and Mechanisms of Enforcement

Many of the rules, regulations, and requirements developed by developers and managers of mixed-income public housing redevelopments are no different from those that govern any rental community or condominium: paying rent and fees on time, keeping noise down after a certain hour at night, maintaining the property. For homeowners, condominium associations establish regulations for their members. These extend to renters living in buildings that also include homeowners and, in many cases, to common areas in and around the buildings. Homeowners' associations thus have wide discretion in setting rules all residents must abide by.[21] Many homeowners see this discretion as important to protecting their investment and maintaining their quality of life. As a white member of a condominium board in Westhaven Park put it, "This is my home, and what do I want, regardless if it's [mixed-income] or not? I didn't want to lower my standards. . . . I wasn't trying to be racial or anything like that. I was just trying to say, I'm paying for a place. I'm not going to lower the standard, [allow] my standard of living to be lowered. So that was kind of [why] maybe we had to create rules and all those sorts of things that we didn't have."

For renters in all units, one set of foundational requirements are the screening criteria, outlined in chapter 4, that guide resident selection and establish the threshold standards for living in these developments. For the most part these requirements—background and credit checks, employment, children's enrollment in school, drug testing—are uniformly required for all renters if they are required at all.[22] Sometimes exceptions are made for relocated public housing residents, some to lower the bar for residents engaged in programs and activities that show they are actively "working to meet" eligibility criteria (as at Park Boulevard and Oakwood Shores), some to protect the "right to return" of public housing residents under the conditions of a consent decree (as at Westhaven Park), and some establishing more stringent requirements, such as social service screening and in-person interviews (as at Park Boulevard). Similarly, regulations codified in leases and associated "house rules" that elaborate expectations for residents' conduct are for the most part meant (at least formally) to extend to all renters, although some exceptions apply only to relocated public housing residents. These include reporting changes in household composition, employment, or income; meeting community service or "self-sufficiency" requirements for all adults in the household (at Westhaven Park and Oakwood Shores);[23] and "zero tolerance" for criminal activity—including both specific criminal acts (such as using or distributing illegal substances) and more general infractions (such as parole violations and the "abuse or pattern of abuse of alcohol")—by the leaseholder or, importantly, any members of the household or their guests.[24]

The list of rules across sites is substantial—"they have a dictionary-sized Rules and Regulations," as one relocated public housing resident at Oakwood Shores put it. Many rules are very specific (fee schedules, pet regulations, barbecue prohibitions, rules on placing objects on balconies or outside unit doors). Others are more generally stated—not "loitering" or gathering in common areas, and taking responsibility for children and guests—or require some interpretation. (What counts as "loitering"? Which areas are designated as "common" for these purposes?) In either case, these rules are cited by both development professionals and residents—particularly relocated public housing residents and other low-income renters—as tools for ensuring compliance and triggering penalties.

While formally applying to all renters (if not to homeowners), and in spite of development professionals' insistence that enforcement is equitable—"a complaint is a complaint, a violation is a violation, the rules and regulations are the same," as one put it—the lion's share of responding to infractions targets low-income renters, especially public housing residents. Indeed, low-income renters are seen as likely to cause fundamentally different problems than homeowners and other higher-income residents. As a development stakeholder at Westhaven Park put it:

There's a huge distinction between owners and renters. So in this building, what the owners do that is annoying to other owners are things that you'd expect in a condo building. You know, they're leaving their trash in the trash room instead of throwing it down the trash chute. They're leaving their pizza boxes out. They—they track in mud from outside. Someone's stealing someone else's newspaper. . . . The renters, on the other hand, you know a tax-credit renter or even a market-rate renter, you know, can still be playing their music too loud, can still, you can still—listen, it happens all the time. You know that the tax, you can get a tax-credit renter that's selling drugs out of their unit.[25]

Compliance with these rules is monitored and enforced through a number of mechanisms, both formal and informal. "When you put all these rules in place," as an African American homeowner at Park Boulevard put it, "you really needed to bring an army to enforce it."

Formal monitoring and enforcement is largely the domain of development team members, especially property management staff, in part through collective engagement with renters at tenant meetings, attended almost exclusively by relocated public housing residents and other low-income renters. These meetings provide a mechanism for sharing information and airing grievances, but the principal focus is on clarifying rules and responsibilities (such as expectations for apartment maintenance, yearly lease renewals, and "neighborly behavior"), explaining how infractions will be handled, and stressing the consequences of lease violations. As a development professional at Oakwood Shores put it, acknowledging the development team's dual (and often difficult) role in both providing support services for relocated public housing residents and enforcing rules and order,[26]

One of the problems with [our combined responsibility for Community Supportive Services] and property management—and we hear this a lot from our residents—is, "You guys are confusing me. Are you the good guy or the bad guy?" And this makes it easy. We're the bad guy, okay? If what you mean by bad guy is who's gonna enforce the lease, who's gonna yell at you when your kids are hanging out in the common areas and your trash didn't make it to the garbage, then one more time you didn't pay your rent, that's us. I would rather say we are the creators and protectors of this space, and we want to promote this networking concept here, but we will be the ones—we're gonna do you a favor. If anyone steps out of line as defined by the lease—Now you signed the lease. That's always the one thing you've got going for you. You signed it. You bought into this covenant, if you will, and we'll make sure that that gets enforced.

Developers and property managers also operate through more individualized engagement, both by surveillance—walking the streets during the day and driving around the site at night, talking to residents about how things are going—and by enforcement: for example, calling residents into the office for meetings, sending notices about expected behavior or reported violations, documenting offenses. And these functions increasingly are done through formal surrogates (such as private security—often off-duty police officers) and electronic surveillance. Indeed, beginning in 2010, building on a CHA initiative to install cameras at CHA properties, all three sites deployed closed-circuit television (CCTV) cameras as both a deterrent to crime and a tool that might aid in prosecution.[27] By far the most extensive system is at Oakwood Shores, where perceived increases in crime and in antisocial behavior by youths have led to particularly vigorous efforts to address residents' concerns. In partial response, 150 cameras have been installed, focused on all rental buildings (not homeowner buildings),[28] parking lots, alleyways, open spaces (except the public parks, where the city has installed cameras), and the perimeter of the development. Beyond providing a record of public activity to review in response to criminal incidents, cameras at Oakwood Shores are monitored by a private outside firm and feed into the city of Chicago CCTV system, which is in turn monitored by the Office of Emergency Management and Communications.[29] In addition, cameras are designed to respond to certain behaviors—such as groups of people standing around for a certain time—with recorded messages warning them away.[30]

Formal mechanisms also include the police: development professionals at each site frequently urge them to increase their presence on the streets and in the parks and, in keeping with the broken windows orientation, to be more vigilant about both serious crimes and a broad range of incivilities—"getting the police more proactive in the community with the guys hanging out," as one development professional put it. Discussion at CAPS meetings too, especially at Oakwood Shores and Westhaven Park, frequently turns to requests for more aggressive policing and additional patrols, asking that youths be checked for identification (one resident, in Oakwood Shores, suggested issuing armbands to identify resident youths) and urging a "zero-tolerance policy" toward loitering. Describing a plan for extra patrols in the neighborhood surrounding Westhaven Park,[31] for example, a police officer noted that it will concentrate on incivilities—drinking, hanging out—"the kind of crap you see every day."

Beyond formal mechanisms, both property management and the police also encourage residents to keep watch and to report infractions. Police, for example, routinely emphasize calling 911, creating phone trees, and joining volunteer patrols. And property management systematically asks residents to monitor infractions (by notes in mailboxes or posting notices to call management about anything questionable). Management also works through relationships it has with specific residents. As a development professional at Westhaven Park explained:

According to my visual inspection, I can look at a building and . . . say, "I need to go visit that person on the second floor," just by seeing. I mean, for me personally, I can look at the outside sidewalk and see if there's been too much traffic inside of the building going on, and when I start noticing, hey, this property has a pickup on traffic, I know there's something wrong, and I need to find out. And the thing is that I don't so much as go over there. I'll call residents inside the building that I have a good relationship with and say, "Hey, what's going on in your building?" But I keep my ear to the community finding out what's going on, and I guess that's a big part of it.

To many relocated public housing residents, this surveillance has a Panopticon quality, and many said they felt uncomfortable about its pervasiveness and the sense that their behavior was under constant scrutiny. As a public housing resident at Park Boulevard put it, "It's like everything you do, they know about it." And this in turn informs behavior—"govern[ing] people by getting them to govern themselves," as Barbara Cruikshank puts it—very much in the mode of poverty governance discussed in chapter 2.[32]

In many cases, relocated public housing residents respond by trying to "blend in," as one at Oakwood Shores explained: "I have found myself that when I talk to the people at market rent or homeowners, it will have to be on a different kind of behavior, and I think it's just psychological, 'cause they don't tell me to or ask me to, but I immediately want to impress them that, you know, I can blend over here with you all."

In other cases, as we will explore below, residents either push back against what they see as unreasonable restrictions or, most commonly, withdraw and stake out a defensive position in these new communities.

Responses

Most people in these communities—development professionals and residents alike—recognize that the offending acts, whether clearly criminal or just uncivil, likely are generated by a relatively few "problem house-holds" and their guests or (particularly in the case of crime) by low-income residents in the surrounding neighborhood who may or may not be connected to current residents. That said, relocated public hous-ing residents and other low-income renters (higher-income residents virtually never distinguish between them)[33] are the principal focus of regulatory regimes. As the leader of a community organization in the neighborhood surrounding Westhaven Park put it:

The target becomes people in public housing; it's just easier to lump them in as a group. . . . The police have told them a dozen times: this is a social situation, you have to figure out ways culturally, socially, to deal with it, you can't police this away, and so those tensions are heightened, because [the relocated public housing residents] know who called the police, know who's giving them grief. . . . It's a clash unlike anything I've seen, and to get anywhere remotely close to that, you'd have to go back to when blacks were trying integrate communities back in the sixties, to get that kind of venom and rabid anger that comes out when people are talking about the neighborhood.

Relocated public housing residents themselves are of two minds about rules and rule enforcement. On the one hand, many recognize their importance generally (as noted above) and believe that enforcing them improves the quality of life (safety, sanitation, quality of the built environment) compared with public housing, especially by reining in disruptive youths or removing tenants they recognize as troublesome. For some, the more restrictive regime is a fair trade for the improvement in living standards. As a relocated public housing resident in Westhaven Park put it, "The rules are what is expected. I mean, what can you say? You come from the projects and you get blessed with a brand-new apart-ment that's built from the ground. What more can you ask for? You come out of the projects where there's rats, roaches, floods, no heat half the time, no lights half the time. So I'm grateful. I have no complaints."

Many, however, find the nature and extent of surveillance and regula-tion invasive, often excessive, and a significant source of stress. Indeed, while most homeowners and market-rate renters we spoke with advo-cated more stringent rules and, especially, more rigorous enforcement—a position shared by some renters of affordable units, as long as they tar-get troublesome tenants—virtually no relocated public housing residents recommended more stringent rules or saw a need for more vigorous en-forcement. Beyond some basic disagreements about the appropriateness of some rules—restricted access to what they view as public space, injunctions against "congregating," prohibitions on barbecuing—there was general

177

concern about how often certain rules singled them out as likely transgressors, were differentially enforced, and were potentially detrimental to both their rights to community enjoyment and their ultimate housing stability. They expressed these concerns, sometimes with resignation, sometimes with rancor, with regard to both private behavior and public space.

Policing Private Behavior

Rules governing private behavior and the mechanisms for enforcing them often overlap with concerns about the use of public space, but they are also oriented toward specific aspects of self-sufficiency, self-control, and lifestyle. These range from employment (or else training and community service) to drug use to personal hygiene to housekeeping. At a condominium association meeting at Westhaven Park, for example, complaints about the smell of cigarettes emanating from people's apartments—the source was explicitly presumed to be relocated public housing residents—led to a proposal to prohibit smoking in apartments by declaring the building a no-smoking zone.[34] At a tenants' meeting at Park Boulevard, development professionals told relocated public housing residents that homeowners had complained about their stepping outside their units "not looking acceptable for public presentation" (uncombed, barefoot, in pajamas) and encouraged them to "take away [homeowners'] ammunition" by thinking beyond the specific rules codified in their lease. Instead, they should remember that "people are watching" and avoid behaviors that would be perceived as negative by their higher-income neighbors, especially in light of the relative benefits they themselves receive: "People are paying $300,000 and $500,000 for these units. You all have the same units. You've been privileged to move into this development."

Indeed, although public housing residents often questioned equitable enforcement, many homeowners and development professionals saw the more stringent requirements as appropriate in light of the benefits received. In the words of a development professional working on the Transformation at the city level:

If I was going to pay your rent and you didn't have to do anything for it and I had no expectation for you, you may go off and be the greatest most quiet person, or you may just party all day long, right? Lots of people who don't have any expectations set on them are just going to end up partying all day long. So because we're subsidizing the rent, I just think they have to come with some expectations of behavior. . . .

I think if it's subsidy without an expectation of behavior, then I think that becomes a problem.

One way of monitoring these expectations for residents' behavior is through periodic unit inspections. Although some residents accept them as necessary and say they help maintain building sanitation and upkeep, others find inspections unfair and intrusive. "People have no business looking in my closets," one relocated public housing resident complained at an Oakwood Shores ombudsman meeting. "I want them to stay out of my house."

Formally, all renters regardless of income or subsidy are required to allow inspection of their units at least annually. In practice, however, unit inspections are disproportionally focused on low-income residents, and they often take place far more frequently than the annual requirement.[35] As a development professional at Westhaven Park noted, "Part of the unit expectation is their units will be inspected at least four times a year, but it's at least twice that, and for some residents it's more than that. . . . Market residents are excluded from that, but our market renters are a small portion and the affordable and public housing units, I mean, they have to open their doors literally every month to inspectors."

The outcome of inspections, along with complaints from other residents and infractions documented by property management, provides the foundation for a range of penalties. Across sites, there is a stated regime of strict enforcement. As a development professional at Park Boulevard put it, "I don't negotiate. The rule's the rule." This is a stance recognized by public housing residents across sites—even in Westhaven Park, where the consent decree and legal representation give relocated public housing residents more leverage to negotiate terms than at the other sites. "It's zero tolerance for every resident," noted one public housing resident there, "Westhaven do not play."

The weight of surveillance and the rigor with which infractions are sought out and penalized have led many relocated public housing residents to feel both confined and under constant threat—"walking on eggshells," as one put it—as well as ultimately demeaned. As a public housing resident at Westhaven Park put it, "Believe me, you are being watched. The cameras, the cameras. And if anything goes wrong they pull you in the office, they're gonna tell you every detail." Or, in the words of a public housing resident at Park Boulevard, "I feel less of a woman than I was before I came here. I was a grown woman before I came. Here, they treat you like a little kid. Every day you're getting a note from your teacher, a note sent home to your mother—you can't do this, you're too loud."

The pressure of neighbors' complaints and managers' responses are often seen as contrasting to the more flexible, tolerant stance toward living with neighbors that many relocated public housing residents believe they themselves take. "We're adaptable to noise, to people walking when we can hear it at 4:00 in the morning," noted a public housing resident leader. "We should tell each other. Maybe we should complain, but we figure it's their business."[36]

Leaseholders' concerns about overzealous and unfair enforcement extend beyond the stigma of having their own behavior scrutinized. They feel that their children are unwelcome in the community and unfairly targeted by efforts to enforce rules, especially those pertaining to public space. Even more worrying for many is that they are held responsible for the actions—indeed, even the presence—of visitors and nonresident relatives. A number of relocated public housing residents commented on rules that define the actions of nonresident children as lease violations and on the effect that has on both family cohesion and a sense of basic security. A resident at Westhaven Park, for example, noted the increasing trend of eviction proceedings owing to criminal acts by nonresident adult children and residents' complaints about them. "My son got caught somewhere out west, and it's causing me to be evicted here," she recounted as an example, "I don't think that's fair." Or, in the words of a relocated public housing resident at Park Boulevard, "I don't think they should have to be scrutinized because of what their children do. If your grown child has committed a crime outside of the area, they are telling you that these people can't come and visit you. . . . They are going to immediately evict you from the property because you have a visit [from a relative who has committed a crime]. I don't agree with that. It separates families. . . . Instead of bringing them together, you're actually isolating people."

In response to general complaints about street-corner gatherings, especially of youths, there have been increased efforts across sites, though most energetically in Westhaven Park and Oakwood Shores, to deal with questionable visitors (including "banning" orders) or to discourage people from "hanging out." As the leader of a local community organization in the neighborhood surrounding Oakwood Shores noted, "We're programmed that when we see a group of young people, particularly teens just hanging out somewhere, it's a cause for concern." This has led, as noted above, to blanket calls for "zero tolerance" toward loitering, particularly aimed at eliminating young people from public spaces and, more recently, at enlisting residents to police their presence. In some cases this occurs through service-oriented efforts to build and engage local resident leadership. In Park Boulevard, for example, development professionals have sought, as one explained, to organize "leadership teams" of resident young people to intervene, "get[ting] the teens to say [to other teenagers congregating in public], Hey, it's not cool to hang out, culturally it's not cool." In others, policing such activity takes a more punitive turn, making the consequences of inaction clear. At one neighborhood meeting in Westhaven Park, for example, a CHA staff member shared with the participants that as he was walking to the meeting he noticed two young men sitting on the front steps of a house. Discovering they didn't live there, he told the leaseholder that "you can't have young black guys hanging out in front of your house," and that she would be held responsible for their behavior and could be evicted if they did something wrong. This message is increasingly sent to relocated public housing residents by property managers and other development professionals across sites.

Privatizing the Public

As this last example suggests, policing individual behavior often follows from concerns about maintaining order in public spaces. These concerns have informed a range of responses, most hinging on different approaches to privatization.[37] On the one hand, as we noted with reference to the tenets of New Urbanism in chapter 2 and the lack of important "third spaces" for interaction discussed in chapter 6, the importance of public and transitional space is generally recognized by development professionals and residents alike. As a professional working on the Transformation at the city level put it, echoing New Urbanist arguments:

Public space creates a convenient space. It's a place where people can come together, pass by each other. That's another reason why, you know, having the sidewalks, having the street grid restored to help promote walking and so that you may encounter your neighbors and interact with your neighbors and just say hello is more important than having these big imposing structures where you don't see anybody or you have kind of less of an opportunity to interact with them. And it's the kind of public space too. You know, Is the public space attractive? Is it safe? Is there something there that attracts different types of people to it so that different types of people can interact?

On the other hand, monetary considerations, concerns about safety, homeowners' preferences for privacy, and disagreements regarding normative expectations for behavior in public spaces have led to both design and management choices that for the most part limit the public spaces available, separate them from the main residential concentrations, and regulate access to these spaces and the uses they can be put to.

The principal focus in design is on providing housing, and most of the space is set aside for private units for rental or for sale. In part this allocation is driven by financial considerations and the desire for density ("If [the developers] want money, they want money, but people need more space, open space," as a subsidized renter at Westhaven Park put it in response to this perception), but it is also driven in part by preferences, especially those of homeowners. As the member of a community organization at Oakwood Shores put it, "It's designed in such a way that [homeowners] really do have their own privacy. I mean, their garages go all the way across their yard. Their kids could play in the yard and you don't even have to be outside, 'cause they're fenced in. So there's no contact where you're coming over the fence or throwing things over the fence and stuff like that. I don't see any of that kind of stuff."

But it is also, importantly, driven by concerns about safety. The design implications of this decision draw on the seminal arguments regarding "defensible space" put forth by Oscar Newman in the 1970s, which were adopted by New Urbanists promoting "traditional neighborhood design" and, in turn, informed thinking about HOPE VI public housing redevelopment nationally. The emphasis here is on promoting a sense of territoriality, ownership, and responsibility, demarcating "safe zones," and increasing informal surveillance.[38] Thus, design across these sites has for the most part privileged private (and privately controlled) space over common areas, including a preference for individual entrances and private balconies as well as the demarcation of common spaces that can be effectively monitored and managed (see figs. 7.3 and 7.4).

Such privatization incorporates both design choices and management strategies. In some cases privatization is explicit, by creating civic space (such as "community meeting" rooms) that are privately managed and staffed or by designating as private particular common spaces that, to the general observer, might reasonably be seen as public space. Both Oakwood Shores and Westhaven Park have created the first type of spaces: access is gained through formal request, approval, and scheduling, and their use is regulated by development staff. The social control gained by having such spaces is noted by a development professional at Oakwood Shores: "The indoor public spaces are easy because the indoor

7.3   Private balconies at Park Boulevard. Photo credit: Sara Voelker.

public spaces we can monitor, and we staff and we maintain [them]. The outdoor public spaces are more challenging just because they require the police to do their job."[39]

Park Boulevard provides a case in point about outdoor spaces. Here designers created a kind of town square, with green space and a playground, around which townhouses are arranged along the long sides, with multi-unit dwellings at the corners (see fig. 7.5). Use of this park, and particularly the playground, has been the subject of some contention. In a dramatic event early in the development's history, several ten- or eleven-year-olds were actually arrested by an "overzealous security guard," in the words of one development professional there, for being too old to play on the equipment and for being too loud. The incident raised issues about who could use this public space and about appropriate policing. Signs were then posted explicitly stating rules of access and use—the park was for Park Boulevard residents only ("the reality is that it is a private park," noted another development professional there; "it's a private park for 150 residents"), and responses to its use became more measured.

As all this suggests, privatizing space in the name of security depends as much on regulation as on formal designation. Indeed, as Evelyn Ruppert points out, the decline of urban public space that several scholars have noted has more to do with regulatory regimes—the "myriad practices (such as laws, regulations, urban design, surveillance, and policing) that seek to guide the conduct of agents"—than with formal ownership.[40] Across sites, regulations have sought to redefine public space by limiting residents' access to common areas not explicitly designated for social uses or by prohibiting their use. This includes both what might generally be assumed to be public spaces (such as streets, parks, playgrounds, alleyways, the areas in front of and behind buildings) and transitional spaces (such as front steps and parking lots) that might be more readily recognized as private but available to residents and their

7.4   Gated play area at Oakwood Shores. Photo credit: Janet Li.

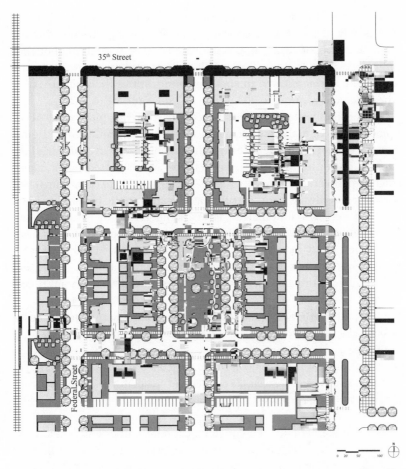

35th Street

Federal Street

0 20' 50' 100' N

7.5   Park Boulevard is designed around a town square area featuring green space and a small
play area.

guests. Thus, across sites prohibitions seek to keep people off the streets
and sidewalks and away from the fronts of buildings and to limit disturbances and curtail visible "hanging out" by controlling the use of parking lots, boulevards, and parks. As a development stakeholder at Park
Boulevard explained, "They're used to being able to stand outside in the
hallway or in front of the building and cuss each other out and all that.
You can't do that here. That's a violation of your lease. In the projects,
you could do that."

Relocated public housing residents and other low-income renters frequently commented on the prohibitions, finding them both draconian

and disproportionately aimed at low-income renters.[41] As a public housing resident at Park Boulevard stated, "They must have been sitting out on their porch or sitting outside on the crate or something, but they put notices in all their mailboxes telling them that was very ghetto. You know: You're not allowed to congregate in front of the property. Well, where do you want me to go? Where do you want me to go?"

Rather than sitting out front or "congregating" in plain view, development professionals, in particular response to the complaints of homeowners, encourage residents to use the private spaces available to them (such as balconies, where they have them) or designated public spaces (such as parks and community rooms, within particular constraints). But parks are not always convenient; as a relocated public housing resident at Westhaven Park complained, "The park that is here—you can't let your seven-year-old walk there by themselves; it's a good four blocks away from where everybody lives." Further, use of park space itself often leads to contention where expectations of "appropriate" use value come into conflict. As an African American homeowner at Oakwood Shores noted:

Well, people barbecued at [the park] at the walking track. I mean—and they do like serious barbecues. One night there was like tons of cars out there, and it's like out of place to me. . . . I mean, [some people] like to walk around that track. And then people are like competing with this barbecue smoke and music and whatever else is going on out there. So it's almost like there are two different groups that are using the park for almost two different purposes.

More fundamentally, these preferences reflect an orientation and expectations about neighborhood spaces as places of sociability that are profoundly different from those shared by many relocated public housing residents and other low-income renters. As a renter of an affordable unit at Westhaven Park explained, "They want us to sit in the back because they thought it's unsightly to have us out here, but we don't see anybody in the back. In the front you can see people coming and going. . . . People drive by, and they stop and they talk, but in the back you not going to get that."

These preferences also contrast with the expectations that relocated public housing residents had experienced in previous public housing. There, public spaces were seen as essential sites for socializing and building community, helping to construct social networks and enduring relationships, in spite of concerns about safety. "You knew the whole— everybody's body, mamas, cousins," as a public housing resident in

Oakwood Shores noted, "their second generations, their third generations." As a public housing resident at Westhaven Park recalled:

And see, what we used to do down there, when we were staying in Henry Horner Homes, is that we had so much green grass area around the buildings that we could just go outside and, like, set up a table and have your barbecue grill and sit out and barbecue and everything, like, right outside 'cause you have so much grassy area. Now it's like you can't do it. I mean, you could still do it, but just space is, like, really limited. You can't do much. They really say not to do it because they'll fine you and you'll get in trouble for it, but people still do it anyway, but it's still a hassle.

In response, as the end of this quotation suggests, while privatizing space and enforcing rules to support it partially curbs the behaviors development professionals and higher-income residents want to limit, a countervailing process reappropriates such privatized space for social interaction, recreation, and leisure. Often individuals or small groups gather in front of buildings or on street corners, sit on front stoops, or pull up chairs to socialize outside. In other cases the appropriation of space is more active—kids running up and down the street and between cars in the parking lots and playing in the alleys or people holding parties on the street to eat, drink, and listen to music. Particularly in the warmer months, homeowners across sites object to these activities; an African American homeowner at Oakwood Shores, for example, complained about "mobs of people" setting up a late-night party behind her building, "totally invad[ing] the parking area." Similarly, an African American renter of a market-rate unit at Westhaven Park complained, "They need a park for the people that are loitering on the street. They are in front of your house. . . . They are congregating in the front with about ten chairs, kids running up and down the street. . . . They use the back [parking lot] as a park, and it's a parking lot—you don't have a party every day in the parking lot."

To some extent these two kinds of appropriation are mutually reinforcing: the privatizing of common areas, a lack of accessible public space, and rules perceived as too restrictive or inconsistently enforced lead residents to informally reclaim such space for social uses; then this socializing in front of buildings, in parking lots, and on the street—as well as some activities in public parks—brings complaints from higher-income residents and censure by property management. But while some residents push back against what they see as unfair restrictions, development professionals recognize that much of this public socializing is due less to large numbers of current residents than to visiting by former residents or by people from the larger neighborhood, sometimes as guests of (a few) current residents, sometimes coming on their own. Many current residents, in contrast, respond to these regulatory regimes by withdrawing, seeking to avoid penalties and choosing to "keep their heads down" and stay out of trouble.[42] As a relocated public housing resident at Westhaven Park put it, "I say it's best to just mind your own business and just speak to people hi and bye and not socialize or fraternize with them; then that way you won't be one of the ones that they calling into the office on."

Such a response reflects the differential impact that rule infractions have on public housing residents and other low-income renters compared with their higher-income neighbors.

Differential Impact

In addition to a general sense of being targeted by what are sometimes seen as inappropriate regulations, relocated public housing residents and other low-income renters complain that the rules are unfairly enforced and that renters have no channel for complaints about their higher-income neighbors. "The only people that have to abide by the rules is us as the low-income people," one public housing resident at Park Boulevard complained; "[homeowners] don't have rules." Or, in the words of a public housing resident leader at Westhaven Park, "It's always them being able to go to somebody and complain about us, but they have the same issues, you know, but there's nobody you can go to and say, well, you know, I don't like my neighbor. Her dog messed in front of my door. Or, her dog always running, always barking in the house."

But perhaps more important is that enforcement has a fundamentally different impact on relocated public housing residents and other low-income renters. This is particularly true for "three-strike" rules across sites and the effort to step up evictions—or the threat of evictions—in response to complaints. Low-income people, after all, have significantly fewer housing options in the market than those with more money, and since relocated public housing residents have made these communities their "permanent" housing choice, eviction from their current units could mean losing their right to public housing subsidy entirely. Thus, besides feeling that their higher-income neighbors are treated more leniently and have more rights, they worry about the potentially serious impact of rule enforcement. For example, a public housing resident at Park Boulevard, where students from the nearby Illinois Institute of Technology live in some homeowner units, expressed this dilemma:

They be running in the hallways, riding up and down on the elevator, and I done told [property management] about that, and [they're] like, well they bought that condo. Yeah, they bought the condo, but they didn't buy the hallway, and they didn't buy the elevator. If it was us, we'll get put out right then and there. . . . If it was us, "Okay, first strike. You've got one more strike and we gonna take you to court and you've got to go."

Indeed, enforcing three-strike provisions and moving quickly toward eviction have become more common across sites over time. This is a shift from earlier in the history of these developments, when the desire to keep apartments rented made development professionals more willing to work through some of residents' less serious problems with neighbors and when the barriers to eviction proceedings—at least for public housing residents—were particularly stringent in an effort to protect their rights under the Relocation Rights Contract. More recently, particularly at Oakwood Shores and to some extent Westhaven Park, development teams have tried to enlist the CHA's help in evicting problem tenants and have started more vigorous enforcement of three-strike provisions. "We have to rack up the lease violations," a development professional at Oakwood Shores noted at a local CAPS meeting; "if you breathe hard, that's a lease violation."

Many evictions have been for nonpayment of rent and, given the recession, these have included market-rate renters. But other eviction proceedings, especially when involving relocated public housing residents and other subsidized renters, have been for rule violations and troublesome behavior. This behavior has included criminal convictions, which are explicitly grounds for eviction (though not without contention, depending on the offender's relationship to the household, as noted above). Many, however, focus on more general problem behavior, from positive drug tests (not a crime, but a lease violation) to unauthorized guests to multiple complaints about noise or other incivilities. "I'm cracking down on residents who allow people that don't live here to come and mess up what you have," a development professional at Westhaven Park noted. "If your guest causes problems, you will reap the repercussions of it." Similarly, at a management meeting at Oakwood Shores, discussion about pending eviction proceedings centered on targeting households responsible for a range of "disturbances"—from substance abuse to loud music to large numbers of visitors to dropping

189

cigarette butts off the balcony. Thus, in responding to complaints about incivilities, managers conflate a broad range of behaviors and actionable lease violations, enlisting residents to make the case. As a development professional at Westhaven Park noted:

If there's a lease-compliance issue, now our residents know to report it to property management. They're supposed to document it and then go the next step to investigate it and see how true it is, [or] not true. Then go [to] the next step, which could be calling the resident in or filing a police report. . . . They have a period of time to adhere or fix the problem. If it's not something—like we have clients that are arguing back and forth, and it's a lot of threats and cursing, you know, there's nothing in the lease that says you can't yell outside to your neighbor. Now is it neighborly? No. If it gets to the point where the person is fearful and feels that it's a threat, then they can make a police report; [then] that becomes a real lease violation.

Conclusion: From Integrationist Aims to Incorporated Exclusion

From the standpoint of safety, order, and the quality of the built environment, the communities emerging on the footprint of public housing complexes under the Plan for Transformation show considerable improvement over what they replaced. While relocated public housing residents and other low-income renters acknowledge these improvements and particularly appreciate the greater safety of the neighborhood and better quality of the housing, homeowners and market-rate renters are not entirely satisfied. Their concerns about safety, disorder, and neighborhood quality of life are largely grounded in complaints about their low-income neighbors, especially public housing residents. This has led to significant contention about both place and space—what kind of community each of these areas will become and how the space can be shared equally or be differentially enjoyed based on residents' income or housing tenure.

The regulatory regimes established to protect and maintain order in these communities are informed by "market norms" and "broken windows" orientations as well as by enduring culture of poverty narratives concerning the urban underclass. Rather than promoting integration of the poor into well-functioning mixed-income neighborhoods, the mechanisms put in place to implement these regimes—both formal and informal, individual and organizational—and the perceptions of differential targeting and inequitable enforcement of rules have more often generated new forms of exclusion and new dynamics of marginaliza-tion. "We're like a little testing mouse," as a relocated public housing resident at Park Boulevard put it; "they just want to see if we're going to make a wrong move. That's why they give us three strikes like we're some kind of animals."

These exclusionary dynamics within the framework of spatial incor-poration have led more to separation than to integration (with social interaction largely limited to within-group exchange), to dynamics of contestation (through conflict over regulatory regimes and the appropri-ation and reappropriation of space), and, particularly for many relocated public housing residents, to withdrawal. For some, withdrawal takes the form of defensiveness in day-to-day choices: "I'm just gonna stay in this shell in my house and mind my own business," as a resident leader at Oakwood Shores described the reactions of some of her friends. "When they come for me, they just come for me." Others make hard choices about managing personal relationships, such as removing adult children from the lease to avoid eviction should they get in trouble. Yet others face a more complete exit, by force or by choice.[43] As a relocated public housing resident described it:

It's the fear of, like, they're under a microscope. You know, you've got to have—you visi-tors can't stay over. You've got to be very careful about what they do. . . . They can't live up to the expectations of the Plan, so we've had several people here that requested to go back to traditional public housing, which was a concern, because if you made it here why not, you know, just continue to be engaged in everything it is? But they gave up. It's like, "I don't want any part of it. I want to go back."

As we will explore in the next chapter, these dynamics of exclusion extend to the nature of integration (or lack of it) in the wider commu-nity, including engagement in civil society—community organizations, neighborhood associations, forums of public deliberation—and to how well the developments, and relocated public housing residents within them, are integrated into the fabric of the larger neighborhood and city.

EIGHT

Development, Neighborhood, and Civic Life: The Question of Broader Integration

The examination of the nature of interaction, regulation, and exclusion in earlier chapters focused on community dynamics playing out largely on the footprint of the new mixed-income developments. These are, after all, the micro-neighborhoods at the center of the integrationist project. They are also the sites where development professionals and other organizational players have the most direct influence over the circumstances that might influence these dynamics. The integrationist aims of the Transformation, however, go beyond the boundaries of the developments, seeking to integrate residents—particularly public housing residents—into the broader neighborhood and the civic life of the city. The redevelopment sites are intended to promote and be connected to broader neighborhood revitalization, and residents of the developments are meant to benefit from these connections and improvements. As a professional who supports the Transformation citywide stated:

Not having access to the broader neighborhood defeats the goal of the Plan for Transformation. Those old developments were isolated. We don't want the new ones to be too. They've got to be really integrated into the rest of the community and actually help catalyze improvement in the surrounding communities. . . . The end goal is not just about the development. It is about knitting it into the fabric of the city, both socially and economically.

This chapter examines how well the broader integration of place and people has been achieved. In the service of this goal, we first describe how the neighborhoods the sites are embedded in are changing socially and economically. Then, drawing on interviews, focus groups, and field observations, we consider the perspectives of residents, development professionals, and leaders of community organizations on how the new developments are connecting with these revitalizing neighborhoods. In doing so, we consider the spatial, social, and organizational mechanisms that could foster relationships between residents of the development and those in the broader neighborhood and assess, in particular, the integration of public housing residents.

As we will make clear, our conclusions about what we have called the incorporated exclusion of public housing residents within the micro-neighborhoods of the mixed-income developments hold true for broader integration as well. Although the redeveloped sites are being physically reconnected to the revitalizing neighborhoods around them, this does not appear to translate into increased integration for low-income residents or their greater engagement in the broader neighborhood and society.

Community Connection and Neighborhood Revitalization

Development teams at all three sites consider their task to be both redeveloping the public housing sites and reconnecting these emergent communities to the neighborhoods around them. Before the Transformation, all three of these neighborhoods—particularly those on the South Side—had strong identities, and all had begun to show signs of revitalization independent of the Transformation. For development professionals, finding ways to leverage and contribute to the momentum of the broader neighborhood was an imperative. Development team members at Oakwood Shores were particularly explicit about their ambitious intentions to contribute to and shape neighborhood revitalization. This is in part explained by the planned scale of the Oakwood Shores site— twice as large as the others in units and land area—as well as by the developers' community-oriented focus and their intent, as one put it, of "building a neighborhood" rather than just developing housing. But regardless of the scale of their ambitions, from early on teams across sites were explicit about their aim to connect the developments to the surrounding community and end the isolation that had characterized the public housing complexes they were replacing. As a development professional at Westhaven Park put it, "It's really important that the entire neighborhood sees the development as a part of their neighborhood and vice versa, that the development sees [itself] as part of a greater neighborhood."

The nature of this task—wholesale demolition, reconstruction, marketing, and repopulating of what had been well-known public housing developments—makes this a challenging ambition. Regarding Oakwood Shores, for example, development team members and leaders of local community organizations were frustrated that the project had to be given an official name and marketed as a "development," fearing (with good reason, as we shall see) that this would make it stand out as a separate complex rather than blending into the broader North Kenwood–Oakland neighborhood.

Physical Integration: Design and Spatial Planning

Developers, the city, and the CHA have gone to considerable effort and expense to physically reconnect the former public housing sites to the neighborhood and cityscape around them. To inform our consideration of neighborhood integration, we return briefly to site design, specifically efforts to connect the developments to the surrounding communities.

The street grid redesign in all three sites had benefits beyond opening the area to traffic and pedestrian flow and establishing a visual sense of connectedness. The reconnected streets and alleys returned to the jurisdiction of the city's streets and sanitation department, meaning that plowing streets and picking up trash would now be the responsibility of the city rather than the CHA. This was part of a larger effort at institutional integration, seeking to end not just the physical disconnectedness of public housing but its institutional isolation. For example, the separate 365-member Chicago Housing Authority Police Department, created in 1989 in hopes of more effectively reducing crime and gang activity in public housing developments, was dissolved at the beginning of the Plan for Transformation. Echoing Mayor Daley's stated commitment to reintegrating public housing residents into the broader city, the CEO of the CHA at the time explained, "By incorporating CHA safety and security into the fabric of the entire city, residents of the CHA will receive the same level of security as other residents in Chicago."[1] The "service connector" approach to social services discussed in chapter 3, in which public housing residents were referred to private, nonprofit organizations for support, is another example of an effort to integrate public housing residents into existing citywide systems. Yet certain approaches by the CHA and development teams, such as hiring private security firms or creating an Office of the Ombudsman to advocate for public housing residents in mixed-income developments, perpetuated their separate treatment.

Although all three developments aimed to reestablish the physical connection with the broader neighborhoods, they took quite different design approaches to this integration. Ultimately, all three retain some features that distinguish the new developments from the neighborhoods around them and maintain the sense that their residents are part of a separate development. At Oakwood Shores, the working group and community leaders put the most pressure on developers to design the new development to "blend in" architecturally with the surrounding neighborhood. Planning discussions called for "traditional architecture" that reflected the local vernacular in building designs and colors. Park space was designed to be connected to the large public park that abuts the development. Boulevards reflected and were connected to the network of boulevards—first established in Daniel Burnham's 1909 master plan for the city of Chicago—that serve as corridors connecting neighborhoods throughout the city.[2] However, two features in particular—lower building density and lower building height—make the development noticeably different from the blocks around it. Some leaders of local community organizations think Oakwood Shores resembles a "suburb in the city," setting it off from its surroundings.[3] In response, later phases of the development have greater density, including two mid-rise buildings.

The developers at both Park Boulevard and Westhaven Park were less interested in mirroring traditional architectural styles, and they sought a distinctive look for their developments. Unlike Oakwood Shores, which sits in the middle of a primarily residential area, both are in neighborhoods with a more significant institutional presence. Park Boulevard is adjacent to the campus of the Illinois Institute of Technology and a block from the headquarters of the Chicago Police Department. Westhaven Park is a few blocks from the massive United Center professional sports complex and near a community college campus.[4] Given this context, developers at Park Boulevard explicitly sought to "simulate a neighborhood" and contracted with seven architectural firms to create designs for portions of the development. Through this diversity of styles, they hoped to avoid the institutional look of other master-planned communities and create a more human-scale, "traditional" urban neighborhood in the New Urbanist mode. Unlike the other two sites, at Park Boulevard the development team was able to exploit the location on a main city thoroughfare to create, at the fringe of the development, mixed-use buildings that now house a Starbucks coffee shop, a bank, and a sandwich shop among other businesses. Thus, while the residential component remains essentially set apart from the surrounding area, the retail establishments connect the development outward and bring people from the surrounding area and the city more broadly onto the fringe of its residential zone.

Westhaven Park has embraced the most contemporary architectural style among the three sites, incorporating some traditional Chicago architectural elements (such as towers and turrets) into a mostly modern design. As Larry Bennett describes it in *The Third City*:

Westhaven Park's architecture is a new urbanist pastiche of row house minimalism trimmed with Industrial Age sheet metal and ornamented with the occasional Victorian peaked roof. . . . The façade materials and color shadings are vivid: variously painted brick, concrete blocks and built in flower boxes. . . . In a nod to one of Mayor Daley's design preferences, low, black painted, faux iron fencing borders some of the small yards fronting some of the dwellings.[5]

Although visually striking, the style also seems fitting for the rapidly gentrifying Near West Side and its nearby warehouse district. The surroundings of Westhaven Park—the massive sports stadium, numerous parking lots, and its distance from denser commercial and residential areas—provide less of a "neighborhood" the development can be connected to both physically and socially. Furthermore, as we described in previous chapters, Westhaven Park has the unique challenge among the city's mixed-income developments of having been designed completely around an earlier redevelopment phase, "The Villages," which houses only public housing residents, maintains a separate physical and social identity, and adds to the challenge of integrating the development into the larger neighborhood.

Overall, then, the development teams have worked to reconnect the developments to the surrounding neighborhoods physically through their basic street grid infrastructure and institutionally through the return of city policing and sanitation services and referrals to private service providers. To varying degrees, the architecture and design of the new sites maintain some aesthetic distinction from the neighborhood, both clearly distancing them from the monotonous and dispiriting appearance of the former public housing developments and attempting to embrace the vitality of the city around them. Before turning to whether and how people living in these contexts experience and perceive this physical reconnection of place, we examine how the neighborhoods around these developments are changing.

Broader Neighborhood Revitalization

Without question, the neighborhoods surrounding the mixed-income public housing redevelopments are changing dramatically. In all three neighborhoods some of this revitalization was in motion for a few years before the launch of Plan for Transformation, and it is possible that the anticipation of their redevelopment accelerated neighborhood development. Sean Zielenbach and others have provided evidence of improvements in the neighborhoods around HOPE VI-funded redevelopments in several cities.[6] This is important context for the questions about the integration and inclusion of low-income households that concern us here. Substantial demographic and economic changes in the broader neighborhood are proceeding in parallel with the changes on the development footprints. In what ways are the neighborhoods changing, how robust are these changes, and what are the implications for the developments and their residents, particularly the relocated public housing residents intended to benefit from access to a revitalizing neighborhood? As we detail below, we find that the area around Westhaven Park shows the strongest revitalization, along with demographic changes that are aligned with the changes at the site. However, although more tenuous neighborhood improvements represent a liability for the success of Oakwood Shores and Park Boulevard, the neighborhood around Westhaven Park has the highest crime rate of the three. Thus characteristics of each of the sites' surrounding neighborhoods present barriers to broader integration.

We examine three broad domains of neighborhood change: demographic change, including population size and racial and ethnic diversity; economic change, including employment, income, homeownership, and loan activity; and changes in crime rates. Our analysis here uses several geographic definitions based on data availability.[7] By "development footprint" we mean the public housing redevelopment site, and by "surrounding area" we mean the census tracts adjacent to the public housing site but not including the development footprint. Where data availability does not allow us to separate the two, we refer to "footprint and its surrounding area." For foreclosure data we refer to the official Chicago community areas within which the developments are situated, and for crime data we refer to the respective police beats.

Demographic Change

If population growth (or decline) is an indication of neighborhood vitality, then comparing changes in population in the three areas surrounding the development sites provides an initial sense of their varying trajectories. As a benchmark, from 2000 to 2010 the city of Chicago experienced a 7 percent decrease in overall population. The area surrounding Westhaven Park, by contrast, remained essentially level over that period, a sign of relative stability (preceded by ten years of substantial growth—a 16 percent population increase from 1990 to 2000). The area surrounding Oakwood Shores mirrored the city's 7 percent decline, while population decline around Park Boulevard was almost twice as steep. Thus, while Westhaven Park benefited from a surrounding area that was holding its population steady, the South Side mixed-income sites had to contend with surroundings where decades of population loss had not yet been reversed.

Although the overall population in the area surrounding Westhaven Park was stable between 2000 and 2010, the racial and ethnic makeup changed dramatically, with a sharp increase in the white, Asian, and Hispanic populations accompanied by a sharp decrease in the African American population (see table 8.1). These demographic changes (excluding the increase in Hispanics) were also seen in the Westhaven Park development footprint over the same period. At Oakwood Shores, there were relatively moderate decreases in the African American population and modest increases in the white population from 2000 to 2010. At Park Boulevard there was a wide divergence between the changing footprint demographics and those in the surrounding area, indicating a possible challenge to establishing social connections between the site and the broader neighborhood. While the footprint saw sharp increases in the white population and sharp decreases in the African American population, the surrounding neighborhood experienced minimal changes in these subgroups. These trends suggest why the emerging white population at the South Side sites, particularly at Park Boulevard, might be less likely to engage with the broader, more stably African American neighborhood, as well as how this broader context shapes attention and attitudes toward issues of race and class both in the neighborhoods and on the development footprints.

Table 8.1 Race and Housing Occupancy (1990–2010)

	Development Footprint			Surrounding Neighborhood		
	1990	2000	2010	1990	2000	2010
Race						
Oakwood Shores						
African American (%)	99.5	98.3	95.5	98.9	97.4	93.9
White (%)	0.2	0.6	1.0	0.4	0.6	2.0
Other (%)	0.3	1.1	3.5	0.7	2.0	4.1
Park Boulevard						
African American (%)	99.7	99.0	77.3	86.2	79.4	79.2
White (%)	0.2	0.2	12.9	8.2	10.2	10.9
Other (%)	0.1	0.8	9.8	5.6	10.4	9.9
Westhaven Park						
African American (%)	99.1	93.7	86.4	96.8	92.1	72.0
White (%)	0.2	0.9	5.9	1.1	3.1	14.5
Other (%)	0.7	5.4	7.7	2.1	4.8	13.5
Housing						
Oakwood Shores						
Owner-occupied (%)	0.8	1.4	10.4	5.2	7.4	15.7
Renter-occupied (%)	74.7	54.4	80.3	68.8	76.4	72.0
Vacant (%)	24.5	44.2	9.3	26.0	16.2	12.3
Park Boulevard						
Owner-occupied (%)	0.8	0.6	16.0	10.3	16.2	23.8
Renter-occupied (%)	80.0	42.7	53.5	69.2	65.6	63.0
Vacant (%)	19.2	56.7	30.5	20.5	18.2	13.2
Westhaven Park						
Owner-occupied (%)	0.7	2.2	12.5	9.1	11.6	19.8
Renter-occupied (%)	47.5	68.5	74.1	71.6	76.5	65.9
Vacant (%)	51.8	29.3	13.4	19.3	11.9	14.3

Source: 1990, 2000, and 2010 Census.

Economic Change

All three development footprints and their surrounding areas experienced similar economic changes between 2000 and 2010: a more highly educated population and an increased proportion of homeowners, lower rates of unemployment (from 42 percent to 17 percent, for example, in the Park Boulevard footprint and surrounding area), and—before the Great Recession—substantial spikes in home purchases and, around Westhaven Park, small business loans (see fig. 8.1).[8] This indicates that more neighborhood residents are well positioned economically, but it does not distinguish between the access to opportunity that middle-class newcomers enjoy and the status of existing and returning low-income households. Are relocated public housing residents benefiting from these positive changes? Trends in median household income suggest the

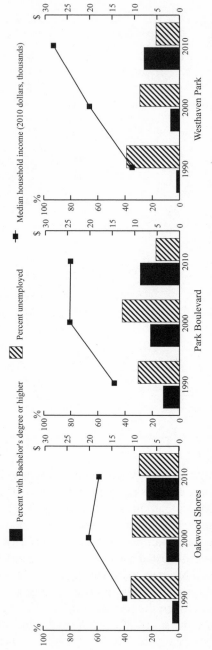

8.1 Educational attainment, unemployment, and income on the development footprints and in the surrounding areas. Source: 1990, 2000, and 2010 Census.

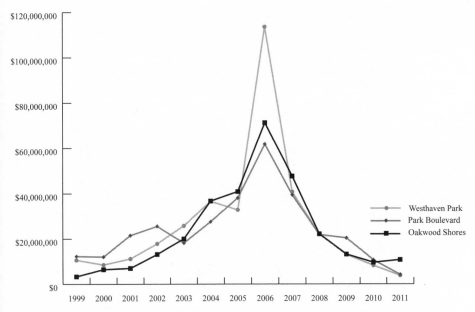

8.2   Total amount of home purchase loans, development footprint and surrounding area. Includes bank-approved and applicant-accepted loans on one- to four-family dwellings. Source: Federal Financial Institutions Examination Council.

answer is no. Despite the increased economic activity, median income remained low in all three areas (roughly half that of the city of Chicago overall), so most likely the higher incomes of incoming households are being offset by continued low incomes among the poor. Median income was flat on the Park Boulevard development footprint and in the surrounding area, and it decreased in real terms in the Oakwood Shores area, where there are three other mixed-income developments nearby (with a substantial proportion of subsidized rental units).[9] Only Westhaven Park's development footprint and the surrounding area saw an increase in median income, of about 40 percent, though it remained well below the city level. We do not have employment and earnings data for relocated public housing residents in our three focal sites, but our analysis of this group throughout the city found high unemployment and low earnings among those who had moved into mixed-income developments (at levels similar to those who had relocated with housing choice vouchers or moved back into traditional public housing). Furthermore, we found no evidence of improvements in earnings or employment among those residents who lived relatively longer in a mixed-income development.[10]

Also important is the fragility of the economic improvements in these neighborhoods, more reason to limit expectations for the developments to integrate with and benefit from revitalization around them. The spike in home purchase and small business loans noted above was followed by a sharp drop, mirroring the economic slowdown across the city and country (see fig. 8.2). And although homeownership is on the rise, in community areas around Oakwood Shores and Park Boulevard the increase was accompanied by an increase in foreclosure rates relative to other neighborhoods in the city. A sharp rise in foreclosure filings in the community area around Oakwood Shores in 2012 made the area the third highest-ranking in the city for foreclosures (compared with ranking twenty-ninth in 2008). Similarly, the Douglas community area around Park Boulevard jumped from twenty-seventh in 2008 to sixth in the city in foreclosure filings. In a further demonstration of its relative economic stability, the Near West Side community area had a far smaller increase in foreclosure filings, which changed its ranking only from fiftieth in the city in 2008 to thirty-ninth in 2012.

Changes in Crime

An important indicator of neighborhood change around the developments is crime statistics. As we noted in chapter 7, total crime decreased substantially in the police beats around the three sites from 2001 to 2011. These decreases were driven by a fall in violent crimes and quality of life crimes; property crimes have held relatively steady over this period in all three areas. Total crime in the beats around Oakwood Shores, although experiencing spikes in 2005 and 2007, was down about 40 percent over that period to a level below the overall city rate. Total crime declined more dramatically around Park Boulevard, by about 250 percent, but remained about 50 percent above the city rate. And total crime at Westhaven Park was down about 31 percent over this same period (also with spikes in 2003, 2006, and 2008). But even this decrease left the area at a little more than twice the city rate, indicating that on this key area of neighborhood life the neighborhood around Westhaven Park presents a greater challenge than those on the South Side (see fig. 7.1).

Public School Performance

A key neighborhood feature in attracting and retaining families with children is high-quality public schools. Historically, the public schools

near the three public housing sites have been among the lowest performing in the city. In general this trend has continued despite the mixed-
income redevelopment and a variety of citywide initiatives to improve
schools. In the neighborhood surrounding Park Boulevard, student attainment at the main elementary school was rated "far below" national
testing standards in 2013, and attainment at the local high school was
rated "below" national standards.[11] Youths at Westhaven Park who attend
school in the area go to one of five public elementary schools: three had
student attainment "far below" national standards, one ranked "below"
national standards, and only one ranked "above" national standards (the
only school that achieved this level of student performance at any of the
three sites). Of the two high school options in the area, one had student attainment "far below" national standards and the other, a charter
school sponsored by the city's professional basketball team, had attainment that met "average" national standards. Elementary schools around
Oakwood Shores were similarly low performing, with attainment "far
below" or "below" national standards—with the key exception of the
charter school within the Oakwood Shores site. This school is operated
by the University of Chicago and outperformed the other neighborhood
schools, though overall student attainment met only "average" standards. (Using an alternative "value-added" measure of student growth
over the school year, the University of Chicago charter school and one
other elementary school near Oakwood Shores had ratings "above" national standards, the only two elementary schools at any of the three
sites to achieve this rating.) The two local high school options for youths
at Oakwood Shores had student attainment levels "below" national standards, though one, a males-only charter school, has received national
recognition for its 100 percent college acceptance rate.

In sum, then, the developments have been physically reconnected to
their surrounding neighborhoods, though in some ways their appearance still sets them apart, and on some key measures the neighborhoods
around them are changing dramatically. This includes changes in their
economic conditions and crime rates, although they are still generally
high poverty and there is instability even among new homeowners. The
racial demographics of the broader areas are changing less rapidly in the
South Side neighborhoods, presenting a possible deterrent to whites'
integrating beyond the development footprint. Finally, it appears from
the generally flat or declining median income levels that low-income
residents are not necessarily benefiting economically from the revitalization, although it is harder to extrapolate from neighborhood indicators
what the social impact on households has been.

Making Connections: Residents' Integration and Engagement in the Broader Neighborhood

We turn now to how the residents of the mixed-income developments, particularly the relocated public housing residents, view these changes and how they are experiencing them. To examine how fully residents of the mixed-income sites are engaging with resources and activities beyond the developments, we first consider the general sense among residents and development professionals of whether there is a growing connection to the neighborhood. We then take a closer look at the formal associations in the neighborhood and the dynamics of participation, inclusion, and exclusion within them.

Connections between the Development and the Neighborhood

In general, development professionals at the three sites are disappointed that the developments remain so disconnected from the neighborhood and that low-income residents are generally failing to venture out into the broader community. This sentiment is particularly strong at Oakwood Shores, where, as we noted, the development team and local leaders of community organizations expressed a strong commitment to ending the isolation of the development by physically reconnecting the site and encouraging residents to see themselves as part of the broader neighborhood. One community organization leader in that neighborhood suggested that the developers could do more to push residents to engage beyond the site:

[The development team] kept wanting us to come there and host a meeting for their people. We said, no, no, no. They have to learn how to come out to community meetings. This isn't the Oakwood Shores community. They're part of a larger community, and you all have to encourage them to go out to other types of meetings. Because what you're doing is reinforcing that public housing mentality where the meeting is held for the residents and they don't know anything outside of those walls.

In this instance the "public housing mentality" is the expectation established through previous CHA practice that activities for public housing residents will be offered on site, obviating the need for them to engage more broadly. A contributing factor may be the branding of the sites as separate developments with an identity and functioning distinct from the rest of the neighborhood. As a leader of another community organization in North Kenwood–Oakland asserted:

In the perfect world, the Transformation sites would be just another part of the greater community, and you wouldn't be distinguishing again, which we are doing, and I think that's part of the mistake in the whole issue of the Transformation. And, again, nobody listens to me when I say this. We keep segregating, unintentionally, residents from the greater community. When we label the development site as something other than the community, we're setting that site apart again, and the community is not Kenwood-Oakland, [but] Oakwood Shores. Some people now are so confused. They think it's another community area, and actually it's just part of the greater area.

This general disappointment among development teams and community organization leaders about the integration of the development into the broader neighborhood is similarly stressed by the residents themselves. In general, residents of the developments, with some differences across income levels, also feel that the developments remained largely disconnected from the neighborhoods. Residents are most divided on this at Park Boulevard, with relocated public housing residents, many of whom have strong ties and familiarity with the neighborhood, more likely than other residents to see the development as "blending in." Park Boulevard has also been slower to build out and is currently much smaller than the other developments, which may help thus far to avoid the sense of being set apart. Furthermore, the historical identity of the Bronzeville neighborhood, and public housing residents' previous ties to it, might be a factor in their greater connectedness as the new development takes shape. White homeowners at Park Boulevard, however, in general do not share this feeling, perhaps in part because the rapid increase in the white population on the development footprint has not been accompanied by such an increase in the broader area.

At Oakwood Shores and Westhaven Park, residents across income levels generally feel that the development is quite separate from the rest of the neighborhood. At Oakwood Shores in particular, the perception that the development "stands out" is widely shared, bearing out community organization leaders' concerns about the branding of the development and its suburban appearance. At Westhaven Park residents express interesting differences in perceptions across income levels and housing tenures. Some relocated public housing residents and market-rate renters think the site blends in, but others disagree. There is more consensus among affordable-rate renters that the development feels disconnected.

Market-rate owners echo the perceptions of the development team that there is little to connect to around the development. "We *are* the neighborhood" was the way one expressed it. To the extent that relocated public housing residents are more likely to be familiar with the broader neighborhood while higher-income newcomers are less likely to feel any sense of connection, this could be an additional point of differentiation among residents of the developments as the communities evolve. However, the familiarity public housing residents feel pertains to the "old" neighborhood, not the emerging one, and our interviews suggest that affective ties to people and place have not necessarily translated into any instrumental benefits or access to opportunities created by the revitalization.

Several factors contribute to residents' disconnectedness and the feeling among some that the development is an "island" within a larger neighborhood. Some of these factors are physical, such as the design of the developments and the lack of amenities and neighborhood infrastructure in the surrounding area. Others are social, such as the sense of enduring stigma and fear about the development among outsiders and a sense among relocated public housing residents that they are not able to participate fully in the revitalization of the broader neighborhood.

There are certainly limited amenities in the surrounding areas, particularly good-quality retail stores, to draw residents out into the community in all three neighborhoods.[12] But beyond this, residents of the mixed-income redevelopments, particularly relocated public housing residents, are perceived by local community organization leaders as not yet willing to cross "boundaries" to get to the few amenities that do exist. In some cases these may be familiar boundaries that delineated gang territory. As one local leader explained:

Kids from Oakwood Shores can feel free to go down to Kennicott Park [Community Center], where we've got all kinds of programs and things going that they should be able to take advantage of, but we haven't gotten there yet. To me that will be a big sign of success, when we no longer have these delineations or boundaries that constrict people of any age and prevent them from feeling free to venture into and to enjoy the greater area. We've got a brand-new beach over there, and you've got kids right here at Oakwood Shores [that have] never been there. They haven't been there yet, and it's right across the street, so to say, I mean, but until people have a greater sense of freedom to move around, I think we are lacking in success in that area as well.

Some community organization leaders are impatient with the lack of connection and frustrated with the mind-set of residents who appear to identify more with their positions at the mixed-income development (a "market-rate homeowner," a "public housing resident") than as residents of the broader neighborhood.

Local schools are one key amenity that could engage residents of the development in the broader neighborhood, particularly those with school-age children. Development professionals, community organization leaders, and residents express a keen sense that, for the most part, the local schools are performing poorly and that those who can do so seek options outside the neighborhood. This is most strongly felt at Park Boulevard. Here the only local elementary school was closed because of low enrollment and reopened (still a low-performing school) twenty blocks away from the development. Among our sample of interviewees and focus group participants, very few parents at Park Boulevard send their children to the local school. At Westhaven Park, opinions among development professionals and residents who expressed a perspective on the local schools were more mixed. The positive sentiments mainly reflect the improvements at a local elementary school that was closed and reopened as a Montessori school. Several development professionals and residents discussed the challenging dynamics that have emerged at the new school, which has emphasized recruiting students from around the city, and low-income parents have resisted enrolling their children there, being skeptical about the unfamiliar Montessori format and resentful of the focus on external recruitment. Development professionals, community organization leaders, and residents at Oakwood Shores have the strongest sense of school improvement, largely due to the opening of the charter elementary school by the Urban Education Institute of the University of Chicago in 2005, followed by the opening of a charter middle school in 2008. Unlike most charter schools in the city, both have a neighborhood attendance boundary, which gives preference to local residents. Despite this neighborhood preference, however, some Oakwood Shores residents have been unable to get their children into the school because of limited openings.

A second factor reinforcing the development's disconnection from the neighborhood is its residents' perception that higher-income residents from the broader area avoid passing through the development except to visit someone who lives there. This is a prime example of complex class differences and tensions at the developments. On the one hand, there are concerns (particularly among higher-income residents) that lower-income residents from the former public housing and surrounding neighborhood continue to walk freely through the new development, which seems intrusive and makes them feel insecure. On the other hand, there is a sense across income levels that the broader population keeps its distance. As a market-rate renter at Westhaven Park complained, "We are disjointed from the area; it feels like a little pocket. People will actually walk around our area rather than walk through it." Furthermore, activities at the developments are not well attended by higher-income residents and do not draw in a diverse set of individuals from the broader neighborhood. Some community leaders think the CHA and the development teams have exacerbated the continued isolation by focusing on initiatives and programming for the residents of the development and failing to be assertive in establishing broader connections. Others are more patient with the slow pace of connection and realize it will take considerably more time for the stigma of the development sites to diminish. As a CHA employee explained, "So I think some of it's going to be time. Just letting it integrate back into the, you know, organically integrate back into the neighborhood, sites that for a long time were you know, neighborhoods in and of itself. . . . They were just sort of places people didn't go from the aspect of the community, and so to undo that is going to take years, maybe decades, to really integrate back in."

A third factor, which we will explore in more detail below as we examine formal neighborhood-level associations as mechanisms for broader integration, is the sense that some people (particularly relocated public housing residents but in some cases renters more generally) are not welcome or "invited" to be a part of activities in the broader neighborhood. As an African American homeowner at Oakwood Shores asserted:

If you're not buying a home, then I don't believe that they're invited in the community. There's nothing that I see that's inviting the community to come and see what's going on basically. It's basically, okay, this is what we're doing. Okay, you stay over there, but we gonna do this over here. And I think because they believe, okay, if you come over here, then you gonna tear this up. And we don't want you to tear nothing up, so we not gonna invite you to come in.

This exclusion, real and perceived, from broader neighborhood activities goes against the stated integrationist goals of mixed-income redevelopment and raises questions about how much low-income residents are benefiting from the local revitalization. While some factors— the branding and internally oriented management of the sites, the lack of amenities in the neighborhood, residents' own mind-sets about their scope of engagement—contribute to ongoing disconnection in a way that affects residents of all backgrounds in the development, it is of greater concern for low-income residents. Higher-income residents are more likely to have strong professional and personal networks throughout the metropolitan area and have no particular need to be connected to local neighborhood resources. Proponents of the mixed-income strategy hoped that low-income households, given their relative social and professional isolation, would benefit from the reintegration of the development site into the broader neighborhood. This does not appear to be happening thus far.

Neighborhood Associations and Integration

We established in chapters 6 and 7 that the on-site mechanisms for letting residents participate in decision making, such as homeowners' and condominium associations and tenant meetings, did not bring residents of different incomes and housing tenures together and contributed to exclusionary dynamics within the developments. What about opportunities for meaningful inclusion and influence within the broader ecology of existing and emerging neighborhood associations and organizations beyond the development?

There is a large literature that examines how promoting participation and deliberative democracy at the neighborhood level may help to ensure more effective engagement of minority and disenfranchised interests and may build greater civic capacity among community members.[13] Empirical studies of efforts to support "neighborhood democracy" have found that opportunities for and constraints on participation are not uniform, and that some residents (homeowners, those with relatively more resources, longer-term residents) are more likely than others to engage and be better represented by organizations.[14] Similarly, institutional interests often have outsized influence on deliberations concerning development, even when citizen review and input are formally structured and operative.[15]

As the Plan for Transformation has played out at the three sites in question here, a wide array of associational mechanisms engage residents in planning and action on behalf of the neighborhoods. These include the Homeowners of Westtown, the Neighborhood Development Network, and the Unification Focus Initiative on the Near West Side and the Bronzeville Area Residents' and Commerce Council and Conservation Community Council in North Kenwood–Oakland. However, in practice these associations provide extremely limited opportunities for relocated public housing residents and other low-income renters to engage. Oriented as they are toward the interests of homeowners and institutions (e.g., increasing housing values; attracting private sector investment), most have engaged renters minimally if at all, and there has been limited integration into them of residents living in the mixed-income developments. When asked about their engagement in neighborhood associations, several residents said they did not know when and where the associations meet. While we know of some homeowners who have been active beyond the development, most residents across income levels say they are not engaged in neighborhood organizations. More important, our extensive observations of meetings of various community associations reveal dynamics of tension and exclusion that generate particularly strong barriers to low-income renters.

The Near West Side, for example, has a long history of neighborhood-level activism and some robust community organizations. The Homeowners of Westtown (HOW), a long-established association formed to advocate for the interests of homeowners, makes its exclusive membership very clear from its name, though area businesses are welcome to join as well. Annual membership dues ($25 per household and $35 per business) provide an additional barrier for those not able or willing to pay. Although renters are not welcomed, some owners from the Westhaven Park development have joined the organization, thus representing a selective avenue of integration of the development population into a broader neighborhood mechanism. This integration is circumscribed and carries some tension, however. Frustrated by the disorganization and slow pace of HOW, some Westhaven Park owners created a new organization, the Neighborhood Development Network (NDN), which quickly launched a broad array of advocacy and social activities and established itself as an influential rival force in the neighborhood. The two associations did collaborate on a campaign to bring a good-quality grocery store to the neighborhood and to prevent another store from expanding its business (because of its branding, "Felony Franks," and its emphasis on hiring former offenders, which both associations saw as counter to the image they were seeking to establish for the neighborhood). However, in general the associations have kept their distance from each other. Unlike HOW, NDN's stated mission includes "bringing together our community, which includes all races and incomes," and association leaders have said they want to engage renters. This inclusive intent notwithstanding, NDN's board comprises mainly homeowners, and its events are attended primarily by higher-income residents. Indeed, NDN social events, such as meet-ups at local restaurants, often require a minimum financial contribution, effectively excluding those without the means to pay. Some neighborhood association leaders also assert that NDN does not partner with other organizations or attend others' events.

Concerned about the conflict between HOW and NDN, the Unification Focus Initiative (UFI) was launched on the Near West Side, spearheaded by the Near West Side Community Development Corporation (NWSCDC). The city department of human relations was engaged by the NWSCDC to help shape the initial activities of the group, concentrating on building connections across organizational silos in the neighborhood. UFI has focused on convening leaders of local organizations to build ties and identify common ground. One of UFI's first projects was to organize the Near West Fest, an annual block party started in 2010 to promote area businesses, civic organizations, and services. Unlike HOW and NDN, UFI has been more deliberate in reaching out to the representatives of low-income residents through the Local Advisory Council, the Horner Residents Committee, and staff at the Major Adams Community Center, which has been a local resource for low-income residents for decades.

Turning to the two mixed-income developments on the South Side, we find that the neighborhood associations also focus primarily on the interests of homeowners and offer limited opportunities for renters to participate. Bronzeville Area Residents' and Commerce Council (BARCC) was formed by a local homeowner and entrepreneur in 2004 to serve "the homeowners, condominium owners, renters, and commerce enterprises of Chicago's historic Bronzeville neighborhood."[16] Despite the mention of renters, the BARCC "theme" makes its priorities clear: "We intend to establish a voice for investors and to accelerate home ownership and commercial development, while making an impact on safer and cleaner streets. We organize forums to educate condominium owners, a group critical to the economic growth of the neighborhood."[17] Furthermore, annual membership dues of $35 for individuals, $50 for businesses, and $250 for condo associations present a clear barrier to entry for low-income residents. BARCC has not actively tried to connect with new residents, renters or homeowners, at any of the Bronzeville Transformation sites.

More specifically oriented toward the North Kenwood–Oakland neighborhood within greater Bronzeville, the Conservation Community Council (CCC), like BARCC, is open to renters but is in large part driven by the interests of homeowners. As we described in chapter 4, the North Kenwood–Oakland neighborhood was designated a "conservation area" by the city of Chicago in 1990. This status, legally established by both state and federal law, enables community residents to work with city planners to develop a conservation plan and monitor and advise the city on ongoing land disposition and development in the area. Membership of the CCC comprises residents whose selection is approved by the alderman and the mayor. Although meetings are open to the community, they tend to be attended mostly by homeowners, occasionally including homeowners from Oakwood Shores.

Beyond these organizations, there are other forums that encourage citizens' engagement in neighborhood issues. And though they are often more inclusive of both homeowners and renters, the tenor of their deliberations and the focus of their recommendations tend to stigmatize low-income renters and further marginalize them. These organizations include two Park Advisory Councils in the Oakwood Shores area and Chicago Alternative Policing Strategy (CAPS) meetings across the three sites. The two park councils provide telling contrasts in resident inclusion, engagement, and effectiveness. Mandrake Park is a larger park that borders the Oakwood Shores development to the south and is used by residents of the broader neighborhood and beyond. The Mandrake Park Advisory Council (MPAC) was formed first, and the elected officers are mostly homeowners (from the broader neighborhood and from the Oakwood Shores development), with one relocated public housing resident. The MPAC has been quite successful at engaging the Park District, local police department representatives, staff of the local alderman's office, and members of the Oakwood Shores development team. There is fair attendance at meetings by relocated public housing residents, but low-income renters who come have complained about a lack of voice and representation. In meetings of the advisory committee and other neighborhood associations, public housing residents assert that MPAC is more motivated by, and responsive to, the needs and views of homeowners. Certainly there are more owned units close to Mandrake Park than near Ellis Park, the other public park near the development. MPAC has successfully advocated for a range of actions regarding the park, including putting up No Parking and Tow Zone signs, restricting barbecuing to certain areas, and establishing new criteria for event permits regarding hours, location, noise, and cleanup. There is some tension among the group's leaders and participants between newer homeowners who push for an emphasis on security through restricting use of the park and longer-term homeowners who advocate positive activities that promote appropriate use of the park. This reflects deeper tensions regarding exclusionary versus inclusionary means of establishing and maintaining community standards and expectations. A local community organization leader described it like this:

The newcomers who are mainly coming that I've been in contact with are the middle- and upper-income families who are buying. And it is my view based on conversations with them that they're looking for change immediately in the community. And where longtime middle- and upper-income residents are—have really bought into the mixed-income community and making sure that public housing residents have a place here, and making sure that affordable or working families have a place here, the folks who are coming in from outside are not really concerned about that.

Ellis Park is on the north side of the development and is used less by the broader community. The officers of the Ellis Park Advisory Council (EPAC), formed soon after the Mandrake Park Council, are all relocated public housing residents and are all African American. A homeowner who was elected among the original slate of officers did not attend any further meetings and was removed from the board. He later informed the group that he was bothered by their disorganization and had joined the Mandrake Park Council. EPAC has struggled to maintain focus and has gotten far less support from the development team, Park District, and local police department. No homeowners attend meetings. While there was initial outreach from MPAC for the two councils to collaborate, EPAC leaders were resistant, wanting to maintain their independence as an association. Thus, for different reasons, neither park council has enabled low-income residents to exert meaningful influence on broader neighborhood matters.[18]

Across sites, CAPS meetings are the public forum that draws most broadly from relocated public housing residents, low- and higher-income renters, and homeowners both in the development and from the surrounding neighborhood. Held monthly in police beats across the city and led by local police officers, CAPS meetings focus on crime and safety, seeking to generate deliberation and problem solving between community members and the police. However, meetings often devolve into complaint sessions for residents and appeals from police for more vigilance from citizens. While promoting relatively broad participation, these forums also frequently generate significant conflict. A neighborhood homeowner at one of the sites who assists with CAPS meetings described the challenging dynamics:

Well, the CAPS experience has been an extremely frustrating experience for me personally, for a couple of different reasons. One is you have two groups who are almost adversarial, naturally adversarial. One who controls and the other group of those individuals who believe they are being controlled through a whole series of historical kinds of events and so forth, especially in this community. The second reason is that people will only come when there is a problem, and they come to chastise those who are supposed to be doing certain kinds of things, and their experience has in most cases not been very positive. So you automatically have two groups of opposing views, okay?

Although major crime issues (gang violence, narcotics sales, burglaries) in the neighborhoods are of common concern, much of the discussion at CAPS meetings—except in response to a specific incident (such as a shooting) that had just occurred—centers on community standards of conduct and complaints about loitering, noise, inappropriate youth behavior, curfew violations, and unruly park activities. The most significant force behind such discussions often is homeowners, and as we have observed repeatedly in all three sites, discussion around such issues is often contentious, with responsibility for transgressions frequently laid—sometimes by implication, sometimes explicitly—on relocated public housing residents. As is made clear through their comments at these meeting, many of the higher-income residents assume that any rule violation must have been committed by a public housing resident. This serves as a justification for aggressive demands and scathing comments. For example, at one meeting, which was attended by a senior official from the housing authority, a Westhaven Park homeowner asked whether the CHA would pay for damages to the buildings, since they were "caused by public housing residents." The CHA official refused to affirm this presumption but told the homeowner the CHA would investigate who might be responsible.

Finally, two other organizations in the North Kenwood–Oakland neighborhood, the Kenwood–Oakland Community Organization (KOCO) and the Bronzeville-Oakland Neighborhood Association (BONA), deserve mention because of their stated emphasis on including low-income renters in neighborhood deliberation and engagement. However, for different reasons neither organization has had much success in engaging renters at Oakwood Shores more broadly. KOCO is a long-standing activist organization dedicated to empowering, and advocating for, low-income families. To demonstrate its seriousness yet maintain a low barrier to entry, KOCO charges $5 for a lifetime membership. However, despite having been very active in the citywide and neighborhood debates about the future of public housing and displacement of public housing residents, KOCO has done little direct outreach to residents in the mixed-income developments and has had limited participation from them. BONA, in contrast, is a new organization launched with the support of the development team at Oakwood Shores, which seeks diverse representation both from within the development and from the broader neighborhood. However, BONA remains composed predominantly of development residents (in particular relocated public housing residents), has struggled to sustain engagement and turnout, and has had limited success in establishing and carrying out a clear agenda. Because of this, the organization has not made significant contributions toward integrating the development into the broader neighborhood.

Stepping back from this organizational landscape, we see several other barriers to the greater integration of low-income renters in civic activities beyond the development. Some of these hurdles are logistical. For example, residents say they know little about available forums and when and where they meet. Furthermore, residents have limited time and energy for such engagement. As one relocated public housing resident told us, "I work seven days a week. And when I come home from one job, I'm too tired." The prevailing disconnectedness between the developments and the neighborhoods discussed throughout this chapter also dampens individual residents' motivation to engage more broadly. Those inclined to participate—particularly those with concerns about problems in the neighborhood or the treatment they or their peers must tolerate—feel resentment at not being taken seriously. As a public housing resident at Park Boulevard asserted, "When we have meetings with homeowners, they show the difference in your face. . . . For instance, if a CHA resident raises a hand in the meeting . . . you hurry up and get your question out . . . they let the homeowner make their point, and they'll shush you up and make it known that you're a CHA resident."

Finally, as is evident from the descriptions of the various associations and forums, intertwined with these factors are explicit exclusionary tactics, such as closed membership and annual dues, as well as more subtle but no less powerful deterrents of stigmatizing and demeaning discourse and policies. Ultimately, relocated public housing residents have to live with the sense that they are not wanted. As a public housing resident from Oakwood Shores put it, "They don't want to mingle with us, they want to just push us out." An owner at Westhaven Park expressed this perspective explicitly at a CAPS meeting: "I did not pay $300,000 for a condo to live next to the projects."

Conclusion

The integrationist aims of the mixed-income development strategy extend beyond creating mixed-income housing on the sites of former public housing complexes. Though it was beyond the scope of their direct influence and control, private developers, CHA staff, and local community organization leaders were explicit about their commitment to reintegrating the developments into their surrounding neighborhoods. On a physical level, they have been generally successful. Although all the developments have design features that continue to set them apart from the neighborhoods around them, the city street grid has been reestablished throughout the complexes, citywide sanitation departments and nonprofit organizations provide services, and there is no longer an obviously institutional appearance that stigmatizes them. The neighborhoods surrounding the developments are revitalizing, though with varying momentum and robustness, and each has elements of fragility (tenuous economic vitality around Oakwood Shores and Park Boulevard and crime around Westhaven Park) that suggest caution about how the pace will be sustained. It also remains to be seen how the differing pace of gentrification and changing racial makeup of the Near West Side as compared with the South Side will affect the dynamics between the developments and their broader neighborhoods.

Development professionals and community organization leaders are largely disappointed with residents' lack of engagement beyond the development, and residents largely experience this disconnection as well. While relocated public housing residents often express familiarity and general connection to the overall neighborhood, given their residential history, for the most part they have not become engaged in its activities. Nor, besides enjoying relatively safer and better-designed surroundings, have they been able to benefit from the changes in these neighborhoods to improve their economic conditions. We also find little evidence of inclusionary democracy. Neighborhood associational mechanisms, whether intentionally or not, marginalize low-income renters, and associations designed to promote inclusion have been largely ineffective. Race and class are enduring features of this social landscape. Those associations led by or composed predominantly of African American renters, such as the Local Advisory Council at Westhaven Park and the Ellis Park Advisory Council at Oakwood Shores, have had limited influence beyond the development. An instructive exception is the court-ordered Horner Residents Committee and residents' legal counsel at Westhaven Park. Although largely centered on the mixed-income public housing redevelopment, it has influenced decisions about off-site housing in the neighborhood and the residents relocated there. Thus the incorporated exclusion that we documented within the new developments is also a defining characteristic of the neighborhoods beyond the three sites and represents a core challenge in the larger quest for the full integration of public housing residents into the city around them.

NINE

The Promise and Perils of Mixed-Income Public Housing Transformation

Chicago's Plan for Transformation exemplifies a major—and still ascendant—policy trend, both nationally and throughout most of the industrialized West, to address concentrated urban poverty and the failures of public housing by focusing on income mixing and social inclusion. It seeks both to relocate public housing residents to less poor, better-functioning neighborhoods and to remake specific urban spaces, once dominated by deteriorating and unsafe public housing complexes, into vibrant, economically diverse communities. To realize these goals, both strategies—dispersal and development—rely on market orientations and private sector and nonprofit actors, supported by state policy and public funding. And both are grounded in a stated emphasis on the benefits of the social and economic integration of the poor as a response to urban poverty. Rather than struggling against concentrated disadvantage, isolated from the resources of the broader city, public housing residents and other low-income households are to be effectively integrated into new communities and thus to gain access to the social, economic, and relational opportunities they provide. And public housing itself is to be similarly integrated into the neighborhoods in which it is embedded and into the market and civic institutions and processes through which they function. In its particular focus on community and the assumptions that lie behind it, mixed-income public housing reform also connects to—adopts and adapts—the efforts of a long line of community-based interventions in the United States, dating at least to the Progressive Era, that have sought to remedy urban poverty and the social problems associated with it. The approach to community-based public housing reform in Chicago has been to engage "community" principally as a target of intervention rather than as a unit of action, emphasizing planning, design principles, and the primacy of development professionals rather than mobilization of community-level actors, processes, and resources. As we have shown, this emphasis has tended to privilege market-oriented goals over social goals, producing new communities where the poor have been spatially incorporated but remain socially and economically excluded.

The Plan for Transformation embraces an ambitious set of goals that are fraught with challenges. Our study has sought to understand and critically examine the goals, the benefits, and the difficulties of this effort, investigating the possibilities and limitations the policy represents for addressing urban poverty, public housing failure, and urban development. To do so, we have taken an in-depth and comprehensive look at mixed-income public housing reform as it is playing out in three communities in Chicago. We have analyzed the arguments and interests that drive mixed-income public housing reform broadly and in the specific context of Chicago's Plan for Transformation. We have considered the strategies engaged and the actors, mechanisms, and processes directed toward the Transformation's goals, looking particularly at new mixed-income communities developed on the footprint of former public housing complexes. And we have investigated in detail the character of the communities emerging on these sites by exploring the experience of residents and the perspectives of development professionals responsible for their build-out and management. We have investigated the dynamics that shape residents' experiences there, the nature and extent of integration achieved, and the benefits and costs to residents of the developments, the larger neighborhoods, and the city. Although we have documented physical transformation, emergent economic revitalization, and improved safety and stability in the targeted areas, we conclude that the Plan for Transformation has thus far fallen considerably short of its social goals of breaking down the barriers that have isolated public housing residents in disadvantage and of integrating them into the physical, social, and economic fabric of the city. This failure raises significant concerns about the likelihood of achieving more broadly shared benefits from the substantial redevelopment that remains to be completed and about the longer-term stability and viability of the existing mixed-income communities.

Our focus on Chicago and these particular three development sites is a considered one. Chicago's endeavor to "transform" public housing is the most ambitious of its kind, substantially exceeding other major efforts in the United States in scale and responding to what was arguably the nation's most disastrous public housing failure. Although the mixed-income development component is only part of the framework of the Transformation, it is in many ways its most central expression, driving relocation and resettlement more broadly, commanding by far the largest share of resources, reclaiming and fundamentally remaking urban neighborhoods where public housing once stood, and representing the most explicit and intentional test of the integrationist goals that lie behind the policy.

In Chicago the mixed-income development component of the Transformation is also particularly ambitious, with a strong emphasis on market-rate homeownership that establishes the foundation for substantial economic diversity within the redeveloped communities and with a substantial emphasis on the spatial integration of market-rate and subsidized, for-sale, and rental units. There is also significant diversity across mixed-income developments and the public housing complexes they are replacing. Our selection of the three sites we study reflects this diversity, allowing us to explore both common themes and divergent dynamics in emerging communities that differ in size, stage of development, density, location, neighborhood context, design, management, organizational infrastructure, income, housing tenure, and racial mix. The sheer scale of the Transformation, while providing a rich opportunity for analysis and comparison, has also raised problems of complexity and manageability. But while Chicago is of particular interest for some of these unique characteristics, the core principles, operations, and dynamics of the mixed-income transformation are common to similar endeavors across the United States and beyond, making our findings here broadly relevant. These include expectations for the benefits of integration; considerations about design and financing; processes of relocation, demolition, construction, population selection, and management; and approaches to community building, place making, and regulation.

Our analysis is based on six years of in-depth fieldwork and allied research over a period when the new communities were being built and populated, organizational arrangements and orientations toward governance and management were being institutionalized, and the dynamics of social interaction and community life were being shaped and solidified. What has been built and what has happened over this time is obviously far from the end of the story. The policy and its implementation continue to roll out, and the communities that have replaced public housing complexes continue to evolve, shaped in part through the intentional actions of development professionals, state and civil society actors, and the organizations they work for and in part through the informal, quotidian actions and responses of individual residents and informal groups.

Some of these actions are driven, or at least informed, by changes at the macro level, some occur in response to more local issues and dynamics. The housing crisis and recession that began in late 2007—the greatest economic downturn in the United States since the Great Depression—fundamentally changed the market conditions redevelopment plans had been based on. Construction of for-sale units stalled, the value of owners' units fell, jobs dwindled, and initial plans for investment, income mix, and unit build-out were revisited. Significant institutional upheavals also took place. Over the course of the Transformation thus far, the CHA has undergone six changes in leadership and several waves of staff turnover and restructuring. In 2011 the city elected Rahm Emmanuel as its new mayor—the first in over two decades—to succeed Richard M. Daley, who was the city's longest-serving mayor and the principal mover behind the Plan for Transformation. With this change in leadership came an effort to reconsider and "recalibrate" the next phase of public housing reform. Building on a series of forums to get input from a broad range of city "stakeholders," the CHA launched a process to shape the "Plan for Transformation 2.0," released in 2013 as *Plan Forward: Communities That Work*. Issued after more than a year of internal deliberation and to much anticipation, *Plan Forward* provides a skeletal outline of the CHA's strategic framework for completing the Plan for Transformation. Although calling for a "reimagination" of the final phase of the effort, *Plan Forward* retains and builds on the original Plan—focusing on "coordinating public and private investments to develop healthy, vibrant communities"—while seeking to respond to changed economic circumstances and the lessons emerging over the first decade of implementation. It calls, for example, for expanding affordable housing options (such as by acquiring and rehabilitating available properties in "vibrant neighborhoods"), finding new ways to provide rental assistance, developing CHA-controlled land for economic development rather than just housing, and expanding services to better support the needs of CHA residents.[1] Some of the proposed strategies may address key issues raised in our study. For example, the plan proposes "an annual community engagement plan and community governance strategy customized to each mixed-income property."[2] But without far more detail, it is difficult to determine the depth of commitment or strategic approaches to some of the critical challenges we have examined. How *Plan Forward* will be operationalized and executed, and to what effect, is yet to be seen.

In this final chapter, we draw some broad conclusions about mixed-income public housing reform in Chicago, explore what they suggest regarding the promise and perils of this approach to concentrated urban poverty, and outline some implications of our findings for both policy and practice. First we step back to briefly review the evidence regarding the effect of poverty deconcentration policies, through both dispersal and development, on their integrationist goals and anticipated outcomes for the poor, then discuss some of the reasons for these outcomes in the context of mixed-income public housing reform. We then suggest approaches that might inform future phases of current efforts as well as future policy and implementation orientations toward housing policy and toward urban poverty more broadly.

Integrationist (and Other) Outcomes

We begin by briefly putting our findings about the shaping of what we have called incorporated exclusion—the limited and contentious nature and effects of the attempts at integration in mixed-income public housing redevelopments—in the context of public housing reform focused on poverty deconcentration. To what extent have such attempts led to the effective integration of the poor into "better" neighborhoods—less poor, less racially segregated, safer, more supportive—and how has this integration affected poor households?

There has been significant research on mobility programs and their effects, but the evidence it provides is mixed. The clearest success has been on basic improvement in neighborhood circumstances, at least for those relocated to suburban neighborhoods under the original Gautreaux program in Chicago and through the distribution of scattered-site public housing across city neighborhoods. In these cases most residents moved to and remain in neighborhoods that are both more economically vibrant and more racially mixed (or majority white), with better schools, services, and amenities than the public housing communities they came from.[3] In other mobility programs findings are more equivocal. In both Moving

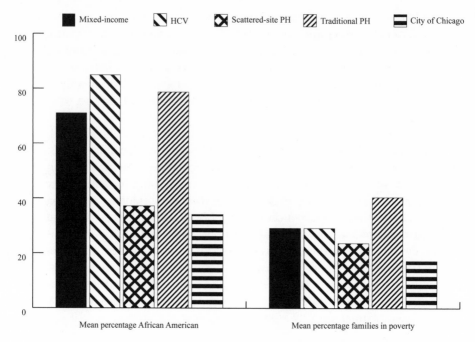

9.1 Census tract characteristics by subsidized housing type, 2008. HCV: Housing Choice voucher; PH: public housing. Source: American Community Survey 2005 to 2009 five-year estimates.

to Opportunity (MTO) and the second round of the Gautreaux program, initial moves to safer, less poor neighborhoods with better infrastructure, services, and amenities were often followed by subsequent moves to high-poverty, racially segregated, socially isolated neighborhoods.[4] Similarly, households relocated using vouchers under the HOPE VI and Housing Choice voucher programs, if they did not move to mixed-income developments replacing public housing complexes, often landed in poor and racially segregated neighborhoods—though they did attain greater neighborhood improvement than those who remained in or returned to renovated public housing.[5] This was largely true in Chicago as well as nationally—census tract poverty rates for movers in Chicago averaged about 29 percent versus about 40 percent for those remaining in or returning to traditional public housing—but voucher holders ended up in neighborhoods even more racially segregated than traditional public housing developments.[6]

Changes in neighborhood were accompanied by some changes in measures of the well-being of those living in relocated households, but again the evidence is mixed. Studies of the families relocated in response to the original Gautreaux ruling found improvements in employment and educational attainment, but the economic benefits of moving to the suburbs were more tenuous than the initial research had suggested.[7] Similarly, residents who relocated within the city as part of the MTO program reported better physical and mental health but no gains in employment or educational attainment, and despite a reduction in risky behavior among young women, delinquent behavior (as well as depression, posttraumatic stress, and conduct disorder) among young men increased.[8] Research has found improved mental health among HOPE VI voucher holders, but also significant economic hardship and no positive effects on employment or income.[9] Indeed, holders of Housing Choice vouchers in Chicago evince a number of disadvantages after relocation compared with others affected by the Transformation. These include lower earnings, greater use of food stamps, and more involvement with the child welfare and juvenile justice systems.[10] And while, on average, public housing families affected by the Transformation have higher earnings than they did before relocation, nine years into the Transformation

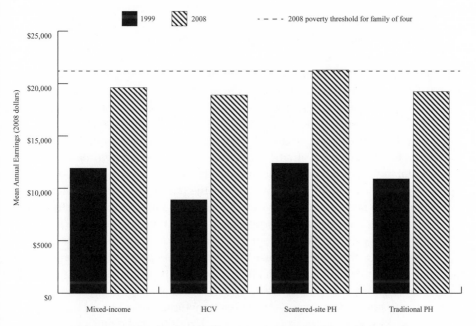

9.2   Mean earnings of working households, 1999 and 2008. HCV: Housing Choice voucher; PH: public housing. Source: Chicago Housing Authority and Illinois Department of Employment Security.

and at the outset of the Great Recession, working households, regardless of housing destination, remained on average at or around the poverty line.

As these indicators already suggest, the integrationist goals of many of these efforts are proving difficult to attain, and research to date suggests that the social processes that might lead to more effective integration and connection are relatively weak and are failing to aid social mobility. As we outlined in chapter 6, most studies of mobility programs suggest that those moving from public housing often remain socially isolated in their new neighborhoods. Relocation has for the most part neither led to significant cross-class interaction between public housing residents and their higher-income neighbors nor significantly enhanced social networks for them, although some studies suggest that scattered-site public housing residents at least become acquainted with some of their higher-income neighbors, even if these relationships are not particularly close and fail to yield instrumental benefits. At least one study suggests that for those relocated under Gautreaux, network relations, including some instrumental exchanges, did eventually improve—after fifteen years.[11]

This is the context of changes brought about by mobility programs in the service of poverty deconcentration, but mixed-income redevelopment approaches differ in how much control they have over reshaping the neighborhood environment and in their explicit focus on promoting and managing integration. The research here is less extensive, but it again suggests there has been limited social interaction that might lead to social mobility and limited effects on relocated public housing residents' well-being. Social interaction in these contexts tends to occur principally among residents with similar social backgrounds, and there is little evidence of cross-class integration, development of social capital, or increased social or economic advancement among the poor.[12] As we have shown, although mixed-income public housing redevelopments have been more effective at changing the physical infrastructure and demographic mix where relocated public housing residents live (on the footprint of the development, if not necessarily in the broader community), there are significant barriers to promoting social interaction among this diverse population, and effective integration has remained elusive, to say the least. Indeed, along with positive changes in safety and improvements in the built environment, these new communities expose poor people—and particularly relocated public housing residents—to different kinds of disadvantage and have generated new forms of exclusion.

Why These Outcomes?

What accounts for these outcomes in mixed-income public housing re-developments, in spite of their explicit goal of social and economic integration? We suggest these effects are due to a combination of theoretical disjunctions and failures of implementation.

As we discussed in chapter 2, a set of theoretical assumptions lie behind the arguments for mixed-income public housing reform. These include theories concerning the importance of neighborhood as both built environment and social space; the potential of community relational networks to promote social capital development and social control; the benefits of middle-class role modeling in influencing the aspirations and behavior of the poor; and the possibility of leveraging market forces and design principles to create inclusive, well-functioning communities. But as our analysis has shown, implementing these ideas in the highly diverse—and highly contrived—communities replacing public housing complexes is difficult. It challenges the application of some of these assumptions and complicates the attempt to bring them to fruition through planned social change. We highlight four related themes.

The first theme concerns the presumed influence of propinquity on relationship building and social capital. If living in concentrated poverty led to constrained relational networks that isolated the poor from "mainstream" individuals and institutions that could provide opportunities for mobility, mixed-income communities were meant to facilitate such access by reducing the distance between the poor and "better connected" individuals. Through both management and design, they were also meant to shape the circumstances whereby residents' interaction as neighbors and in local institutions would support the development of social capital and the potential for social mobility. These goals did not require intimate relations or meaningful friendships between the poor and more affluent neighbors, but they did assume that propinquity would lead to some instrumental interactions fostering "weak ties" and the social capital they represent.

To some extent spatial proximity did make interaction easier, but cross-class exchanges for the most part have been both limited and either extremely casual, failing to yield instrumental benefits for the poor, or contentious, contributing to conflict between low- and higher-income residents. This conflict has led the latter to demand more surveillance, stricter regulations on the behavior of their low-income neighbors, and more stringent rule enforcement. To be fair, development professionals did not rely merely on the presumed power of propinquity to foster relationship building, but promoting engagement across income and housing tenure groups has for the most part proved difficult. These efforts have been confounded by both the compartmentalizing of participation—different groups sorting themselves into different activities and organizations, due in part to individual choice and constraints and in part to structural arrangements—and by mounting contention, exclusion, and stigma.

These dynamics have largely been driven by the significant social distance between public housing residents and other low-income renters, on the one hand, and homeowners and market-rate renters on the other. Rather than the groups' coming together around common goals as neighbors with relatively equal status, in ways that might break down barriers of prejudice and promote integration (as contact theory suggests),[13] the extreme differences in socioeconomic status (income, employment, education) between the poorest residents in these communities and those owning homes or renting at market rate militated against connection, and the difficulties of bridging status differences have proved formidable. Indeed, inclinations to privilege negative contact experiences and expectations have outweighed opportunities to revise such expectations.[14] These circumstances are complicated by racial dynamics and, in particular, by the enduring power of an urban underclass narrative in which institutionalized assumptions regarding a culture of poverty—a pattern of values, beliefs, and behaviors presumably embraced by the underclass in opposition to mainstream values of work and self-sufficiency—remains salient. The economic diversity within the African American population in these sites, and prevailing tensions around issues of class and culture, add further complexity as a secondary marginalization has surfaced.[15] Thus some low-income blacks feel judged by and alienated not only from whites but also from more affluent blacks.

The second theme has to do with expectations for how having middle-class "role models" will affect the poor. This orientation reflects both some acceptance of the culture of poverty thesis and a privileging of individual, behavior-focused approaches to addressing poverty over those directed more to institutionalized barriers and structural factors blocking access to social and economic mobility. As we have shown, while policy makers, development professionals, and higher-income residents often invoked exposure to the values and workday routines of middle-class neighbors as a way to shift the aspirations and behaviors of the poor, most relocated public housing residents and other low-income renters did not see a disjunction between their own values and aspirations and those of their higher-income neighbors. To the extent that they changed their behaviors or reconsidered what their future might hold, public housing residents emphasized the pressures of new responsibilities for demonstrating self-sufficiency and maintaining lease compliance and, to a lesser extent, new opportunities (for example, for job training). The benefits of living in these new mixed-income communities were generally seen as stemming from improvements in safety and the built environment rather than from the behavioral cues they might take from their higher-income neighbors. While one should not underestimate the benefits of structural changes that provide for safer and higher-quality neighborhoods, attention to broader issues of capacity, opportunity, and access has not been enough to move most public housing residents to self-sufficiency, let alone promote significant social and economic mobility. Indeed, at the threshold of the Great Recession fewer than half of relocated public housing families in mixed-income developments in Chicago had any income from employment, in spite of the requirement of employment eligibility in most mixed-income sites.[16] And while enforcing responsibility toward achieving self-sufficiency and accountability may be a good motivator, greater attention to the other side of that equation—the nature of economic opportunity and the factors that condition access to it—is clearly necessary and has proved even more difficult with the economic downturn. In addition, surveillance to monitor behavior and ensure accountability—and punitive zero-tolerance policies and rule enforcement in response to a broad range of infractions examined in chapter 7—has contributed to exclusion and withdrawal rather than promoting integration and upward mobility.

The third theme relates to faith in what James DeFilippis calls "spatial solutions to social problems."[17] Mixed-income development strategies rely to a large extent on remaking local environments as a solution to a complicated set of interwoven social and economic problems, in an effort to replace an urban landscape characterized by economic and (often) racial segregation with one that promotes integration. This spatial orientation connects assumptions about the importance of neighborhood as both space and place with assumptions about the potential of design to shape the built environment so as to promote social cohesion and social control. To carry out these ideas, mixed-income public housing redevelopments rely on New Urbanist design principles. But, as we have seen, they have tended to apply these principles selectively, with greater emphasis on design that contributes to "defensible" space and less on creating public and civic space. Indeed, through both design and management these mixed-income communities have privileged privatization along with the policing or formal management of common space to minimize spontaneous socializing that might lead to (real or perceived) problems. In any case, while spatial arrangements can certainly contribute to social dynamics—making incidental encounters easy or difficult, creating secure or potentially dangerous spaces, promoting shared use or privileging privacy—there are limits to what spatial strategies and the built environment can do. They cannot stand in for or fully shape the social, economic, and political processes required to bridge significant social distance and address inequalities of access and opportunity.

The final issue is connected with the presumed alliance of market means and social goals and the potential to leverage the former in service of the latter. As we noted in chapter 5, development professionals largely see the turn to market approaches to public housing reform as symbiotic with the social policy goals of moving public housing residents from concentrated urban poverty to self-sufficiency and integrating them into new, safe, and well-functioning communities. The anticipated risks of mixed-income development were considered too great to motivate developers unless they were also committed to the social goals, and creating communities that would draw market investment and both attract and retain middle-class residents was seen as necessarily contributing to the well-being of low-income residents. Certainly other investments would be required, including a range of social and support services to help relocated public housing residents be "successful" in these new environments, but development professionals argued for the basic compatibility of pursuing social policy goals through market mechanisms and state-supported private development. These expectations notwithstanding, the pervasive market orientation of these projects—the reliance on market actors and focus on "market norms," the stress on private provision of services and private property, the exigencies of making these communities profitable, and concerns about maintaining investment levels and protecting exchange value—has led to privileging the preferences and anxieties of higher-income residents. This in turn has led to regulatory regimes—rules, surveillance, and enforcement—that disproportionally target low-income residents and place relocated public housing residents, in particular, at risk, given their more tenuous hold on housing rights and housing subsidies should they be evicted. Although there is significant agreement among both residents (across income and tenure status) and development professionals about the need for rules and adherence to community norms, there is also disagreement about where to draw the line between what is acceptable and what should be prohibited, about how these distinctions should be made, about reasonable strategies for ensuring compliance, and about when enforcement is fairly and uniformly applied. In protecting what development professionals often describe as "market norms," these regulatory regimes essentially become mechanisms of poverty governance that reproduce marginalization and create new dynamics of social exclusion within the context of spatial incorporation in mixed-income communities.

Implications

Although the expectations for integration in mixed-income public housing redevelopments and the benefits it was meant to provide for the poor have largely not been realized, tolerating isolated enclaves of concentrated urban poverty is clearly not the answer. And while these efforts, particularly with regard to improvements in safety and the built environment and the beginnings of neighborhood revitalization, have generated some clear benefits, these benefits have not been shared equally. The vast majority of public housing residents relocated to make way for these new mixed-income communities have not returned to the new developments. Ten years into the Transformation, only about 13 percent of the nearly 10,000 residents still living in CHA (not senior) subsidized housing (and only 8 percent of the nearly 17,000 leaseholders in the system at the start of the Transformation) were living in mixed-income redeveloped sites.[18] Instead, most have either moved to other neighborhoods using Housing Choice vouchers (about 40 percent) that landed them in communities less poor than the public housing complexes from which they came but still largely very low income and racially segregated or returned to traditional, renovated public housing (about 32 percent).[19] And many of those who did return to the redeveloped sites, while benefiting from infrastructure improvements and significant reduction in crime, have in numerous ways been marginalized within these communities, subjected to routine surveillance and regulation and excluded from many of the benefits that integration was meant to provide. Promoting effective integration and responding to poverty and inequality require other tools, investments, and orientations. Some of these can be targeted to more effective implementation of mixed-income development schemes themselves, with limitations. Other actions need to be directed to different issues and at different levels of intervention.

Implications for Mixed-Income Public Housing Redevelopment

In the context of mixed-income development schemes, our findings suggest several actions that might contribute to better social integration, promote social mobility, and create more inclusive communities.

A first imperative is for greater clarity and communication among the numerous actors at each mixed-income public housing redevelopment about the social goals in that particular site and neighborhood. Given current circumstances, opportunities, and challenges, and knowing what is known now about the dynamics of race and class in mixed-income communities, there should be early planning conversations among the development team, resident leaders, and other community partners, raising these questions: What are the intentions for integration and social inclusion? How are they to be achieved? What are the roles and responsibilities of various actors in pursuing them? Given the emerging insights about various roles, which actors are best placed to carry them out effectively and what additional resources and capacity are necessary? In light of the "theoretical disjunctions" we identified above regarding unfulfilled expectations for social capital, role modeling, spatial design, and market forces, how should key actors reshape their strategic implementation to promote greater social inclusion and mobility among the poor? In Chicago, we have seen little evidence of such strategic conversations. Experienced practitioners should be asked for technical assistance and consultation about promising practices in other developments, and opportunities for peer-to-peer conversations among developers, service providers, property managers, and resident leaders from different cities should be encouraged by the sponsors of these efforts.

Another possible direction concerns social distance. The residents of mixed-income public housing redevelopments we examined in Chicago have a particularly wide span of socioeconomic status: the distance between the poorest residents (relocated public housing residents) and the wealthiest (market-rate homeowners) is dramatic. Moderating this distance, perhaps through unit design and price points that allow for a broader array of incomes between poles, might mitigate the extreme social distance between the poorest and the most affluent. Market conditions have forced the Park Boulevard developers to move in this direction from their initial bifurcated design, and the social impact appears promising but remains to be seen. And it should be kept in mind that socioeconomic proximity alone is not a guarantee of harmonious relations.

Indeed, some of the most strident critics of the "ghetto behavior" of re-located public housing residents were other low-income renters trying to distance themselves from that kind of activity and to avoid being seen in the same light by development professionals and their higher-income neighbors. The "optimal" proportions of social mix will certainly vary depending on redevelopment context, informed by the size of the development and its financing streams, the existing mix and market conditions in the local neighborhood, and the skills, philosophy, and commitment to "managing inclusion" of the developer and particularly the property management team. But armed with existing knowledge, these decisions should be driven less by financing or "relocation politics"—demands and compromises regarding unit distribution and set-asides among the housing authority, development professionals, and resident advocates—and more strategically in terms of establishing the conditions for a well-functioning community. In cities and neighborhoods where the housing market recovers sufficiently to make for-sale units once again feasible as a component of mixed-income development, stipulations should be incorporated to encourage owner-occupancy rather than investment purchases or leasing by homeowners, and special attention should be paid to anticipating and managing owner-renter tensions. (We will elaborate when we discuss issues of governance below.)

Beyond this, more direct attention needs to be paid to promoting self-sufficiency, social mobility, wealth, and status among public housing residents and other low-income renters. This should include more robust efforts to promote human capital development (education, vocational training, acquiring "soft skills" that contribute to workforce engagement and job retention) and more intensive workforce engagement strategies that connect public housing residents to specific employers, maintain connections, and provide some ongoing support to ensure success—or at least increase the odds.[20] Opportunity Chicago, as mentioned in chapter 3, was a major workforce initiative designed to support the Plan for Transformation that broke important new ground along these lines. This five-year initiative, spearheaded by the city, the CHA, and the Partnership for New Communities, surpassed its goals by placing 5,185 relocated public housing residents in jobs while helping them increase their skills and earnings. However, despite the success in employment placement, individual annual earnings remained low, at under $11,000.[21] The program was geared toward public housing residents broadly, with no specific strategies for the mixed-income developments, so data are not available on its exact impact in these sites. The implication here is that the operational and strategic lessons from that initiative—systems integration, wraparound services, literacy-workforce programming—should be refined, applied, adapted, and targeted to ongoing and future mixed-income development efforts.

There might also be opportunities for employment support to be directly connected to the redevelopment process. Development professionals note that one of the benefits of these mixed-income public housing redevelopments has been the number of jobs created, particularly for construction, but also in allied tasks and services. Training public housing residents for some of these jobs, and negotiating community benefit agreements (establishing expectations for local hiring) with employers drawn to invest in the revitalizing communities might contribute more directly to new employment for low-income community residents. The federal Section 3 program is intended to connect public housing residents to employment and contracting opportunities in redevelopments, but resident leaders and advocates have been disappointed by its impact in the Plan for Transformation, owing to high competition for the limited jobs available, their generally short-term nature, and criticisms about a lack of transparency. The CHA's *Plan Forward* promises "a recalibrated Section 3 program to support economic self-sufficiency among low-income families and support entrepreneurship."[22] A more intensive assessment should be done of the most successful uses of the Section 3 program around the country, and a strategic adaptation to future mixed-income development projects should be implemented. In Chicago, the CHA should be held accountable for following through on this commitment to recalibrate its use of Section 3.

Efforts to address social distance might also include helping public housing families and other low-income residents develop longer-term assets, such as by cash transfers (whether conditional or unconditional), individual development accounts (matched savings accounts specifically designed to encourage low-income individuals to save) and, for some, homeownership supports (such as rent-to-own arrangements, help with down payments, financial counseling, and low-interest fixed-term loans).[23] Two of the mixed-income sites in Chicago (Oakwood Shores and Roosevelt Square, the redevelopment of ABLA Homes on the city's Near West Side) incorporated homeownership opportunities for some public housing residents in their unit mix in collaboration with the CHA's Choose-to-Own program. The number of units allocated under this scheme was very small, however, and was further curtailed by the stalled production of for-sale units in general. Still, the effort showed some early promise; there were, for example, no foreclosures in any of the units sold to public housing residents at Oakwood Shores. Asset-building strategies such as individual development accounts and the federal Family Self-Sufficiency program,[24] which provides a range of social and financial counseling services to families selected into the program and connects them to an interest-bearing escrow account to make saving easier, could also be adapted to mixed-income developments.

If successful, these inputs could help low-income renters achieve greater self-sufficiency and support ultimate social mobility while also raising their status and stake in these communities. There are obvious complications in implementing these ideas, in part because at least some public housing residents in these contexts face significant challenges (extremely limited skills and education, disability, long-term dislocation from the workforce) and in part because resources are severely constrained, with the lion's share going to construction and physical development rather than to social services and community supports. But greater attention and additional resources need to go toward addressing inequality beyond developing housing and promoting income mix. And it is clear that, to achieve real results, social mobility programming will need to be a long-term investment with extensive post-occupancy support for residents who need it, a far more extensive commitment than the one year of pre-occupancy support originally proposed by the CHA.

Another line of action might be to revise approaches to building community. At one level this includes greater attention to transparency. As we noted in chapter 4, marketing materials generally did not state explicitly that properties were part of a mixed-income redevelopment of public housing, and some homeowners moved into these communities without a clear understanding of this. More clarity up front, and a procedure to establish expectations and concerns early in the game, might mitigate tensions down the road. As an African American owner of a market-rate unit at Westhaven Park put it,

I think maybe next time when you have a mixed-income area that you are trying to develop, if you're truly trying to minimize conflict and if you truly want to have a sense of community, you need to bring people that's going to be part, that can be potentially part of that community to the table and discuss [it]. . . . See, that's the problem. No one wants to have a real candid conversation. So if you don't have a real candid conversation, you're not going to have real candid answers. You're going to get fake 'cause you had a fake development.

This is no easy task, and it is obviously risky given the need to attract market-rate renters and owners. But greater transparency might also draw a population more inclined to living in a diverse setting and more tolerant of the complexity of urban life in such settings.

Community-building efforts also need to reevaluate the opportunities for participation, deliberation, and governance in these communities to provide for more engagement of low-income residents and more attention to their points of view. One goal here is to collectively establish community norms that protect order, safety, and sound investment without overly restricting individual freedom and access to public space, and without punitive responses visited disproportionately on the poor. Since property managers tend to be responsible for monitoring residents' behavior, they should receive training and capacity building in this regard. Another approach is to promote opportunities for engagement and interaction in which community members of all backgrounds can contribute to deliberation and shape responses around a range of issues and through multiple mechanisms. Establishing more inclusive forums—resident associations, neighborhood associations—to support deliberation and decision making among residents across incomes and housing tenures may be a key element of more equitable, and ultimately more sustainable, mixed-income communities. The complexity of such an agenda where there is significant inequality is not to be underestimated. It likely requires both intentionality (ensuring disadvantaged groups' meaningful representation and participation) and attention to building capacity (training, communication, leadership development) both to help low-income residents advocate for themselves and to help professionals and higher-income residents engage effectively where there is significant socioeconomic, and to some extent racial and ethnic, diversity.[25] Given the complexity and sensitivity of these discussions, development staff might consider securing external assistance to design and moderate the forums. The role the Chicago Department of Human Relations played in helping to convene neighborhood leaders on the Near West Side is an example of the assistance that could be provided by those with this expertise and capacity.

While new mechanisms might be created for this kind of dialogue, existing forums could also be encouraged to become more inclusive. Technically, the private developers are members of the condominium associations, representing those units they own and rent out. At Westhaven Park the developer used this influence to advocate for relocated public housing residents to be represented at the regular meetings of the condominium board of one multi-unit building on site. Representation was minimal (two residents) and selective, and the public housing residents were not given a vote, but their participation has gone some way toward opening communication and easing tensions in the building. Tenant meetings could also be used more effectively as forums for input and dialogue among residents rather than simply sessions for disseminating information and reviewing rules. And working groups could be restructured to encourage residents to participate more substantively, beyond the two residents drawn from the old Local Advisory Council leadership. Finally, the ombudsman position created by the CHA to advocate for public housing residents in the mixed-income development, while serving as an outlet for individual grievances, does not allow for sustaining broad participation and has obvious limitations, relying as it does on a centralized, CHA-staffed function to promote residents' input that might, after all, contest CHA priorities and authority. Building an effective and constructive collective governance capacity among relocated public housing residents requires support beyond the ombudsman, and it demands independence from the CHA. In all these cases, additional avenues for inclusion could employ effective democratic means for selecting participants, offer training to enable effective participation, support activities that promote information exchange, and strengthen the potential to organize in response to collectively recognized challenges.[26]

A third component of renewed efforts at community building should be a reorientation to spatial arrangements and expectations. Rather than being integrated, mixed-use communities, the sites are essentially residential (commercial development, for example, is largely left to later phases, and most park space is either on the periphery of the developments or associated with condominium governance, raising issues of access). As we have noted, the more communal, civic space is limited in favor of private spaces, the more likely it is that some residents will appropriate available areas—front steps, street corners, parking lots—for social activities that others find objectionable. Public spaces need to be allocated and integrated within neighborhoods, encouraging general access to them and collective agreement about their use. This includes fostering an appreciation of the benefits of public space and a recognition that in the city such space will have varied uses. It also requires cultivating and strengthening the organizational infrastructure of these communities—organizational "places" that welcome shared use, such as stores, coffee shops, recreational facilities, and schools. The retail storefront developed at Park Boulevard is a good illustration. Examples of missed opportunities include the Abraham Lincoln Center at Oakwood Shores and the Major Adams Community Center at Westhaven Park. Both have a long history of serving as a vital resource to a public housing population, but despite their convenient location on the footprint of the mixed-income development, they have not repositioned themselves as "neutral" gathering places for the new population. The Donoghue charter elementary school at Oakwood Shores has also not become a resource for the mixed-income population at the site. This is in part due to timing (the new school was opened and populated before families began to move back into the development) and in part to demographics (there are relatively fewer higher-income families with school-age children). But both the school leaders and the developer acknowledge that they could have done more to link the school and the development. Greater attention to creating and promoting public and civic space and local organizational resources may diversify the spaces available to residents, integrate their activities into the broader community, and provide more "neutral" arenas where residents may find some common ground—or be more comfortable with difference. This comfort with difference, what Iris Marion Young describes as "the being together of strangers," is a critical part of the urban experience: accepting and embracing diversity and discovering that people of different backgrounds, interests, resources, and priorities have the desire and capacity to simply live together as neighbors.[27]

Finally, more attention needs to be paid, and more resources dedicated, to providing social services and supports for residents with intensive needs and to supplying, particularly for youths, "primary supports" that offer normative contexts and resources to foster social and individual development.[28] A fundamental problem development professionals faced was the sometimes severe personal and family issues some public housing residents struggled with, which in the most extreme cases made them difficult and disruptive tenants.

Social services might be tailored based on residents' characteristics and needs and might range from less intensive but ongoing support (for example, with employment and financial management) to more intensive case management, counseling, and wraparound services.[29] Susan Popkin and her colleagues, for example, examined the outcomes for participants in a small demonstration program within the Transformation who received intensive case management and support services, and the research provides compelling evidence that social and economic conditions may improve for adults who receive such support.[30] Building on these findings, the Housing Opportunities and Services Together initiative, now being implemented in both mixed-income and traditional public housing developments in several US cities, is a leading example of fully integrating services for high-needs households into public housing redevelopments.[31]

We have noted that in spite of the perceived promise that young people would be a "bridge" between lower- and higher-income families by associating with peers from different backgrounds, young people (particularly older youths) have instead contributed to tension and conflict that is driven by concerns about safety and adherence to norms of behavior, in turn driving the regulatory responses described in chapter 7. In addition to the limited contexts where the daily lives of young people from different backgrounds intersect, these communities generally lack youth programs, after-school activities, jobs, and other ways for youths to engage constructively in their free time.[32]

Broader Implications

Beyond efforts to make mixed-income public housing redevelopments themselves more effective in promoting integration and delivering the other benefits they are meant to generate for low-income residents, addressing urban poverty and accomplishing effective integration of the poor requires action well beyond the reform of public housing— although increasing the supply of affordable housing in ways that don't contribute to the concentration of poverty is clearly an important component. Indeed, given the relative paucity of quality affordable housing in Chicago and other major US cities, a foundational focus on expanding affordable housing options is a critical part of meeting the needs of the poor. The demolition of thousands of "hard" units of public housing, the housing policy shift toward Housing Choice vouchers, and the privatizing of remaining (and new) hard units through mixed-income development, project-based voucher projects, and the Rental Assistance Demonstration program[33] raise fundamental questions about the long-term commitment to public housing in the United States. With resources and public support for public housing construction and rehabilitation dwindling, many of these strategies aim to leverage resources from the private sector. But given the enduring scale of the need for safe, quality housing for very low and extremely low income families, there is reason for concern that relying on privatizing will ultimately increase the deficit of housing for the poor.

In addition to providing housing itself, coupling affordable housing development with broader efforts at community development may fill some of the needs of low-income populations without resorting to wholesale demolition and redevelopment, moving people to less-poor neighborhoods, or promoting an influx of middle-class residents to spur development.[34] Beyond mobility and explicit income mixing, therefore, attention should be paid to supporting broader housing and community development that can reinforce stability and opportunity in poor and working-class neighborhoods. This requires resources, but it does not necessarily require major top-down policy interventions; community development corporations and other local organizations and initiatives may offer capacity, knowledge, and experience that can be leveraged and supported. In addition, federal community development block grant funding, which municipalities often allocate piecemeal or diffusely, could be strategically targeted in alignment with affordable housing efforts to bolster social supports. For example, the Housing Choice and project-based voucher programs and inclusionary zoning efforts focus primarily on affordable housing access, and they might have a greater effect on social mobility if combined with strong employment and asset-building programs.[35]

To the extent that mobility programs can help people find affordable housing in less poor and less racially segregated neighborhoods, they are more likely to do so when they include effective support to ensure and sustain these moves. The first round of the Gautreaux program, and at least the initial moves under MTO (when such supports were provided), suggests some potential along these lines.[36] With the depth of current research and experience about the pros and cons of various relocation options—traditional public housing, scattered-site housing, Housing Choice vouchers, mixed-income developments—relocation counselors should be able to help households make more informed decisions about which option is the best fit given their particular circumstances, capacities, and preferences. Other strategies more focused on supply, such as scattered-site public housing and inclusionary zoning policies, have the potential to increase affordable housing in more economically advantaged neighborhoods and to produce this housing in neighborhoods with particular advantages, such as residential stability, good schools, and access to jobs. Contrary to the fears of many homeowners that lead to NIMBY-driven opposition, a significant body of research shows that scattered-site public housing and affordable housing set-asides need not, and most often do not, have a negative impact on property values, property taxes, out-migration of current residents, or crime.[37] (This evidence might also allay some of the fears of homeowners in mixed-income public housing redevelopment sites.) There are limits to these strategies, of course. Inclusionary zoning, for example, often produces a relatively small proportion of affordable set-asides compared with market-rate units being developed (generally 10–20 percent), and it often defines affordability at 60 percent of the area median income (in Chicago, about twice the poverty line). It therefore reaches only a portion of the population in need of affordable housing. And neither scheme is likely, by itself, to address the question of social integration, although the community dynamics leading to incorporated exclusion that we have documented in mixed-income redevelopments of public housing sites tend to be less fraught in these other contexts.[38] Indeed, given the expense and operational demands of wholesale mixed-income redevelopment, inclusionary zoning, scattered-site public housing, and project-based vouchers may be more practical alternatives for innovative place-based poverty deconcentration policy. Strategic advances in this arena would include significantly boosting the availability of these units for low-income households, adding robust programs and supports to foster social mobility and inclusion to these housing-focused programs, and dedicating more research and evaluation to learning about these methods.

Beyond this, although our study provides less direct insight into the potential and limitations of other kinds of policy interventions, it is very clear that the central reliance on housing policy and expectations for income mixing are insufficient to address—are not in fact really *designed* to address—other structural factors that create and reproduce urban poverty. Inequalities in access to quality education, the absence of living-wage employment for those with limited education and skills, and a range of institutional barriers that face the urban poor (such as discrimination, incarceration, lack of access to higher education) all contribute to the persistence of urban poverty and the difficulty of plotting a path toward self-sufficiency and social and economic mobility. As historian Michael Katz notes, although it is clearly an important contributor to the well-being of poor families, housing policy "does not substitute for policies that tackle poverty head on, policies that have been off the table for decades."[39]

Some recent public policy developments, such as the launching of the Obama administration's Promise and Choice Neighborhoods programs, have sought to address some of these limitations. Choice Neighborhoods, for example, which builds on and expands the efforts begun under HOPE VI, includes support for both affordable housing and economic development on the footprint of public housing (or other HUD-assisted housing) developments and in the neighborhoods around them. It also concentrates on social services, schools, issues of crime and safety, public assets and transportation, and community commercial and economic development. Interim evaluation findings on the first sites where Choice Neighborhoods was implemented document the complexity of these multifaceted efforts.[40] The mixed-income strategic enhancements we recommended above regarding social mix, upward mobility, community building, the design of public space, and integration of services for high-needs residents can all be applied to ongoing and future Choice Neighborhoods projects. Furthermore, given the scope and complexity of the Choice Neighborhoods design, the grantee cities will need to galvanize a long-term commitment of public will and resources to sustain the redevelopment well beyond the five-year grant period and put in place a high-capacity collaboration anchored by strong coordination and leadership from the mayor's office. The federal government will need to fortify its interagency coordination to leverage and align funding, streamline bureaucratic procedures and requirements, and broaden agency expertise across topical areas (e.g., education, workforce development, asset strategies). It will also need to require more extensive up-front planning from grantees on issues like informal social control, governance, and resident engagement and to make well-designed and timely technical assistance on these issues readily available.

Besides place-based efforts like Promise and Choice Neighborhoods (and the recently launched Promise Zones, which revives the Clinton-era Empowerment Zone strategy of packaging tax incentives, technical assistance, and other job creation strategies toward neighborhood revitalization), the stimulus funding that began in 2009 with passage of the American Recovery and Reinvestment Act has led to investments in infrastructure, education, and technology that have indirectly addressed the problems of urban poverty (what Hilary Silver calls Obama's "stealth urban policy").[41] In addition to place-based efforts that contribute to community revitalization and development and target investment in local institutions and local economic opportunity, policy needs to work at different levels to address poverty more broadly and more directly, including fueling living-wage employment, strengthening educational opportunity, offering opportunities to build wealth, and addressing the fundamental drivers of extreme social inequality.

Conclusion

Chicago's Plan for Transformation is the country's largest attempt at mixed-income public housing reform. The benefits to the city and its impact on neighborhood regeneration are notable: the ominous landscape of public housing towers is gone for good, former crisis zones of crime and violence are far safer and more stable, and vast tracts of concentrated poverty have been transformed into revitalizing communities. The real estate development community has certainly benefited from the infusion of resources and large-scale opportunities, although it has been a high-risk venture that some development companies have not survived. Higher-income residents have benefited from the "reclaiming" of the inner city as an option for those seeking attractive housing and an urban lifestyle near downtown amenities, though they have found the social environment challenging and though homeowners, like many across the nation, are having to ride out a decline in property values.

But what about the urban poor? It was their marginalization and exclusion that was the rallying cry for the $3.2 billion (and counting) Transformation. Drawing on our findings to weigh in on the debate between proponents and critics of the Plan for Transformation, we conclude that the shift to a market-driven approach to public housing reform has deployed precious public resources to provide only limited benefits to the vulnerable households displaced through the initiative. While acknowledging the clear need to change the 1999 status quo in public housing, the remarkable physical transformation of the target developments, and the improved circumstances of some individual households, the benefits to the urban poor in Chicago have not outweighed the tremendous operational and individual costs of the Transformation. Most relocated public housing families still live in great poverty in their destination neighborhoods, and the few who have returned to the redeveloped communities have not been effectively integrated or reaped the presumed benefits of integration. Furthermore, the sustainability of the Transformation is highly uncertain given the unfinished status of the mixed-income developments, the social and financial challenges that remain to be tackled, and the lack of detail and substance in the city's "recalibrated" plan for the next phase.

The Plan for Transformation has led to dramatic changes in the urban landscape and significant physical improvements in highly distressed neighborhoods formerly dominated by public housing. This achievement has required considerable political will and risk as well as extraordinary public- and private-sector resources and persistence. But these changes have not brought significant social and economic advantages for most relocated public housing residents, and considerable vital work remains to be done. Today's situation, where most relocated residents have reconcentrated in high-poverty neighborhoods and many of those who gained a place in mixed-income developments remain socially and economically marginalized, is not a strong platform for Chicago's future. To accept this outcome is to swap one version of isolation and exclusion for another, create new resentments that undermine social cohesion and social mobility, and risk disillusioning the general public about large-scale efforts at social transformation, thus unraveling the tenuous gains made by individuals and neighborhoods.

On a more hopeful note, those implementing mixed-income public housing redevelopment, both in future phases of the Chicago experience and where it is under way in other contexts, can learn from the challenges encountered so far. Efforts can be reshaped to attend to these challenges along the lines of the recommendations outlined above. Explicit recognition of both the promise and the limitations of these efforts can lay the groundwork for alternative orientations—including addressing poverty and inequality head on. And the resilience and fortitude of low-income families plus the dedication and commitment of development professionals, advocates, and activists can continue to drive the quest for effective solutions to urban poverty and for a more livable, just, and equitable urban reality.

Acknowledgments

This book represents the culmination of an eight-year journey that has been made possible with the support of many individuals and institutions. Above all we thank the hundreds of residents of Oakwood Shores, Park Boulevard, and Westhaven Park who allowed us into their homes, meetings, and community gatherings and shared their insights and perspectives about living in the new mixed-income developments replacing public housing in these neighborhoods.

We have been fortunate to have two fabulous project directors work with us in carrying out this project. Amy Khare joined the project in its design phase, helped launch and complete the first phase of data collection, analysis, and associated publications, and has remained a valued collaborator and a dear friend. Sara Voelker joined us as a research assistant, then directed the second phase of research and skillfully coordinated the development of the book manuscript, graciously adjusting her career plans so she could see the project through the very end of the grant period. Amy and Sarah were joined by an extensive, evolving group of project staff over time. Brenda Copley and Ranada Harrison helped coordinate fieldwork and conducted many hours of interviews and meeting observations. Our research assistants on the University of Chicago team have included Naomi Bartz, Marisa Berwald, Lia Bosma, Rachel Boyle, Julia Conte, Jim Crawford, Mike DiDomenico, Marnie Flores, Erin Kelley, Nicole Lasky, David LaSuer, Janet Li, Matt Maronick, Christopher Mills, Danielle Raudenbush, Hasan Reza, Michaeljit Sandhu, Florian Sichling, and Danielle Washington. Our

Case Western Reserve University team has included Taryn Gress, April Hirsh, Jung-Eun Kim, Jess Rudolph, and Michael Salwiesz. We also thank our anonymous reviewers and others we invited to read manuscript drafts; we appreciate their careful review and helpful suggestions. We are grateful to staff members at the University of Chicago Press for their interest in and support of this project, in particular our editor Tim Mennel, editorial associate Nora Devlin, Alice Bennett, and the broader team responsible for moving this book from manuscript to publication.

Our thanks also go to the executives and staff of the Chicago Housing Authority, who fully supported our research and periodically made themselves available to discuss the implications of our emerging findings. In particular we thank Cindy Blumenthal, Laura Broussard, Sharon Gist-Gilliam, Meghan Harte, Mary Howard, Latrice Jefferson, Lewis Jordan, Linda Kaiser, Anna Lee, Bill Little, Kellie O'Connell Miller, Terry Peterson, Ella Renfro, Gloria Seabrook, Andy Teitelman, Tim Veenstra, Bryce White, and Charles Woodyard.

We could not have conducted this project without the collaboration of the development teams at each of the mixed-income sites. In particular we thank Delrice Adams, Felicia Dawson, Bill Goldsmith, Vorricia Harvey, Toby Herr, Peter Levavi, James Miller, Lee Pratter, Rich Sciortino, Danielle Walters, Joseph Williams, and Lisa Young. A range of other civic and policy leaders were also generous with their time and support, including Julie Brown, Rita Fry, Andy Geer, Lawrence Grisham, Maria Hibbs, Jamie Kalven, Leroy Kennedy, Hoy McConnell, Alex Polikoff, Roberto Requejo, Robin Snyderman, and Bill Wilen. We also received valuable engagement and assistance from resident and community leaders at each of the developments and surrounding neighborhoods, including in particular Todd Barnett, Pat Dowell, Ernest Gates, Bernita Johnson-Gabriel, Amy Knapp, Shirley Newsome, Crystal Palmer, Andre Perrin, Toni Preckwinkle, Francine Washington, Greg Washington, and Sandra Young.

This project would also not have been possible without the generous funding provided by the John D. and Catherine T. MacArthur Foundation. We are particularly grateful to Alaina Harkness, Craig Howard, Ianna Kachoris, Susan Lloyd, Julia Stasch, and Michael Stegman. We also received significant support from the Annie E. Casey Foundation and would like to thank Ryan Chao, Salin Geevarghese, Bob Giloth, and Charles Rutheiser. Of course, the findings and conclusions presented here are ours alone and do not necessarily reflect the opinions of the funders of this research.

Finally, we are both deeply grateful to our wives and children—Me'lani, Layla, Malik, and Ayande Joseph and Kit, Hannah, and Nick Chaskin—as well as to our extended families, friends, and colleagues for their ongoing understanding, engagement, encouragement, and support. A special thank you to colleagues at the University of Ghana at Legon where Mark spent a sabbatical semester as we were finishing work on this manuscript.

Appendix: Methods and Data

This book takes a mixed-method, comparative case study approach, drawing on document analysis, administrative data, public source neighborhood data, and, most centrally, extensive fieldwork on three mixed-income communities replacing public housing complexes. Our fieldwork, conducted over the course of six years, included in-depth interviews with a range of people living in these new communities—relocated public housing residents, other subsidized renters, renters of market-rate units, and homeowners living in both market-rate and "affordable" housing—as well as development professionals and community key informants involved in some way in the Transformation at either the local or the citywide level. It also included observations of a broad range of meetings and community events and, in the third wave of data collection, focus group discussions with residents of different incomes and housing tenures. Our emphasis on fieldwork and in-depth qualitative interviews was guided by our desire to understand, in nuanced detail, the nature of the communities being built on the footprint of public housing developments and to appreciate the lived experience of both relocated public housing residents and their neighbors in these new communities. Through this detailed exploration we sought in particular to interrogate and interpret the ideas, inputs, processes, and dynamics—the "hows" and "whys"—behind the effort to integrate public housing residents into new, mixed-income communities as a response to concentrated urban poverty.

Study Sites

Our analysis focuses on three sites—Oakwood Shores, Park Boulevard, and Westhaven Park—which together provide variations in design, developer characteristics, organizational arrangements, community-building strategies, models of management and service provision, and neighborhood characteristics that allow for comparative analysis of the implementation of mixed-income development and of the experiences of residents. Oakwood Shores replaces Ida B. Wells Homes/Madden Park, the oldest public housing development in Chicago. It is the largest of the three sites and the only one that embodies the transformation of a primarily low-rise development. Park Boulevard represents the transformation of Stateway Gardens, a high-rise public housing development along the State Street corridor. Its plan is unique in that it calls for a larger proportion of homeownership (42 percent) than the other sites, and it includes a new nonprofit organization to manage social services and community building in the development. The redevelopment of Henry Horner Homes into Westhaven Park started before the Plan for Transformation. Because units produced in the initial pre-Transformation phase were only for public housing residents, ultimately the new development will have a larger proportion of former public housing residents (63 percent) than any other site. It is also the only one of the three that is on the West Side of Chicago and one of only two mixed-income developments in the city that operate under a consent decree offering greater legal protections to relocated public housing residents.

Resident Interviews

In-depth interviews were conducted with a panel of eighty-five residents living in the mixed-income developments. Residents to be interviewed were randomly selected from occupancy lists in each development. Respondents included residents across income levels and housing tenures: thirty-five relocated public housing residents, ten renters of affordable units, eleven renters of market-rate units, fifteen owners of affordable units,[1] and fourteen owners of market-rate units. Resident respondents at Oakwood Shores and Westhaven Park were interviewed

Table A.1 Resident Characteristics, Interview Sample

	Overall	RPH	TC RTR	TC FS	MKT RTR	MKT FS
Number of respondents	85	35	10	15	11	14
Female (%)	74.1	88.6	100.0	60.0	63.6	42.9
Race						
African American (%)	83.5	100.0	100.0	60.0	100.0	42.8
White (%)	8.2	0	0	20.0	0	28.6
Other (%)	8.3	0	0	20.0	0	28.6
Average age	43	44	46	37	46	38
Married (%)	20.2	5.7	20.0	26.7	30.0	42.9
Education level						
High school graduate or GED (%)	82.4	60.0	90.0	100.0	100.0	100.0
Bachelor's degree or higher (%)	40.0	0	20.0	80.0	63.6	92.9
Employed (%)	69.4	42.9	70.0	93.3	90.9	92.9
With children in household (%)	48.2	65.7	50.0	20.0	36.4	42.9
Annual income						
Under $20,000 (%)	40.0	85.7	40.0	0	0	0
Over $70,000 (%)	21.2	0	10.0	33.3	27.3	64.3

RPH: Relocated public housing residents in units with a public housing subsidy.
TC RTR: Renters in nonpublic housing units subsidized with tax credits.
TC FS: Owners in units subsidized with tax credits.
MKT RTR: Renters in units priced at market rate.
MKT FS: Owners in units priced at market rate.

twice, approximately eighteen months apart, in 2007 and 2008. Owing to construction and occupancy delays at Park Boulevard, residents there were interviewed only once, in 2008.

Demographic information from the random sample of residents interviewed suggests that relocated public housing residents are predominantly African American and are most likely to have children living with them (see table A.1). They have relatively low levels of education and employment, and most have an annual income of less than $20,000. Like relocated public housing residents, renters of affordable units are likely to be African American and low-income, with modestly higher levels of education and employment, and are nearly as likely to have children in the household. Owners of affordable units are more likely than market-rate renters but less likely than market-rate owners to earn more than $70,000 annually, and like market-rate owners are in general highly educated. They are also more likely than market-rate owners, but less likely than renters of market-rate units, to be African American.

Resident interviews were guided by a semi-structured instrument comprising primarily open-ended questions covering a broad range of topics, including the respondents' satisfaction with their units, development, and neighborhood; their experience with and assessment of social interactions within and across income levels; their evaluation of community dynamics; their experience with rules, safety, and public behavior; their engagement in development and neighborhood activities, meetings, and organizations; their understanding of how decisions get made and who participates in these decisions; and their perspectives on neighborhood change and how living in the mixed-income community has affected them personally. Respondents were also asked a limited number of closed-response questions on, for example, social interaction and demographics.

Interviews were audiotaped digitally and transcribed in their entirety, then coded for analysis based on a set of deductively derived thematic codes and refined based on inductive interim analysis. Coding and analysis were done using NVivo qualitative analysis software. Interview transcripts were initially double-coded to ensure intercoder reliability, and then every fifth coded transcript was reviewed to ensure continued reliability. Summary matrices of responses were created to allow for systematic comparison of perspectives across resident "type" as defined by site, income level, and housing tenure.

Focus Groups

In 2011, we conducted focus groups with a new sample of 102 residents. Invitations to participate were mailed to a random sample of residents drawn from updated developer occupancy lists, and slots were reserved for the first ones to respond. Participants were grouped according to site, income, and housing tenure and included fifty relocated public housing residents, twenty-one affordable renters, seventeen market-rate renters, and fourteen affordable and market-rate owners. Two groups of relocated public housing residents were convened at each site. Affordable and market-rate owners were combined to form one group at each site because they were demographically similar and described similar experiences and perspectives in the resident interviews. Groups of affordable and market-rate renters were held only at Oakwood Shores and Westhaven Park because there were no occupied affordable or market-rate rental units at Park Boulevard at the time.

Demographic information from the sample of focus group participants is very similar to that from the interview sample, with a few exceptions. Employment rates are lower overall and for most groups, though relocated public housing residents are still the least likely to be employed (43 percent) and market-rate renters, affordable owners, and market-rate owners have the highest employment rates (75 percent, 100 percent, and 89 eighty-nine respectively). Relocated public housing residents and affordable renters in the focus group sample were also less likely to have children in their households than their counterparts in the interview sample (44 percent and 43 percent), though more likely than other resident groups in the focus group sample.

A focus group discussion guide was developed based on findings from the two waves of resident interviews and designed to explore residents' perspectives as openly as possible while ensuring comparability across groups. Topics explored included residents' expectations and experiences of living in a mixed-income development, the nature of community dynamics within the development, the relationship between the development and the surrounding neighborhood, opportunities for residents to participate in groups and organizations and their impact in the community, and residents' outlook for the future of the development and neighborhood.

Focus groups were audiotaped digitally, and the facilitator produced summary memos for each group based on a careful review of the audiotape. The summary memos were then coded for analysis using NVivo software and the coding and analysis scheme described above.

Key Informant Interviews

In addition to resident interviews and focus groups, we conducted in-depth interviews with a panel of eighty-five professional key informants over the course of three waves in 2007, 2008, and 2010. These individuals were selected because they were either members of the development teams (developers, service providers, and property managers at the mixed-income sites), key community leaders and informants (such as service providers, community activists, and public officials active in the neighborhoods where the developments are being built), or informants knowledgeable about the Transformation at the city level (including officials with the CHA and public housing activists working on the Transformation).

Professional stakeholder interviews were also guided by a semi-structured instrument comprising open-ended questions about a range of topics including the respondents' functions within the development or community, their assessment of the nature of interaction and community-building among residents, their sense of their own role (if any) in helping to promote a well-functioning community, their expectations and assessment of the relationship between the development and the surrounding neighborhood, and any particular challenges they experienced or observed as part of the larger process. They were also asked to reflect on their expectations and goals for mixed-income development and the policy context within which the Transformation was taking place.

Interviews were audiotaped digitally and transcribed in their entirety, then coded for analysis using NVivo software and the coding scheme described above for resident interviews. Summary matrices of responses were created to allow for systematic comparison of perspectives across respondent "types" as defined by site and respondent role.

Field Observations

Data from the field observation of community meetings, programs, and events were used to contextualize interview and focus group data within the specific dynamics of each site, and they provided both a check on and new insight into the dynamics described by the sample of respondents. We conducted approximately five hundred observations during six years of fieldwork at the three mixed-income developments. These included on-site meetings of (primarily low-income) renters organized and facilitated by property management to discuss safety, rules, and services and to provide a forum for residents to voice their concerns, and also meetings of homeowner associations responsible for managing and maintaining the for-sale property at the developments. We observed broader neighborhood meetings as well, including new and existing groups organized to address issues such as business development, youth leadership, and safety and security. We also observed the operations of governing bodies responsible for aspects of development oversight, including working group meetings (responsible for monitoring development plans and implementation and comprising representatives from the CHA, the development team, property management, public housing advocates, elected officials, and public housing resident leadership); management team meetings (meetings of development, property management, and service providers to review relocated public housing residents' lease compliance, working-to-meet eligibility criteria, and social service needs); and meetings of the Horner Residents Committee (a group of public housing resident representatives and their legal counsel responsible for approving all decisions related to the redevelopment process at Westhaven Park). Finally, we observed a number of public meetings and events, including Community Alternative Policing Strategy (CAPS) meetings (organized by police in each beat to provide information on crime trends and respond to residents' concerns about crime and quality of life issues) and Park Advisory Council meetings (organized by the Chicago Park District and facilitated by area residents to address issues of safety and programming in neighborhood park space), as well as community-building events organized by development teams and their partners, such as community cleanups, beautification projects, and social gatherings.

All observations yielded field notes that documented the nature of the event, its content, the number and types of participants, and participant dynamics during the course of the event. Field notes were coded and analyzed using NVivo software and the coding scheme described above. For periodic meetings (working group, management team, resident meetings, CAPS), field notes were also synthesized into narrative memos that described the content, participation, and changing dynamics at these meetings over time.

Document Review

Documents relevant to the progress of the Transformation and the three mixed-income developments were collected and reviewed over the course of the study. These documents were produced by the CHA, the developers, their partners, and other stakeholders, and they included annual CHA plans and reports, maps, marketing materials, community newsletters, and progress reports on site build-out, unit sales, and service provision. We also conducted bimonthly reviews of public media sources for articles related to the development sites, communities, and the Transformation. We used these documents to track key events and decisions at each of the sites and for the Transformation citywide. We also reviewed historical documents, including city and neighborhood plans for the areas encompassing and surrounding the development sites.

Administrative Data

In addition to the qualitative research conducted at the three mixed-income developments, we partnered with Chapin Hall at the University of Chicago to complete a quantitative analysis of nearly seventeen thousand households living in CHA housing at the start of the Transformation.[2] We used CHA leaseholder records and state administrative data to compare the demographics and well-being of households living in different housing contexts at the start of the Transformation and ten years later.

The CHA provided data files containing residential histories, demographic characteristics of individual child and adult household members (birth date, gender, relation to household head), and current address and subsidized housing type as of November 2008 for all households that were granted a right to return to CHA housing owing to their active leaseholder status in October 1999, when the Plan for Transformation was announced. Additional household composition data were obtained from the US Department of Housing and Urban Development's (HUD's) Multifamily Tenant Characteristics System (MTCS). HUD matched the November 2008 CHA leaseholder records to 1999 CHA leaseholder records in the MTCS and provided individual-level records for all child and adult household members as of 1999.

Individual-level records for 1999 and 2008 were linked through probabilistic matching to the integrated database (IDB) at Chapin Hall. The IDB contains administrative records from a variety of state and local agencies in Illinois, including the Illinois Department of Children and Family Services, the Illinois Department of Human Services, the Illinois Department of Employment Security, and the Cook County Juvenile Court. These data were used to measure labor force participation, receipt of Temporary Assistance for Needy Families (TANF) and food stamps, and involvement with child welfare services (child abuse or neglect investigations, foster care placements) and the juvenile justice system.

Neighborhood-Level Data

We also used data from several public sources to track broader neighborhood change over the course of the Transformation. Indicators evaluated include crime rates, home purchase loans, small business loans, foreclosures, population and socioeconomic characteristics (race, educational attainment, employment, and income) and housing characteristics (tenure and residential stability). For population and housing characteristics, we compared change over time at two geographical levels for each site. The "development footprint" level is constructed using census block data and follows the actual boundaries of the developments. The "surrounding area" level is constructed using census tract data, and the boundaries include census tracts containing and contiguous to the development footprint except those that lie across a major physical barrier, such as an interstate highway, major thoroughfare, or railway (see figs. A.1–A.3). For home purchase loans, small business loans, and population and housing data not available at the census block level (educational attainment, employment, income, and residential stability), we analyzed the combined development footprint and surrounding area levels.

Crime data were retrieved from the city of Chicago data portal, an online catalog of datasets from city departments, including the Chicago Police Department. Reported crime in police beats containing the three mixed-income developments and the city as a whole was collected for the period January 1, 2001, through December 31, 2011. Incidents were then coded into three groups according to Illinois Uniform Crime Reporting classification numbers: violent crime (homicide, criminal sexual assault, robbery, and aggravated assault and battery), property crime (burglary, theft, motor vehicle theft, and arson), and "quality of life" crime (vandalism, defacement of property, narcotics possession and distribution, prostitution, and gambling). Annual and quarterly crime rates were calculated for each group and development site and the city of Chicago using population data from the US Census and American Community Survey.

Information on home purchase loans, reported under the Home Mortgage Disclosure Act, was obtained from the Federal Financial Institutions Examination Council (FFIEC). The number and amount of bank-approved and applicant-accepted loans on one- to four-family dwellings was totaled for census tracts containing the footprint and surrounding area of each mixed-income development. Data were reported annually and collected for the years 1999 through 2011.

Information on small business loans, reported in accordance with the Community Reinvestment Act, was also obtained from the FFIEC. The number and amount of small business loans originating in census tracts containing the footprint and surrounding area of each mixed-income development were totaled for the years 1996 through 2011.

Data on foreclosures were collected by Record Information Services and obtained from the Woodstock Institute data portal. Annual foreclosure filings per thousand mortgageable properties were reported for the years 2008 to 2012 in community areas containing each of the

A.1   Oakwood Shores, development footprint and surrounding area.

A.2   Park Boulevard, development footprint and surrounding area.

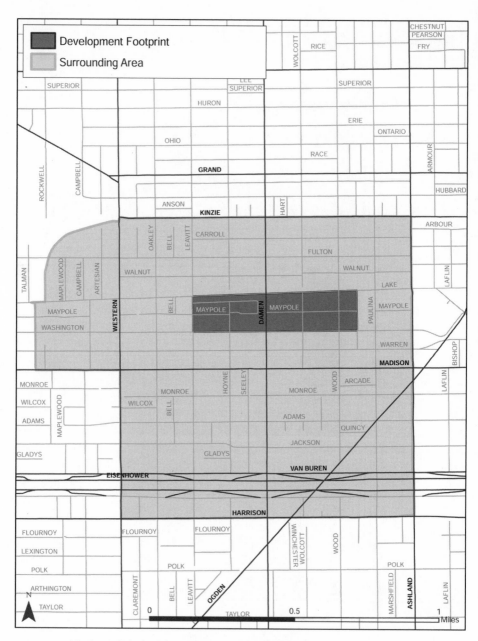

A.3 Westhaven Park, development footprint and surrounding area.

mixed-income developments. Annual rankings of foreclosure rates in these communities were calculated based on the foreclosure rates in all seventy-seven Chicago community areas.

Population and housing characteristics were obtained from the 1990, 2000, and 2010 US Census and the 2010 American Community Survey five-year estimates. Population counts and socioeconomic measures were used to calculate the total population, racial composition, educational attainment for the population twenty-five years and older (percentage high school graduate/GED recipient, percentage bachelor's degree or higher), unemployment rate for the population sixteen years and older, and median household income (reported in 2010 dollars). Unit counts and housing measures were used to calculate the housing tenure (percentage owner-occupied, percentage renter-occupied), vacancy rates, and residential stability (households moved in previous five years). Indicators were calculated for the development footprint and surrounding area levels for 1990, 2000, and 2010.

Confidentiality

Throughout the book, we include direct quotations from residents and key informants. To protect respondents' confidentiality, we identify them only by their income level and housing tenure (and, when relevant, race) and by the development where they live or work; we identify key informants by their professional roles. The identity of individuals making statements in closed meetings that we were allowed to observe with the agreement of the participants is also protected. Public figures who are important to the history of these neighborhoods and developments are occasionally named in the context of their past contributions.

Notes

1. The residents in these conversations had lived in the new development for from at least one year to as many as four years. All names are pseudonyms. CHA refers to the Chicago Housing Authority.

CHAPTER ONE

1. Hirsch, *Making the Second Ghetto*; Massey and Kanaiaupuni, "Public Housing and the Concentration of Poverty."
2. Though not a state, Puerto Rico, a United States territory generally included in the definition of the United States, has the second largest public housing authority, after New York City.
3. See, for example, Bowly, *Poorhouse*; Hirsch, *Making the Second Ghetto*; Hunt, *Blueprint for Disaster*; Popkin et al., *Hidden War*; Venkatesh, *American Project*.
4. See, for example, Kotlowitz, *There Are No Children Here*; Wiseman, *Public Housing*.
5. Hunt, *Blueprint for Disaster*; Popkin et al., *Hidden War*.
6. "The Plan for Transformation," Chicago Housing Authority, accessed September 10, 2012, http://www.thecha.org/pages /the_plan_for_transformation/22.php.
7. Indeed, although earlier efforts at public housing reform— most notably the Gautreaux program in Chicago—were organized around explicit goals for *racial* desegregation, the framing of contemporary policies, including the federal HOPE VI and Moving to Opportunity programs (discussed below) and the Plan for Transformation, are essentially silent on the issue of race, focusing instead on income

integration—even though in many cities, Chicago among them, the public housing population is largely if not exclusively African American. Khare, Joseph, and Chaskin, "Enduring Significance of Race"; Polikoff, *Waiting for Gautreaux*; Turner, Popkin, and Rawlings, *Public Housing and the Legacy of Segregation.*

8. Bennett, Smith, and Wright, *Where Are Poor People to Live?* Bloom, *Public Housing That Worked*; Briggs, Popkin, and Goering, *Moving to Opportunity*; Goetz, *Clearing the Way*; Goetz, *New Deal Ruins*; Hunt, *Blueprint for Disaster*; Rubinowitz and Rosenbaum, *Crossing the Class and Color Lines*; Vale, *From the Puritans to the Projects*; Vale, *Purging the Poorest.*

9. Klemek, *Transatlantic Collapse of Urban Renewal*; Mollenkopf, *Contested City.*

10. Bluestone and Harrison, *Deindustrialization of America.*

11. World War I also increased industrial production and temporarily interrupted immigration flows from Europe, which had provided the main source of industrial labor, creating opportunities that began to draw southern blacks to the North. Grossman, *Land of Hope.*

12. Ibid.

13. Hirsch, *Making the Second Ghetto.*

14. Massey and Denton, *American Apartheid*; Squires, *From Redlining to Reinvestment*; Sugrue, *Origins of the Urban Crisis.*

15. Jackson, *Crabgrass Frontier.*

16. Wilson, *Truly Disadvantaged.*

17. The processes of deindustrialization and demographic change, including the relation between "white flight" from the cities and the dynamics of race, racial tension, and racist policy and community responses are obviously highly complex. On deindustrialization in the United States generally, see Bluestone and Harrison, *Deindustrialization of America.* On the effects of economic restructuring on the inner city and concentrated poverty, see Wilson, *Truly Disadvantaged*, and Wilson, *When Work Disappears.* On the role of racial segregation see Massey and Denton, *American Apartheid.* For an in-depth analysis of the dynamics among race, protest, and deindustrialization in Detroit—arguably the most dramatic example of deindustrialization and urban decline in the United States—see Sugrue, *Origins of the Urban Crisis.*

18. Doussard, Peck, and Theodore, "After Deindustrialization"; Jargowsky, *Poverty and Place.*

19. Massey and Denton, *American Apartheid.*

20. E.g., Kasarda, "City Jobs"; Ricketts and Sawhill, "Defining and Measuring the Underclass"; Wilson, *Truly Disadvantaged.*

21. Wilson, *Truly Disadvantaged.*

22. Fair market rent standards are set annually by HUD using data from the Decennial Census, American Community Survey, American Housing Survey, and telephone surveys. They are specific to the geographic area,

include rent and tenant-paid utilities, and represent the amount below which 40 percent of standard-quality units are rented. The FY2013 fair market rent for a two-bedroom unit in Chicago was set at $966 (see "Fair Market Rents," HUD, accessed November 26, 2013, www.huduser.org /portal/datasets/fmr.html).

23. Jane Roessner, *A Decent Place to Live*; Wyly and Hammel, "Capital's Metropolis."

24. Katz, "Origins of HOPE VI."

25. Omnibus Consolidated Rescissions and Appropriations Act of 1996, Pub. L. No. 104–134, 110 Stat. 1321 (1996).

26. Arthurson, "Creating Inclusive Communities"; Joseph, Chaskin, and Webber, "Addressing Poverty through Mixed-Income Development"; Kearns and Mason, "Mixed Tenure Communities and Neighbourhood Quality"; Kleit, "Role of Neighborhood Social Networks." As we shall discuss, this integration imperative also has its critics, who question the underlying assumptions that posit the need for higher-income residents in order to achieve beneficial conditions for low-income families; Pattillo, *Black on the Block*; Vale, "Ideological Origins of Affordable Home Ownership Efforts."

27. Hunt, *Blueprint for Disaster*.

28. About 30 percent of the 25,000 planned replacement units will be in mixed-income developments, thus establishing an upper bound on the number of possible returnees. As of 2008, only about 13 percent of the nearly 10,000 residents still living in CHA (non-senior) subsidized housing were living in mixed-income redeveloped sites, compared with 40 percent living in voucher units, 32 percent in traditional, renovated public housing units, and 16 percent in scattered-site housing. In addition, over 6,000 residents with the "right to return" were no longer accounted for in the CHA system. The circumstances of half of these were unknown by the CHA; others had been evicted, were deceased, were living in unsubsidized housing but waiting to return, or chose to remain in unsubsidized housing. A few had moved to senior housing. See Chaskin et al., "Public Housing Transformation." These numbers, it is important to note, include only *leaseholders*; individuals living in CHA units but not on the lease, such as relatives and friends in need of housing, are not included and have no right to return. The number of people this latter category represents is unknown, but such "doubling up" is common among low-income families who have trouble finding affordable housing. See Skobba and Goetz, "Mobility Decisions of Very Low-Income Households."

29. About two-thirds of the total investment in the Transformation (approximately $3.2 billion as of December 2009) has been in the mixed-income developments, and about one-third has been in rehabilitation of senior and family public housing. The total cost of vouchers in 2009 was approximately $505 million, including both existing vouchers and the expansion of vouchers under the Transformation. See Chicago Housing Authority,

Plan for Transformation at 10; Chicago Housing Authority, *FY2009 Moving to Work Annual Report*.

30. Vale and Graves, *Chicago Housing Authority's Plan for Transformation*, 40.

31. We discuss the complex financing of mixed-income developments in chapter 4. For simplicity, we refer to three types of units throughout the book: replacement public housing units, which are financed through an ongoing Annual Contributions Contract with the Department of Housing and Urban Development; "affordable units," which are subsidized, often with the use of federal low-income housing tax credits; and market-rate units, which have no subsidy. We will use this categorization, even though replacement public housing units are also certainly meant to be "affordable" to low-income households.

32. Chicago Housing Authority, *Annual Plan for Transformation FY2003*, 2.

33. Epp, "Emerging Strategies for Revitalizing Public Housing Communities"; Naparstek, Dooley, and Smith, *Community Building in Public Housing*; Von Hoffman, "High Ambitions."

34. Cameron, "Gentrification, Housing Redifferentiation and Urban Regeneration."

35. Initial policy requirements for one-to-one replacement of demolished units were repealed by Congress in 1998, at the same time the HOPE VI program was authorized. Thus, replacement units have been planned with the intent to replace, in essence, only those units *occupied* (as opposed to those in existence) at the time of the announcement of the Plan. See Hunt, *Blueprint for Disaster*; Smith, "Chicago Housing Authority's Plan for Transformation."

36. Popkin et al., "Decade of HOPE VI"; Vale and Graves, *Chicago Housing Authority's Plan for Transformation*; Venkatesh, *American Project*; Venkatesh and Celimli, "Tearing Down the Community."

37. In 1996, residents of the Cabrini-Green development filed suit against the CHA, contending that residents had been denied the right to participate in the planning for the site's redevelopment under a HOPE VI grant. Demolition was halted for four years while resident leaders and the CHA negotiated a consent decree that established a plan to redevelop the site as a mixed-income community; Wright, Wheelock, and Steele, "Case of Cabrini-Green." In response to another resident lawsuit filed in 2003, the CHA agreed to modify the relocation process to avoid steering displaced residents to majority African American communities characterized by high rates of poverty and crime, low-performing schools, and inadequate services; Fry, *Independent Monitor's Report*.

38. Bennett, Smith, and Wright, *Where Are Poor People to Live*? Briggs, "Moving Up versus Moving Out"; Joseph, Chaskin, and Webber, "Addressing Poverty through Mixed-Income Development"; Kleit, "Role of Neighborhood Social Networks;" Pattillo, *Black on the Block*.

39. See, for example, Bennett, "Downtown Restructuring"; Fraser and Kick,

"Role of Public, Private, Non-profit and Community Sectors"; Lees, "Gentrification and Social Mixing"; Peck, Theodore, and Brenner, "Neoliberal Urbanism"; Smith and Stovall, "'Coming Home' to New Homes and New Schools."

40. E.g., Hackworth, *Neoliberal City.*

41. Peck, Theodore, and Brenner, "Neoliberal Urbanism," 58.

42. Goetz, "Where Have All the Towers Gone?" Hyra, *New Urban Renewal*; Hyra, "Conceptualizing the New Urban Renewal"; Smith, "Chicago Housing Authority's Plan for Transformation."

43. Leaseholders who were living in CHA housing at the time the Plan for Transformation was announced have a legal guarantee of one of four permanent housing choices: a newly built unit in a mixed-income development, a permanent Housing Choice voucher, a rehabilitated scattered-site unit, or a rehabilitated unit in a traditional CHA development. After residents have signed a lease for one of these units, they receive a notice that their right to return has been satisfied and they are guaranteed assistance with subsequent moves only if there are changes to household composition; Chicago Housing Authority, *CHA Leaseholder Housing Choice and Relocation Rights Contract.*

44. Chicago Housing Authority, *FY2013 Moving to Work Annual Report*; Chicago Housing Authority, *FY2014 Moving to Work Annual Plan.*

45. We distinguish here between "leaseholders" and the broader population of people living in CHA housing at the time the Transformation was announced, many of whom, as "unofficial" or "unauthorized" residents, were without rights to relocation assistance or future public housing subsidies of any sort. Even among leaseholders *with* a right to return, over 3,000 (about 18 percent of the pre-Transformation public housing families living in non-senior housing developments) remain unaccounted for by the CHA (Chaskin et al., "Public Housing Transformation").

46. Vale and Graves, *Chicago Housing Authority's Plan for Transformation.*

47. Briggs, Popkin, and Goering, *Moving to Opportunity*; Feins and Shroder, "Moving to Opportunity"; Kling et al., "Moving to Opportunity and Tranquility"; Ludwig et al., "What Can We Learn about Neighborhood Effects?" Orr et al., *Moving to Opportunity: Interim Impacts Evaluation.*

48. Briggs, Popkin, and Goering, *Moving to Opportunity*; Oakley and Burchfield, "Out of the Projects, Still in the Hood"; Rosenbaum and Zuberi, "Comparing Residential Mobility Programs"; Sampson, "Moving to Inequality"; Varady and Walker, "Using Housing Vouchers to Move to the Suburbs"; Varady et al., "Geographic Concentration of Housing Vouchers."

49. Popkin et al., "Public Housing Transformation and Crime."

50. In some larger redevelopments, some public housing units have remained in place, principally in response to legal action that led to their redevelopment (e.g., at the Henry Horner Homes) or retention (e.g., at Cabrini Green).

51. Chaskin and Joseph, "Building 'Community' in Mixed-Income Developments"; Chaskin, Khare, and Joseph, "Participation, Deliberation, and Decision Making"; Graves, "Structuring of Urban Life."
52. Atlanta and San Francisco are notable here as the other cities engaging in citywide public housing transformation strategies.
53. On "social mixing" policies connected with public (or "social") housing regeneration, see, e.g., Arthurson, "Creating Inclusive Communities"; Atkinson and Kintrea, "Owner-Occupation, Social Mix, and Neighbourhood Impacts"; August, "Social Mix and Canadian Public Housing Redevelopment"; Bailey et al., *Creating and Sustaining Mixed Income Communities*; Berube, *Mixed Communities in England*; Bolt and van Kempen, "Successful Mixing?" Lees, "Gentrification and Social Mixing"; Musterd and Andersson, "Housing Mix, Social Mix, and Social Opportunities"; Ruming, Mee, and McGuirk, "Questioning the Rhetoric of Social Mix."
54. Klemek, *Transatlantic Collapse of Urban Renewal*.
55. Doussard, Peck, and Theodore, "After Deindustrialization," 186.
56. Abu-Lughod, *America's Global Cities*.
57. Doussard, Peck, and Theodore, "After Deindustrialization."
58. Hirsch, *Making the Second Ghetto*; Hunt, *Blueprint for Disaster*; Rosenbaum, Stroh, and Flynn, "Lake Parc Place"; Wyly and Hammel, "Capital's Metropolis."
59. Mathieson et al., "Social Exclusion: Meaning, Measurement and Experience;" Sen, "Social Exclusion: Concept, Application, and Scrutiny"; Silver, "Social Exclusion and Social Solidarity."
60. Schram, Fording, and Soss, "Neo-liberal Poverty Governance."
61. *Incorporation* here is distinguished from terms like *assimilation* and *acculturation*, both of which imply a somewhat unidirectional process of accommodation to majority cultural expectations and "becoming like" or "fitting into" the dominant culture. Integration and incorporation, in contrast, have been embraced as more value-neutral terms, though each with somewhat different emphases. The distinctions among these terms remain a topic of some debate. See, for example, Cook, "Is Incorporation of Unauthorized Immigrants Possible?" Ramakrishnan, "Incorporation versus Assimilation"; and Rumbaut, "Assimilation and Its Discontents."

CHAPTER TWO

1. Indeed, in Atlanta these reforms have essentially led to the end of the city's "traditional" public housing—properties built, managed, and maintained by the public housing authority. With the exception of some seniors still in public housing, eligible families and individuals will receive subsidies either as vouchers or attached to units in mixed-income developments. See Atlanta Housing Authority, *FY2005 Moving to Work Annual Plan*.

2. Vale, *Purging the Poorest*, 30. See also Bennett, "Downtown Restructuring," and Goetz, *Clearing the Way*.
3. Smith and Stovall, " 'Coming Home' to New Homes and New Schools," 135; see also Bennett, "Downtown Restructuring"; Bridge, Butler, and Lees, *Mixed Communities*; Fraser and Kick, "Role of Public, Private, Non-profit and Community Sectors"; Imbroscio, " '[U]nited and Actuated by Some Common Impulse of Passion'"; and Smith, "Mixed-Income Communities."
4. Soss, Fording, and Schram, *Disciplining the Poor*.
5. An earlier elaboration of the relation between these theories and the rationale for mixed-income development responses to urban poverty and the failures of public housing can be found in Joseph, Chaskin, and Webber, "Theoretical Basis for Addressing Poverty through Mixed-Income Development."
6. See, for example, Booth, *Life and Labour of the People in London*; Burgess, "Growth of the City"; Mayhew, *London Labour and the London Poor*; Shaw and McKay, *Juvenile Delinquency*; Suttles, *Social Order of the Slum*; Thrasher, *Gang*; and Zorbaugh, *Gold Coast and the Slum*.
7. Wilson, *Truly Disadvantaged*.
8. Ibid.; Wilson, *When Work Disappears*.
9. Bell, *Faces at the Bottom of the Well*; Hacker, *Two Nations*; Massey and Denton, *American Apartheid*; Neckerman and Kirschenman, "Hiring Strategies, Racial Bias, and Inner-City Workers"; Pager, "Mark of a Criminal Record."
10. Jargowsky, *Poverty and Place*; Kasarda, "Urban Change and Minority Opportunities"; Ricketts and Sawhill, "Defining and Measuring the Underclass"; Wilson, *Truly Disadvantaged*; Wilson, *When Work Disappears*.
11. Wilson, *Truly Disadvantaged*, 60.
12. Wilson, "Cycles of Deprivation"; Wilson, *Truly Disadvantaged*.
13. Among the most influential of these conservative critiques was Charles Murray's *Losing Ground*. See also Mead, *New Politics of Poverty*, and Wilson, *Thinking about Crime*. On the culture of poverty and its critiques, see Duneier, *Slim's Table*; Katz, *"Underclass" Debate*; Lewis, *La Vida*; Lewis, "Culture of Poverty"; Newman, *No Shame in My Game*; Small and Newman, "Urban Poverty after *The Truly Disadvantaged*"; and Valentine, *Culture and Poverty*.
14. Moynihan, *Negro Family*. In more recent work, Wilson revisits the importance of culture in sustaining racial inequality and expresses his determination to "take culture seriously as one of the explanatory variables in the study of race and urban poverty." Wilson, *More Than Just Race*, 3.
15. See also Anderson, *Streetwise*.
16. Akers et al., "Social Learning and Deviant Behavior"; Bandura, *Social Learning Theory*; Brewer and Wann, "Observational Learning Effectiveness."
17. Joseph, Chaskin, and Webber, "Theoretical Basis for Addressing Poverty through Mixed-Income Development"; Putnam, *Making Democracy Work*.

18. See, for example, Duneier, *Slim's Table*; Hannerz, *Soulside*; Katz, *"Underclass Debate"*; Newman, *No Shame in My Game*; Small and Newman, "Urban Poverty after *The Truly Disadvantaged*"; and Valentine, *Culture and Poverty*.

19. Duneier, *Slim's Table*; Joseph, Chaskin, and Webber, "Theoretical Basis for Addressing Poverty through Mixed-Income Development"; Newman, *No Shame in My Game*.

20. Rosenbaum, Stroh, and Flynn, "Lake Parc Place."

21. See, for example, Brooks-Gunn, Duncan, and Aber, *Neighborhood Poverty*, vol. 1; Elliott et al., "Effects of Neighborhood Disadvantage on Adolescent Development"; Jencks and Mayer, "Social Consequences of Growing Up in a Poor Neighborhood"; Leventhal and Brooks-Gunn, "Neighborhoods They Live In"; Rankin and Quane, "Social Contexts and Urban Adolescent Outcomes"; and Sampson, *Great American City*.

22. See, for example, the debate between Ludwig et al., "What Can We Learn about Neighborhood Effects," and Sampson, "Moving to Inequality"; Jencks and Mayer, "Social Consequences of Growing Up in a Poor Neighborhood"; and Sampson, *Great American City*.

23. For reviews, see Gephart, "Neighborhoods and Communities as Contexts for Development," and Sampson, Morenoff, and Gannon-Rowley, "Assessing 'Neighborhood Effects.'" On the relation between neighborhood poverty and high rates of child abuse, for example, see Coulton et al., "Community Level Factors and Child Maltreatment Rates," and Garbarino and Crouter, "Defining the Community Context for Parent-Child Relations." On neighborhood effects and teenage and out-of-wedlock births, see Anderson, "Neighborhood Effects on Teenage Pregnancy"; Coulton and Pandey, "Geographic Concentration of Poverty"; and Crane, "Epidemic Theory of Ghettos." On the relation between neighborhood context and school achievement and development, see Chase-Lansdale et al., "Neighborhood and Family Influences"; Crane, "Epidemic Theory of Ghettos"; and Darling and Steinberg, "Community Influences on Adolescent Achievement and Deviance." On neighborhood effects, adolescent behavior, delinquency, and crime, see Coulton and Pandey, "Geographic Concentration of Poverty"; Sampson and Groves, "Community Structure and Crime"; and Spencer et al., "Neighborhood and Family Influences."

24. Sampson, "What 'Community' Supplies."

25. For reviews see Chaskin, "Perspectives on Neighborhood and Community"; Chaskin, "Theories of Community"; and Sampson, "What 'Community' Supplies."

26. Firey, "Sentiment and Symbolism"; Hunter, *Symbolic Communities*; Park, "Human Ecology."

27. Kasarda and Janowitz, "Community Attachment in Mass Society"; Shaw and McKay, *Juvenile Delinquency*; Suttles, *Social Construction of Communities*; Warren, *Community in America*.

28. Sampson, "What 'Community' Supplies"; Sampson, Morenoff, and Gannon-Rowley, "Assessing 'Neighborhood Effects'"; Small, *Villa Victoria.*

29. DeFilippis, Fisher, and Shragge, "Neither Romance nor Regulation"; Molotch, "City as a Growth Machine"; Sites, Chaskin, and Parks, "Reframing Community Practice for the 21st Century"; Suttles, *Man-Made City.*

30. Sampson, *Great American City*, 47.

31. Sampson, Morenoff, and Gannon-Rowley, "Assessing 'Neighborhood Effects.'"

32. Chaskin and Joseph, "Building 'Community' in Mixed-Income Developments."

33. Bourdieu, "Forms of Capital"; Coleman, "Social Capital in the Creation of Human Capital"; Hanifan, "Rural School Community Center"; Hanifan, *Community Center*; Hannerz, *Soulside*; Jacobs, *Death and Life of Great American Cities*; Putnam, *Making Democracy Work*; Putnam, *Bowling Alone.*

34. One critique of the use of social capital in the literature, for example, has been the way it is often invoked as a broadly normative, positive construct, almost always assuming benefits for society—in spite of the value-neutral treatment given it by both Coleman's and Bourdieu's early formulations. Rather than being an "unqualified good," as Portes points out, social capital can potentially promote inequality (given its uneven distribution), constrain individual advancement in light of membership obligations and "downward leveling norms" within groups, or lead to exclusionary practices. In addition to these considerations, the idea of social capital has been criticized on theoretical grounds as tautological, employing a circular logic that posits it as simultaneously both cause and effect; for the way the notion of social capital appropriates and (uncritically) translates social dynamics and values into economic ones, for the way its ambiguities allow it to be invoked by actors across the ideological spectrum and allow support for vastly different policy agendas, and for the ways a focus on social capital can suppress attention to conflict, depoliticize the nature of poverty and marginalization, and suggest responses to them that shift the burden of change to the poor, relieving the state of responsibility, see, for example, Portes, "Social Capital"; Cohen and Prusak, *In Good Company*; Edwards and Foley, "Civil Society and Social Capital Beyond Putnam"; Foley and Edwards, "Escape from Politics?" Portes and Landolt, "Downside of Social Capital"; and Woolcock, "Social Capital and Economic Development."

35. Burt, "Structural Holes versus Network Closure," 31; Coleman, "Social Capital in the Creation of Human Capital," 98.

36. Briggs, "Moving Up versus Moving Out"; Gittell and Vidal, *Community Organizing*; Putnam, *Bowling Alone.*

37. Granovetter, "Strength of Weak Ties"; Granovetter, *Getting a Job.* Ronald Burt, exploring the strategic engagement of networks by firms to increase their competitiveness argues that it is not the strength of the tie that

matters, but the structural position of "players" within network arrangements that allows them to bridge "structural holes"—the gaps between "nonredundant contacts" that link different networks of actors—providing additional access to information, resources, and opportunity; Burt, *Structural Holes*.

38. Lin, *Social Capital*, 37. Lin's examples here are with regard to people with relatively high positions in the social hierarchy, but since the general point concerns "congruence" within hierarchical strata, the inverse is also true.

39. Briggs, "Brown Kids in White Suburbs," 178; Elliott, "Social Isolation and Labor Market Insulation"; Lin and Dumin, "Access to Occupations through Social Ties"; Lin, Vaughn, and Ensel, "Social Resources and Occupational Status Attainment"; Rankin and Quane, "Neighborhood Poverty"; Stoloff, Glanville, and Bienenstock, "Women's Participation in the Labor Force."

40. Chaskin and Joseph, "Social Interaction in Mixed-Income Developments."

41. Granovetter, *Getting a Job*.

42. Lin, Vaughn, and Ensel, "Social Resources and Occupational Status Attainment"; Lin and Dumin, "Access to Occupations through Social Ties."

43. Stoloff, Glanville, and Bienenstock, "Women's Participation in the Labor Force."

44. Fischer, *To Dwell Among Friends*; McPherson, Smith-Lovin, and Cook, "Birds of a Feather"; Wellman, "Community Question"; Wellman and Wortley, "Different Strokes from Different Folks."

45. Fleming, Baum, and Singer, "Social Support and the Physical Environment"; Keane, "Socioenvironmental Determinants of Community Formation"; Wilner, *Human Relations in Interracial Housing*; Wilner, Walkley, and Cook, "Residential Proximity and Intergroup Relations"; Wimmer and Lewis, "Beyond and Below Racial Homophily"; Yancey, "Architecture, Interaction, and Social Control."

46. See, for example, Gans, "Balanced Community"; Hipp and Perrin, "Formation of Neighborhood Ties"; Lazarsfeld and Merton, "Friendship as Social Process"; McPherson, Smith-Lovin, and Cook, "Birds of a Feather"; and Michelson, *Man and His Urban Environment*. We will return to the importance of homophily (the tendency of people to associate with others "like themselves") and the promise of contact theory (that intergroup conflict can be reduced and positive interaction supported through contact over time) and review the evidence for the assumptions about spatial proximity's promoting network development in the context of poverty deconcentration in chapter 6 when we turn to the question of social interaction in mixed-income communities replacing public housing.

47. Allport, *Nature of Prejudice*; Lin, *Social Capital*; Pettigrew, "Intergroup Contact Theory."

48. Lin, *Social Capital*; Joseph, Chaskin, and Webber, "Theoretical Basis for Addressing Poverty through Mixed-Income Development."

49. Benson and Lund, *Neighborhood Distribution of Local Public Services*; Burnett, "Neighborhood Participation, Political Demand Making and Local Outputs"; Judd and Mushkatel, "Inequality of Urban Services"; Peterson, *City Limits*; Pinch, "Inequality in Pre-school Provision"; Smith, *Mixed-Income Housing Developments*.

50. Sampson, Raudenbush, and Earls, "Neighborhoods and Violent Crime," 918.

51. Khadduri, "Deconcentration"; Sampson, Raudenbush, and Earls, "Neighborhoods and Violent Crime."

52. See, for example, Crenson, *Neighborhood Politics*; Logan and Molotch, *Urban Fortunes*; and Verba, Scholzman, and Brady, *Voice and Equality*.

53. Logan and Molotch, *Urban Fortunes*; Lefebvre, *Writings on Cities*.

54. Joseph, Chaskin, and Webber, "Addressing Poverty through Mixed-Income Development."

55. Sampson, *Great American City*, 37.

56. Shaw and McKay, *Juvenile Delinquency*; see also Bursik and Grasmick, *Neighborhoods and Crime*; Chaskin, *Youth Gangs and Community Intervention*; Kornhauser, *Social Sources of Delinquency*; and Sampson, *Great American City*.

57. Freudenburg, "Density of Acquaintanceship"; Sampson and Groves, "Community Structure and Crime."

58. Coleman, "Social Capital in the Creation of Human Capital," S106.

59. Sampson, Raudenbush, and Earls, "Neighborhoods and Violent Crime," 918.

60. Jacobs, *Death and Life of Great American Cities*, 35.

61. Anderson, *Streetwise*; Furstenberg, "How Families Manage Risk and Opportunity."

62. Sampson, Raudenbush, and Earls, "Neighborhoods and Violent Crime"; Sampson, Morenoff, and Earls, "Beyond Social Capital."

63. Freudenberg, "Density of Acquaintanceship"; Sampson, "Local Friendship Ties"; Sampson and Groves, "Community Structure and Crime"; Sampson and Raudenbush, "Systematic Social Observation of Public Spaces"; Sampson, Raudenbush, and Earls, "Neighborhoods and Violent Crime."

64. Logan and Molotch, *Urban Fortunes*; Sampson, Raudenbush, and Earls, "Neighborhoods and Violent Crime."

65. Sampson, Raudenbush, and Earls, "Neighborhoods and Violent Crime."

66. Gans, *Urban Villagers*; Kornhauser, *Social Sources of Delinquency*; Shaw and McKay, *Juvenile Delinquency*; Merry, *Urban Danger*.

67. Bursik and Grasmick, *Neighborhoods and Crime*; Hunter, "Private, Parochial and Public Orders."

68. Carr, "New Parochialism"; Chaskin and Joseph, "Uses and Expectations of Space and Place"; Fischer, *To Dwell Among Friends*; Freeman, *There Goes the 'Hood*; Pattillo, *Black on the Block*.

69. Additional benefits claimed include promoting sustainability, encouraging walking and reducing reliance on automobiles, strengthening community

identity, promoting citizen responsibility, and supporting economic health. See Leccese and McCormick, *Charter of the New Urbanism.*

70. See, for example, Bohl, "New Urbanism and the City"; Calthorpe, *Next American Metropolis*; Katz, *New Urbanism*; and Talen, *Charter of the New Urbanism.*

71. Larsen, "New Urbanism's Role in Inner-City Neighborhood Revitalization."

72. See, for example, Ellis, "The New Urbanism: Critiques and Rebuttals," 261; Deitrick and Ellis, "New Urbanism in the Inner City"; Fung, "Beyond and Below the New Urbanism"; Garde, "Designing and Developing New Urbanist Projects"; Miles and Song, "'Good' Neighborhoods in Portland, Oregon"; Podobnik, "New Urbanism and the Generation of Social Capital"; Podobnik, "Assessing the Social and Environmental Achievements of New Urbanism."

73. Pyatok, "Martha Stewart vs. Studs Terkel?: New Urbanism and Inner City Neighborhoods That Work," 42; Bohl, "New Urbanism and the City," 780. See, for example, Day, "New Urbanism and the Challenges of Designing for Diversity"; Fainstein, "New Directions in Planning Theory"; Hanlon, "Success by Design"; Harvey, "New Urbanism and the Communitarian Trap"; and Larsen, "New Urbanism's Role in Inner-City Neighborhood Revitalization."

74. Hanlon, "Success by Design"; Johnson and Talen, "Affordable Housing in New Urbanist Communities"; Larsen, "New Urbanism's Role in Inner-City Neighborhood Revitalization"; Lund, "Testing the Claims of New Urbanism"; Sander, "Social Capital and New Urbanism"; Talen, "Social Goals of New Urbanism"; Talen, "Affordability in New Urbanist Development"; Trudeau, "Typology of New Urbanism Neighborhoods"; Trudeau and Malloy, "Suburbs in Disguise."

75. Talen, "Affordability in New Urbanist Development," 489.

76. Bohl, "New Urbanism and the City."

77. Congress for the New Urbanism and US Department of Housing and Urban Development, *Principles for Inner-City Neighborhood Design.*

78. Ibid., 3.

79. Ibid., 3, 10.

80. Ibid., 20; Comitta, chapter 18; Plater-Zyberk, chapter 11; Solomon, chapter 19; all in Talen, *Charter of the New Urbanism.*

81. See Daly and Silver, "Social Exclusion and Social Capital," for a critical review and discussion of the relation between these two constructs. The following consideration of social exclusion as it might apply to the analysis of mixed-income public housing reform was first elaborated in Chaskin, "Integration and Exclusion."

82. Daly and Silver, "Social Exclusion and Social Capital."

83. In spite of this, although state initiated, the reforms that are actually generated from a social exclusion discourse within the broader context of neoliberalism nevertheless take on many of the same properties as those closely

associated with social capital generation, including the invocation of "civil society" and the use of community and voluntary organizations to shape and implement interventions. This is increasingly the case in the context of fiscal austerity adopted by some states in response to the economic downturn beginning in 2008, with a concomitant withdrawal of state-led efforts in favor of voluntary responses.

84. Daly and Silver, "Social Exclusion and Social Capital."

85. As Hilary Silver points out, social exclusion arguments draw variously on Durkheimian ideas about social cohesion, Weberian notions of exclusionary closure, and Marxian orientations toward class division, and these different orientations are reflected in the policy responses to social inclusion in different states. As a policy framework, social exclusion was catalyzed initially in France in the 1970s, where it was to call attention to a portion of the population disconnected from mainstream society and outside the protection of social insurance schemes owing to a broad range of factors including, but moving well beyond, poverty alone—from disability to delinquency to drug addiction to discrimination—and exacerbated by challenges to social cohesion in the wake of civil unrest and in the context of growing unemployment and inequality. See Silver, "Social Exclusion and Social Solidarity"; Burchardt, LeGrand, and Piachaud, "Social Exclusion in Britain, 1991–1995"; Davies, "Social Exclusion Debate"; Mathieson et al., "Social Exclusion: Meaning, Measurement and Experience"; Room, "Poverty and Social Exclusion."

86. Bowring, "Social Exclusion: Limitations of the Debate"; Mathieson et al., "Social Exclusion: Meaning, Measurement and Experience"; Sen, "Social Exclusion: Concept, Application, and Scrutiny"; Silver, "Social Exclusion and Social Solidarity."

87. Hilary Silver, in a seminal effort to unpack some of this complexity, suggests three "paradigms" that frame the meaning and use of social exclusion in different contexts. The *solidarity* paradigm, grounded in French republicanism and Durkheimian notions of the social order, sees social exclusion as a breakdown of social cohesion that requires normative and cultural integration of the excluded. The *specialization* paradigm, more common in English-speaking liberal democracies, sees exclusion as a consequence of social stratification based in the economic division of labor, in which certain individuals engaged in voluntary exchanges across social spheres may encounter discrimination or other "barriers to free movement between spheres." Finally, the *monopoly* paradigm, more common among the European left, draws on Marxian and (especially) Weberian notions of class, status, and the workings of power relations within a coercive social order; it sees exclusion as the product of exclusionary closure driven by monopoly interests, particularly in the market. Silver, "Social Exclusion and Social Solidarity," 543; see also Mathieson et al., "Social Exclusion: Meaning, Measurement and Experience."

88. Mathieson et al., "Social Exclusion: Meaning, Measurement and Experience." See also Wacquant, *Urban Outcasts*, 249–50, who dismisses the construct of social exclusion (along with "the underclass") as a "wooly and spongy term," unstable and incoherent, hiding more than it reveals.

89. Beall, "Globalization and Social Exclusion in Cities"; Davies, "Social Exclusion Debate"; Levitas, *Inclusive Society?* Silver, "Social Exclusion and Social Solidarity."

90. Sen, "Social Exclusion: Concept, Application, and Scrutiny," 8.

91. Daly and Silver, "Social Exclusion and Social Capital."

92. Briggs, Popkin, and Goering, *Moving to Opportunity*; Goetz, *Clearing the Way*; Joseph, Chaskin, and Webber, "Addressing Poverty through Mixed-Income Development."

93. Bowring, "Social Exclusion: Limitations of the Debate," 312.

94. Wacquant, *Urban Outcasts*, 232.

95. Soss, Fording, and Schram, *Disciplining the Poor*; Schram, Fording and Soss, "Neo-liberal Poverty Governance."

96. Piven and Cloward, *Regulating the Poor*; Wacquant, *Punishing the Poor*.

97. Brenner and Theodore, "Cities and the Geographies of 'Actually Existing Neoliberalism'"; Hackworth, *Neoliberal City*; Harvey, *Brief History of Neoliberalism*; Peck and Tickell, "Neoliberalizing Space."

98. Soss, Fording, and Schram, *Disciplining the Poor*, 22.

99. Mead, "Telling the Poor What to Do," 99.

100. Soss, Fording, and Schram, *Disciplining the Poor*, 6; Wacquant, *Punishing the Poor*.

101. Soss, Fording, and Schram, *Disciplining the Poor*, 25.

102. Ibid., 283; Wacquant, *Punishing the Poor*.

103. Cruikshank, *Will to Empower*.

104. Ibid., 39; see also Foucault, "Governmentality"; Gordon, "Governmental Rationality"; Rose, "Death of the Social?" Rose, O'Malley, and Valverde, "Governmentality"; Soss, Fording, and Schram, *Disciplining the Poor*.

105. Rose, O'Malley, and Valverde, "Governmentality," 89; Cruikshank, *Will to Empower*; Soss, Fording, and Schram, *Disciplining the Poor*.

106. Hackworth, *Neoliberal City*, 48.

107. Soss, Fording, and Schram, *Disciplining the Poor*, 16.

CHAPTER THREE

1. In first half of the nineteenth century, for example, Alexis de Tocqueville commented on Americans' propensity for forming both civic and political associations and the ways local communities tended to exercise "executive functions" through them to get things done; *Democracy in America*; cf. Crenson, *Neighborhood Politics*.

2. See, for example, Halpern, *Rebuilding the Inner City*; O'Connor, "Swimming Against the Tide."

3. Davis, *Spearheads for Reform*; Halpern, *Rebuilding the Inner City*; Katz, *In the Shadow of the Poorhouse*; O'Connor, "Swimming Against the Tide."

4. Garvin and Cox, "History of Community Organizing." Although the urban ecological framework that guided these early explanations of city growth remained influential for understanding urban dynamics and community functioning today, subsequent scholarship has both refined and challenged some of its basic claims. Two issues in particular are worth highlighting here. One concerns a fundamental challenge to the assumptions regarding the nature of "organic" change that drives urban processes, stressing instead the critical roles played by particular forms of agency, conflict, and the dynamics of investment as promoted by both capital and policy actors. See, e.g., Castells, *Urban Question*; Gottdiener and Feagin, "Paradigm Shift in Urban Sociology"; Harvey, *Social Justice and the City*; Molotch, "City as a Growth Machine"; Suttles, *Man-Made City*; and Zukin, "Decade of the New Urban Sociology." Another approach focuses on the social organization and dynamics of interaction *within* neighborhoods and their relation to larger units, including the social construction of space and the ways individuals and groups define and negotiate it. Gerald Suttles, for example, working very much in the early Chicago school mode of investigation, describes slum neighborhoods as characterized by "ordered segmentation" among component groups defined by space, race, ethnicity, sex, and age that are either reflected in or thrown into opposition by local institutions (e.g., churches, schools, commercial establishments, recreational facilities, voluntary organizations). In these contexts (and in contrast with Park's metaphor of a mosaic), the behaviors of each group within the neighborhood are shaped very much in response to the behavior patterns of other component groups; Suttles, *Social Order of the Slum*.

5. Halpern, *Rebuilding the Inner City*.

6. These included advocating for better city services and municipal reform, engaging in legislative campaigns, and promoting investments in neighborhood improvements, from parks and playgrounds to libraries and the expanded use of schools as social centers. This advocacy was largely driven by movement leaders (Jane Addams famously among them) lobbying for policy reform rather than by mobilizing neighborhood residents to push for social change. See Davis, *Spearheads for Reform*; Garvin and Cox, "History of Community Organizing"; Halpern, *Rebuilding the Inner City*; Katz, *In the Shadow of the Poorhouse*.

7. Fisher, *Let the People Decide*; Halpern, *Rebuilding the Inner City*.

8. Fisher, "From Grass-Roots Organizing to Community Service"; Fisher, *Let the People Decide*; Mooney-Melvin, *Organic City*; Miller, "Role and Concept of Neighborhood."

9. Fisher, *Let the People Decide*.

10. Ibid.; Schlossman and Sedlak, *Chicago Area Project*.

11. See Mollenkopf, *Contested City*, which also notes the role these efforts played in aligning various interests at the local level, creating or recruiting

a range of organizational mechanisms (from labor unions to agencies established to deliver programs) for mobilizing political constituencies and building political power by consolidating them into a Democratic electoral alliance.

12. Mollenkopf, *Contested City*.

13. Clark, "Conversation with James Baldwin."

14. Frieden and Kaplan, *Politics of Neglect*; Haar, *Between the Idea and the Reality*; Halpern, *Rebuilding the Inner City*; Kravitz and Kolodner, "Community Action"; Marris and Rein, *Dilemmas of Social Reform*; Mollenkopf, *Contested City*; Moynihan, *Maximum Feasible Misunderstanding*; O'Connor, "Swimming Against the Tide."

15. Mollenkopf, *Contested City*.

16. Pierce and Steinbach, *Corrective Capitalism*; see also Berndt, *New Rulers in the Ghetto*; Faux, *CDCs*; Ford Foundation, *Community Development Corporations*.

17. See, for example, Hackworth, *Neoliberal City*; Harvey, *Brief History of Neoliberalism*; Klemek, *Transatlantic Collapse*; Peck and Tickell, "Neoliberalizing Space."

18. See, for example, Kubisch et al., *Voices from the Field*; Kubisch et al., *Voices from the Field II*; Kubisch et al., *Voices from the Field III*; and Chaskin et al., *Building Community Capacity*.

19. Despite the conceptual emphasis both on an asset orientation that focuses inward on marshaling and enhancing communities' capacities to drive and sustain change and on a structural orientation that focuses outward on reconnecting poor communities to resources, systems, and opportunities from which they have become isolated, the practical emphasis of most CCIs has been internal and local. And although community organizing is often invoked as an important strategy, most CCIs have made limited use of it—at least in the form of organizing for political action—privileging instead forms of "consensus" organizing that focus on partnerships between community actors and those in power. See Chaskin and Karlström, *Beyond the Neighborhood*, and Dewar, "Aligning with Outside Resources and Power."

20. Promise Neighborhoods is modeled explicitly on the Harlem Children's Zone, a CCI dedicated to moving children out of poverty through a holistic set of services, schools and educational programs, and community building, and Choice Neighborhoods draws on CCI models in its explicit focus on multisectoral, multidimensional neighborhood change. See Kubisch, "Structures, Strategies, Actions, and Results of Community Change Efforts."

21. Naparstek, Dooley, and Smith, *Community Building in Public Housing*; Naparstek et al., *HOPE VI: Community Building Makes a Difference*.

22. Chaskin, "Theories of Community."

23. These three "models of community organization practice" are drawn from Jack Rothman's well-known typology, "Three Models of Community Organization Practice" and "Approaches to Community Intervention." Rothman's terminology differs slightly, referring to social planning, locality

development, and social action. Following William Sites and his colleagues, we use "community development" here because it aligns better with common usage among both scholars and professionals (although with different relative emphasis on participatory deliberative processes, on the one hand, and particular outputs, on the other), and "community organizing" because it clearly stresses community as the organizing principle and unit of action and because it has generally been adopted in the field to describe community-based social mobilization strategies. See Sites, Chaskin, and Parks, "Reframing Community Practice."

24. Bowly, *Poorhouse*; Hirsch, *Making the Second Ghetto*; Hunt, *Blueprint for Disaster*.
25. Hirsch, *Making the Second Ghetto*, 11.
26. Hunt, *Blueprint for Disaster*.
27. Vale, *Purging the Poorest*.
28. For more on the early history of public housing in Chicago see Bowly, *Poorhouse*; Fuerst and Hunt, *When Public Housing Was Paradise*; Hirsch, *Making the Second Ghetto*; and Hunt, *Blueprint for Disaster*.
29. Vale, *Purging the Poorest*, 33.
30. Hirsch, *Making the Second Ghetto*; Hunt, *Blueprint for Disaster*; Kotlowitz, *There Are No Children Here*; Venkatesh, *Robert Taylor Homes*.
31. Hunt, *Blueprint for Disaster*.
32. Ibid.; Klemek, *Transatlantic Collapse*; Vale, *Purging the Poorest*.
33. Hirsch, *Making the Second Ghetto*; Hunt, *Blueprint for Disaster*.
34. Hunt, *Blueprint for Disaster*.
35. Ibid., 201; see also Vale, who notes that "largely as a reaction to the pressures of the civil rights movement, the leadership of most large American cities inexorably retenanted 'the projects' with the least advantaged and most economically desperate urban dwellers"; *Purging the Poorest*, 17.
36. Vale, *Purging the Poorest*.
37. Hunt, *Blueprint for Disaster*, 204.
38. Katz, "Origins of HOPE VI."
39. H.R. Rep. No. 104–437 (1995).
40. See, for example, Venkatesh, *Robert Taylor Homes*.
41. The LACs operated under the aegis of a Central Advisory Council, elected from LAC leadership across the system, that represented the interests of public housing residents to the housing authority.
42. Chaskin, Khare, and Joseph, "Participation, Deliberation, and Decision Making"; Hunt, *Blueprint for Disaster*; Venkatesh, *American Project*; Wright, "Community Resistance to CHA Transformation."
43. Bennett, "Downtown Restructuring"; Hunt, *Blueprint for Disaster*; Wright, "Community Resistance to CHA Transformation."
44. The Habitat Company served in this instrumental role, approving all the new construction under the Plan for Transformation, until 2011 when the local courts lifted the receivership.

45. Briggs, "Moving Up versus Moving Out"; Goering and Feins, *Choosing a Better Life?* Rosenbaum, "Changing the Geography of Opportunity"; Varady and Walker, "Housing Vouchers and Residential Mobility."

46. Joseph, "Is Mixed-Income Development an Antidote to Urban Poverty?" Joseph, Chaskin, and Webber, "Theoretical Basis for Addressing Poverty through Mixed-Income Development"; Kleit, "HOPE VI New Communities."

47. Goetz, "Politics of Poverty Deconcentration"; Goetz, "Housing Dispersal Programs"; Varady and Walker, "Housing Vouchers and Residential Mobility."

48. Hogan, *Scattered-Site Housing.*

49. Vale, *Purging the Poorest.*

50. Goetz, "Politics of Poverty Deconcentration."

51. For more on the Gautreaux program see DeLuca, "Continuing Relevance of the Gautreaux Program"; DeLuca and Rosenbaum, "If Low-Income Blacks Are Given a Chance"; DeLuca et al., "Gautreaux Mothers and Their Children"; Keels, "Residential Attainment of Now-Adult Gautreaux Children"; Keels et al., "Fifteen Years Later"; Polikoff, *Waiting for Gautreaux*; Rubinowitz and Rosenbaum, *Crossing the Class and Color Lines.*

52. MTO was implemented in five cities: Baltimore, Boston, Chicago, New York, and Los Angeles. For more on the MTO program see, for example, Briggs, Popkin, and Goering, *Moving to Opportunity*; Orr et al., *Moving to Opportunity: Interim Impacts Evaluation.*

53. Goetz, "Housing Dispersal Programs"; Popkin et al., *Decade of HOPE VI*; Sard and Staub, *House Bill Makes Significant Improvement in HOPE VI Public Housing Revitalization Program*; Vale, *Purging the Poorest.*

54. For more on the mixed-income approach, see Cisneros and Engdahl, *From Despair to Hope*; Epp, "Emerging Strategies for Revitalizing Public Housing Communities"; Goetz, *Clearing the Way*; Joseph, "Is Mixed-Income Development an Antidote to Urban Poverty?" Joseph, Chaskin, and Webber, "Theoretical Basis for Addressing Poverty through Mixed-Income Development"; Khadduri, "Deconcentration"; Kleit, "HOPE VI New Communities"; Rosenbaum, Stroh, and Flynn, "Lake Parc Place"; Schwartz and Tajbakhsh, "Mixed-Income Housing: Unanswered Questions"; and Von Hoffman, "High Ambitions." Mixed-income housing has also been built independent of public housing redevelopment across the country. See, for example, Brophy and Smith, "Mixed-Income Housing: Factors for Success," and Smith, *Mixed-Income Housing Developments.*

55. See, for example, Bailey et al., *Creating and Sustaining Mixed Income Communities*; Berube, *Mixed Communities in England*; Musterd and Andersson, "Housing Mix, Social Mix, and Social Opportunities"; and Silverman, Lupton, and Fenton, *Good Place for Children.*

56. Ceraso, "Is Mixed-Income Housing the Key?"

57. Ryan et al., *All in Together.*

58. Barnett, *Redesigning Cities*; Brophy and Smith, "Mixed-Income Housing: Factors for Success"; Baron, "Evolution of HOPE VI as a Development Program"; Breitbart and Pader, "Establishing Ground"; Pader and Breitbart, "Transforming Public Housing"; Roessner, *Decent Place to Live*; Schubert and Thresher, *Lessons from the Field*.

59. National Commission on Severely Distressed Public Housing, *Final Report*; Wexler, "HOPE VI: Market Means/Public Ends."

60. Ceraso, "Is Mixed-Income Housing the Key?" Schill, "Chicago's Mixed Income New Communities Strategy."

61. Rosenbaum, Stroh, and Flynn, "Lake Parc Place," 713.

62. For more on the HOPE VI program see Cisneros and Engdahl, *From Despair to Hope*; HOPE VI Improvement and Reauthorization Act, Hearing on S. 289, before the Committee on Banking, Housing, and Urban Affairs, Subcommittee on Housing, Transportation, and Community Development (2007) (testimony of Susan J. Popkin); Popkin et al., *A Decade of HOPE VI*; Sard and Staub, *House Bill Makes Significant Improvement in HOPE VI Public Housing Revitalization Program*.

63. Omnibus Consolidated Rescissions and Appropriations Act of 1996, Pub. L. No. 104–134, 110 Stat. 1321, Title II (1996).

64. Katz, "Origins of HOPE VI," 15.

65. Turbov, "Public Housing Redevelopment"; Cisneros and Engdahl, *From Despair to Hope*.

66. Turbov, "Public Housing Redevelopment," 174.

67. Baron, "Evolution of HOPE VI," 33.

68. Turbov, "Public Housing Redevelopment."

69. "Revitalization of Severely Distressed Public Housing, 2011 Summary Statement and Initiatives," HUD, accessed December 13, 2011, http://hud.gov /offices/cfo/reports/2011/cjs/rodph-hopeIV2011.pdf.

70. Kingsley, "Appendix A."

71. Buron et al., *HOPE VI Resident Tracking Study*; HOPE VI Improvement and Reauthorization Act, Hearing on S. 289, before the Committee on Banking, Housing, and Urban Affairs, Subcommittee on Housing, Transportation, and Community Development (2007) (testimony of Susan J. Popkin); Popkin et al., *Decade of HOPE VI*; Turbov and Piper, *HOPE VI and Mixed-Finance Redevelopments*; Zielenbach, "Assessing Economic Change."

72. Baron, "Evolution of HOPE VI as a Development Program"; US Department of Housing and Urban Development, *HOPE VI Program Authority*; Wexler, "HOPE VI: Market Means/Public Ends."

73. Bowly, *Poorhouse*; Ceraso, "Is Mixed-Income Housing the Key?" Rosenbaum, Stroh, and Flynn, "Lake Parc Place"; Wilen, "Horner Model."

74. Hunt, *Blueprint for Disaster*; Flynn McRoberts and John Kass, "Demolishing Some High-Rises Job 1," *Chicago Tribune*, June 1, 1995; Patrick Reardon, "Old Leader Leaves," *Chicago Tribune*, June 1, 1995.

75. Bowly, *Poorhouse*.
76. Chicago Housing Authority and US Department of Housing and Urban Development, *Moving to Work Demonstration Agreement*, 2.
77. Chicago Housing Authority, *Annual Plan for Transformation FY2003*, 2.
78. For more on the Atlanta transformation, see Boston, "Effects of Revitalization"; Salama, "Redevelopment of Distressed Public Housing"; and Vale, *Purging the Poorest*.
79. Hunt, *Blueprint for Disaster*; Smith, "Chicago Housing Authority's Plan for Transformation."
80. Two other important service programs that were a part of the Plan for Transformation, Opportunity Chicago from 2006 to 2010 and the Chicago Family Case Management Demonstration (CFCMD) from 2007 to 2010, are not covered in depth here because they did not directly serve residents in the mixed-income developments, which are our focus. For more on Opportunity Chicago see Parkes et al., *Opportunity Chicago*, and for more on the CFCMD see Popkin et al., *Overview of the Chicago Family Case Management Demonstration*, and Popkin and Davies, *Improving the Lives of Public Housing's Most Vulnerable Families*.
81. The MTW Program allowed HUD to grant federal exceptions to PHAs in order to achieve greater cost effectiveness in federal expenditures, give incentives to working families, and increase housing choices for low-income families (Omnibus Consolidated Rescissions and Appropriations Act of 1996, Pub. L. No. 104–134, 110 Stat. 1321, Title II, Sec. 204 [1996]).
82. Chicago Housing Authority, *FY 2000 Moving to Work Annual Report*.
83. More than ten development partnerships have been selected by the CHA to implement the various mixed-income redevelopments. These partnerships include local and national developers, for-profit and non-profit companies, and companies new to mixed-income housing and others with deep experience in multiple cities; for more detail see Joseph, "Creating Mixed-Income Developments in Chicago."
84. Cunningham, Popkin and Burt, *Public Housing Transformation and the "Hard to House."*
85. Claire Bushey, "Housing Agency Struggles to Speed Up Residents' Return," *Chi-Town Daily News*, June 18, 2008, http://www.chitowndailynews.org/2008/06/18/Housing-agency-struggles-to-speed-up-residents-return-14858.html; Antonio Olivo, "Rules Leave New CHA Homes Empty," *Chicago Tribune*, February 16, 2005; Antonio Olivo, "Report Hits CHA for Losing Residents," *Chicago Tribune*, July 22, 2005; Brian J. Rogal, "Uncertain Prospects," *Chicago Reporter*, March 1, 2005.
86. Metropolitan Planning Council, *CHA Plan for Transformation July 2003 Progress Report*.
87. Those households retaining their right to return were then given a number of temporary relocation housing options including relocating to another on-site unit, transferring to another public housing development, or taking

a temporary voucher for a rental unit in the private market. These households were also asked to indicate their top three choices for their "permanent" housing from among the range of developments that would be rehabilitated as traditional public housing, demolished and replaced with mixed-income housing, or preserved as scattered-site housing throughout the city. Once a household was placed in one of their permanent housing options, the CHA would satisfy its obligation to provide housing and would not be required to fulfill any future transfer requests.

88. For more detail on resident relocation in Chicago, see Joseph, "Creating Mixed-Income Developments"; Levy and Gallagher, *HOPE VI and Neighborhood Revitalization*; Polikoff, *Third Side*; Popkin, "Glass Half Empty?" Venkatesh, *Robert Taylor Homes*; Venkatesh and Celimli, "Tearing Down the Community"; and Williams, Fischer, and Russ, *Temporary Relocation, Permanent Choice*.

89. In practice, the decision about what to do if the resident fails to meet the criteria after a year has been left to the property managers at each site, and it appears that in most cases, as long as the household is not causing problems for other residents at the development, their lease is extended.

90. Sullivan, *Independent Monitor's Report*.

91. Ibid. For more on the barriers to relocation that face a substantial proportion of the public housing population, see Cunningham, Popkin, and Burt, *Public Housing Transformation and the "Hard to House."*

92. Joseph, "Creating Mixed-Income Developments"; Joseph and Chaskin, "Mixed-Income Developments and Low Rates of Return."

93. Note that the CHA has had seven CEOs since the start of the Transformation, and while this has added to the instability and sense of constantly changing policy, the leadership changes also provided opportunities for reshaping strategies that were not working.

CHAPTER FOUR

1. Chicago is renowned for its array of neighborhoods, many of them well delineated with clear boundaries, character, and history; Hunter, *Symbolic Communities*; Park, Burgess, and McKenzie, *City*; Sampson, *Great American City*. In the 1930s, University of Chicago sociologist Ernest Burgess famously identified seventy-five "community areas" in Chicago, designations that are still relevant for residents, planners, and researchers, though they serve neither as administrative units for city service delivery nor as representative units of city government. And while community areas are often referred to in identifying community contexts within the city, there are also smaller neighborhoods—similarly named and recognized—whose boundaries lie within or overlap with those of the official (now seventy-seven) community areas. In our analysis, we use the term *neighborhood* to refer to locally recognized geographic areas around the mixed-income

development sites: Bronzeville, North Kenwood–Oakland, and the Near West Side. Bronzeville encompasses several community areas. North Kenwood–Oakland combines one community area with part of another. Only one of the neighborhoods in question, the Near West Side, is coterminous with a community area as originally defined by Burgess.

2. Sampson, *Great American City*, 9.

3. Bennett, *Third City*.

4. New Homes for Chicago is an affordable housing program through which the city provides land and other subsidies for private developers to build new homes in neighborhoods throughout the city, particularly in areas that need revitalizing.

5. Boyd, "Defensive Development"; Hyra, *New Urban Renewal*.

6. Hyra, *New Urban Renewal*; Pattillo, *Black on the Block*.

7. Bronzeville is also known as the black metropolis of Drake and Cayton's famous *Black Metropolis*. See also Hyra, *New Urban Renewal*, and Von Hoffman, *House by House*.

8. Pattillo, *Black on the Block*.

9. Drake and Cayton, *Black Metropolis*; Hyra, *New Urban Renewal*.

10. Boyd, "Defensive Development"; Von Hoffman, *House by House*.

11. Street, *Racial Oppression in the Global Metropolis*.

12. Bowly, *Poorhouse*.

13. Chicago Housing Authority, *Plan for Transformation: Improving Public Housing in Chicago and the Quality of Life*.

14. In 2010 Preckwinkle was elected president of the Cook County Board—the county that encompasses the city of Chicago.

15. Bowly, *Poorhouse*.

16. Chicago Housing Authority, *Plan for Transformation: Improving Public Housing in Chicago and the Quality of Life*; Popkin et al., *HOPE VI Panel Study*; Popkin, Cunningham, and Woodley, *Residents at Risk*.

17. The Mid-South Planning and Development Commission was formed in 1990 with the support of the city Department of Planning and Development. A series of community meetings, planning charrettes, and task force efforts led to the release in 1993 of the Mid-South Strategic Development Plan, "Restoring Bronzeville."

18. "Kenwood Oakland Community Organization," accessed February 13, 2012, http://www.kocoonline.org.

19. Illinois law allows for city boards (in Chicago's case, the Community Development Commission) to designate conservation areas in communities in danger of becoming "slum and blighted areas" owing to a variety of factors, including deterioration of existing buildings, overuse of housing, obsolete and inadequate community facilities, lack of sound community planning, rising delinquency and crime rates, and large out-migration of residents; Urban Community Conservation Act, 315 ILCS 25 (1953). Area residents are appointed to Conservation Community Councils (CCC) to

work with the city to develop and implement a conservation plan for the
area that will prevent further deterioration largely through preservation
and renewal rather than demolition (Pattillo, *Black on the Block*). North
Kenwood–Oakland's council consists of fifteen community members appointed by the mayor. The two other mixed-income developments in the
community conservation area are Lake Park Crescent and Jazz on the Boulevard. Another influential layer of community-based collaboration and
planning in North Kenwood–Oakland was launched in 2003, when the
Quad Communities Development Corporation (QCDC) was formed as part
of the New Communities Program (NCP). NCP is a comprehensive community development initiative being implemented in sixteen neighborhoods
across the city, managed by the Local Initiative Support Corporation and
funded by the John D. and Catherine T. MacArthur Foundation. Vision-
ing sessions with over two hundred community members informed the
development of a "quality of life plan" that identified priority strategies
for North Kenwood–Oakland and two bordering neighborhoods. The plan,
which used the earlier Mid-South Plan as a framing document, explicitly
called for more education, training, and jobs for returning public housing
residents and stressed the need to realize a "socially cohesive neighborhood that welcomes families of every ethnicity and income level." QCDC,
which Alderman Preckwinkle helped establish, oversees the implementation of the NCP quality-of-life plan with the goal of creating a "sustainable,
healthy, mixed-income neighborhood" and has focused on commercial
and retail development, school improvement, employment, and housing;
Barry and Riley, *Quad Communities*, 12; Greenberg et al., *Creating a Platform
for Sustained Neighborhood Improvement*.

20. Campbell, *Mid-South Strategic Development Plan*.
21. Kimball Hill Homes, the largest privately owned home builder in the nation at the time, declared bankruptcy in 2009 at the height of the housing
market crisis and dropped out of the partnership.
22. In 2012 the Chicago Housing Authority ended its contract with TCB for
providing social service at Oakwood Shores.
23. The affordable rental and for-sale units are financed with a combination
of federal, state, and city programs, including the Low Income Housing
Tax Credit, Affordable Housing Tax Credit, and tax increment financing
programs. The specific financing sources and stipulations vary by mixed-
income site, depending on what was allocated to the developer. These
programs have requirements that units be rented or sold to households
earning a certain percentage of area median income, typically 50 to 80 percent for rental units and up to 120 percent for for-sale units.
24. Seligman, *Block by Block*.
25. Hunt, *Blueprint for Disaster*; Fuerst and Hunt, *When Public Housing Was
Paradise*.
26. Barry, *More Than Bricks and Mortar*.

27. Von Hoffman, *House by House*.

28. Wilen, "Horner Model"; Henry Horner Mothers Guild v. Chicago Housing Authority, class action complaint, 91 C 3316 (N.D. Ill. 1991).

29. *Henry Horner Mothers Guild*, at 21.

30. Henry Horner Mothers Guild v. Chicago Housing Authority, consent decree, 91 C 3316, 1, 3 (N.D. Ill. 1995).

31. Wilen, "Horner Model."

32. In 1987 the city announced a plan to build a new 75,000-seat stadium for the Chicago Bears football team on the Near West Side. The neighborhood was already home to the Chicago Stadium, home of the professional basketball and ice hockey teams, and the Chicago Bears Stadium plan called for demolishing 328 homes housing approximately 1,500 people, mostly low-income, elderly African Americans. Community residents organized to oppose the plan and created their own redevelopment plan, called "The Better Alternative," that envisioned affordable housing and community amenities—a park, library, and community center—in place of the stadium. They staged public protests and shared their plan with city leaders. The stadium plan stalled and eventually died over funding shortfalls and property disputes. About the same time, plans surfaced for a larger basketball and hockey arena to replace the Chicago Stadium. The city used "The Better Alternative" plan as the basis for negotiations and eventually reached an agreement that included some replacement housing for displaced residents and financing that led to the creation of the Mabel Manning Library (opened in 1994) and the James Jordan Boys and Girls Club and Family Life Center (opened in 1996). The new stadium, the United Center, opened in 1994 in the midst of the basketball team's six national championships. See Barry, *More Than Bricks and Mortar*; Finkel, *West Haven*; and Von Hoffman, *House by House*.

33. Like the Quad Communities area on the South Side, the West Haven neighborhood was selected to participate in the New Communities Program and also adopted the goal of creating a mixed-income community that would welcome new residents without displacing current ones; Finkel, *West Haven*.

34. Chaskin, Khare, and Joseph, "Participation, Deliberation, and Decision Making"; Chicago Housing Authority, *Plan for Transformation: Improving Public Housing in Chicago and the Quality of Life* (Chicago: Chicago Housing Authority, 2000).

35. Chaskin, Khare, and Joseph, "Participation, Deliberation and Decision Making."

36. Wilen, "Horner Model."

37. Richard Baron, founding partner of McCormack Baron Salazar, helped persuade the Department of Housing and Urban Development to launch the HOPE VI program in the early 1990s; Cisneros and Engdahl, *From Despair to Hope*.

38. Chicago Housing Authority, *FY2009 Moving to Work Annual Report*.

39. Authors' calculation based on 207 HOPE VI revitalization grants from 1993 to 2010 listed in National Initiative on Mixed-Income Communities mixed-income development database at nimc.case.edu.
40. The affordable housing resources included $102 million in HOME and Community Development Block Grant allocations, $55 million in tax increment financing funds, $19 million in Low-Income Housing Tax Credit allocations, and $7 million in donation tax credits; Chicago Housing Authority, *Plan for Transformation at 10*.
41. The Partnership for New Communities was established and capitalized by a group of local foundations and corporations to provide supplemental funding for workforce development and economic revitalization in support of the Transformation. It operated from 2001 to 2012.
42. In addition to funding the research this book is based on, the MacArthur Foundation has provided grants for a longitudinal study of the relocation experiences of CHA residents and ongoing evaluation of resident services models and outcomes.
43. A HOPE VI grant was awarded for the phase 1 redevelopment at Westhaven Park before the mixed-income phase of development. In July 2000 the Oakwood Shores HOPE VI application was ranked first in the nation; Chicago Housing Authority, *Plan for Transformation Year 2*.
44. Approved by Congress as a component of tax reform legislation during the Reagan administration, the LIHTC provides tax incentives for private-sector investment in affordable rental housing. HUD allocates tax credits to each of the states, which then hold competitions for local developers to bid for an allocation of funds for specific affordable housing proposals; Cummings and DiPasquale, "Low-Income Housing Tax Credit."
45. Dye and Merriman, "Effects of Tax Increment Financing on Economic Development."
46. Chicago Housing Authority, *FY2007 Moving to Work Annual Report*. Although the plan was innovative and creative in a design sense, the use of so many architects created practical difficulties and added to construction costs by incorporating so many different building styles.
47. Wilen, "Horner Model."
48. Joseph, "Creating Mixed-Income Developments"; Joseph and Chaskin, "Mixed-Income Developments and Low Rates of Return."
49. Of the relocated public housing residents currently living at each development who previously lived in that development, the highest proportion is at Park Boulevard (74 percent), followed by Oakwood Shores (63 percent) and Westhaven Park (47 percent); Chicago Housing Authority, *The Plan for Transformation: An Update on Relocation*.
50. This unplanned feature of renters living in for-sale units, most prevalent at Park Boulevard but present at the other two sites as well, complicates the social dynamics on site in several ways, including creating a cohort of renters who are not formally under the auspices of property management and

thus are disconnected both from site staff and from fellow tenants, shifting the tenure mix on site (exacerbating the shift already created by the for-sale construction freeze).

CHAPTER FIVE

1. By "development professionals," we are referring broadly to those working on the design and implementation of the mixed-income development, including real estate developers, property managers, social service providers, and staff at the Chicago Housing Authority.
2. An earlier analysis of community building strategies in these mixed-income communities can be found in Chaskin and Joseph, "Building 'Community' in Mixed-Income Developments."
3. Vale, *Purging the Poorest.*
4. Bennett, Smith, and Wright, *Where Are Poor People to Live?*
5. This goal was less prominently mentioned by development team members at Westhaven Park, likely owing to the less stringent screening criteria there under the consent decree.
6. One might argue that this agenda should also include changing owners' and market-rate residents' perspectives on their low-income neighbors, but development professionals in these sites focused almost exclusively on public housing residents and other low-income residents.
7. Metropolitan Planning Council, *CHA Plan for Transformation, July 2003 Progress Report.*
8. A more extensive analysis of the opportunities and dynamics of participatory deliberation in these mixed-income communities can be found in Chaskin, Khare, and Joseph, "Participation, Deliberation, and Decision Making."
9. For a more detailed analysis, see ibid.
10. In place of the LACs, the CHA created and staffed an internal office of the ombudsman, a citywide mechanism for providing support and advocacy for relocated public housing residents in the new developments. Ironically, when the ombudsman staff held meetings on site they were, at least in some cases that we observed, open only to public housing residents, thus generating exactly the separation that CHA supposedly was seeking to avoid.
11. Gans, *Urban Villagers*; Kleit, "HOPE VI New Communities."

CHAPTER SIX

1. A third theoretical framework, regarding social control and grounded in social disorganization theory, also has implications for social interaction and rests on assumptions about relational networks, but it is oriented toward

somewhat different ends and lies more centrally behind the issues to be investigated in chapter 7.

2. Briggs, "Brown Kids in White Suburbs."
3. Anderson, *Streetwise*; Wilson, *Truly Disadvantaged.*
4. Bandura, "Self-Efficacy."
5. E.g., Kasarda, "City Jobs"; Lewis, "Culture of Poverty"; Murray, *Losing Ground.*
6. Katz, *"Underclass" Debate*; Valentine, *Culture and Poverty.*
7. Duneier, *Slim's Table*; Lamont and Small, "How Culture Matters"; Newman, *No Shame in My Game*; Small and Newman, "Urban Poverty after *The Truly Disadvantaged.*"
8. E.g., Bott, "Observation of Play Activities."
9. E.g., Burt, "General Social Survey Network Items"; Duncan, Featherman, and Duncan, *Socioeconomic Background and Achievement*; Laumann, *Bonds of Pluralism.*
10. E.g., Gans, *Urban Villagers*; Hipp and Perrin, "Formation of Neighborhood Ties"; Ibarra, "Race, Opportunity, and Diversity of Social Circles"; Kleit and Carnegie, "Integrated or Isolated?" Mark, "Culture and Competition"; McPherson and Smith-Lovin, "Homophily in Voluntary Organizations"; Ruef, Aldrich, and Carter, "Homophily, Strong Ties, and Isolation."
11. See McPherson, Smith-Lovin, and Cook, "Birds of a Feather," for review.
12. Lazarsfeld and Merton, "Friendship as Social Process"; McPherson, Smith-Lovin, and Cook, "Birds of a Feather." Homophilous relationships are also shaped and reproduced by key contexts (such as neighborhoods and organizations), by propinquity (which reduces barriers to interaction), and by a range of "tie-generating mechanisms"—from shared and reciprocal friendships to institutional processes that sort individuals into elite or less-privileged contexts—through which contact can be promoted and that may be more influential in tie formation than, for example, racial homophily alone. See Hipp and Perrin, "Formation of Neighborhood Ties"; Kleit and Carnegie, "Integrated or Isolated?" McPherson, Smith-Lovin, and Cook, "Birds of a Feather"; Wimmer and Lewis, "Beyond and Below Racial Homophily."
13. McPherson, Smith-Lovin, and Cook, "Birds of a Feather."
14. Pettigrew and Tropp, "Test of Intergroup Contact."
15. Allport, *Nature of Prejudice*; Pettigrew, "Intergroup Contact Theory," 67.
16. Pettigrew, "Intergroup Contact Theory."
17. Emerson, Kimbro, and Yancey, "Contact Theory Extended."
18. See Pettigrew and Tropp, "Test of Intergroup Contact," for a recent meta-analysis.
19. Pettigrew and Tropp, "Test of Intergroup Contact."
20. Barlow et al., "Contact Caveat"; Putnam, "*E Pluribus Unum*"; Quillian, "Prejudice as a Response to Perceived Group Threat."

21. Barlow et al., "Contact Caveat," 1630.
22. Paolini, Harwood, and Rubin, "Negative Intergroup Contact," 1725.
23. E.g., Clampet-Lundquist, "HOPE VI Relocation"; Clampet-Lundquist, "Social Ties, Perceived Safety, and Public Housing Relocation"; Curley, "Relocating the Poor"; Fauth, Leventhal, and Brooks-Gunn, "Seven Years Later"; Greenbaum et al., "Deconcentration and Social Capital."
24. DeLuca, "Continuing Relevance of the Gautreaux Program."
25. Mendenhall, "Pathways to Economic Independence."
26. Kleit, "Role of Neighborhood Social Networks"; Kleit, "Job Search Networks."
27. Briggs, "Brown Kids in White Suburbs"; cf. Hogan, *Scattered-Site Housing*.
28. Briggs, Popkin, and Goering, *Moving to Opportunity*; Cove et al., *Escaping from Poor Neighborhoods*.
29. Buron et al., *HOPE VI Resident Tracking Study*; Chaskin and Joseph, "Social Interaction in Mixed-Income Developments"; Graves, "Structuring of Urban Life"; Graves, "Mixed Outcome Developments"; Mark L. Joseph, "Early Resident Experiences at a New Mixed-Income Development in Chicago," *Journal of Urban Affairs* 30, no. 3 (2008): 229–57; Kleit, "HOPE VI New Communities"; Kleit and Carnegie, "Integrated or Isolated?" Tach, "More Than Bricks and Mortar."
30. Rosenbaum, Stroh, and Flynn, "Lake Parc Place."
31. Arthurson, "Operationalising Social Mix"; Atkinson and Kintrea, "Owner-Occupation"; Jupp, *Living Together*; Tach, "More Than Bricks and Mortar."
32. Kleit, "HOPE VI New Communities."
33. An earlier and much more limited exploration of these dynamics in two of the sites examined here can be found in Chaskin and Joseph, "Social Interaction in Mixed-Income Developments."
34. Pettigrew, "Intergroup Contact Theory."
35. There is considerable contention from higher-income residents, particularly homeowners, about how fully they were made aware of the nature of income mixing planned for the developments, in terms of both the high proportion of relocated public housing residents and the level of physical integration on blocks and within buildings. One-third of the buyers of affordable units and half of the buyers of market-rate units in our interview sample said that they did not know at the time of purchase that the development was mixed-income or that they didn't receive a clear description from the developers and sales team of what the mix would be. These concerns were reiterated by participants in our randomly drawn homeowner focus groups as well.
36. Chaskin, Sichling, and Joseph, "Youth in Mixed-Income Communities"; Pattillo, *Black on the Block*.
37. For clarity, we will indicate the race of the homeowners and market-rate renters we quote. All relocated public housing residents and renters of affordable units in our respondent sample are African American.
38. These characteristics are often conflated, since, as we noted earlier,

homeowners are less likely to be African American in these sites, except at Oakwood Shores.

39. Interactions like these are also sometimes described by African American homeowners, although except at Oakwood Shores relatively few home-owners in these sites are African American—and there are relatively few homeowners in Oakwood Shores as a proportion of the overall population.
40. Pattillo, *Black on the Block*, 99.
41. The names in this quotation are pseudonyms.
42. Freudenburg, "Density of Acquaintanceship."
43. See also Graves, "Mixed Outcome Developments."
44. Pettigrew, "Intergroup Contact Theory."
45. Simmel, "Metropolis and Urban Life"; Tönnies, *Gemeinschaft und Gessel-schaft*; Wirth, "Urbanism as a Way of Life."
46. Wellman, "Community Question."
47. Kasarda and Janowitz, "Community Attachment in Mass Society"; Sampson, "What 'Community' Supplies"; Suttles, *Social Construction of Communities*.
48. Campbell and Lee, "Sources of Personal Neighbor Networks"; Lee, Camp-bell, and Miller, "Racial Differences in Urban Neighboring."
49. The ways residents of these communities draw conclusions about "who's who" based on a range of visual and behavioral cues will be discussed below.
50. Bandura, "Self-Efficacy"; Granovetter, *Getting a Job*.
51. Small, "Weak Ties."
52. As we noted in chapter 4, although initial plans did not include rental units beyond those set aside for relocated public housing residents, some for-sale units were ultimately rented out by the developer, mostly to stu-dents attending the nearby Illinois Institute of Technology, and some homeowners rented out their units.
53. Bohl, "New Urbanism and the City"; Congress for the New Urbanism and US Department of Housing and Urban Development, *Principles for Inner-City Neighborhood Design*.
54. Talen, *New Urbanism and American Planning*.
55. Leccese and McCormick, *Charter of the New Urbanism*; Talen, "Social Goals of New Urbanism."
56. Talen, "Social Goals of New Urbanism," 179–80.
57. Hipp and Perrin, "Formation of Neighborhood Ties"; McPherson, Smith-Lovin, and Cook, "Birds of a Feather"; Wimmer and Lewis, "Beyond and Below Racial Homophily."
58. Hipp and Perrin, "Beyond and Below Racial Homophily," calculate that a 10 percent increase in the value of a resident's home (a measure of social distance) has the same effect on tie formation as a 5.6 percent increase in spatial distance.
59. The developer of this site ultimately brokered a negotiated settlement and the furniture was returned, with agreement that residents and their guests

would use it only for short-term purposes, such as when waiting for a friend. As we will explore in detail in chapter 7, these tensions around the purpose, "publicness," and appropriate use of common space are often at the center of cross-group conflict in these communities, and they often serve to bring on increasingly restrictive efforts to control access to these spaces and shape rules for their use.

60. These exceptions will be discussed further in chapters 7 and 8. Key among them are meetings organized under the Chicago Alternative Policing (CAPS) program, which brings local residents together with police and other public officials to raise issues about crime and security and discuss solutions (see Skogan and Hartnett, *Community Policing, Chicago Style*; Fung, *Empowered Participation*). As we will see, although they do provide somewhat broader-based participation, they also often generate conflict rather than consensus between groups.

61. The CHA established the Office of the Ombudsman at its central offices downtown as a replacement for elected LACs no longer operating in mixed-income developments. The ombudsman mediates and responds to relo-cated public housing residents' concerns about their experience in the mixed-income communities.

62. This is basically an inversion of the use of the culture of poverty frame-work. Rather than being used to explain "underclass" values and behavior, it is drawn on as an institutionalized narrative that informs the behavior of homeowners toward their low-income neighbors. On cognitive frames see, e.g., Bourdieu, *Outline of a Theory of Practice*; Goffman, *Stigma*; Lamont and Small, "How Culture Matters"; Small, *Villa Victoria*. On culture as "sym-bolic boundaries," see Lamont and Fournier, *Cultivating Differences*; Lamont and Small, "How Culture Matters."

63. Cohen, *Boundaries of Blackness*; see also Pattillo, *Black on the Block*; Smith and Stovall, "'Coming Home' to New Homes and New Schools." For more on the specific dynamics of race in these mixed-income public housing redevelopments, see Khare, Joseph, and Chaskin, "Enduring Significance of Race."

CHAPTER SEVEN

1. See, for example, Anderson, *Streetwise*; Massey and Denton, *American Apart-heid*; Pattillo, *Black on the Block*; Sugrue, *Origins of the Urban Crisis*; Wilson, *Truly Disadvantaged*.
2. This chapter builds on and substantially expands an earlier analysis of these dynamics; see Chaskin and Joseph, "Uses and Expectations of Space and Place."
3. Kelling and Wilson, "Broken Windows." We will examine the broken win-dows thesis and how it plays out in these contexts later in the chapter.
4. See, for example, Garbarino and Crouter, "Defining the Community Con-

text for Parent-Child Relations," on child abuse; Coulton and Pandey, "Geographic Concentration of Poverty," and Anderson, "Neighborhood Effects on Teenage Pregnancy," on teen and out-of-wedlock births; Crane, "Epidemic Theory of Ghettos," on dropout rates; Sampson and Groves, "Community Structure and Crime," and Coulton and Pandey, "Geographic Concentration of Poverty," on crime and delinquency; and Holloway and Mulherin, "Effect of Adolescent Neighborhood Poverty," on unemployment. On neighborhood effects more broadly, see Gephart, "Neighborhoods and Communities as Contexts for Development," and Sampson, Morenoff, and Gannon-Rowley, "Assessing 'Neighborhood Effects,'" for reviews.

5. Chaskin and Joseph, "Building 'Community' in Mixed-Income Developments"; Fischer, *To Dwell Among Friends*; Freeman, *There Goes the 'Hood*; Pattillo, *Black on the Block*.

6. Pattillo, "Sweet Mothers and Gangbangers."

7. Pattillo, *Black on the Block*, 264; see also Freeman, *There Goes the 'Hood*, and Hyra, *New Urban Renewal*.

8. The discourse on gentrification is complex, contributing competing views of the determinants of the process (supply versus demand), outcomes (regeneration versus displacement), and value assessments ("emancipatory" versus "revanchist") (Lees, "Reappraisal of Gentrification"). As Lance Freeman makes clear, different people within gentrifying contexts have different perspectives on its benefits and harms, and in some cases residents see both positive and negative aspects at once (*There Goes the 'Hood*; see also Pattillo, *Black on the Block*). Such observations have led some to suggest the need for a more "complex and ambivalent normative assessment" of gentrification (Cameron, "Gentrification, Housing Redifferentiation and Urban Regeneration," 2374). Debates about whether mixed-income developments such as the one we are examining here can be considered "positive gentrification" are particularly lively in Europe, where "social mixing" development schemes, in many ways analogous to the Plan for Transformation and HOPE VI-associated efforts more broadly, have been ascendant. Proponents see them as public policy seeking to harness private capital and market forces to attract higher-income residents and generate neighborhood revitalization while reducing segregation and fostering inclusion of the poor and ethnic minorities; critics argue that they are essentially state-sanctioned and -assisted processes that lead to the same kinds of displacement and other negative outcomes for the poor that have given the term gentrification such a negative connotation. See, for example, Bridge, Butler, and Lees, *Mixed Communities*; Butler, "For Gentrification?" Davidson, "Spoiled Mixture"; and Lees, "Gentrification and Social Mixing."

9. As we previously noted, however, the number of CHA residents who in fact "return" to the mixed-income redevelopments is notably small, a very small proportion of the total number of CHA residents relocated by the Transformation. See chapter 1, note 28.

10. These include the shooting of Hadiyah Pendleton, a fifteen-year-old honors student killed in the crossfire of a retaliatory gang shooting, which generated national attention on gang violence in Chicago more broadly and garnered specific attention from President Obama.

11. Seemingly innocuous activities like older men playing chess, for example, were often understood by development professionals as cover for the illegal acts of others. As one development professional explained at a meeting, "This is not nice chess."

12. In response to perceived increases in crime and antisocial behavior in the neighborhood surrounding Oakwood Shores, for example, the development team began to convene "safety and security meetings" attended by both low-income renters and homeowners as well as by representatives of the CHA and police from the two districts where Oakwood Shores sits. In the spring of 2011, a series of shootings in the community, including five incidents in April, generated energetic efforts to push police to combat both crime and disorder more forcefully and to vigilantly enact a range of sanctions, surveillance measures, and heightened enforcement by property management—some focused on criminal behavior, but many on more broadly defined incivilities. We will explore these responses in more detail later in this chapter.

13. The list of such behaviors respondents noted goes on: leaving shoes outside apartment doors, walking down the street eating a bowl of cereal, stepping outside in bare feet or in pajamas. While some take the relative merits of their set of use values for granted (one homeowner at Park Boulevard, for example, commented about a resident who had to be corrected about the propriety of putting a sign on her apartment door asking guests to take their shoes off before entering, "She just didn't know that it wasn't proper to do that. She didn't know any better"), others recognize that such different expectations for behavior are fundamentally about preference.

14. As we will explore below, rules and processes specific to the development are largely the responsibility of property management. Existing and emerging organizations that play some role in shaping norms, promoting regulation, and monitoring enforcement are varied and include, at the development level, condominium associations, management committees, working groups, and the CHA Office of the Ombudsman. At the level of the broader community they include the police, established neighborhood organizations, and public forums such as CAPS meetings and Parks Advisory Councils.

15. Bursik and Grasmick, *Neighborhoods and Crime.*

16. Kelling and Wilson, "Broken Windows."

17. LaGrange, Ferraro, and Supancic, "Perceived Risk and Fear of Crime"; Lewis and Maxfield, "Fear in the Neighborhoods"; Perkins et al., "Physical Environment of Street Crime"; Skogan, *Disorder and Decline*; Taylor and

Covington, "Community Structural Change and Fear of Crime"; Taylor and Hale, "Testing Alternative Models of Fear of Crime."

18. Sampson and Raudenbush, "A New Look at Disorder," 610; Janowitz, "Sociological Theory and Social Control."

19. Indeed, Kelling and Wilson raise—and largely dismiss—the question of rights in their argument for aggressive suppression of incivilities. In reminiscing about an earlier era in which police primarily maintained order rather than solved crimes, they claim that they asserted "authority by acting, sometimes violently, on behalf of the community. Young toughs were roughed up, people were arrested 'on suspicion' or for vagrancy, and prostitutes and petty thieves were routed. 'Rights' were something enjoyed by decent folk, and perhaps also by the serious professional criminal, who avoided violence and could afford a lawyer" ("Broken Windows").

20. For example, one homeowner and leader of a neighborhood organization in the neighborhood surrounding Oakwood Shores, while explicitly arguing at one meeting for a "broken windows" response to unruly youths in the neighborhood, argues at another that imposing too-strict rules on the use of a public parkway would violate First Amendment rights. Similar tensions are frequently encountered by development professionals, who need to balance the pressures of responding to the preferences of their market-rate clients with their responsibility to help relocated public housing residents successfully integrate into these neighborhoods and progress toward "self-sufficiency."

21. This is most clearly true for buildings that accommodate both owned and rented units, which constitute a small portion of the buildings on each site (developers also sit on their boards, representing the rental units they own). But homeowners' interests and concerns have significant influence beyond the governance of their individual condominium associations, and they often put pressure on developers and property management to respond to problems in the development more broadly.

22. As we noted in chapter 4, Westhaven Park has only recently established work requirements—which are now systemwide for CHA-subsidized residents regardless of the type of housing they live in—and Park Boulevard has not established drug-testing requirements for residents.

23. There are exemptions to this rule, for example, for those who are employed, disabled, or elderly.

24. This rule, commonly referred to as "one strike," is in adherence to HUD's requirements for all public housing leases, and any infraction of rules under this policy is grounds for immediate eviction from public housing, even if it is a first offense and even if no household member is aware of the activity (see Code of Federal Regulations, Housing and Urban Development, title 24, sec. 966.4). Indeed, in addition to HUD requirements, many of the rules established at mixed-income redevelopment sites are developed to

comply with regulations attached to a wide variety of funding streams and institutions supporting the redevelopment. (See also note 34 below.)

25. "Tax-credit renter" refers to renters of affordable units, the middle tier of the three categories of units as we have categorized them in this book.

26. Although this tension is relevant for development teams as a whole across sites, it is particularly strongly felt at Oakwood Shores, given The Community Builders' organizational structure, in which responsibility for supportive services and property management rested with the same organization until 2012, when the Chicago Housing Authority ended its contract with TCB for providing social services to relocated public housing residents.

27. At this time the Chicago Housing Authority provided federal stimulus dollars to all mixed-income and traditional public housing developments for installing cameras. Developer-owner entities at Oakwood Shores, Park Boulevard, and Westhaven Park contributed additional funds, and homeowners and business owners paid a special assessment for exterior cameras at Park Boulevard.

28. According to one development professional at Oakwood Shores, although homeowners wanted cameras to be focused on their buildings as well, the CHA would not pay for these additional cameras, and homeowners were unwilling to do so themselves.

29. Chicago's video surveillance network has been called the most "extensive and integrated" in the nation. In 2012 an official with the Office of Emergency Management and Communication estimated that the city had access to twenty thousand public and private cameras through its system, including cameras owned and operated by the Police Department, Housing Authority, Transit Authority, Public Schools, and Park District; Schwartz, "Chicago's Video Surveillance Cameras," 47.

30. Indeed, early in the deployment of these cameras, two members of our research team who stopped for several minutes to observe activity at a playground on the site triggered the camera's warning system, summoning a member of the on-site security team.

31. These extra patrols, in response to pressure from organized homeowners' groups, were funded in part by the CHA.

32. Cruikshank, *Will to Empower*, 39.

33. Similarly, although development professionals clearly recognize the difference between relocated public housing residents and other subsidized renters (in large part because they have different responsibilities toward each), the work of property management staff in monitoring rule compliance and responding to infractions, including through the tenants' meetings described above, focuses on both categories of residents. In contrast, renters of affordable units have a strong tendency to distance themselves from public housing residents. They are often as vociferous as higher-income residents in complaining about them, and they are quick to dissociate themselves from their values and behaviors. This may be in part a response

to shared stigma and an effort to manage that stigma through distancing themselves; see, e.g., Goffman, *Stigma*; Link and Phelan, "Conceptualizing Stigma"; and McCormick, Joseph, and Chaskin, "New Stigma of Relocated Public Housing Residents." Their stance toward public housing residents is exacerbated by the sense among many of them that the relocated public housing residents enjoy relatively greater benefits, including outlets for grievances (through the ombudsman or former LAC leadership), special services, and legal protections. This may be most sharply felt at Westhaven Park, given the consent decree in place there. As one renter of an affordable unit there recounted, "I called the CHA main office to complain about my CHA neighbor, and they told me that CHA have more rights than I do. . . . No matter what I say and do it doesn't matter." At the same time, renters of affordable units are often painted with the same brush as relocated public housing residents and bear the brunt of exclusion or marginalization in similar ways.

34. This suggestion was not implemented here—although it has been at Park Boulevard—on the grounds that doing so singled out relocated public housing residents engaged in a legal activity. The winning argument in this case was pushed by development professionals against that of some condominium owners: "You can't do different things, make different rules for CHA residents. I think the owners are more likely to smoke pot. . . . Smoking [cigarettes] is not illegal. What if they cooked Indian food or chit-lins or something else that smells? What if a person has dog allergies?" The conflict around such behaviors is further illustrated by the argument, made by several relocated public housing residents in this building (and acknowl-edged by the development professional in attendance), that while public housing residents are the target of a range of complaints about noise, smell, and sanitation, they are also sometimes blamed for the behavior of owners, such as smoking marijuana in *their* units.

35. One reason for this is that a number of institutions provide financing to subsidize units (e.g., the CHA, HUD, and banks and state agencies holding low-income housing tax credits), and each claims oversight privileges to frequently check on their investment; it is thus not just property managers who are targeting public housing residents for inspection.

36. A public housing advocate involved in the Transformation also stresses this point, and how far individual complaints get generalized to the popula-tion of relocated public housing residents: "The market-rate owners in that building were driving these concerns, and it wasn't about this neighbor or that neighbor, it was about public housing residents as a category. . . . But the point that was so interesting to me [was] that the market-rate people were really inexperienced. . . . You know, I mean it's hard for people to live together, and the membrane between my private domestic space and your private domestic space is a highly volatile thing, you know, between neighbors, and so there is that piece of this in some ways, even though all

of the discourse is about the sort of remedial project for public housing residents. You have lots of public housing residents who were much more sophisticated about living with other people, about being tolerant, about not depending on authority structures to negotiate and resolve neighborhood, neighbor-to-neighbor issues."

37. The privatizing of urban space has been noted as an effect of neoliberal urban reform, and with it the concomitant decrease in the "civic functions" that open public space can perform in favor of more highly regulated spaces that restrict use to specific activities and behavior. The arguments behind such restrictions often focus on the primacy of maintaining order. Don Mitchell, for example, focusing on the ways privatizing has limited urban dwellers' "right to the city," is particularly concerned with the curtailment of rights to use public space for political mobilizing and expression and with restrictions on the rights of access and use for the homeless who, having no "private" space to retreat to, are particularly victimized by the ways property rights "hedge in space, bound it off, and restrict its usage." Mitchell, *Right to the City*, 33. In this way, he argues, the homeless are effectively denied their rights as citizens. As the analysis here suggests, however, the dynamics of privatizing and their extension to formerly "public" spaces—including streets—can extend to some of the most basic daily activities as well as curtail citizens' rights to participation and protest (see also Mitchell and Staeheli, "Clean and Safe?").

38. Leccese and McCormick, *Charter of the New Urbanism*; Newman, *Defensible Space*; Newman, *Creating Defensible Space*; Popkin et al., *Decade of HOPE VI*.

39. Oakwood Shores is unique among the three sites in that two large public parks are adjacent to the development, providing significantly more public space than at the other two sites but also contributing to worries about safety, since it is often in the parks that violent crime occurs, and the parks are not within the control of development teams.

40. Ruppert, "Rights to Public Space," 273; Lofland, *Public Realm*. On the decline of public space more generally see Harvey, "Social Justice, Postmodernism and the City"; Mitchell, *Right to the City*; Sorkin, *Variations on a Theme Park*; and Zukin, *Cultures of Cities*.

41. Indeed, some homeowners also recognize that such behaviors are differently perceived and acted on depending on who is involved. As one homeowner at Westhaven Park noted, "Well, if you're low income, I think that they look at you differently. . . . If a whole bunch of low-income people were just like hanging out in front of a building, it looks a little different than if me and four or five other people that are owners are hanging out in front of the building. It just looks different, so people can say whatever they want."

42. This is especially so at Oakwood Shores and Park Boulevard, where the public housing residents are less well organized and lack the benefit of

the consent decree that strengthens Westhaven Park residents' hand in negotiation.

43. In many cases, rather than fully evicting residents, development teams and the CHA will seek to reassign residents voluntarily from mixed-income public housing redevelopments to traditional public housing.

CHAPTER EIGHT

1. Melita M. Garza, "CHA Dumps Cop Force in Revamp," *Chicago Tribune*, October 13, 1999.
2. Burnham and Bennett, *Plan of Chicago*; Kling, "Wide Boulevards, Narrow Visions."
3. This criticism clearly reflects some of the critiques of New Urbanist orientations outlined in chapter 2.
4. See figures 4.1 to 4.3 in chapter 4.
5. Bennett, *Third City*, 148.
6. Zielenbach, "Assessing Economic Change"; Zielenbach, "Catalyzing Community Development"; Zielenbach and Voith, "Local Market Dynamics." See also Turbov and Piper, *HOPE VI and Mixed-Finance Redevelopments*.
7. With census block group data (population demographics and housing), home mortgage data (on home purchase loans), and community reinvestment act data (small business loans), we are able to compare change at the "development footprint" level with change in the development's "surrounding area." We use an approximation of the "development footprint" constructed with the census block groups that contain the actual development boundaries (see methodological appendix for maps). We define the "surrounding area" using the census tracts that are contiguous to the development footprint (except those on the other side of a significant physical divider such as a major thoroughfare) and subtracting the census block groups that we used for the development footprint. With data available only at the census tract level (educational attainment, employment status, and residential stability) we provide an analysis of the surrounding neighborhood including the development footprint, but we cannot separate the two with any precision. We must also use larger geographic units to examine two other areas of neighborhood change: foreclosure data are available only for the Chicago community area, and crime data are available only by police beats.
8. The development footprint and the neighborhood surrounding Westhaven Park showed similar improvements in the unemployment rate, from 29 percent to 17 percent, but this was not the case in and around Oakwood Shores, where unemployment changed only from 34 percent to 29 percent from 2000 to 2010.
9. These developments are Lake Parc Place, Lake Park Crescent, and Jazz on the Boulevard.

10. Chaskin et al., "Public Housing Transformation."
11. Public school performance data are available at http://cps.edu/Schools /Find_a_school/Pages/schoollocator.aspx.
12. There have been recent efforts to address this issue. In 2013, for example, the city of Chicago announced that, along with The Community Builders, it would develop a 30,000-square-foot arts and recreation center adjacent to Oakwood Shores, and in 2014 the city announced that a grocery store was planned for the Oakwood Shores site.
13. See, for example, Berry, Portney, and Thomson, *Rebirth of Urban Democracy*; Briggs, *Democracy as Problem Solving*; Chaskin et al., *Building Community Capacity*; Chaskin, Khare, and Joseph, "Participation, Deliberation, and Decision Making"; Cohen and Rogers, *Associations and Democracy*; Fung, *Empowered Participation*; Ostrander, "Agency and Initiative by Community Associations"; Pateman, *Participation and Democratic Theory*; Sirianni, *Investing in Democracy*; Yates, *Neighborhood Democracy*; Young, *Justice and the Politics of Difference*.
14. Berry, Portney, and Thomson, *Rebirth of Urban Democracy*; Chaskin, "Fostering Neighborhood Democracy"; Crenson, *Neighborhood Politics*; Verba, Schlozman, and Brady, *Voice and Equality*.
15. Berry, Portney, and Thomson, *Rebirth of Urban Democracy*.
16. "Mission and Background," Bronzeville Area Residents' and Commerce Council, accessed November 20, 2013, http://www.thebarcc.org/about.php.
17. Ibid.
18. The city's announcement in late 2013 that a 30,000-square-foot arts and recreation center would be built at Ellis Park portends increased activity and resident engagement for EPAC and a higher profile in the broader neighborhood.

CHAPTER NINE

1. Chicago Housing Authority, *Plan Forward: Communities That Work*; http:// www.thecha.org/filebin/pdf/PressReleases/13–04–19_CHA-FINAL-ONLINE _FINAL.pdf.
2. CHA, *Plan Forward*, 17.
3. DeLuca, "Continuing Relevance of the Gautreaux Program"; DeLuca and Rosenbaum, "If Low-Income Blacks Are Given a Chance"; DeLuca et al., "Gautreaux Mothers and Their Children"; Duncan and Zuberi, "Mobility Lessons from Gautreaux and Moving to Opportunity"; Galster et al., *Why Not in My Backyard?* Hogan, *Scattered-Site Housing*; Keels et al., "Fifteen Years Later"; Keels, "Residential Attainment of Now-Adult Gautreaux Children"; Rubinowitz and Rosenbaum, *Crossing the Class and Color Lines*. This has not been the case with all dispersion efforts driven by desegregation lawsuits, however. See, for example, Goetz, "Desegregation Lawsuits and Public Housing Dispersal"; Popkin, Cunningham, and Woodley, *Residents at Risk*.

4. Boyd, "Defensive Development"; Boyd et al., "Durability of Gains"; Briggs et al., *Moving to Opportunity*; Kling et al., "Moving to Opportunity and Tranquility"; Ludwig et al., "What Can We Learn about Neighborhood Effects?" Orr et al., *Moving to Opportunity*; Feins and Shroder, "Moving to Opportunity"; Sampson, "Moving to Inequality"; Rosenbaum and Zuberi, "Comparing Residential Mobility Programs."

5. Basolo, "Examining Mobility Outcomes"; Buron et al., *HOPE VI Resident Tracking Study*; Popkin et al., "Has Hope VI Transformed Residents' Lives?" Popkin, "Glass Half Empty?" Kingsley, Johnson, and Pettit, "Patterns of Section 8 Relocation"; Oakley and Burchfield, "Out of the Projects."

6. Chaskin et al., "Public Housing Transformation."

7. Rubinowitz and Rosenbaum, *Crossing the Class and Color Lines*; DeLuca et al., "Gautreaux Mothers and Their Children."

8. Orr et al., *Moving to Opportunity*; Briggs, Popkin, and Goering, *Moving to Opportunity*; Kessler et al., "Associations of Housing Mobility Interventions."

9. Popkin, "Glass Half Empty?" Goetz, "Housing Dispersal Programs"; Clampet-Lundquist, "HOPE VI Relocation"; Curley, "Relocating the Poor."

10. Chaskin et al., "Public Housing Transformation."

11. Kleit, "Role of Neighborhood Social Networks"; Kleit and Carnegie, "Integrated or Isolated?" DeLuca, "Continuing Relevance of the Gautreaux Program."

12. Buron et al., *HOPE VI Resident Tracking Study*; Kleit, "HOPE VI New Communities"; Levy, McDade, and Bertumen, "Mixed-Income Living"; Graves, "Mixed Outcome Developments"; Graves, "Structuring of Urban Life"; Chaskin et al., "Public Housing Transformation"; Chaskin and Joseph, "Social Interaction in Mixed-Income Developments"; Kleit and Carnegie, "Integrated or Isolated?"

13. Allport, *Nature of Prejudice*; Pettigrew, "Intergroup Contact Theory"; Pettigrew and Tropp, "Meta-analytic Test of Intergroup Contact."

14. Barlow et al., "Contact Caveat"; Paolini, Harwood, and Rubin, "Negative Intergroup Contact"; Quillian, "Prejudice as a Response to Perceived Group Threat."

15. Cohen, *Boundaries of Blackness*; Khare, Joseph, and Chaskin, "Enduring Significance of Race."

16. Chaskin et al., "Public Housing Transformation."

17. DeFilippis, "On Spatial Solutions"; Bohl, "New Urbanism and the City." This is also a general critique of New Urbanism, on which, as we have shown, mixed-income public housing redevelopments are in part based.

18. Joseph and Chaskin, "Mixed-Income Developments and Low Rates of Return."

19. The remaining 16 percent now live in scattered-site housing, but more than 6,000 residents with the "right to return" were no longer accounted for in the CHA system. Half of these remain unaccounted for, while the rest have been identified as individuals who either were evicted, died, were

living in unsubsidized housing but waiting to return, or chose to remain in unsubsidized housing. A few had moved to senior housing. See Chaskin et al., "Public Housing Transformation." These numbers, it is important to note, include only *leaseholders*; individuals living in CHA units but not listed on the lease, such as relatives and friends in need of housing, are not included and have no right to return. The number of people in this latter category is unknown, but such "doubling up" is common among low-income families who have trouble finding affordable housing. See Skobba and Goetz, "Mobility Decisions of Very Low-Income Households."

20. Fraser, Chaskin, and Bazuin, "Making Mixed-Income Neighborhoods Work"; Popkin, "Glass Half Empty?"

21. Parkes et al., *Opportunity Chicago.*

22. CHA, *Plan Forward*, 17.

23. Angelucci et al., "The Impact of Oportunidades on Consumption, Savings and Transfers"; Baird et al., "Relative Effectiveness of Conditional and Unconditional Cash Transfers"; Fraser, Chaskin, and Bazuin, "Making Mixed-Income Neighborhoods Work"; McKernan and Sherraden, *Asset Building and Low-Income Families*; Sherraden, *Assets and the Poor*; Sherraden, *Inclusion in the American Dream*; Schreiner and Sherraden, *Can the Poor Save?*

24. Ficke and Piesse, *Evaluation of the Family Self-Sufficiency Program*; Sard, "Family Self-Sufficiency Program"; Silva et al., "Evaluation of the Family Self-Sufficiency Program."

25. Briggs, "Brown Kids in White Suburbs"; Chaskin, "Democracy and Bureaucracy"; Chaskin, Khare, and Joseph, "Participation, Deliberation, and Decision Making"; Young, *Justice and the Politics of Difference.*

26. Chaskin, Khare, and Joseph, "Participation, Deliberation, and Decision Making."

27. Young, *Justice and the Politics of Difference.*

28. Whalen and Wynn, "Enhancing Primary Services for Youth."

29. Theodos et al., "Challenge of Targeting Services."

30. Popkin et al., *CHA Residents and the Plan for Transformation.*

31. Popkin et al., "Planning the Housing Opportunities and Services Together Demonstration."

32. Chaskin, Sichling, and Joseph, "Youth in Mixed-Income Communities."

33. See www.hud.gov/rad.

34. Pattillo, "Investing in Poor Black Neighborhoods."

35. Joseph, "Mixed-Income Symposium Summary and Response."

36. Briggs, Popkin, and Goering, *Moving to Opportunity*; DeLuca, "Continuing Relevance of the Gautreaux Program"; DeLuca and Rosenbaum, "If Low-Income Blacks Are Given a Chance"; DeLuca et al., "Gautreaux Mothers and Their Children"; Feins and Shroder, "Moving to Opportunity"; Keels et al., "Fifteen Years Later"; Kling et al., "Moving to Opportunity and Tranquility"; Ludwig et al., "What Can We Learn?" Orr et al., *Moving to Opportunity.*

37. Briggs, Darden, and Aidala, "In the Wake of Desegregation"; Galster et al., *Why Not in My Backyard?* Goetz, Lam, and Heitlinger, *There Goes the Neighborhood?*" Santiago and Galster, "Assessing the Property Value Impacts"; Hogan, *Scattered-Site Housing*; Massey et al., *Climbing Mount Laurel*; Silver, "Mixing Policies."

38. Hogan, *Scattered-Site Housing*; Kleit, "Housing, Social Networks, and Access to Opportunity"; Kleit, "Role of Neighborhood Social Networks"; Kleit, "Neighborhood Relations"; Larsen, "Scattered-Site and Aggregate Public Housing."

39. Katz, "Narratives of Failure?"

40. Urban Institute, *Developing Choice Neighborhoods*.

41. Silver, "Obama's Urban Policy," 6; Katz, "Obama's Metro Presidency."

APPENDIX

1. The affordable rental and for-sale units are financed through a combination of federal, state, and city programs, including the Low Income Housing Tax Credit, Affordable Housing Tax Credit, and tax increment financing. The specific financing sources and stipulations vary by mixed-income site, depending on what was allocated to the developer. These programs require that units be rented or sold to households earning a certain percentage of area median income, typically 50 percent to 80 percent for rental units and up to 120 percent for for-sale units.

2. A more complete analysis of these data can be found in Chaskin et al., "Public Housing Transformation."

References

Abu-Lughod, Janet L. *New York, Chicago, Los Angeles: America's Global Cities*. Minneapolis: University of Minnesota Press, 1999.

Akers, Ronald L., Marvin D. Krohn, Lonn Lanza-Kaduce, and Marcia Radosevich. "Social Learning and Deviant Behavior: Specific Test of a General Theory." *American Sociological Review* 44 (1979): 636–55.

Allport, Gordon. *The Nature of Prejudice*. Cambridge, MA: Addison-Wesley, 1954.

Amos, Hawley H. "Human Ecology, Space, Time, and Urbanization." In *Urban Patterns: Studies in Human Ecology*, edited by George A. Theodorson, 111–14. University Park: Pennsylvania State University Press, 1982.

Anderson, Elijah. "Neighborhood Effects on Teenage Pregnancy." In *The Urban Underclass*, edited by Christopher Jencks and Paul E. Peterson, 375–98. Washington, DC: Brookings Institution Press, 1991.

———. *Streetwise: Race, Class, and Change in an Urban Community*. Chicago: University of Chicago Press, 1990.

Angelucci, Manuela, Orazio Attanasio, and Vicenzo Di Mario. "The Impact of Oportunidades on Consumption, Savings and Transfers." *Fiscal Studies* 33 (2012): 305–34.

Arthurson, Kathy. "Creating Inclusive Communities through Balancing Social Mix: A Critical Relationship or Tenuous Link?" *Urban Policy and Research* 20 (2002): 245–61.

———. "Operationalising Social Mix: Spatial Scale, Lifestyle and Stigma as Mediating Points in Resident Interaction." *Urban Policy and Research* 28 (2010): 49–63.

Atkinson, Rowland, and Keith Kintrea. "Owner-Occupation, Social Mix, and Neighbourhood Impacts." *Policy and Politics* 28 (2000): 93–108.

Atlanta Housing Authority. *FY2005 Moving to Work Annual Report*. Atlanta: Atlanta Housing Authority, 2004.

August, Martine. "Social Mix and Canadian Public Housing Redevelopment: Experiences in Toronto." *Canadian Journal of Urban Research* 17 (2008): 82–100.

Bailey, Nick, Anna Haworth, Tony Manzi, Primali Paranagamage, and Marion Roberts. *Creating and Sustaining Mixed Income Communities*. London: University of Westminster, 2006.

Baird, Sarah, Francisco H. G. Ferreira, Berk Özler, and Michael Woolcock. "Relative Effectiveness of Conditional and Unconditional Cash Transfers for Schooling Outcomes in Developing Countries: A Systematic Review." *Campbell Systematic Reviews* 2013:8.

Bandura, Albert. "Self-Efficacy: Towards a Unifying Theory of Behavioral Change." *Psychological Review* 84 (1977): 191–215.

———. *Social Learning Theory*. Englewood Cliffs, NJ: Prentice Hall, 1977.

Barlow, Fiona Kate, Stefania Paolini, Anne Pedersen, Matthew J. Hornsey, Helena R. M. Radke, Jake Harwood, Mark Runi, and Chris G. Sibley. "The Contact Caveat: Negative Contact Predicts Increased Prejudice More Than Positive Contact Predicts Reduced Prejudice." *Personality and Social Psychology Bulletin* 38 (2012): 1629–43.

Barnett, Jonathan. *Redesigning Cities: Principles, Practice, Implementation*. Chicago: Planners Press, 2003.

Baron, Richard D. "The Evolution of HOPE VI as a Development Program." In *From Despair to Hope: HOPE VI and the New Promise of Public Housing in America's Cities*, edited by Henry G. Cisneros and Lora Engdahl, 31–47. Washington, DC: Brookings Institution Press, 2009.

Barry, Patrick. *More Than Bricks and Mortar: A Quality of Life Plan for West Haven*. Chicago: New Communities Initiative, 2002.

Barry, Patrick, and Lisa Riley. *Quad Communities: Connecting Past, Present and Future*. Chicago: New Communities Program, 2005.

Basolo, Victoria. "Examining Mobility Outcomes in the Housing Choice Voucher Program: Neighborhood Poverty, Employment, and Public School Quality." *Cityscape* 15, no. 2 (2013): 135–54.

Beall, Jo. "Globalization and Social Exclusion in Cities: Framing the Debate with Lessons from Africa and Asia." *Environment and Urbanization* 14 (2002): 41–51.

Bell, Derrick A. *Faces at the Bottom of the Well: The Permanence of Racism*. New York: Basic Books, 1992.

Bennett, Larry. "Downtown Restructuring and Public Housing in Contemporary Chicago: Fashioning a Better World-Class City." In *Where Are Poor People to Live? Transforming Public Housing Communities*, edited by Larry Bennett, Janet L. Smith, and Patricia A. Wright, 282–300. Armonk, NY: M. E. Sharpe, 2006.

———. *The Third City: Chicago and American Urbanism*. Chicago: University of Chicago Press, 2010.

Bennett, Larry, Janet L. Smith, and Patricia A. Wright, eds. *Where Are Poor People to Live? Transforming Public Housing Communities*. Armonk, NY: M. E. Sharpe, 2006.

Benson, Charles S., and Peter B. Lund. *Neighborhood Distribution of Local Public Services*. Berkeley: University of California, Institute of Governmental Studies, 1969.

Berndt, Harry E. *New Rulers in the Ghetto: The Community Development Corporation and Urban Poverty*. Westport, CT: Greenwood Press, 1977.

Berry, Jeffrey M., Kent E. Portney, and Ken Thomson. *The Rebirth of Urban Democracy*. Washington, DC: Brookings Institution, 1993.

Berube, Alan. *Mixed Communities in England: A U.S. Perspective on Evidence and Policy Prospects*. Washington, DC: Brookings Institution, 2005.

Bloom, Nicholas D. *Public Housing That Worked: New York in the Twentieth Century*. Philadelphia: University of Pennsylvania Press, 2008.

Bluestone, Barry, and Bennett Harrison. *The Deindustrialization of America: Plant Closings, Community Abandonment, and the Dismantling of Basic Industry*. New York: Basic Books, 1982.

Bohl, Charles C. "New Urbanism and the City: Potential Applications and Implications for Distressed Inner-City Neighborhoods." *Housing Policy Debate* 11 (2000): 761–801.

Bolt, Gideon, and Ronald van Kempen. "Successful Mixing? Effects of Urban Restructuring Policies in Dutch Neighbourhoods." *Journal of Economic and Social Geography* 102 (2011): 361–68.

Booth, Charles. *Life and Labour of the People in London*. London: Macmillan, 1902.

Boston, Thomas D. "The Effects of Revitalization on Public Housing Residents." *Journal of the American Planning Association* 71 (2005): 393–407.

Bott, Helen. "Observation of Play Activities in a Nursery School." *Genetic Psychology Monographs* 4 (1928): 44–88.

Bourdieu, Pierre. "The Forms of Capital." In *Handbook of Theory and Research for the Sociology of Education*, edited by John G. Richardson, 241–59. New York: Greenwood Press, 1986.

———. *Outline of a Theory of Practice*. Cambridge: Cambridge University Press, 1977.

Bowly, Devereux. *The Poorhouse: Subsidized Housing in Chicago, 1895–1976*. Carbondale: Southern Illinois University, 2012.

Bowring, Finn. "Social Exclusion: Limitations of the Debate." *Critical Social Policy* 20 (2000): 307–30.

Boyd, Melody, Kathryn Edin, Susan Clampet-Lundquist, and G. Duncan. "The Durability of Gains from the Gautreaux Two Residential Mobility Program: A Qualitative Analysis of Who Stays and Who Moves from Low-Poverty Neighborhoods." *Housing Policy Debate* 20 (2010): 119–46.

Boyd, Michelle. "Defensive Development: The Role of Racial Conflict in Gentrification." *Urban Affairs Review* 43 (2008): 751–76.

Breitbart, Myrna M., and Ellen J. Pader. "Establishing Ground: Representing Gender and Race in a Mixed Housing Development." *Gender, Place and Culture* 2 (1995): 5–20.

Brenner, Neil, and Nik Theodore. "Cities and the Geographies of 'Actually Existing Neoliberalism.'" *Antipode* 34 (2002): 349–79.

Brewer, Keri R., and Daniel L. Wann. "Observational Learning Effectiveness as a Function of Model Characteristics: Investigating the Importance of Social Power." *Social Behavior and Personality* 26 (1998): 1–10.

Bridge, Gary, Tim Butler, and Loretta Lees. *Mixed Communities: Gentrification by Stealth?* Bristol, UK: Policy Press, 2011.

Briggs, Xavier de Souza. "Brown Kids in White Suburbs: Housing Mobility and the Many Faces of Social Capital." *Housing Policy Debate* 9 (1998): 177–221.

———. *Democracy as Problem Solving: Civic Capacity in Communities across the Globe.* Cambridge, MA: MIT Press, 2008.

———. "Doing Democracy Up-Close: Culture, Power, and Communication in Community Building." *Journal of Planning Education and Research* 18 (1998): 1–13.

———. "Moving Up versus Moving Out: Neighborhood Effects in Housing Mobility Programs." *Housing Policy Debate* 8 (1997): 195–234.

Briggs, Xavier de Souza, Joe T. Darden, and Angela Aidala. "In the Wake of Desegregation: Early Impacts of Scattered-Site Public Housing on Neighborhoods in Yonkers, New York." *Journal of the American Planning Association* 65, no. 1 (1999): 27–49.

Briggs, Xavier de Souza, Susan J. Popkin, and John M. Goering. *Moving to Opportunity: The Story of an American Experiment to Fight Ghetto Poverty.* New York: Oxford University Press, 2010.

Brooks-Gunn, Jeanne, Greg J. Duncan, and Lawrence J. Aber, eds. *Neighborhood Poverty.* Vol. 1, *Context and Consequences for Children.* New York: Russell Sage Foundation, 1997.

Brophy, Paul C., and Rhonda N. Smith. "Mixed-Income Housing: Factors for Success." *Cityscape* 3 (1997): 3–31.

Burchardt, Tania, Julian Le Grand, and David Piachaud. "Social Exclusion in Britain, 1991–1995." *Social Policy and Administration* 33 (1999): 227–44.

Burgess, Ernest W. "The Growth of the City." In *Urban Patterns: Studies in Human Ecology,* edited by George A. Theodorson, 35–41. University Park: Pennsylvania State University Press, 1982. Originally published 1925.

Burnett, Alan. "Neighborhood Participation, Political Demand Making and Local Outputs in British and North American Cities." In *Public Service Provision and Urban Development,* edited by Andrew Kirby, Paul Knox, and Steven Pinch, 316–62. London: Croom Helm, 1984.

Burnham, Daniel H., and Edward H. Bennett. *Plan of Chicago.* Chicago: Commercial Club, 1909.

Buron, Larry, Susan J. Popkin, Diane Levy, Laura E. Harris, and Jill Khadduri. *The HOPE VI Resident Tracking Study: A Snapshot of the Current Living Situation of*

Original Residents from Eight Sites. Washington, DC: U.S. Department of Housing and Urban Development, 2002.

Bursik, Robert, and Harold G. Grasmick. *Neighborhoods and Crime: The Dimensions of Effective Community Control*. New York: Lexington Books, 1993.

Burt, Ronald S. "General Social Survey Network Items." *Connections* 8 (1985): 119–23.

———. *Structural Holes: The Social Structure of Competition*. Cambridge, MA: Harvard University Press, 1992.

———. "Structural Holes versus Network Closure as Social Capital." In *Social Capital: Theory and Research*, edited by Nan Lin, Karen S. Cook, and Ronald S. Burt, 31–56. New York: Aldine de Gruyter, 2001.

Butler, Tim. "For Gentrification?" *Environment and Planning A* 39 (2007): 162–81.

Calthorpe, Peter. *The Next American Metropolis: Ecology, Communities, and the American Dream*. New York: Princeton Architectural Press, 1993.

Campbell, Karen E., and Barrett A. Lee. "Sources of Personal Neighbor Networks: Social Integration, Need, or Time?" *Social Forces* 70 (1992): 1077–1100.

Campbell, Wendell. *Mid-South Strategic Development Plan: Restoring Bronzeville*. Chicago: Mid-South Planning Commission, 1993.

Cameron, Stuart. "Gentrification, Housing Redifferentiation and Urban Regeneration: 'Going for Growth' in Newcastle upon Tyne." *Urban Studies* 40 (2003): 2367–82.

Carr, Patrick J. "The New Parochialism: The Implications of the Beltway Case for Arguments concerning Informal Social Control." *American Journal of Sociology* 108 (2003): 1249–91.

Castells, Manuel. *The Urban Question: A Marxist Approach*. Cambridge, MA: MIT Press, 1977.

Ceraso, Karen. "Is Mixed-Income Housing the Key?" *Shelterforce* 1995. http://www.nhi.org/online/issues/80/mixhous.html. Accessed October 15, 2013.

Chase-Lansdale, P. Lindsay, Rachel A. Gordon, Jeanne Brooks-Gunn, and Pamela K. Klebanov. "Neighborhood and Family Influences on the Intellectual and Behavioral Competence of Preschool and Early School-Age Children." In *Neighborhood Poverty*, vol. 1, *Contexts and Consequences for Children*, edited by Jeanne Brooks-Gunn, Greg Duncan, and Lawrence J. Aber, 79–118. New York: Russell Sage Foundation, 1997.

Chaskin, Robert J. "Democracy and Bureaucracy in a Community Planning Process." *Journal of Planning Education and Research* 24, no. 4 (2005): 408–19.

———. "Fostering Neighborhood Democracy: Legitimacy and Accountability within Loosely Coupled Systems." *Nonprofit and Voluntary Sector Quarterly* 32 (2003): 161–89.

———. "Integration and Exclusion: Urban Poverty, Public Housing Reform, and the Dynamics of Neighborhood Restructuring." *Annals of the American Academy of Political and Social Science* 647 (2013): 237–67.

———. "Perspectives on Neighborhood and Community: A Review of the Literature." *Social Service Review* 71 (1997): 521–47.

―――. "Theories of Community." In *The Handbook of Community Practice*, edited by Marie Weil, Michael S. Reisch, and Mary L. Ohmer, 105–22. Thousand Oaks, CA: Sage Publications, 2012.

―――, ed. *Youth Gangs and Community Intervention: Research, Practice, and Evidence*. New York: Columbia University Press, 2010.

Chaskin, Robert J., Prudence Brown, Sudhir Venkatesh, and Avis Vidal. *Building Community Capacity*. New York: Aldine de Gruyter, 2001.

Chaskin, Robert J., and Sunil Garg. "The Issue of Governance in Neighborhood-Based Initiatives." *Urban Affairs Review* 32 (1997): 631–61.

Chaskin, Robert J., and Mark L. Joseph. "Building 'Community' in Mixed-Income Developments: Assumptions, Approaches, and Early Experiences." *Urban Affairs Review* 45 (2010): 299–335.

―――. " 'Positive' Gentrification, Social Control and the 'Right to the City' in Mixed-Income Communities: Uses and Expectations of Space and Place." *International Journal of Urban and Regional Research* 37 (2013): 480–502.

―――. "Social Interaction in Mixed-Income Developments: Relational Expectations and Emerging Reality." *Journal of Urban Affairs* 33 (2011): 209–37.

Chaskin, Robert J., Mark L. Joseph, Sara Voelker, and Amy Dworsky. "Public Housing Transformation and Resident Relocation: Comparing Destinations and Household Characteristics in Chicago." *Cityscape* 14 (2012): 183–214.

Chaskin, Robert J., and Mikael Karlström. *Beyond the Neighborhood: Policy Engagement and Systems Change in the New Communities Program*. New York: MDRC, 2012.

Chaskin, Robert J., Amy T. Khare, and Mark L. Joseph. "Participation, Deliberation, and Decision Making: The Dynamics of Inclusion and Exclusion in Mixed-Income Developments." *Urban Affairs Review* 48 (2012): 863–906.

Chaskin, Robert J., Florian Sichling, and Mark L. Joseph. "Youth in Mixed-Income Communities Replacing Public Housing Complexes: Context, Dynamics and Response." *Cities* 35 (2013): 423–31.

Chicago Housing Authority. *Annual Plan for Transformation FY2003*. Chicago: Chicago Housing Authority, 2002.

―――. *CHA Leaseholder Housing Choice and Relocation Rights Contract*. Chicago: Chicago Housing Authority, 2001.

―――. *FY2000 Moving to Work Annual Report*. Chicago: Chicago Housing Authority, 2001.

―――. *FY2007 Moving to Work Annual Report*. Chicago: Chicago Housing Authority, 2008.

―――. *FY2009 Moving to Work Annual Report*. Chicago: Chicago Housing Authority, 2010.

―――. *FY2012 Moving to Work Annual Report*. Chicago: Chicago Housing Authority, 2013.

―――. *FY2013 Moving to Work Annual Plan*. Chicago: Chicago Housing Authority, 2014.

———. *FY2014 Moving to Work Annual Plan*. Chicago: Chicago Housing Authority, 2015.

———. *Plan for Transformation: Improving Public Housing in Chicago and the Quality of Life*. Chicago: Chicago Housing Authority, 2000.

———. *The Plan for Transformation: An Update on Relocation*. Chicago: Chicago Housing Authority, 2011.

———. *The Plan for Transformation at 10: Goals and Progress of the Plan*. Chicago: Chicago Housing Authority, 2009.

———. *Plan for Transformation Year 2: Moving to Work Annual Plan FY2001*. Chicago: Chicago Housing Authority, 2000.

Chicago Housing Authority and the US Department of Housing and Urban Development. *Moving to Work Demonstration Agreement*. Chicago: Chicago Housing Authority and US Department of Housing and Urban Development, 2000.

Cisneros, Henry G., and Lora Engdahl, eds. *From Despair to Hope: HOPE VI and the New Promise of Public Housing in America's Cities*. Washington, DC: Brookings Institution Press, 2009.

Clampet-Lundquist, Susan. "'Everyone Had Your Back': Social Ties, Perceived Safety, and Public Housing Relocation." *City and Community* 9 (2010): 87–108.

———. "HOPE VI Relocation: Moving to New Neighborhoods and Building New Ties." *Housing Policy Debate* 15 (2004): 415–47.

Clark, Kenneth B. "A Conversation with James Baldwin." In *Conversations with James Baldwin*, edited by Fred L. Standley and Louis H. Pratt, 38–45. Jackson: University Press of Mississippi, 1989. Originally published 1963.

Cohen, Cathy J. *The Boundaries of Blackness: AIDS and the Breakdown of Black Politics*. Chicago: University of Chicago Press, 1999.

Cohen, Don, and Laurence Prusak. *In Good Company: How Social Capital Makes Organizations Work*. Boston: Harvard Business School Press, 2001.

Cohen, Joshua, and Joel Rogers. *Associations and Democracy*. New York: Verso, 1995.

Coleman, James S. "Social Capital in the Creation of Human Capital." *American Journal of Sociology* 94 (1988): S95–S120.

Comitta, Thomas J. Chapter 18. In *Charter of the New Urbanism: Congress for the New Urbanism*, edited by Emily Talen, 171–78. New York: McGraw-Hill, 2013.

Congress for the New Urbanism and US Department of Housing and Urban Development. *Principles for Inner-City Neighborhood Design: Creating Communities of Opportunity*. Washington, DC: US Department of Housing and Urban Development, 2000.

Cook, Maria Lorena. "Is Incorporation of Unauthorized Immigrants Possible? Inclusion and Contingency for Non-status Migrants and Legal Immigrants." In *Outsiders No More? Models of Immigrant Political Incorporation*, edited by Jennifer Hochschild, Jacqueline Chattopadhyay, Claudine Gay, and Michael Jones-Correa, 43–64. New York: Oxford University Press, 2013.

Coulton, Claudia J., Jill E. Korbin, Marilyn Su, and Julian Chow. "Community Level Factors and Child Maltreatment Rates." *Child Development* 66 (1995): 1262–76.

Coulton, Claudia J., and Shanta Pandey. "Geographic Concentration of Poverty and Risk to Children in Urban Neighborhoods." *American Behavioral Scientist* 35 (1992): 238–57.

Cove, Elizabeth, Margery Austin Turner, Xavier de Souza Briggs, and Cynthia Duarte. *Can Escaping from Poor Neighborhoods Increase Employment and Earnings?* Washington, DC: Urban Institute, 2008.

Crane, Jonathan. "The Epidemic Theory of Ghettos and Neighborhood Effects on Dropping Out and Teenage Childbearing." *American Journal of Sociology* 96 (1991): 1226–59.

Crenson, Matthew A. *Neighborhood Politics.* Cambridge, MA: Harvard University Press, 1983.

Cruikshank, Barbara. *The Will to Empower: Democratic Citizens and Other Subjects.* Ithaca, NY: Cornell University Press, 1999.

Cummings, Jean L., and Denise DiPasquale. "The Low-Income Housing Tax Credit: An Analysis of the First Ten Years." *Housing Policy Debate* 10 (1999): 251–307.

Cunningham, Mary K., Susan J. Popkin, and Martha R. Burt. *Public Housing Transformation and the "Hard to House."* Washington, DC: Urban Institute, 2005.

Curley, Alexandra M. "Relocating the Poor: Social Capital and Neighborhood Resources." *Journal of Urban Affairs* 32 (2010): 79–103.

Daly, Mary, and Hilary Silver. "Social Exclusion and Social Capital: A Comparison and Critique." *Theory and Society* 37 (2008): 537–66.

Darling, Nancy, and Laurence Steinberg. "Community Influences on Adolescent Achievement and Deviance." In *Neighborhood Poverty*, vol. 2, *Policy Implications in Studying Neighborhoods*, edited by Jeanne Brooks-Gunn, Greg Duncan, and Lawrence J. Aber, 120–31. New York: Russell Sage Foundation, 1997.

Davidson, Mark. "Spoiled Mixture: Where Does State-Led Positive Gentrification End?" *Urban Studies* 45 (2008): 2385–2405.

Davies, Jonathan S. "The Social Exclusion Debate: Strategies, Controversies and Dilemmas." *Policy Studies* 26 (2005): 3–27.

Davis, Allen F. *Spearheads for Reform: The Social Settlements and the Progressive Movement, 1890–1914.* New Brunswick, NJ: Rutgers University Press, 1984.

Day, Kristen. "New Urbanism and the Challenges of Designing for Diversity." *Journal of Planning Education and Research* 23 (2003): 83–95.

DeFilippis, James. "Commentary: On Spatial Solutions to Social Problems." *Cityscape* (2013): 69–72.

DeFilippis, James, Robert Fisher, and Eric Shragge. "Neither Romance nor Regulation: Re-evaluating Community." *International Journal of Urban and Regional Research* 30 (2006): 673–89.

Deitrick, Sabina, and Cliff Ellis. "New Urbanism in the Inner City." *Journal of the American Planning Association* 70 (2004): 426–42.

DeLuca, Stefanie. "The Continuing Relevance of the Gautreaux Program for Housing Mobility: Recent Evidence." In *Keeping the Promise: Preserving and Enhancing Housing Mobility in the Section 8 Housing Choice Voucher Program*, edited by Philip Tegeler, Mary K. Cunningham, and Margery Austin Turner, 25–42. Washington, DC: Poverty and Race Research Action Council, 2005.

DeLuca, Stefanie, Greg Duncan, Micere Keels, and Ruby Mendenhall. "Gautreaux Mothers and Their Children: An Update." *Housing Policy Debate* 20 (2010): 7–25.

DeLuca, Stefanie, and James E. Rosenbaum. "If Low-Income Blacks Are Given a Chance to Live in White Neighborhoods, Will They Stay? Examining Mobility Patterns in a Quasi-Experimental Program with Administrative Data." *Housing Policy Debate* 14 (2003): 305–45.

Dewar, Tom. "Aligning with Outside Resources and Power." In *Voices from the Field III: Lessons and Challenges from Two Decades of Community Change Efforts*, edited by Anne Kubisch, Patricia Auspos, Prudence Brown, and Tom Dewar, 77–85. Washington, DC: Aspen Institute, 2010.

Doussard, Marc, Jamie Peck, and Nik Theodore. "After Deindustrialization: Uneven Growth and Economic Inequality in 'Postindustrial' Chicago." *Economic Geography* 85 (2009): 183–207.

Drake, St. Clair, and Horace R. Cayton. *Black Metropolis: A Study of Negro Life in a Northern City*. New York: Harcourt, Brace, 1945.

Duncan, Greg J., and Anita Zuberi. "Mobility Lessons fromGautreaux and Moving to Opportunity." *Northwestern Journal of Law and Social Policy* 1, no. 1 (2006): 110.

Duncan, Otis Dudley, David L. Featherman, and Beverly Duncan. *Socioeconomic Background and Achievement*. New York: Seminar Press, 1972.

Duneier, Mitchell. *Slim's Table: Race, Respectability, and Masculinity in America*. Chicago: University of Chicago Press, 1992.

Dye, Richard F., and David F. Merriman. "The Effects of Tax Increment Financing on Economic Development." *Journal of Urban Economics* 47 (2000): 306–28.

Edwards, Bob, and Michael W. Foley. "Civil Society and Social Capital Beyond Putnam." *American Behavioral Scientist* 42 (1998): 124–39.

Elliott, Delbert, William J. Wilson, David Huizing, Robert J. Sampson, Amanda Elliott, and Bruce Rankin. "The Effects of Neighborhood Disadvantage on Adolescent Development." *Journal of Research in Crime and Delinquency* 33 (1996): 389–426.

Elliott, James R. "Social Isolation and Labor Market Insulation: Network and Neighborhood Effects on Less-Educated Urban Workers." *Sociological Quarterly* 40 (1999): 199–216.

Ellis, Cliff. "The New Urbanism: Critiques and Rebuttals." *Journal of Urban Design* 7 (2002): 261–91.

Emerson, Michael O., Rachel Tolbert Kimbro, and George Yancey. "Contact Theory Extended: The Effects of Prior Racial Contact on Current Social Ties." *Social Science Quarterly* 83 (2002): 745–61.

Epp, Gayle. "Emerging Strategies for Revitalizing Public Housing Communities." *Housing Policy Debate* 7 (1996): 563–88.

Fainstein, Susan S. "New Directions in Planning Theory." *Urban Affairs Review* 35 (2000): 451–78.

Fauth, Rebecca, Tama Leventhal, and Jeanne Brooks-Gunn. "Seven Years Later: Effects of a Neighborhood Mobility Program on Poor Black and Latino Adults' Well-Being." *Journal of Health and Social Behavior* 49 (2008): 119–30.

Faux, Geoffrey P. *CDCs: New Hope for the Inner City*. New York: Twentieth Century Fund, 1971.

Feins, Judith, and Mark Shroder. "Moving to Opportunity: The Demonstration's Design and Its Effects on Mobility." *Urban Studies* 42 (2005): 1275–99.

Ficke, Robert C., and Andrea Piesse. *Evaluation of the Family Self-Sufficiency Program: Retrospective Analysis, 1996–2000*. No. 39010. HUD USER, Economic Development. Westat: Rockville, MD, 2004.

Finkel, Ed. *West Haven: Rising Like the Phoenix*. Chicago: New Communities Program, 2007.

Firey, Walter. "Sentiment and Symbolism as Ecological Variables." In *Urban Patterns: Studies in Human Ecology*, edited by George A. Theodorson, 129–36. University Park: Pennsylvania State University Press, 1982.

Fischer, Claude S. *To Dwell Among Friends: Personal Networks in Town and City*. Chicago: University of Chicago Press, 1982.

Fisher, Robert. "From Grass-Roots Organizing to Community Service: Community Organization Practice in the Community Center Movement." In *Community Organization for Urban Social Change: A Historical Perspective*, edited by Robert Fisher and Peter Romanofsky, 33–58. Westport, CT: Greenwood Press, 1981.

———. *Let the People Decide: Neighborhood Organizing in America*. New York: Twayne, 1994.

Fleming, Raymond, Jerome Baum, and Jerome E. Singer. "Social Support and the Physical Environment." In *Social Support and Health*, edited by Sheldon Cohen and Leonard S. Lyme, 327–45. Orlando, FL: Academic Press, 1985.

Foley, Micheal W., and Bob Edwards. "Escape from Politics? Social Theory and the Social Capital Debate." *American Behavioral Scientist* 40 (1997): 550–61.

Ford Foundation. *Community Development Corporations: A Strategy for Depressed Urban and Rural Areas*. New York: Ford Foundation, 1973.

Foucault, Michel. "Governmentality." In *The Foucault Effect: Studies in Governmentality*, edited by Graham Burchell, Colin Gordon, and Peter Miller, 87–104. Chicago: University of Chicago Press, 1991.

Fraser, James C., Robert J. Chaskin, and Joshua Theodore Bazuin. "Making Mixed-Income Neighborhoods Work for Low-Income Households." *Cityscape* 15, no. 2 (2013): 83–100.

Fraser, James C., and Edward L. Kick. "The Role of Public, Private, Non-profit and Community Sectors in Shaping Mixed-Income Housing Outcomes in the U.S." *Urban Studies* 44 (2007): 2357–77.

Freeman, Lance. *There Goes the 'Hood: Views of Gentrification from the Ground Up.* Philadelphia: Temple University Press, 2006.

Freudenburg, William R. "The Density of Acquaintanceship: An Overlooked Variable in Community Research?" *American Journal of Sociology* 92 (1986): 27–63.

Frieden, Bernard J., and Marshall Kaplan. *The Politics of Neglect: Urban Aid from Model Cities to Revenue Sharing.* Cambridge, MA: MIT Press, 1975.

Fry, Rita A. *Independent Monitor's Report to the Chicago Housing Authority and the Central Advisory Council regarding Year 6 of the CHA Plan for Transformation.* Chicago: Author, 2005.

Fuerst, J. S., and D. Bradford Hunt. *When Public Housing Was Paradise: Building Community in Chicago.* Westport, CT: Praeger, 2003.

Fung, Archon. "Beyond and Below the New Urbanism: Citizen Participation and Responsive Spatial Reconstruction." *Boston College Environmental Affairs Law Review* 28 (2001): 615–35.

———. *Empowered Participation: Reinventing Urban Democracy.* Princeton, NJ: Princeton University Press, 2006.

Furstenberg, Frank F. "How Families Manage Risk and Opportunity in Dangerous Neighborhoods." In *Sociology and the Public Agenda*, edited by William J. Wilson, 231–58. Newbury Park, CA: Sage Publications, 1993.

Gallagher, Megan, Chantal Hailey, Elizabeth Davies, Larry Buron, and Christopher Hayes. *CHA Residents and the Plan for Transformation.* Washington, DC: Urban Institute, 2013.

Galster, George C., Peter A. Tatian, Anna M. Santiago, Kathryn L. S. Pettit, and Robin E. Smith, *Why Not in My Backyard? Neighborhood Impacts of Deconcentrating Assisted Housing.* New Brunswick, NJ: Center for Urban Policy Research, 2003.

Gans, Herbert J. "The Balanced Community: Homogeneity or Heterogeneity in Residential Areas?" *Journal of the American Institute of Planners* 27 (1961): 176–84.

———. *The Urban Villagers: Group and Class in the Life of Italian-Americans.* New York: Free Press of Glencoe, 1962.

Garbarino, James, and Ann Crouter. "Defining the Community Context for Parent-Child Relations: The Correlates of Child Maltreatment." *Child Development* 49 (1978): 604–16.

Garde, Ajay. "Designing and Developing New Urbanist Projects in the United States: Insights and Implications." *Journal of Urban Design* 11 (2006): 33–54.

Garvin, Charles D., and Fred M. Cox. "A History of Community Organizing since the Civil War with Special Reference to Oppressed Communities." In *Strategies of Community Intervention*, edited by Jack Rothman, John L. Erlich, and John E. Tropman, 65–100. Itasca, IL: Peacock, 2001.

Gephart, Martha A. "Neighborhoods and Communities as Contexts for Development." In *Neighborhood Poverty*, vol. 1, *Contexts and Consequences for Children*, edited by Jeanne Brooks-Gunn, Greg J. Duncan, and J. Lawrence Aber, 1–43. New York: Russell Sage Foundation, 1997.

Gittell, Ross J., and Avis Vidal. *Community Organizing: Building Social Capital as a Development Strategy*. Thousand Oaks, CA: Sage Publications, 1998.

Goering, John M., and Judith D. Feins. *Choosing a Better Life? Evaluating the Moving to Opportunity Social Experiment*. Washington, DC: Urban Institute Press, 2003.

Goetz, Edward G. *Clearing the Way: Deconcentrating the Poor in Urban America*. Washington, DC: Urban Institute Press, 2003.

———. "Desegregation Lawsuits and Public Housing Dispersal: The Case of Hollman vs. Cisneros in Minneapolis." *Journal of the American Planning Association* 70, no. 3 (2004): 282–99.

———. "Housing Dispersal Programs." *Journal of Planning Literature* 18 (2003): 3–16.

———. *New Deal Ruins: Race, Economic Justice, and Public Housing Policy*. Ithaca, NY: Cornell University Press, 2013.

———. "The Politics of Poverty Deconcentration and Housing Demolition." *Journal of Urban Affairs* 22 (2000): 157–73.

———. "Where Have All the Towers Gone? The Dismantling of Public Housing in U.S. Cities." *Journal of Urban Affairs* 33 (2011): 267–87.

Goetz, Edward Glenn, Hin Kin Lam, and Anne Heitlinger. *There Goes the Neighborhood? The Impact of Subsidized Multi-family Housing on Urban Neighborhoods*. Minneapolis: Center for Urban and Regional Affairs, University of Minnesota, 1996.

Goffman, Erving. *Stigma: Notes on the Management of Spoiled Identity*. New York: Simon and Schuster, 1986. Originally published 1963.

Gordon, Colin. "Governmental Rationality: An Introduction." In *The Foucault Effect: Studies in Governmentality*, edited by Graham Burchell, Colin Gordon, and Peter Miller, 1–51. Chicago: University of Chicago Press, 1991.

Gottdiener, M., and Joe R. Feagin. "The Paradigm Shift in Urban Sociology." *Urban Affairs Review* 24 (1988): 163–87.

Granovetter, Mark S. *Getting a Job: A Study of Contacts and Careers*. Chicago: University of Chicago Press, 1995. Originally published 1974.

———. "The Strength of Weak Ties." *American Journal of Sociology* 78 (1973): 1360–80.

Graves, Erin M. "Mixed Outcome Developments: Comparing Policy Goals to Resident Outcomes in Mixed-Income Housing." *Journal of the American Planning Association* 77 (2011): 143–53.

———. "The Structuring of Urban Life in a Mixed-Income Housing Community." *City and Community* 9 (2010): 109–31.

Greenbaum, Susan, Wendy Hathaway, Cheryl Rodriguez, Ashley Spalding, and Beverly Ward. "Deconcentration and Social Capital: Contradictions of a Poverty Alleviation Policy." *Journal of Poverty* 12 (2008): 201–28.

Greenberg, David M., Nandita Verma, Keri-Nicole Dillman, and Robert J. Chaskin. *Creating a Platform for Sustained Neighborhood Improvement: Interim Findings from Chicago's New Communities Program*. New York: MDRC, 2010.

Grossman, James R. *Land of Hope: Chicago, Black Southerners, and the Great Migration.* Chicago: University of Chicago Press, 1989.

Haar, Charles M. *Between the Idea and the Reality: A Study in the Origin, Fate and Legacy of the Model Cities Program.* Boston: Little, Brown, 1975.

Hacker, Andrew. *Two Nations: Black and White, Separate, Hostile, Unequal.* New York: Scribner, 1992.

Hackworth, Jason R. *The Neoliberal City: Governance, Ideology, and Development in American Urbanism.* Ithaca, NY: Cornell University Press, 2007.

Halpern, Robert. *Rebuilding the Inner City: A History of Neighborhood Initiatives to Address Poverty in the United States.* New York: Columbia University Press, 1995.

Hanifan, L. J. *The Community Center.* Boston: Silver, Burdett, 1920.

———. "The Rural School Community Center." *Annals of the American Academy of Political and Social Science* 67 (1916): 130–38.

Hanlon, James. "Success by Design: HOPE VI, New Urbanism, and the Neoliberal Transformation of Public Housing in the United States." *Environment and Planning A* 42 (2010): 80–98.

Hannerz, Ulf. *Soulside: Inquiries into Ghetto Culture and Community.* New York: Columbia University Press, 1969.

Harvey, David. *A Brief History of Neoliberalism.* New York: Oxford University Press, 2005.

———. "The New Urbanism and the Communitarian Trap." *Harvard Design Magazine*, no. 1(1997): 1–3.

———. "Social Justice, Postmodernism and the City." *International Journal of Urban and Regional Research* 16 (1992): 588–601.

———. *Social Justice and the City.* Baltimore: Johns Hopkins University Press, 1973.

Hipp, John R., and Andrew J. Perrin. "The Simultaneous Effect of Social Distance and Physical Distance on the Formation of Neighborhood Ties." *City and Community* 8 (2009): 5–25.

Hirsch, Arnold R. *Making the Second Ghetto: Race and Housing in Chicago, 1940–1960.* Cambridge: Cambridge University Press, 1983.

Hogan, James. *Scattered-Site Housing: Characteristics and Consequences.* Washington, DC: US Department of Housing and Urban Development, Office of Policy Development and Research, 1996.

Holloway, Steven R., and Stephen Mulherin. "The Effect of Adolescent Neighborhood Poverty on Adult Employment." *Journal of Urban Affairs* 26 (2004): 427–54.

Hunt, D. Bradford. *Blueprint for Disaster: The Unraveling of Chicago Public Housing.* Chicago: University of Chicago Press, 2009.

Hunter, Albert. "Private, Parochial and Public Orders: The Problem of Crime and Incivility in Urban Communities." In *The Challenge of Social Control: Citizenship and Institution Building in Modern Society,* edited by Gerald D. Suttles and Mayer N. Zald, 230–45. Norwood, NJ: Ablex, 1985.

———. *Symbolic Communities: The Persistence and Change of Chicago's Local Communities*. Chicago: University of Chicago Press, 1974.

Hyra, Derek S. "Conceptualizing the New Urban Renewal: Comparing the Past to the Present." *Urban Affairs Review* 48 (2012): 498–527.

———. *The New Urban Renewal: The Economic Transformation of Harlem and Bronzeville*. Chicago: University of Chicago Press, 2008.

Ibarra, Herminia. "Race, Opportunity, and Diversity of Social Circles in Managerial Networks." *Academy of Management Journal* 38 (1995): 673–703.

Imbroscio, David. "'[U]nited and Actuated by Some Common Impulse of Passion': Challenging the Dispersal Consensus in American Housing Policy Research." *Journal of Urban Affairs* 30 (2008): 111–30.

Jackson, Kenneth T. *Crabgrass Frontier: The Suburbanization of the United States*. New York: Oxford University Press, 1985.

Jacobs, Jane. *The Death and Life of Great American Cities*. New York: Random House, 1961.

Janowitz, Morris. "Sociological Theory and Social Control." *American Journal of Sociology* 81 (1975): 82–108.

Jargowsky, Paul A. *Poverty and Place: Ghettos, Barrios, and the American City*. New York: Russell Sage Foundation, 1997.

Jencks, Christopher, and Susan E. Mayer. "The Social Consequences of Growing Up in a Poor Neighborhood." In *Inner-City Poverty in the United States*, edited by Laurence E. Lynn and Michael G. H. McGeary, 111–86. Washington, DC: National Academy Press, 1990.

Johnson, Jennifer S., and Emily Talen. "Affordable Housing in New Urbanist Communities: A Survey of Developers." *Housing Policy Debate* 19 (2008): 583–613.

Joseph, Mark L. "Creating Mixed-Income Developments in Chicago: Developer and Service Provider Perspectives." *Housing Policy Debate* 20 (2010): 91–118.

———. "Early Resident Experiences at a New Mixed-Income Development in Chicago." *Journal of Urban Affairs* 30 (2008): 229–57.

———. "Is Mixed-Income Development an Antidote to Urban Poverty?" *Housing Policy Debate* 17 (2006): 209–34.

———. "Mixed-Income Symposium Summary and Response: Implications for Antipoverty Policy. *Cityscape* 15, no. 2 (2013): 215–21.

Joseph, Mark L., and Robert J. Chaskin. "Mixed-Income Developments and Low Rates of Return: Insights from Relocated Public Housing Residents in Chicago." *Housing Policy Debate* 22 (2012): 377–405.

Joseph, Mark L., Robert J. Chaskin, and Henry S. Webber. "A Theoretical Basis for Addressing Poverty through Mixed-Income Development." *Urban Affairs Review* 42 (2007): 369–409.

Judd, Dennis R., and Alvin H. Mushkatel. "Inequality of Urban Services: The Impact of the Community Development Act." In *The Politics of Urban Public Services*, edited by Richard C. Rich, 127–39. Lexington, MA: Lexington Books, 1982.

Jupp, Ben. "Living Together: Community Life on Mixed Estates." London: Demos, 1999.

Kasarda, John D. "City Jobs and Residents on a Collision Course: The Urban Underclass Dilemma." *Economic Development Quarterly* 4 (1990): 313–19.

———. "Urban Change and Minority Opportunities." In *The New Urban Reality*, edited by Paul E. Peterson, 33–67. Washington, DC: Brookings Institution, 1985.

Kasarda, John D., and Morris Janowitz. "Community Attachment in Mass Society." *American Sociological Review* 39 (1974): 328–39.

Katz, Bruce. "Obama's Metro Presidency." *City and Community* 9, no. 1 (2010): 23–31.

———. "The Origins of HOPE VI." In *From Despair to Hope: HOPE VI and the New Promise of Public Housing in America's Cities*, edited by Bruce Katz, Henry G. Cisneros, and Lora Engdahl, 15–30. Washington, DC: Brookings Institution Press, 2009.

Katz, Michael B. *In the Shadow of the Poorhouse: A Social History of Welfare in America*. New York: Basic Books, 1986.

———. "Narratives of Failure? Historical Interpretations of Federal Urban Policy." *City and Community* 9 (2010): 13–22.

———. *The "Underclass" Debate: Views from History*. Princeton, NJ: Princeton University Press, 1993.

Katz, Peter. *The New Urbanism: Toward an Architecture of Community*. New York: McGraw-Hill, 1994.

Keane, Carl. "Socioenvironmental Determinants of Community Formation." *Environment and Behavior* 23 (1991): 27–46.

Kearns, Ade, and Phil Mason. "Mixed Tenure Communities and Neighbourhood Quality." *Housing Studies* 22 (2007): 661–91.

Keels, Micere. "Residential Attainment of Now-Adult Gautreaux Children: Do They Gain, Hold or Lose Ground in Neighborhood Ethnic and Economic Segregation?" *Housing Studies* 23 (2008): 541–64.

Keels, Micere, Greg Duncan, Stefanie DeLuca, Ruby Mendenhall, and James E. Rosenbaum. "Fifteen Years Later: Can Residential Mobility Programs Provide a Long-Term Escape from Neighborhood Segregation, Crime, and Poverty?" *Demography* 42 (2005): 51–73.

Kelling, George L., and James Q. Wilson. "Broken Windows: The Police and Neighborhood Safety." *Atlantic Monthly* 29 (1982). http://www.theatlantic.com/magazine/archive/1982/03/broken-windows/304465/. Accessed August 12, 2013.

Kessler, Ronald C., et al. "Associations of Housing Mobility Interventions for Children in High-Poverty Neighborhoods with Subsequent Mental Disorders during Adolescence." *Journal of the American Medical Association* 311, no. 9 (2014): 937–48.

Khadduri, Jill. "Deconcentration: What Do We Mean? What Do We Want?" *Cityscape* 5 (2001): 69–84.

Khare, Amy T., Mark L. Joseph, and Robert J. Chaskin. "The Enduring Significance of Race in Mixed-income Developments." *Urban Affairs Review* 50 (2014): 1–30.

Kingsley, G. Thomas. "Appendix A." In *From Despair to Hope: HOPE VI and the New Promise of Public Housing In America's Cities*, edited by Henry G. Cisneros and Lora Engdahl, 299–306. Washington, DC: Brookings Institution Press, 2009.

Kingsley, G. T., Jennifer Johnson, and Kathryn L. S. Pettit. "Patterns of Section 8 Relocation in the Hope VI Program." *Journal of Urban Affairs* 25 (2003): 427–47.

Kleit, Rachel G. "HOPE VI New Communities: Neighborhood Relationships in Mixed-Income Housing." *Environment and Planning A* 37 (2005): 1413–41.

———. "Housing, Social Networks, and Access to Opportunity: The Impact of Living in Scattered-Site Public Housing." PhD diss., University of North Carolina at Chapel Hill, 1999.

———. "Job Search Networks and Strategies in Scattered-Site Public Housing." *Housing Studies* 17 (2002): 83–100.

———. "Neighborhood Relations in Suburban Scattered-Site and Clustered Public Housing." *Journal of Urban affairs* 23, no. 3–4 (2001): 409–30.

———. "The Role of Neighborhood Social Networks in Scattered-Site Public Housing Residents' Search for Jobs." *Housing Policy Debate* 12 (2001): 541–74.

Kleit, Rachel G., and Nicole Carnegie. "Integrated or Isolated? The Impact of Public Housing Redevelopment on Social Network Homophily." *Social Networks* 33 (2011): 152–65.

Klemek, Christopher. *The Transatlantic Collapse of Urban Renewal: Postwar Urbanism from New York to Berlin*. Chicago: University of Chicago Press, 2011.

Kling, Jeffrey, Jeffrey B. Liebman, Lawrence Katz, and Lisa Sanbonmatsu. "Moving to Opportunity and Tranquility: Neighborhood Effects on Adult Economic Self-Sufficiency and Health from a Randomized Housing Voucher Experiment." Harvard University KSG Faculty Research Working Paper Series RWP04–035, 2004.

Kling, Samuel. "Wide Boulevards, Narrow Visions: Burnham's Street System and the Chicago Plan Commission, 1909–1930." *Journal of Planning History* 12 (2013): 245–68.

Kornhauser, Ruth R. *Social Sources of Delinquency: An Appraisal of Analytic Models*. Chicago: University of Chicago Press, 1978.

Kotlowitz, Alex. *There Are No Children Here: The Story of Two Boys Growing Up in the Other America*. New York: Doubleday, 1991.

Kravitz, Sanford, and Ferne K. Kolodner. "Community Action: Where Has It Been? Where Will It Go?" *Annals of the American Academy of Political and Social Science* 385 (1969): 30–40.

Kubisch, Anne. "Structures, Strategies, Actions, and Results of Community Change Efforts." In *Voices from the Field III: Lessons and Challenges from Two*

Decades of Community Change Efforts, edited by Anne Kubisch, Patricia Auspos, Prudence Brown, and Tom Dewar, 15–50. Washington, DC: Aspen Institute, 2010.

Kubisch, Anne, Patricia Auspos, Prudence Brown, Robert J. Chaskin, Karen Fulbright-Anderson, and Ralph Hamilton. *Voices from the Field II: Reflections on Comprehensive Community Change*. Washington, DC: Aspen Institute, 2002.

Kubisch, Anne, Patricia Auspos, Prudence Brown, and Tom Dewar. *Voices from the Field III: Lessons and Challenges from Two Decades of Community Change Efforts*. Washington, DC: Aspen Institute, 2010.

Kubisch, Anne, Prudence Brown, Robert J. Chaskin, Janice Hirota, Mark L. Joseph, Harold Richman, and Michelle Roberts. *Voices from the Field: Learning from the Early Work of Comprehensive Community Initiatives*. Washington, DC: Aspen Institute, 1997.

LaGrange, Randy L., Kenneth F. Ferraro, and Michael Supancic. "Perceived Risk and Fear of Crime: Role of Social and Physical Incivilities." *Journal of Research in Crime and Delinquency* 29 (1992): 311–34.

Lamont, Michèle, and Marcel Fournier. *Cultivating Differences: Symbolic Boundaries and the Making of Inequality*. Chicago: University of Chicago Press, 1992.

Lamont, Michèle, and Mario Luis Small. "How Culture Matters: Enriching Our Understanding of Poverty." In *The Colors of Poverty: Why Racial Disparities Persist*, edited by Ann Chih Lin and David R. Harris, 76–102. New York: Russell Sage Foundation, 2008.

Larsen, Kristin. "New Urbanism's Role in Inner-City Neighborhood Revitalization." *Housing Studies* 20 (2005): 795–813.

Larsen, Larissa. "A Comparison of Chicago's Scattered Site and Aggregate Public Housing Resident's Psychological Self-evaluations." PhD diss., University of Illinois at Champaign-Urbana, 1998.

Laumann, Edward O. *Bonds of Pluralism: The Form and Substance of Urban Social Networks*. New York: Wiley, 1973.

Lazarsfeld, Paul F., and Robert K. Merton. "Friendship as Social Process: A Substantive and Methodological Analysis." In *Freedom and Control in Modern Society*, edited by Morroe Berger, Theodore Abel, and Charles H. Page, 18–66. New York: Van Nostrand, 1954.

Leccese, Michael, and Kathleen McCormick. *Charter of the New Urbanism*. New York: McGraw-Hill, 2000.

Lee, Barrett A., Karen E. Campbell, and Oscar Miller. "Racial Differences in Urban Neighboring." *Sociological Forum* 6 (1991): 525–50.

Lees, Loretta. "Gentrification and Social Mixing: Towards an Inclusive Urban Renaissance?" *Urban Studies* 45 (2008): 2449–70.

———. "A Reappraisal of Gentrification: Towards a 'Geography of Gentrification.'" *Progress in Human Geography* 24 (2000): 389–408.

Lefebvre, Henri. *Writings on Cities*. Translated and edited by Eleonore Kaufman and Elizabeth Lebas. Oxford: Blackwell, 1996.

Lemann, Nicholas. *The Promised Land: The Great Black Migration and How It Changed America*. New York: Knopf, 1991.

Leventhal, Tama, and Jeanne Brooks-Gunn. "The Neighborhoods They Live In: The Effects of Neighborhood Residence on Child and Adolescent Outcomes." *Psychological Bulletin* 126 (2000): 309–37.

Levitas, Ruth. *The Inclusive Society? Social Exclusion and New Labour*. Houndmills, UK: Macmillan, 1998.

Levy, Diane K., Zach McDade, and Kassie Bertumen. "Mixed-Income Living: Anticipated and Realized Benefits for Low-Income Households." *Cityscape* (2013): 15–28.

Levy, Diane K., and Megan Gallagher. *HOPE VI and Neighborhood Revitalization*. Washington, DC: Urban Institute, 2006.

Lewis, Dan A., and Michael G. Maxfield. "Fear in the Neighborhoods: An Investigation of the Impact of Crime." *Journal of Research in Crime and Delinquency* 17 (1980): 160–89.

Lewis, Oscar. "The Culture of Poverty." In *On Understanding Poverty: Perspectives from the Social Sciences*, edited by Daniel P. Moynihan, 187–200. New York: Basic Books, 1969.

———. *La Vida: A Puerto Rican Family in the Culture of Poverty, San Juan and New York*. New York: Random House, 1966.

Lin, Nan. *Social Capital: A Theory of Social Structure and Action*. Cambridge: Cambridge University Press, 2001.

Lin, Nan, and Mary Dumin. "Access to Occupations through Social Ties." *Social Networks* 8 (1986): 365–85.

Lin, Nan, John C. Vaughn, and Walter M. Ensel. "Social Resources and Occupational Status Attainment." *Social Forces* 59 (1981): 1163–81.

Link, Bruce G., and Jo C. Phelan. "Conceptualizing Stigma." *Annual Review of Sociology* 27 (2001): 363–85.

Lofland, Lyn H. *The Public Realm: Exploring the City's Quintessential Social Territory*. New York: Adline de Gruyter, 1998.

Logan, John R., and Harvey L. Molotch. *Urban Fortunes: The Political Economy of Place*. Berkeley: University of California Press, 1987.

Ludwig, Jens, Jeffrey R. Kling, Lawrence F. Katz, Lisa Sanbonmatsu, Jeffrey B. Liebman, Greg J. Duncan, and Ronald C. Kessler. "What Can We Learn about Neighborhood Effects from the Moving to Opportunity Experiment?" *American Journal of Sociology* 114 (2008): 144–88.

Lund, Hollie. "Testing the Claims of New Urbanism: Local Access, Pedestrian Travel, and Neighboring Behaviors." *Journal of the American Planning Association* 69 (2003): 414–29.

Mark, Noah P. "Culture and Competition: Homophily and Distancing Explanations for Cultural Niches." *American Sociological Review* 68 (2003): 319–45.

Marris, Peter, and Martin Rein. *Dilemmas of Social Reform: Poverty and Community Action in the United States*. Chicago: University of Chicago Press, 1982.

Massey, Douglas S., Len Albright, Rebecca Casciano, Elizabeth Derickson, and David N. Kinsey. *Climbing Mount Laurel: The Struggle for Affordable Housing and Social Mobility in an American Suburb.* Princeton, NJ: Princeton University Press, 2013.

Massey, Douglas S., and Nancy A. Denton. *American Apartheid: Segregation and the Making of the Underclass.* Cambridge, MA: Harvard University Press, 1993.

Massey, Douglas S., and Shawn M. Kanaiaupuni. "Public Housing and the Concentration of Poverty." *Social Science Quarterly* 74 (1993): 109–22.

Mathieson, Jane, Jennie Popay, Etheline Enoch, Sarah Escorel, Mario Hernandez, Heidi Johnston, and Laetitia Rispel. "Social Exclusion: Meaning, Measurement and Experience and Links to Health Inequalities." *WHO Social Exclusion Knowledge Network, Background Paper* 1 (2008): 1–91.

Mayhew, Henry. *London Labour and the London Poor.* London: Griffin, Bohn, 1861.

McCormick, Naomi J., Mark L. Joseph, and Robert J. Chaskin. "The New Stigma of Relocated Public Housing Residents: Challenges to Social Identity in Mixed-Income Developments." *City and Community* 11 (2012): 285–308.

McKenzie, Roderick D. "The Scope of Human Ecology." In *Urban Patterns: Studies in Human Ecology*, edited by George A. Theodorson, 28–34. University Park: Pennsylvania State University Press, 1982.

McKernan, Signe-Mary, and Michael Wayne Sherraden, eds. *Asset Building and Low-Income Families.* Washington, DC: Urban Insitute, 2008.

McPherson, J. Miller, and Lynn Smith-Lovin, "Homophily in Voluntary Organizations: Status Distance and the Composition of Face-to-Face Groups." *American Sociological Review* 52 (1987): 370–79.

McPherson, J. Miller, Lynn Smith-Lovin, and James M. Cook. "Birds of a Feather: Homophily in Social Networks." *Annual Review of Sociology* 27 (2001): 415–44.

Mead, Lawrence M. *The New Politics of Poverty: The Nonworking Poor in America.* New York: Basic Books, 1992.

———. "Telling the Poor What to Do." *Public Interest* 132 (1998): 97–112.

Mendenhall, Ruby. "Pathways to Economic Independence: Qualitative Results from the Gautreaux Residential Mobility Program." Paper presented at the fall conference for the Association of Public Policy Analysis and Management, Atlanta, Georgia, October 28–30, 2004.

Merry, Sally E. *Urban Danger: Life in a Neighborhood of Strangers.* Philadelphia: Temple University Press, 1981.

Metropolitan Planning Council. *CHA Plan for Transformation July 2003 Progress Report.* Chicago: Metropolitan Planning Council, 2003.

Michelson, William M. *Man and His Urban Environment: A Sociological Approach, with Revisions.* Reading, MA: Addison-Wesley, 1976.

Miles, Rebecca, and Yan Song. " 'Good' Neighborhoods in Portland, Oregon: Focus on both Social and Physical Environments." *Journal of Urban Affairs* 31 (2009): 491–509.

Miller, Zane L. "The Role and Concept of Neighborhood in American Cities." In *Community Organization for Urban Social Change: A Historical Perspective*, edited by Robert Fisher and Peter Romanofsky, 3–32. Westport, CT: Greenwood Press, 1981.

Mitchell, Don. *The Right to the City: Social Justice and the Fight for Public Space*. New York: Guilford Press, 2003.

Mitchell, Don, and Lynn Staeheli. "Clean and Safe? Property Redevelopment, Public Space and Homelessness in San Diego." In *The Politics of Public Space*, edited by Setha Low and Neil Smith, 143–75. New York: Routledge, 2006.

Mollenkopf, John H. *The Contested City*. Princeton, NJ: Princeton University Press, 1983.

Molotch, Harvey. "The City as a Growth Machine: Toward a Political Economy of Place." *American Journal of Sociology* 82 (1976): 309–32.

Mooney-Melvin, Patricia. *The Organic City: Urban Definition and Community Organization, 1880–1920*. Lexington: University Press of Kentucky, 1987.

Moynihan, Daniel P. *Maximum Feasible Misunderstanding: Community Action in the War on Poverty*. New York: Free Press, 1969.

———. *The Negro Family: The Case for National Action*. Washington, DC: US Department of Labor, Office of Policy Planning and Research, 1965.

Murray, Charles A. *Losing Ground: American Social Policy, 1950–1980*. New York: Basic Books, 1984.

Musso, Juliet, Christopher Weare, Thomas Bryer, and Terry L. Cooper. "Toward 'Strong Democracy' in Global Cities? Social Capital Building, Theory-Driven Reform, and the Los Angeles Neighborhood Council Experience." *Public Administration Review* 71 (2011): 102–11.

Musterd, Sako, and Roger Andersson. "Housing Mix, Social Mix, and Social Opportunities." *Urban Affairs Review* 40 (2005): 761–90.

Naparstek, Arthur, Dennis Dooley, and Robin Smith. *Community Building in Public Housing: Ties That Bind People and Their Communities*. Washington, DC: US Department of Housing and Urban Development, 1997.

Naparstek, Arthur, Susan R. Freis, G. Thomas Kingsley, Dennis Dooley, and Howard E. Lewis. *HOPE VI: Community Building Makes a Difference*. Washington, DC: US Department of Housing and Urban Development, 2000.

National Commission on Severely Distressed Public Housing. *Final Report of the National Commission on Severely Distressed Public Housing*. Washington, DC: National Commission on Severely Distressed Public Housing, 1992.

National Congress for Community Economic Development. *Changing the Odds: The Achievements of Community-Based Development Corporations*. Washington, DC: National Congress for Community Economic Development, 1991.

———. *Tying It All Together: The Comprehensive Achievements of Community-Based Development Organizations*. Washington, DC: National Congress for Community Economic Development, 1995.

Neckerman, Kathryn M., and Joleen Kirschenman. "Hiring Strategies, Racial Bias, and Inner-City Workers." *Social Problems* 38 (1991): 433–47.

Newman, Katherine S. *No Shame in My Game: The Working Poor in the Inner City*. New York: Knopf, 1999.

Newman, Oscar. *Creating Defensible Space*. Washington, DC: US Department of Housing and Urban Development, Office of Policy Development and Research, 1996.

———. *Defensible Space: Crime Prevention through Urban Design*. New York: Macmillan, 1972.

Oakley, Deirdre, and Keri Burchfield. "Out of the Projects, Still in the Hood: The Spatial Constraints on Public Housing Residents' Relocation in Chicago." *Journal of Urban Affairs* 31 (2009): 589–614.

O'Connor, Alice. "Swimming Against the Tide: A Brief History of Federal Policy in Poor Communities." In *Urban Problems and Community Development*, edited by Ronald F. Ferguson and William T. Dickens, 77–138. Washington, DC: Brookings Institution Press, 1999.

Orr, Larry L., Judith D. Feins, Robin Jacob, Erik Beecroft, Abt Associates Inc., Lisa Sanbonmatsu, Lawrence L. Katz, Jeffrey B. Liebman, and Jeffrey R. Kling. *Moving to Opportunity: Interim Impacts Evaluation*. Washington, DC: US Department of Housing and Urban Development, Office of Policy Development and Research, 2003.

Ostrander, Susan A. "Agency and Initiative by Community Associations in Relations of Shared Governance: Between Civil Society and Local State." *Community Development Journal* 48 (2013): 511–24.

Pader, Ellen J., and Myrna M. Breitbart. "Transforming Public Housing: Conflicting Visions for Harbor Point." *Places* 8 (1993): 34–41.

Pager, Devah. "The Mark of a Criminal Record." *American Journal of Sociology* 108 (2003): 937–75.

Paolini, Stefania, Jake Harwood, and Mark Rubin. "Negative Intergroup Contact Makes Group Memberships Salient: Explaining Why Intergroup Conflict Endures." *Personality and Social Psychology Bulletin* 36 (2010): 1723–38.

Park, Robert E. *Human Communities: The City and Human Ecology*. Glencoe, IL: Free Press, 1952.

———. "Human Ecology." In *Urban Patterns: Studies in Human Ecology*, edited by George A. Theodorson, 20–27. University Park: Pennsylvania State University Press, 1982. Originally published 1936.

Park, Robert E., Ernest W. Burgess, and Roderick D. McKenzie. *The City*. Chicago: University of Chicago Press, 1967.

Parkes, Rhae, Emily Holt, Kimary Lee, Nik Theodore, and David Cook. *Opportunity Chicago: 2006–2010, Improving Access to Employment for Public Housing Residents in Chicago*. Chicago: Partnership for New Communities, 2012.

Pateman, Carole. *Participation and Democratic Theory*. Cambridge: Cambridge University Press, 1970.

Pattillo, Mary. *Black on the Block: The Politics of Race and Class in the City*. Chicago: University of Chicago Press, 2007.

———. "Investing in Poor Black Neighborhoods 'As Is.'" In *Public Housing and the*

Legacy of Segregation, ed. Margery Austin Turner, Susan J. Popkin, and Lynette Rawlings, 31–46. Washington, DC: Urban Institute Press, 2009.

———. "Sweet Mothers and Gangbangers: Managing Crime in a Black Middle-Class Neighborhood." *Social Forces* 76 (1998): 747–74.

Peck, Jamie, Nik Theodore, and Neil Brenner. "Neoliberal Urbanism: Models, Moments, Mutations." *SAIS Review of International Affairs* 29 (2009): 49–66.

Peck, Jamie, and Adam Tickell. "Neoliberalizing Space." *Antipode* 34 (2002): 380–404.

Perkins, Douglas D., Abraham Wandersman, Richard C. Rich, and Ralph B. Taylor. "The Physical Environment of Street Crime: Defensible Space, Territoriality and Incivilities." *Journal of Environmental Psychology* 13 (1993): 29–49.

Peterson, Paul E. *City Limits*. Chicago: University of Chicago Press, 1981.

Peterson, Paul, and J. David Greenstone. "Racial Change and Citizen Participation: The Mobilization of Low-Income Communities through Community Action." In *A Decade of Federal Antipoverty Programs: Achievements, Failures, and Lessons*, edited by Robert H. Haveman, 241–84. New York: Academic Press, 1977.

Pettigrew, Thomas F. "Intergroup Contact Theory." *Annual Review of Psychology* 65 (1998): 65–85.

Pettigrew, Thomas F., and Linda R. Tropp. "A Meta-analytic Test of Intergroup Contact." *Journal of Personality and Social Psychology* 90 (2006): 751–83.

Pierce, Neal R., and Carol Steinbach. *Corrective Capitalism: The Rise of America's Community Development Corporations*. New York: Ford Foundation, 1987.

Pinch, Steven. "Inequality in Pre-school Provision: A Geographical Perspective." In *Public Service Provision and Urban Development*, edited by Andrew Kirby, Paul L. Knox, and Steven Pinch, 231–82. London: Croom Helm, 1984.

Piven, Frances F., and Richard A. Cloward. *Regulating the Poor: The Functions of Public Welfare*. New York: Pantheon Books, 1971.

Plater-Zyberk, Elizabeth. Chapter 11. In *Charter of the New Urbanism: Congress for the New Urbanism*, edited by Emily Talen, 109–16. New York: McGraw-Hill, 2013.

Podobnik, Bruce. "Assessing the Social and Environmental Achievements of New Urbanism: Evidence from Portland, Oregon." *Journal of Urbanism* 4 (2011): 105–26.

———. "New Urbanism and the Generation of Social Capital: Evidence from Orenco Station." *National Civic Review* 91 (2002): 245–55.

Polikoff, Alexander. *The Third Side: A Mid-course Report on Chicago's Transformation of Public Housing*. Chicago: Business and Professional People for the Public Interest, 2009.

———. *Waiting for Gautreaux: A Story of Segregation, Housing, and the Black Ghetto*. Evanston, IL: Northwestern University Press, 2006.

Popkin, Susan J. "A Glass Half Empty? New Evidence from the HOPE VI Panel Study." *Housing Policy Debate* 20 (2010): 43–63.

Popkin, Susan J., Mary K. Cunningham, and William T. Woodley. *Residents at Risk: A Profile of Ida B. Wells and Madden Park*. Washington, DC: Urban Institute, 2003.

Popkin, Susan J., and Elizabeth Davies. *Improving the Lives of Public Housing's Most Vulnerable Families*. Washington, DC: Urban Institute, 2013.

Popkin, Susan J., Megan Gallagher, Chantal Hailey, Elizabeth Davies, Larry Buron, and Christopher Hayes. *CHA Residents and the Plan for Transformation*. Washington, DC: Urban Institute, 2013.

Popkin, Susan J., Victor E. Gwiasda, Lynn M. Olson, Dennis P. Rosebaum, and Larry Buron. *The Hidden War: Crime and the Tragedy of Public Housing in Chicago*. New Brunswick, NJ: Rutgers University Press, 2000.

Popkin, Susan J., Bruce Katz, Mary K. Cunningham, Karen D. Brown, Jeremy Gustafson, and Margery A. Turner. *A Decade of HOPE VI: Research Findings and Policy Challenges*. Washington, DC: Urban Institute, 2004.

Popkin, Susan J., Diane K. Levy, and Larry Buron. "Has Hope VI Transformed Residents' Lives? New Evidence From the Hope VI Panel Study." *Housing Studies* 24 (2009): 477–502.

Popkin, Susan J., Diane K. Levy, Laura E. Harris, Jennifer Comey, Mary K. Cunningham, Larry Buron, and William Woodley. *HOPE VI Panel Study: Baseline Report*. Washington, DC: Urban Institute, 2002.

Popkin, Susan J., Michael J. Rich, Leah Hendey, Joe Parilla, and George Galster. "Public Housing Transformation and Crime: Making the Case for Responsible Relocation." *Cityscape* 14 (2012): 137–60.

Popkin, Susan J., Molly M. Scott, Joe Parilla, Elsa Falkenburger, Marla McDaniel, and Shinwon Kyung. "Planning the Housing Opportunity and Services Together Demonstration: Challenges and Lessons Learned." *HOST Brief* 1 (2012).

Popkin, Susan J., Brett Theodos, Lisa Getsinger, and Joe Parilla. *An Overview of the Chicago Family Case Management Demonstration*. Washington, DC: Urban Institute, 2010.

Portes, Alejandro. "Social Capital: Its Origins and Applications in Modern Sociology." *Annual Review of Sociology* 24 (1998): 1–24.

Portes, Alejandro, and Patricia Landolt. "The Downside of Social Capital." *American Prospect* 26 (1996): 18–21.

Putnam, Robert D. *Bowling Alone: The Collapse and Revival of American Community*. New York: Simon and Schuster, 2000.

———. "*E Pluribus Unum*: Diversity and Community in the Twenty-First Century." *Scandinavian Political Studies* 30 (2007): 137–74.

———. *Making Democracy Work: Civic Traditions in Modern Italy*. Princeton, NJ: Princeton University Press, 1993.

Pyatok, Michael. "Martha Stewart vs. Studs Terkel? New Urbanism and Inner City Neighborhoods That Work." *Places* 13 (2000): 40–43.

Quillian, Lincoln. "Prejudice as a Response to Perceived Group Threat: Population Composition and Anti-immigrant and Racial Prejudice in Europe." *American Sociological Review* 60 (1995): 586–611.

Ramakrishnan, S. Karthick. "Incorporation versus Assimilation: The Need for Conceptual Differentiation." In *Outsiders No More? Models of Immigrant Political Incorporation*, edited by Jennifer Hochschild, Jacqueline Chattopadhyay, Claudine Gay, and Michael Jones-Correa, 27–42. New York: Oxford University Press, 2013.

Rankin, Bruce H., and James M. Quane. "Neighborhood Poverty and the Social Isolation of Inner-City African American Families." *Social Forces* 79 (2000): 139–70.

———. "Social Contexts and Urban Adolescent Outcomes: The Interrelated Effects of Neighborhoods, Families, and Peers on African American Youth." *Social Problems* 49 (2002): 79–100.

Ricketts, Erol R., and Isabel V. Sawhill. "Defining and Measuring the Underclass." *Journal of Policy Analysis and Management* 7 (1987): 316–25.

Roessner, Jane. *A Decent Place to Live: From Columbia Point to Harbor Point, A Community History*. Boston: Northeastern University Press, 2000.

Room, Graham. "Poverty and Social Exclusion: The New European Agenda for Policy and Research." In *Beyond the Threshold: The Measurement and Analysis of Social Exclusion*, edited by Graham Room, 1–9. Bristol, UK: Policy Press, 1995.

Rose, Nikolas. "The Death of the Social? Re-figuring the Territory of Government." *Economy and Society* 25 (1996): 327–56.

Rose, Nikolas, Pat O'Malley, and Mariana Valverde. "Governmentality." *Annual Review of Law and Social Science* 2 (2006): 83–104.

Rosenbaum, James E. "Changing the Geography of Opportunity by Expanding Residential Choice: Lessons from the Gautreaux Program." *Housing Policy Debate* 6 (1995): 231–69.

Rosenbaum, James E., Linda K. Stroh, and Cathy A. Flynn. "Lake Parc Place: A Study of Mixed-Income Housing." *Housing Policy Debate* 9 (1998): 703–40.

Rosenbaum, James E., and Anita Zuberi. "Comparing Residential Mobility Programs: Design Elements, Neighborhood Placements, and Outcomes in MTO and Gautreaux." *Housing Policy Debate* 20 (2010): 27–41.

Rothman, Jack. "Approaches to Community Intervention." In *Strategies of Community Intervention*, edited by Jack Rothman, John L. Erlich, and John E. Tropman, 27–64. Itasca, IL: Peacock, 2001.

———. "Three Models of Community Organization Practice." In *Strategies of Community Organization*, edited by Fred M. Cox, John L. Erlich, Jack Rothman, and John E. Tropman, 25–44. Itasca, IL: Peacock, 1974.

Rubinowitz, Leonard S., and James E. Rosenbaum. *Crossing the Class and Color Lines: From Public Housing to White Suburbia*. Chicago: University of Chicago Press, 2000.

Ruef, Martin, Howard E. Aldrich, and Nancy M. Carter. "The Structure of Founding Teams: Homophily, Strong Ties, and Isolation Among U.S. Entrepreneurs." *American Sociological Review* 68 (2003): 195–222.

Rumbaut, Ruben G. "Assimilation and Its Discontents: Ironies and Paradoxes."

In *The Handbook of International Migration: The American Experience*, edited by Charles Hirschman, Philip Kasinitz, and Josh DeWind, 172–97. New York: Russell Sage Foundation, 1999.

Ruming, Kristian J., Kathleen J. Mee, and Pauline M. McGuirk. "Questioning the Rhetoric of Social Mix: Courteous Community or Hidden Hostility?" *Australian Geographical Studies* 42 (2004): 234–48.

Ruppert, Evelyn. "Rights to Public Space: Regulatory Reconfigurations of Liberty." *Urban Geography* 27 (2006): 271–92.

Ryan, William, Allan Sloan, Mania Seferi, and Elaine Werby. *All in Together: An Evaluation of Mixed-income Multi-family Housing*. Boston: Housing Finance Authority, 1974.

Salama, Jerry J. "The Redevelopment of Distressed Public Housing: Early Results from HOPE VI Projects in Atlanta, Chicago, and San Antonio." *Housing Policy Debate* 10 (1999): 95–142.

Sampson, Robert J. *Great American City: Chicago and the Enduring Neighborhood Effect*. Chicago: University of Chicago Press, 2012.

———. "Local Friendship Ties and Community Attachment in Mass Society: A Multilevel Systemic Model." *American Sociological Review* 53 (1988): 766–79.

———. "Moving to Inequality: Neighborhood Effects and Experiments Meet Structure." *American Journal of Sociology* 114 (2008): 189–231.

———. "What 'Community' Supplies." In *Urban Problems and Community Development*, edited by Ronald F. Ferguson and William T. Dickens, 241–92. Washington, DC: Brookings Institution Press, 1999.

Sampson, Robert J., and W. Byron Groves. "Community Structure and Crime: Testing Social-Disorganization Theory." *American Journal of Sociology* 94 (1989): 774–802.

Sampson, Robert J., Jeffrey D. Morenoff, and Felton Earls. "Beyond Social Capital: Spatial Dynamics of Collective Efficacy for Children." *American Sociological Review* 64 (1999): 633–60.

Sampson, Robert J., Jeffrey D. Morenoff, and Thomas Gannon-Rowley. "Assessing 'Neighborhood Effects': Social Processes and New Directions in Research." *Annual Review of Sociology* 28 (2002): 443–78.

Sampson, Robert J., and Stephen W. Raudenbush. "Systematic Social Observation of Public Spaces: A New Look at Disorder in Urban Neighborhoods." *American Journal of Sociology* 105 (1999): 603–51.

Sampson, Robert J., Stephen W. Raudenbush, and Felton Earls. "Neighborhoods and Violent Crime: A Multilevel Study of Collective Efficacy." *Science* 277 (1997): 918–24.

Sander, Thomas H. "Social Capital and New Urbanism: Leading a Civic Horse to Water?" *National Civic Review* 91 (2002): 213–34.

Santiago, Anna M., and George C. Galster. "Assessing the Property Value Impacts of the Dispersed Housing Subsidy Program in Denver." *Journal of Policy Analysis and Management* 20 (2001): 65–88.

Sard, Barbara. *The Family Self-Sufficiency Program: HUD's Best Kept Secret for Promoting Employment and Asset Growth.* Washington, DC: Center on Budget and Policy Priorities, 2001.

Sard, Barbara, and Leah Staub. *House Bill Makes Significant Improvement in HOPE VI Public Housing Revitalization.* Washington, DC: Center on Budget and Policy Priorities, 2008.

Schill, Michael H. "Chicago's Mixed Income New Communities Strategy: The Future Face of Public Housing?" In *Affordable Housing and Urban Redevelopment in the United States*, edited by Willem van Vliet, 135–57. Thousand Oaks, CA: Sage Publications, 1997.

Schlossman, Steven, and Michael Sedlak. *The Chicago Area Project Revisited.* Santa Monica, CA: Rand Corporation, 1983.

Schram, Sanford F., Richard C. Fording, and Joe Soss. "Neo-liberal Poverty Governance: Race, Place and the Punitive Turn in U.S. Welfare Policy." *Cambridge Journal of Regions, Economy and Society* 1 (2008): 17–36.

Schreiner, Mark, and Michael Sherraden. *Can the Poor Save? Saving and Asset Building in Individual Development Accounts.* New York: Transaction, 2006.

Schubert, Michael F., and Alison Thresher. *Lessons from the Field: Three Cases of Mixed-Income Housing Development.* Chicago: University of Illinois at Chicago, Great Cities Institute, 1996.

Schwartz, Adam. "Chicago's Video Surveillance Cameras: A Pervasive and Poorly Regulated Threat to Our Privacy." *Northwestern Journal of Technology and Intellectual Property* 11 (2013): 47–60.

Schwartz, Alex, and Kian Tajbakhsh. "Mixed-Income Housing: Unanswered Questions." *Cityscape* 3 (1997): 71–92.

Seligman, Amanda I. *Block by Block: Neighborhoods and Public Policy on Chicago's West Side.* Chicago: University of Chicago Press, 2005.

Sen, Amartya. "Social Exclusion: Concept, Application, and Scrutiny." *Asian Development Bank, Social Development Papers* 1 (2000): 1–54.

Shaw, Clifford R., and Henry D. McKay. *Juvenile Delinquency and Urban Areas: A Study of Rates of Delinquents in relation to Differential Characteristics of Local Communities in American Cities.* Chicago: University of Chicago Press, 1942.

Sherraden, Michael. *Assets and the Poor: A New American Welfare Policy.* Armonk, NY: M. E. Sharpe, 1991.

———, ed. *Inclusion in the American Dream: Assets, Poverty, and Public Policy.* New York: Oxford University Press, 2005.

Silva, Lalith, Imesh Wijewardena, Michelle Wood, and Bulbul Kaul. "Evaluation of the Family Self-Sufficiency Program: Prospective Study." Prepared for US Department of Housing and Urban Development, Office of Policy Development and Research, 2011.

Silver, Hilary. "Commentary: Mixing Policies: Expectations and Achievements. *Cityscape* 15, no. 2 (2013): 73–82.

———. "Obama's Urban Policy: A Symposium." *City and Community* 9 (2010): 3–12.

———. "Social Exclusion and Social Solidarity: Three Paradigms." *International Labour Review* 133 (1994): 531–78.

Silverman, Emily, Ruth Lupton, and Alex Fenton. *A Good Place for Children? Attracting and Retaining Families in Inner Urban Mixed Income Communities.* York, UK: Joseph Rowntree Foundation, 2005.

Simmel, Georg, "The Metropolis and Urban Life." In *Georg Simmel on Individuality and Social Forms*, edited by Donald N. Levine, 324–39. Chicago: University of Chicago Press, 1971.

Sirianni, Carmen. *Investing in Democracy: Engaging Citizens in Collaborative Governance.* Washington, DC: Brookings Institution Press, 2009.

Sites, William, Robert J. Chaskin, and Virginia Parks. "Reframing Community Practice for the 21st Century: Multiple Traditions, Multiple Challenges." *Journal of Urban Affairs* 29 (2007): 519–41.

Skobba, Kimberly, and Edward G. Goetz. "Mobility Decisions of Very Low-Income Households." *Cityscape* 15 (2013): 155–72.

Skogan, Wesley G. *Disorder and Decline: Crime and the Spiral of Decay in American Neighborhoods.* New York: Free Press, 1990.

Skogan, Wesley G., and Susan M. Hartnett. *Community Policing, Chicago Style.* New York: Oxford University Press, 1997.

Small, Mario Luis. *Villa Victoria: The Transformation of Social Capital in a Boston Barrio.* Chicago: University of Chicago Press, 2004.

———. "Weak Ties and the Core Discussion Network: Why People Regularly Discuss Important Matters with Unimportant Alters." *Social Networks* 35 (2013): 470–83.

Small, Mario Luis, and Katherine Newman. "Urban Poverty after *The Truly Disadvantaged*: The Rediscovery of the Family, the Neighborhood and Culture." *Annual Review of Sociology* 27 (2001): 23–45.

Smith, Alastair. *Mixed-Income Housing Developments: Promise and Reality.* Cambridge, MA: Harvard University, Joint Center for Housing Studies, 2002.

Smith, Janet L. "The Chicago Housing Authority's Plan for Transformation." In *Where Are Poor People to Live? Transforming Public Housing Communities*, edited by Larry Bennett, Janet L. Smith, and Patricia A. Wright, 93–124. Armonk, NY: M. E. Sharpe, 2006.

———. "Mixed-Income Communities: Designing Out Poverty or Pushing Out the Poor?" In *Where Are Poor People to Live? Transforming Public Housing Communities*, edited by Larry Bennett, Janet L. Smith, and Patricia A. Wright, 59–81. Armonk, NY: M. E. Sharpe, 2006.

Smith, Janet L., and David Stovall. "'Coming Home' to New Homes and New Schools: Critical Race Theory and the Politics of Containment." *Journal of Education Policy* 23 (2008): 135–52.

Solomon, Daniel. Chapter 19. In *Charter of the New Urbanism: Congress for the New Urbanism*, edited by Emily Talen, 181–86. New York: McGraw-Hill, 2013.

Sorkin, Michael. *Variations on a Theme Park: The New American City and the End of Public Spaces.* New York: Hill and Wang, 1992.

Soss, Joe, Richard C. Fording, and Sanford Schram. *Disciplining the Poor: Neoliberal Paternalism and the Persistent Power of Race*. Chicago: University of Chicago Press, 2011.

Spencer, Margaret B., Steven P. Cole, Stephanie M. Jones, and Dena P. Swanson. "Neighborhood and Family Influences on Young Urban Adolescents' Behavior Problems: A Multi-sample, Multi-site Analysis." In *Neighborhood Poverty*, vol. 1, *Contexts and Consequences for Children*, edited by Jeanne Brooks-Gunn, Greg Duncan, and Lawrence J. Aber, 200–218. New York: Russell Sage Foundation, 1997.

Squires, Gregory D. *From Redlining to Reinvestment: Community Responses to Urban Disinvestment*. Philadelphia: Temple University Press, 1992.

Street, Paul Louis. *Racial Oppression in the Global Metropolis: A Living Black Chicago History*. Lanham, MD: Rowman and Littlefield, 2007.

Stoloff, Jennifer A., Jennifer L. Glanville, and Elisa J. Bienenstock. "Women's Participation in the Labor Force: The Role of Social Networks." *Social Networks* 21 (1999): 91–108.

Stoutland, Sara E. "Community Development Corporations: Mission, Strategy and Accomplishments." In *Urban Problems and Community Development*, edited by Ronald F. Ferguson and William T. Dickens, 193–240. Washington, DC: Brookings Institution Press, 1999.

Sugrue, Thomas J. *The Origins of the Urban Crisis: Race and Inequality in Postwar Detroit*. Princeton, NJ: Princeton University Press, 1996.

Sullivan, Thomas. *Independent Monitor's Report No. 5 to the Chicago Housing Authority and the Central Advisory Council*. Chicago: Author, 2003.

Suttles, Gerald D. *The Man-Made City: The Land-Use Confidence Game in Chicago*. Chicago: University of Chicago Press, 1990.

———. *The Social Construction of Communities*. Chicago: University of Chicago Press, 1972.

———. *The Social Order of the Slum: Ethnicity and Territory in the Inner City*. Chicago: University of Chicago Press, 1968.

Tach, Laura M. "More Than Bricks and Mortar: Neighborhood Frames, Social Processes, and the Mixed-Income Redevelopment of a Public Housing Project." *City and Community* 8 (2009): 269–99.

Talen, Emily. "Affordability in New Urbanist Development: Principle, Practice, and Strategy." *Journal of Urban Affairs* 32 (2010): 489–510.

———, ed. *Charter of the New Urbanism: Congress for the New Urbanism*. 2nd ed. New York: McGraw-Hill, 2013.

———. *New Urbanism and American Planning: The Conflict of Cultures*. New York: Routledge, 2005.

———. "The Social Goals of New Urbanism." *Housing Policy Debate* 13 (2002): 165–88.

Taylor, Ralph B., and Jeanette Covington. "Community Structural Change and Fear of Crime." *Social Problems* 40 (1993): 374–97.

Taylor, Ralph B., and Margaret Hale. "Testing Alternative Models of Fear of Crime." *Journal of Criminal Law and Criminology* 77 (1986): 151–89.

Theodos, Brett, Susan J. Popkin, Joe Parilla, and Liza Getsinger. "The Challenge of Targeting Services: A Typology of Public-Housing Residents." *Social Service Review* 86, no. 3 (2012): 517–44.

Thrasher, Frederic M. *The Gang: A Study of 1,313 Gangs in Chicago*. Chicago: University of Chicago Press, 1927.

Tocqueville, Alexis de. *Democracy in America*. Edited by Jacob P. Mayer, translated by George Lawrence. Garden City, NY: Doubleday, 1969.

Tönnies, Ferdinand. *Gemeinschaft und Gesselschaft*. New York: Harper and Row, 1965.

Trudeau, Dan. "A Typology of New Urbanism Neighborhoods." *Journal of Urbanism* 6 (2013): 113–38.

Trudeau, Dan, and Patrick Malloy. "Suburbs in Disguise? Examining the Geographies of the New Urbanism." *Urban Geography* 32 (2011): 424–47.

Turbov, Mindy. "Public Housing Redevelopment as a Tool for Revitalizing Neighborhoods: How and Why Did It Happen and What Have We Learned?" *Northwestern Journal of Law and Social Policy* 1 (2006):167–201.

Turbov, Mindy, and Valerie Piper. *HOPE VI and Mixed-Finance Redevelopments: A Catalyst for Neighborhood Renewal*. Washington, DC: Brookings Institution, 2005.

Turner, Margery Austin, Susan J. Popkin, and Lynette Rawlings. *Public Housing and the Legacy of Segregation*. Washington, DC: Urban Institute Press, 2009.

Urban Institute. *Developing Choice Neighborhoods: An Early Look at Implementation in Five Sites*. Interim Report. Washington, DC: Urban Institute, 2013.

US Department of Housing and Urban Development. *HOPE VI Program Authority and Funding History*. Washington, DC: US Department of Housing and Urban Development, 2007.

Vale, Lawrence J. *From the Puritans to the Projects: Public Housing and Public Neighbors*. Cambridge, MA: Harvard University Press, 2000.

———. "The Ideological Origins of Affordable Home Ownership Efforts." In *Chasing the American Dream: New Perspectives on Affordable Homeownership*, edited by William M. Rohe and Harry L. Watson, 15–40. Ithaca, NY: Cornell University Press, 2007.

———. *Purging the Poorest: Public Housing and the Design Politics of Twice-Cleared Communities*. Chicago: University of Chicago Press, 2013.

Vale, Lawrence J., and Erin Graves. *The Chicago Housing Authority's Plan for Transformation: What Does the Research Show So Far?* Chicago: John D. and Catherine T. MacArthur Foundation, 2010.

Valentine, Charles A. *Culture and Poverty: Critique and Counter-proposals*. Chicago: University of Chicago Press, 1968.

Varady, David P., and Carole Walker. "Housing Vouchers and Residential Mobility." *Journal of Planning Literature* 18 (2003): 17–30.

————. "Using Housing Vouchers to Move to the Suburbs: How Do Families Fare?" *Housing Policy Debate* 14 (2003): 347–82.

Varady, David P., Xinhao Wang, Yimei Wang, and Patrick Duhaney. "The Geographic Concentration of Housing Vouchers, Blacks, and Poverty over Time: A Study of Cincinnati, Ohio, USA." *Urban Research and Practice* 3 (2010): 39–62.

Venkatesh, Sudhir. *American Project: The Rise and Fall of a Modern Ghetto*. Cambridge, MA: Harvard University Press, 2000.

————. *The Robert Taylor Homes Relocation Study*. New York: Columbia University, Center for Urban Research and Policy, 2002.

Venkatesh, Sudhir, and Isil Celimli. "Tearing Down the Community." *Shelterforce* 138 (20044). http://www.nhi.org/online/issues/sf138.html.

Verba, Sidney, Kay L. Schlozman, and Henry E. Brady. *Voice and Equality: Civic Voluntarism in American Politics*. Cambridge, MA: Harvard University Press, 1995.

Vidal, Avis C. *Rebuilding Communities: A National Study of Urban Community Development Corporations*. New York: New Schools for Social Research, 1992.

Von Hoffman, Alexander. "High Ambitions: The Past and Future of American Low-Income Housing Policy." *Housing Policy Debate* 7 (1996): 423–46.

————. *House by House, Block by Block: The Rebirth of America's Urban Neighborhoods*. New York: Oxford University Press, 2003.

Wacquant, Loïc. *Punishing the Poor: The Neoliberal Government of Social Insecurity*. Durham, NC: Duke University Press, 2009.

————. *Urban Outcasts: A Comparative Sociology of Advanced Marginality*. Cambridge, MA: Polity, 2008.

Warren, Roland L. *The Community in America*. Chicago: Rand McNally, 1978.

Wellman, Barry. "The Community Question: The Intimate Networks of East Yonkers." *American Journal of Sociology* 84 (1979): 1201–31.

Wellman, Barry, and Scot Wortley. "Different Strokes from Different Folks: Community Ties and Social Support." *American Journal of Sociology* 96 (1990): 558–88.

Wexler, Harry J. "HOPE VI: Market Means/Public Ends: The Goals, Strategies, and Midterm Lessons of HUD's Urban Revitalization Demonstration Program." *Journal of Affordable Housing and Community Development Law* 10, no. 3 (2001): 195–233.

Whalen, Samuel P., and Joan R. Wynn. "Enhancing Primary Services for Youth through an Infrastructure of Social Services." *Journal of Adolescent Research* 10 (1995): 88–110.

Wilen, Willam P. "The Horner Model: Successfully Redeveloping Public Housing." *Northwestern Journal of Law and Social Policy* 1 (2006): 62–95.

Williams, Kale, Paul Fischer, and Mary Ann Russ. *Temporary Relocation, Permanent Choice: Serving Families with Rent Vouchers during the Chicago Housing Authority Plan for Transformation*. Chicago: Metropolitan Planning Council, 2003.

Wilner, Daniel M. *Human Relations in Interracial Housing: A Study of the Contact Hypothesis*. Minneapolis: University of Minnesota Press, 1955.

Wilner, Daniel M., Rosabelle P. Walkley, and Stuart W. Cook. "Residential Proximity and Intergroup Relations in Public Housing Projects." *Journal of Social Issues* 8 (1952): 45–69.

Wilson, James Q. *Thinking about Crime*. New York: Basic Books, 1975.

Wilson, William J. "Cycles of Deprivation and the Underclass Debate." *Social Service Review* 59 (1985): 541–59.

———. *More Than Just Race: Being Black and Poor in the Inner City*. New York: Norton, 2009.

———. *The Truly Disadvantaged: The Inner City, the Underclass, and Public Policy*. Chicago: University of Chicago Press, 1987.

———. *When Work Disappears: The Work of the New Urban Poor*. New York: Knopf, 1996.

Wimmer, Andreas, and Kevin Lewis. "Beyond and Below Racial Homophily: ERG Models of a Friendship Network Documented on Facebook." *American Journal of Sociology* 116 (2010): 583–642.

Wirth, Louis. "Urbanism as a Way of Life." *American Journal of Sociology* 44 (1938): 1–24.

Wiseman, Frederick, dir. *Public Housing*. DVD. Cambridge, MA: Zipporah Films, 1997.

Woolcock, Michael. "Social Capital and Economic Development: Toward a Theoretical Synthesis and Policy Framework." *Theory and Society* 27 (1998): 151–208.

Wright, Patricia A. "Community Resistance to CHA Transformation: The History, Evolution, Struggles, and Accomplishments of the Coalition to Protect Public Housing." In *Where Are Poor People to Live? Transforming Public Housing Communities*, edited by Larry Bennett, Janet L. Smith, and Patricia A. Wright, 125–67. Armonk, NY: M. E. Sharpe, 2006.

Wright, Patricia A., Richard M. Wheelock, and Carol Steele. "The Case of Cabrini-Green." In *Where Are Poor People to Live? Transforming Public Housing Communities*, edited by Larry Bennett, Janet L. Smith, and Patricia A. Wright, 168–84. Armonk, NY: M. E. Sharpe, 2006.

Wyly, Elvin K., and Daniel J. Hammel. "Capital's Metropolis: Chicago and the Transformation of American Housing Policy." *Geografiska Annaler*, ser. B, *Human Geography* 82 (2000): 181–206.

Yancey, William L. "Architecture, Interaction, and Social Control." In *Environment and the Social Sciences: Perspectives and Applications*, edited by Joachim F. Wohlwill and Daniel H. Carson, 126–36. Washington, DC: American Psychological Association, 1972.

Yates, Douglas. *Neighborhood Democracy: The Politics and Impacts of Decentralization*. Lexington, MA: Lexington Books, 1973.

Young, Iris M. *Justice and the Politics of Difference*. Princeton, NJ: Princeton University Press, 1990.

Zielenbach, Sean. "Assessing Economic Change in HOPE VI Neighborhoods." *Housing Policy Debate* 14 (2003): 621–56.

———. "Catalyzing Community Development: HOPE VI and Neighborhood Revitalization." *Journal of Affordable Housing and Community Development Law* 13 (2003): 40–80.

Zielenbach, Sean, and Richard Voith. "HOPE VI and Neighborhood Economic Development: The Importance of Local Market Dynamics." *Cityscape* 12 (2010): 99–131.

Zorbaugh, Harvey W. *The Gold Coast and the Slum: A Sociological Study of Chicago's Near North Side.* Chicago: University of Chicago Press, 1929.

———. "The Natural Areas of the City." In *Urban Patterns: Studies in Human Ecology,* edited by George A. Theodorson, 50–54. University Park: Pennsylvania State University, 1982. Originally published 1926.

Zukin, Sharon. *The Cultures of Cities.* Cambridge: Blackwell, 1995.

———. "A Decade of the New Urban Sociology." *Theory and Society* 9 (1980): 575–601.

Index

Page numbers followed by *t* indicate a table; those followed by *f* indicate a figure. Housing complexes and developments named in the index are located in Chicago unless otherwise indicated.